The Political Economy of Comparative Development into the 21st Century

The Political Economy of Comparative Development into the 21st Century

Essays in Memory of John C.H. Fei, Volume 1

Edited by

Gustav Ranis
Frank Altschul Professor of International Economics and Director, Yale Center for International and Area Studies, Yale University, USA

Sheng-Cheng Hu
Research Fellow and Director, Institute of Economics, Academia Sinica, Taiwan and Professor of Economics (Joint Appointment), National Taiwan University, Taiwan

Yun-Peng Chu
Research Fellow and Director, Sun Yet-Sen Institute for Social Sciences and Philosophy, Academia Sinica, Taiwan and Adjunct Professor of Economics, National Taiwan University, Taiwan

Edward Elgar
Cheltenham, UK • Northampton, MA, USA

Published by
Edward Elgar Publishing Limited
Glensanda House
Montpellier Parade
Cheltenham
Glos GL50 1UA
UK

Edward Elgar Publishing, Inc.
6 Market Street
Northampton
Massachusetts 01060
USA

A catalogue record for this book
is available from the British Library

Library of Congress Cataloguing in Publication Data

Essays in memory of John C.H. Fei / edited by Gustav Ranis, Sheng-Cheng Hu, Yun-Peng Chu.
"Selected papers presented … at the conference … held at the Academia Sinica, Taipei, Taiwan, on August 1 and 2, 1997 … jointly sponsored by Yale University … [et al.]"—Pref.
Includes bibliographical references.

ISBN 1 85898 878 0 (v. 1)
ISBN 1 85898 879 9 (v. 2)
1. Taiwan—Economic conditions—1945—Congresses. 2. Economic history—1945—Congresses. 3. Economic development—Congresses. I. Fei, John C.H. II. Ranis, Gustav. III. Hu, Sheng-Cheng, 1940– IV. Chu, Yun-Peng.
HC430.5 .P65 1999
338.95124'9—dc21

98–29702
CIP

ISBN 1 85898 878 0

Printed and bound in Great Britain by
Biddles Ltd, Guildford and King's Lynn

Contents

List of Figures vii
List of Tables ix
List of Contributors xiii
Preface xv

Part I Overview

1. As the Centruy Turns: Analytics, Empirics and Politics of Development 3
T.N. Srinivasan

Part II Sources of Development

2. The Sources of East Asian Economic Growth 45
Lawrence J. Lau

3. Can Capital Fundamentalism be Revived? A General Equilibrium Approach to Growth Accounting 77
Kenneth S. Lin and Hsiu-Yun Lee

4. Incomplete Currency Markets and Growth: Some Evidence from Southeast Asia and the Lessons from Japan and Taiwan 107
Pan A. Yotopoulos

5. Initial Pre-takeoff Conditions and Stages of Growth 143
Anthony Y.C. Koo

6. A Dual-Dual Framework to Analyze Intersectoral Relationships throughout the Development Process 157
Erik Thorbecke

7. Changing Industrial Structure and Economic Development: Prewar Japan Revisited 189
Tetsushi Sonobe and Keijiro Otsuka

Part III Income Distribution and Development

8. Growth and Changes in Inequality in Labor-absorbing Economies 213
Chau-Nan Chen and Yun-Peng Chu

9. Income Distribution and Development in Newly Industrialized Countries 253
Irma Adelman

10. Changes in Inequality and Welfare in a Developing Country Experiencing Hyperinflation 279
John P. Formby and Jacob Kaliyati

Part IV Institution and Development

11. Growth, Poverty and Inequality in the Philippines 313
Arsenio M. Balisacan

12. The Founding of the Bretton Woods Institutions: A View from the 1990s 335
Anne O. Krueger

13. Democracy, Conflict and Development – Three Cases 355
Frances Stewart and Meghan O'Sullivan

Index 387

Figures

2.1	The concept of a production function – the single-output, single-input case	47
2.2	The concept of technical progress – the single-output, single-input case	47
2.3	Decomposition of the sources of economic growth	48
2.4	Percentage of total R&D expenditure in GDP	54
2.5	Human capital	56
2.6	R&D capital	56
2.7	Tangible capital stock per labor hour	64
2.8	School years per labor hour	64
2.9	R&D capital stock per labor hour	65
3.1	Per capita real GDP and its linear time trend	93
3.2	Linear time trend residual versus annual growth rate	94
4.1	Shifts in Japanese industrial structure and patterns of trade, 1930-75	130
5.1	A Rostow contour	151
5.2	A Kuznets contour	152
5A.1	Taiwan's export pattern, 1949-88	156
6.1	Dual-dual framework according to technology and form of organization, and physical environment and type of production	159
6.2	Migration pattern under a bimodal agricultural structure and an unimodal agricultural structure	166
6.3	Early development phase	170
6.4	Family farm configuration in early development phase	173
6.5	Middle development phase product exchange: emergence of four distinct configurations	179
6.6	Phase 3. Mature development phase: predominance of industry and service sectors	185
7.1	Trends in wage-rental ratio and capital-labor ratio, semi-log scale	196

7.2 Changes in employment shares of heavy and machinery industries 198
7.3 Trends in horse power per worker in manufacturing industries 200
7.4 Trends in real value added per worker by industry 202
8.1 Effects of changes in terms of trade on changes in inequality in Taiwan: 1968-72 222
10.1 Lorenz dominance and inequality 285
10.2 First-order dominance – per capita food expenditures 286
10.3 First-order dominance – food-share expenditures 289
11.1 Cumulative distribution of real per capita consumption 318
11.2 Real mean consumption versus poverty 325

Tables

2.1	Average annual rates of growth of output and measured inputs	51
2.2	Relative contributions of the sources of economic growth	53
3.1	Statistical properties of growth rates	95
3.2	Empirical results for reduced-form ARMA models	97
3.3	Estimates in various growth models	101
4.1	Countries ranked by value of the *RER* index, 1985	112
4.2	Cross-section/time-series regressions on growth, all countries, 1970, 1975, 1980 and 1985	115
4.3	Cross-section/time-series regressions on growth, Southeast Asian countries, 1970, 1975, 1980 and 1985	116
4.4	Taiwan: rate of growth of GNP and financial statistics, 1953-91	123
4.5	Ownership of consumer durables, 1957-80	131
4.6	Comparisons of income levels between farm households and urban worker households in Japan	135
5.1	Orders of magnitude of major components of the British economy	151
7.1	Changes in employment share by industrial sector	199
7.2	Changes in horse power per worker by industrial sector	199
7.3	Decomposition of the growth of the average capital-labor ratio	201
7.4	Decomposing of labor productivity growth for 1931-38	203
7.5	Intra-industry growth rates of labor productivity for 1931-38	203
8.1	Decomposition of Gini coefficient in Taiwan: 1964-68	219
8.2	Decomposition of Gini coefficient in Taiwan: 1968-72	220
8.3	Income inequality in Japan, 1960-89	224
8.4	Relative income of agricultural households in Japan by scale of farm, 1957-81	225
8.5	Monthly wage income in Hong Kong	230
8.6	Choo's estimate of inequality of household income in Korea	233

8.7	Ratio of nonagricultural to agricultural income in annual farm household income	234
8.8	Gini of household income in Korea	236
8.9	Household income inequality and employment in Malaysia	238
8.10	Income distribution in the Philippines	243
9.1	Rotated factor matrix for share of income accruing to the poor in 1990	262
9.2	Rotated factor matrix for share of population in absolute poverty in 1990	263
9.3	Rotated factor matrix for share of income accruing to the middle-income group in 1990	268
9.4	Rotated factor matrix for concentration and the share of income accruing to the rich in 1990	271
10.1	An overview of the Peruvian living standard surveys	291
10.2	Lorenz dominance comparisons for Peru 1985-86 and 1991 per capita total consumption expenditure equivalence	293
10.3	Summary of Lorenz dominance comparisons of per capita consumption expenditures in Peru	294
10.4	Lorenz dominance and inequality in Peru using four different equivalence scales	296
10.5a	First-order dominance comparisons of inflation-adjusted household food expenditure in Peru, 1985-86 and 1991	297
10.5b	First-order dominance comparisons of household food expenditure shares and welfare in Peru, 1985-86 and 1991	298
10.6	Summary of first-order dominance comparisons of food expenditure shares and welfare in Peru	299
10.7	Mobility matrices of per capita household consumption in Lima, 1985-86 to 1990	301
10.8	Mobility matrices of per capita household consumption in Lima, 1990-1991	303
11.1	Poverty estimates based on two approaches	316
11.2	Poverty reduction, Philippines versus other developing countries	319
11.3	Consumption growth and inequality	320
11.4	Simulated poverty measures	321
11.5	Regional poverty profile, 1985 and 1994	322
11.6	Decomposition of poverty change between 1985 and 1994, by region	324
11.7	Poverty determination functions	328
13.1	Size and location of largest ethnic groups in Kenya and Uganda	358
13.2	Violence in Kenya and Uganda, estimated deaths	360

13.3 Economic performance in Kenya and Uganda 367
13.4 Social developments in Kenya and Uganda, 1962-97 368
13.5 Government expenditure and revenue, Uganda and Kenya 370

Contributors

Irma Adelman, *Professor in the Graduate School, Department of Agricultural and Resource Economics, University of California, Berkeley, CA, USA*

Arsenio M. Balisacan, *Professor of Economics, University of the Philippines, Quezon, Philippines*

Chau-Nan Chen, *Member of Academia Sinica and Research Fellow, Sun Yat-Sen Institute for Social Sciences and Philosophy, Academia Sinica, Taipei, Taiwan ROC*

Yun-Peng Chu, *Research Fellow and Director, Sun Yat-Sen Institute for Social Sciences and Philosophy, Academia Sinica, Taipei, Taiwan ROC*

John P. Formby, *Hayes Professor of Economics, University of Alabama, Tuscalloosa, AL, USA*

Jacob Kaliyati, *Economist, Zimbabwe Institute of Development, Zimbabwe*

Anthony Y.C. Koo, *Member of Academia Sinica, Taipei, Taiwan ROC and Professor of Economics, Michigan State University, East Lansing, MI, USA*

Anne O. Krueger, *Professor of Economics and the Herald L. and Caroline L. Ritch Professor of Humanities Sciences, Stanford University, Stanford, CA, USA*

Lawrence J. Lau, *Member of Academia Sinica and Kwoh-Ting Li Professor of Economic Development, Stanford University, Stanford, CA, USA*

Hsiu-Yun Lee, *Associate Professor of Economics, National Chung-Cheng University, Chiayi, Taiwan ROC*

Kenneth S. Lin, *Professor of Economics, National Taiwan University, Taipei, Taiwan ROC*

Meghan O'Sullivan, *Queen Elizabeth House, International Development Centre, University of Oxford, Oxford, UK*

Keijiro Otsuka, *Associate Professor of Economics, Tokyo Metropolitan University, Tokyo, Japan*

Tetsushi Sonobe, *Associate Professor of Economics, Tokyo Metropolitan University, Tokyo, Japan*

T.N. Srinivasan, *Samuel C. Park, Jr. Professor of Economics, Economic Growth Center, and Chairman, Department of Economics, Yale University, New Haven, CT, USA*

Frances Stewart, *Professor and Director, Queen Elizabeth House, International Development Centre, University of Oxford, Oxford, UK*

Erik Thorbecke, *H.E. Babcock Professor of Economics and Food Economics, Cornell University, Ithaca, NY, USA*

Pan A. Yotopoulos, *Professor of Economics, Food Research Institute, Stanford University, Stanford, CA, USA*

Preface

This book contains selected papers presented or related to the issues discussed at the conference entitled 'The Economics and Political Economy of Development at the Turn of the Century: Conference in Memory of John C.H. Fei', held at Academia Sinica, Taipei, Taiwan, on August 1-2, 1997. The conference was jointly sponsored by Yale University, Academia Sinica, National Taiwan University, Chung-Hua Institution for Economic Research, Taiwan Institute of Economic Research and Taiwan Research Institute, with additional financial support from the National Science Council, the Ministry of Education, the Council for Economic Planning and Development, and the Far Eastern Foundation, Taiwan, ROC.

John C.H. Fei (1923-96) was a great teacher and economist. He contributed significantly to economic development theory, and is best known for his analysis of labor surplus, dualistic economies. He also contributed significantly during the past decade to research on Taiwan and on the reform of mainland China's economic system. Professor Fei received his BA from Yenching University, Peking in 1945, his MA in Economics from the University of Washington in 1948, and his PhD from the Massachusetts Institute of Technology in 1952. In the early 1950s he was an instructor at MIT and served as a senior economic researcher at the Harvard Economic Research Project. From 1955 to 1962 he was an associate professor at Antioch College, Ohio. After this, he was based primarily at Yale University, first as an associate professor (until 1965), then full professor (1969-93), and finally as professor emeritus (1993-96). During the period 1965-69, he was the Carl Mark Chair Professor at Cornell University. He also served as a consultant on numerous occasions for such organizations as Agency of Industrial Development (AID), and the United Nations Development Program. President Teng-Hui Lee of ROC who inaugurated the Conference was about to appoint Professor Fei as his Personal Advisor at the time of his death.

Throughout his career, Professor Fei was devoted to Taiwan, and returned to the country many times. In 1972, he became a Member of Academia Sinica. From 1980 to 1982, he was the Director of the Taiwan Institute of Economic Research and consultant for the National Science

Council. After 1993, he served as Chairman of the Board of Trustees for the Chung-Hua Institution for Economic Research. He also taught at National Taiwan University and Soochow University.

This book is dedicated to the memory of John C.H. Fei. His teachings and writings remain with us, and the issues to which he devoted his life continue to be relevant and important in the field of economics today, as can be seen by the range of issues covered in this book.

The editors wish to thank Professors Chi-fu Chang, Gregory Chow, Mei-lei Chu, Yih-chyi Chuang, Richard Eckaus, Thomas Gold, Yujiro Hayami, Michael Hsiao, Chau-chi Huang, Fun-mey Huang, Feng-fuh Jiang, Chi-yuan Liang, Jyh-wen Lin, Jun-ji Shih, Percy Vaughn, Henry Wan, and Shu-jen Yeh for helpful comments and suggestions.

Part I Overview

1. As the Century Turns: Analytics, Empirics and Politics of Development

T.N. Srinivasan

1 INTRODUCTION

I first met John Fei when I had just finished my graduate work in economics at Yale in 1962 and began teaching there. After returning to India in 1964, I came back to Yale in 1980, and joined John at the Economic Growth Center. During more than two decades of our association since then, we used to tell each other often, not entirely in jest, that the only two developing economies that mattered were China and India, and each is the only relevant and appropriate comparator for the other! My interest in learning about Chinese development was warmly welcomed by John. Indeed, John and I visited China together in January 1989 with the support of the Ford Foundation to advise the People's Bank of China on a proposed collaborative research project on inflation in China. After our very enjoyable visit, during which I was witness to the respect that many senior officials in China paid to John, we put up a research proposal to the Henry Luce Foundation for financing. Unfortunately, the Luce Foundation did not choose to fund our research collaboration with the People's Bank. However, the failure to attract research support did not dim our enthusiasm for exchanging ideas with each other on problems of development in general, and of China and India in particular, until his retirement. In fact, I made a modest effort in comparing Chinese and Indian agricultural and foreign trade policies with contributions from Justin Lin and Yun Win Sung (Srinivasan 1994a).

John Fei's research covered a wide spectrum and even included exploration of Chinese culture, particularly as a foundation for industrial capitalism and unification.[1] One can, however, distinguish three broad areas in his research. The first, of course, is the theory of development and growth including his celebrated work on the dual economy, in collaboration with Gustav Ranis. The second is the theory and measurement of inequality, with applications to Taiwan. The third is economic history. In many of his contributions, particularly those linking culture, history and economic performance, John showed great insight when he looked at the role of institutions, broadly speaking, in development.

John's contributions to growth theory are many. Even now I vividly recall with pleasure the many discussions we had on the paper 'Growth with Fluctuations' on which he was working with a graduate student, Deborah Reed, just prior to his retirement from Yale. I am sure he would have been pleased that, with its revival starting with the seminal papers of Lucas (1988) and Romer (1986), growth theory is currently at the frontier of research in theoretical and empirical economics.

Macroeconomic time-series data for an increasing number of countries, in particular from the painstaking work of Summers and Heston (1988, 1991) on purchasing power parity (PPP) adjusted data, have become widely accessible. This has stimulated empirical research, starting with Baumol (1986) and Barro (1991), on the determinants of development and growth. Although John was not an applied econometrician, his work on Taiwan is certainly empirical. He would have been keenly interested in the expanding empirical literature on growth.

John's work on Taiwan and on China enriched our understanding of the economics of this ancient civilization. The growth performance of East Asian countries (Japan, Hong Kong, Korea, Taiwan and Singapore) and their followers (Indonesia and Thailand) in Southeast Asia has been outstanding in contrast to the lackluster achievements of the rest of the developing world. John would not have been surprised that East Asian experience has figured prominently, not only in the recent empirical literature on growth as is to be expected, but also in motivating new theoretical approaches to growth as, for example, in the work of Lucas (1993).

John Fei would also have been enthused by the recent revival of institutional economics, a field that went out of fashion long ago because much of the analysis of institutions then was historical and anecdotal rather than formal (Lin and Nugent 1995). Transactions cost approach to economics indeed goes back to the great institutional economist John R. Commons, who long ago insisted that 'the ultimate unit of activity must include in itself the three principles of conflict, mutuality and order. This unit is a transaction' (1934, p. 4). This approach proved fruitful in studying the contrasting economic performance in their history of erstwhile colonies of Spain and Portugal in the Western Hemisphere and that of the former British colonies such as Australia, Canada and the

United States, as well as the role of institutions and their change in economic performance (North 1990a and Olson 1982). Analytical rigor was brought to bear on the transactions cost approach in formal modeling of the analysis of organizations (for example, Milgrom and Roberts 1992, Tirole 1994). This approach is now being applied to the analysis of politics as well (North 1990b, Dixit 1996). Again it is no surprise that East Asian development has been analyzed from the perspective of comparative institutional analysis (Aoki et al. 1997a).

Among the factors that might affect growth is the distribution among the relevant socioeconomic groups of the gains from growth and the costs of bringing it about. For example, the vastly overrated study of the World Bank (1993) claims that the authoritarian and paternalistic regimes of the high-performing East Asian economies followed 'the principle of shared growth', in order to legitimize themselves and to win the support of the society at large. John, who in his work on Taiwan emphasized its egalitarian growth, would certainly have approved the attention paid to distributional issues in the recent empirical literature on growth. However, the good theorist and an admirer of Simon Kuznets that he was, he would also have noted that in economic theory one cannot find an unambiguous and unidirectional causal relation between income and social inequalities and economic growth. One can easily postulate that, through the mechanism of savings and investment, greater inequality would promote *greater* growth; just as easily, one can postulate that, as the World Bank (1993) suggests, greater equality promotes more rapid growth. Of course, the famous Kuznets hypothesis is about causation going the other way — as incomes increase with growth, inequality first increases and then decreases. Indeed, notwithstanding the tall claims about 'shared growth' in East Asia, as I note below, in the empirical growth literature the influence of inequalities on growth is often statistically insignificant or ambiguous, and tests of the Kuznets hypothesis have yielded ambiguous results as well.

In celebrating John Fei's life and contributions to economics of growth and development, I thought that it would be appropriate to reflect on how the recent theoretical and empirical literature on economics and politics of growth has changed our earlier understanding of the development and growth process and its determinants. In particular, what are the lessons from the literature and development experience of the last five decades on the roles of the state, market and other institutions in the development process? What have we learned about the importance for rapid growth of openness to foreign trade, technology and capital flows? Does the accumulated evidence suggest that a democratic political framework is not an impediment to growth as it was once thought to be?

In what follows, first, I relate the 'new' growth theory to its neoclassical antecedents and argue that at least some of the implications of neoclassical growth theory that the 'new' growth theorists wished to escape from arose from a misleading characterization of the former (Section 2). Nevertheless, the recent growth literature has brought many new insights to the growth process. Second, I delve into the institutional underpinnings of development, in particular contrasting 'market failure', 'market-friendly' and 'market-enhancing' views of the role of the state in development (Section 3). Third, I summarize the findings from the recent empirical literature on the determinants of growth, including openness and on democracy and development (Section 4). I offer a few concluding remarks in Section 5.

2 GROWTH THEORIES: OLD AND NEW [2]

Theorizing about long-run growth revived after a hiatus of over two decades since the last spurt in the 1950s and 1960s. In the largely neoclassical growth theoretic literature of the 1960s and earlier, one could distinguish three strands.

The first strand is *positive* or, better still, *descriptive* theory aimed at explaining the stylized facts of long-run growth in industrialized countries (particularly in the United States) such as a steady secular growth of aggregate output, relative constancy of the share of savings, investment, labor and capital income in aggregate output. Solow's (1956, 1957) celebrated articles and later work by Jorgenson and Griliches (1966) and others are examples of descriptive growth theory and related empirical analysis. As Stiglitz (1990) remarked, by showing that the long-run steady- state growth rate could be unaffected by the rate of savings (and investment) and, even in the short run, that the rate of growth was mostly accounted for by the rate of labor-augmenting technical progress, Solow challenged the then conventional wisdom.

The second strand is *normative* theory which drew its inspiration from Ramsey's (1928) classic paper on optimal saving. In contrast to the descriptive models in which the aggregate savings rate was exogenously specified (usually as a constant over time), the normative models derived time-varying savings rates from the optimization of an intertemporal social welfare function. There were mainly two variants of such normative models: one-sector models (Koopmans 1965 and Cass 1965) and two-sector models (Srinivasan 1962, 1964 and Uzawa 1964).

The third strand of theory is primarily neither descriptive nor normative though it is related to both. Harrod's (1939) dynamic extension of the Keynesian model (with its constant marginal propensity to save) raised the issue of stability of the growth path by contrasting two growth rates: the *warranted* rate of growth that would be consistent with maintaining the savings-investment equilibrium and the *natural* growth rate as determined by the growth of the labor force and technical change. In this model, unless the economy's behavioral and technical parameters keep it on the knife edge of equality between warranted and natural growth rates, there would be either growing underutilization of capacity if the warranted rate exceeds the natural rate or growing unemployment if the natural rate exceeds the warranted rate. Indeed this knife-edge property resulting from Harrod's assumption that capital and labor are used in fixed proportions led Solow to look for growth paths converging to a steady state by replacing Harrod's technology with a neoclassical technology of positive elasticity of substitution between labor and capital. Von Neumann's (1945) model is also part of the third strand. In this model production technology is characterized by a finite set of constant returns to scale activities with inputs being committed at the beginning, outputs emerging at the end, of each discrete production period. There are no non-produced factors of production such as labor or exhaustible natural resources. In the 'primal' version, von Neumann characterized the vector of activity levels that permitted the maximal rate of *balanced growth* (that is, growth in which outputs of all commodities grew at the same rate) given that the outputs of each period were to be plowed back as inputs in the next period. In the 'dual' version, a vector of commodity prices and an interest rate were derived which had the properties that the value of output of each activity was no higher than the value of inputs inclusive of interest and that the interest rate was the lowest possible. Under certain assumptions about the technology, von Neumann showed that the maximal growth rate of output of the primal was equal to the (minimal) interest rate of the dual.

Barring a few exceptions, in the neoclassical growth models production technology was assumed to exhibit constant returns to scale and in many, though not all, models smooth substitution among inputs with strictly diminishing marginal rates of substitution between any two inputs along an isoquant was also posited. Analytical attention was focussed on conditions ensuring the existence and uniqueness of steady-state growth paths along which all inputs and outputs grew at the same rate the steady-state being the path to which all transitional paths starting from any given initial conditions and satisfying the requirements of specified descriptive rates of accumulation or of intertemporal welfare optimality converged. The steady state growth rate was the *exogenous* rate of growth of labor force in efficiency units so that in the absence of (exogenous) labor-augmenting technical progress, output per worker was constant along the steady state.

Turning to the exceptions, Solow (1956) himself drew attention to the possibility that a steady state need not even exist and even if one existed it need not be unique. Indeed, output per worker could grow indefinitely even in the absence of labor-augmenting technical progress, if the marginal product of capital was bounded below by a sufficiently high positive number. Also, there could be multiple steady states, some of which were unstable if the production technology exhibited nonconvexities. There were also exceptions to the exogeneity of technical progress and of the rate of growth of output along a steady state. Kaldor and Mirrlees (1962) endogenized technical progress (and hence the rate of growth of output) by relating productivity of workers operating newly produced equipment to the rate of growth of investment per worker. And there was the celebrated model of Arrow (1962) of 'learning by doing', in which factor productivity was an increasing function of cumulated output or investment. Uzawa (1965) also endogenized technical progress by postulating that the rate of growth of labor-augmenting technical progress was a concave function of the ratio of labor employed in the education sector to total employment. The education sector was assumed to use labor as the only input. Uzawa's model has influenced recent contributions to growth theory. Besides, in the literature on induced innovation (Ahmad 1966, Boserup 1965, Kennedy 1964) technical change was, by definition, endogenous.

The recent revival of growth theory started with the influential papers of Lucas (1988) and Romer (1986). Lucas motivated his approach by arguing that neoclassical growth theory cannot account for observed differences in growth across countries and over time and its evidently counterfactual prediction that international trade should induce rapid movements toward equality in capital-labor ratios and factor prices. He argued that

> In the absence of differences in pure technology then, and under the assumption of no factor mobility, the neoclassical model predicts a strong tendency to income equality and equality in growth rates, tendencies we can observe within countries and, perhaps, within the wealthiest countries taken as a group, but which simply cannot be seen in the world at large. When factor mobility is permitted, this prediction is powerfully reinforced. (Lucas 1988, pp. 15-16)

He then goes on to suggest that the one factor isolated by the neoclassical model, namely, variation across countries in technology,

> has the potential to account for wide differences in income levels and growth rates ... when we talk about differences in 'technology' across countries we are not talking about knowledge in general, but about the knowledge of particular people, or particular subcultures of people. If so, then while it is not exactly wrong to describe these differences [as] exogenous ... neither is it useful to do so. We want a formalism that leads us to think about individual decisions to acquire knowledge, and about the consequences of these decisions for productivity.

He draws on the theory of 'human capital' to provide such a formalism: each individual acquires productivity-enhancing skills by devoting time to such acquisition and away from paying work. The acquisition of skills by a worker not only increases his or her productivity but by increasing the average level of skills in the economy as a whole, it has a spillover effect on the productivity of all workers by increasing the average level of skills in the economy as a whole.[3]

Romer also looked for an alternative to the neoclassical model of long-run growth to escape from its implications that 'initial conditions or current disturbances have no long-run effect on the level of output and consumption in the absence of technical change, per capita output should converge to a steady-state value with no per capita growth' (Romer 1986, pp. 1002 3). His is 'an equilibrium model of endogenous technological change in which long-run growth is driven primarily by the accumulation of knowledge by forward-looking, profit-maximizing agents' (p. 1003). While the production of new knowledge is through a technology that exhibits diminishing returns, 'the creation of new knowledge by one firm is assumed to have a positive external effect on the production possibilities of other firms ... [so that] production of consumption goods as a function of stock of knowledge exhibits increasing returns; more precisely, knowledge may have an increasing marginal product' (p. 1003).

It should be noted that the spillover effect of the average stock of human capital per worker in the Lucas model and of knowledge in the Romer model are externalities unperceived (and hence not internalized) by individual agents. However for the economy *as a whole* they generate increasing scale economies even though the perceived production function of each agent exhibits constant returns to scale. Thus, by introducing nonconvexities through the device of a Marshallian externality, Lucas and Romer were able to work with intertemporal competitive (albeit a socially nonoptimal) equilibrium. Thus both avoid facing the problem that research and development (R&D) that lead to technical progress are 'naturally associated with imperfectly competitive markets, as Schumpeter (1942) had forcefully argued' (Stiglitz 1990, p. 25). Later work by others (for example, Grossman and Helpman 1991) formulated models in which firms operating in an imperfectly competitive markets undertook R&D.

In sorting out the differences between neoclassical and recent growth models it is useful to start with a simplified version of Solow's (1956) growth model.

$$\text{Output: } Y(t) \equiv K(t)^a L(t)^b + cK(t) \tag{1.1}$$

where: $0 < a < 1, 0 < b < 1, a + b \geq 1, \; c \geq 0$

$$\text{Net investment: } \dot{K}(t) = sY(t) - \delta K(t) \tag{1.2}$$

$$\text{Labor force: } L(t) = e^{nt} \tag{1.3}$$

Now as long as $nb \neq (sc - \delta)(1 - a)$, there exists a unique steady-state solution for $K(t)$ with its rate of growth being $(sc - \delta)$ if $(sc - \delta)(1 - a) > nb$ and $(nb)/(1 - a)$ if $(sc - \delta)(1 - a) < nb$. Three special cases are of interest.

The first case is one in which $a + b = 1$ and $c = 0$. The production function exhibits *constant returns to scale* and the marginal product of capital *diminishes to zero* as the capital-labor ratio increases indefinitely. Along the unique steady state, capital stock, consumption and output grew at the same *exogenous* rate, n, the rate of growth of the labor force.

The second is one in which $c = 0$ and $a + b > 1$. The production function exhibits increasing scale economies, and the property that the marginal product of capital diminishes to zero (because $0 < a < 1$) as the capital-labor ratio increases indefinitely. Along the unique steady state, capital stock grows at the rate $(nb)/(1 - a) > n$ and output per worker grows at the rate $[n(a + b - 1)]/(1 - a) > 0$. Thus, with increasing scale economies, there is *positive* but *exogenous* growth in per worker output in the long-run steady state.

The third is the case in which $a + b = 1$ and $c > 0$. The production function now exhibits constant returns to scale, but the marginal product of capital is bounded below by $c > 0$. If c is sufficiently large so that $(sc - \delta)(1 - a) > nb = n(1 - a)$ or $sc > (n + \delta)$, then in the steady state capital stock grows at the rate $(sc - \delta) > n$ and output per worker grows at the rate $(sc - \delta - n)a > 0$.

Almost all contributors to the 'old' neoclassical growth theory were in fact working with production functions, as in the first case, with *constant returns to scale and the absence of a positive floor* to the marginal product of capital. Indeed, it is this combination that is responsible for the steady-state implications of neoclassical growth models from which the 'new' growth theorists wished to escape.

It is clear from the second case that although increasing scale economies yield a positive rate of growth in per worker output in the steady state, this rate is *exogenous*. As such, increasing scale economies alone are *not sufficient* to generate endogenous growth.

In the third case, since the savings rate s could be endogenous, one obtains positive, *endogenously* determined growth in per worker output in the long run. This case demonstrates that increasing scale economies are not *necessary* to generate *endogenous and positive growth* of output per worker in the long run. It is enough if a sufficient high positive rate lower than the marginal product exists, although there are no scale economies.

It should now be evident from the third case that one can generate long-run growth effects of trade liberalization if the production function is such that there is a sufficiently high floor for the marginal product of capital. This can be demonstrated with two well-known models, the one-sector Harrod-Domar model and the two-sector Fel'dman-Mahalanobis model.

Consider the simplest version of the work-horse of early development planning, namely, the Harrod Domar (1957) model in which capital is the sole factor of production.[4] Output Y at any time t is the product of capital stock K in existence at that time and a constant output-capital ratio β. The economy is assumed to be closed to foreign trade. A constant proportion s of output is assumed to be saved and invested so that, given a constant proportional rate of depreciation at the rate δ per unit of time of capital stock, the growth rate g of the economy is $s\beta - \delta$. As long as s is exogenous, so is the growth rate g.

Let me introduce foreign trade into the model in a very simple way by supposing that the economy can trade with the rest of the world at a constant terms of trade of π ($\pi > 1$) units of investment per unit of output in contrast with domestic terms of trade of unity under autarky. In other words, while under autarky, the economy can transform each unit of output into one unit of consumption or one unit of investment, with trade it gets the same consumption but more (that is, π ($\pi > 1$)) investment per unit of output. Implicit in this way of introducing trade is that the economy is too small to influence the world relative price (in terms of home output) of investment good and that it has a comparative advantage in its home output or equivalently, consumption good. Thus with capital as its sole factor of production this Ricardian economy specializes in producing consumption good under free trade.

Let us as well make savings (equivalently consumption c_t) endogenous (and thus growth endogenous) through the maximization of intertemporal welfare

$$W \equiv \int_0^\infty e^{-\rho t} u(c_t)dt \tag{1.4}$$

where, for simplicity of analysis, assume that the instantaneous felicity function $u(c_t)$ is $(c^{1-\sigma}-1)/(1-\sigma)$(with $\sigma>0$). Assume, again for simplicity, that international lending or borrowing is infeasible, so that trade has to be balanced at each t. Thus W is to be maximized subject to the constraint investment goods imports equal the value of exports or

$$\dot{K}_t + \delta K_t = \pi[\beta K_t - c_t] \tag{1.5}$$

and the non-negativity constraints $c_t \geq 0,\ \dot{K}_t + \delta K_t \geq 0$.

An optimal solution to this problem exists, and is unique, as long as $\rho + (\sigma - 1)(\pi\beta - \delta) > 0$. It is given by:

$$K_t = K_0 e^{gt} \text{ and } c_t = \left[\frac{\rho + (\sigma - 1)(\pi\beta - \delta)}{\pi\sigma}\right] K_0 e^{gt} \tag{1.6}$$

where

$$g = \left(\frac{\pi\beta - \delta - \rho}{\sigma}\right) \tag{1.7}$$

The *short- and long-run growth rate* g of consumption and capital stock will be positive as long as $\pi\beta - \delta - \rho > 0$. Now $\partial g / \partial \pi = \beta / \sigma > 0$. Since opening the economy to trade involves an increase in the relative price of the consumption good in which the economy has comparative advantage from its value of 1 under autarky to $\pi > 1$ under free trade, it follows from $\partial g / \partial \pi > 0$ that the short- and long-run growth rate of the economy, namely, g, is increased by such opening. *Thus, trade liberalization (which in this case is moving to free trade from autarky) has positive growth effects.*[5]

Now the gross domestic product (GDP) valued in units of *investment goods* is

$$(\dot{K}_t + \delta K_t) + \pi c_t = \beta\pi K_0 e^{gt} \tag{1.8}$$

Clearly as π under free trade is raised above its autarky value of unity, there is a *positive level effect* (through $\beta\pi$) *and* a *positive* growth effect (through g) on GDP (from the move to free trade). The value of GDP in units of *consumption goods* (or equivalently output) is $\beta K_0 e^{gt}$. As such, moving to free trade has only a growth effect (through the effect of the rise in π on g), but no level effect on GDP in units of consumption good.

It is seen from (1.6) that moving to free trade has a positive growth effect, but an ambiguous level effect (it is positive, zero or negative accordingly as $(\sigma-1)\delta-\rho$ is positive, zero or negative), on consumption in physical units. This reflects the conflict between a *positive* income effect and a negative substitution effect as the economy moves to freer trade, arising from the rise in relative price of consumption good in which the economy has comparative advantage. The *value* of consumption, in terms of investment goods, is

$$\pi c_t = \left[\frac{\rho + (\sigma-1)(\pi\beta-\delta)}{\sigma}\right] K_0 e^{gt}.$$

Hence, moving to free trade has a *positive growth effect* on it as well. The *level effect* is *positive if and only if* the intertemporal elasticity of substitution $1/\sigma < 1$. However, whether or not the level effect on consumption is positive (either in value or in physical units), it can be shown that intertemporal welfare W increases under free trade relative to autarky, the reason being that even if the *level effect* on consumption of a move to free trade is negative, the positive *growth effect* is more than enough to raise W under free trade above its autarky level.

One of the influential development models was formulated independently by Fel'dman (1928) for the Soviet Union and independently by the physicist-statistician Mahalanobis (1955) for India. It is a model of a closed economy in which there are two sectors, one of which produces a consumption good, and the other, a capital good. Capital is the only factor of production, and the output of each sector is the product of the stock of capital in existence in that sector and its output-capital ratio. While the *flow* of output of the investment goods sector can be allocated in any fashion to augment the *stock* of capital in either sector, capital, once installed in that sector, cannot be shifted to the other sector. It turns out that the long-run growth rate of the economy depends only on the output-capital ratio of the capital goods sector and the proportion of the output of that sector that is invested in it and it is increasing in both. As such a Soviet-style 'heavy-industry' strategy that plowed a greater share of investment into the capital goods industry increased long-run growth at the expense of current consumption.

I have analyzed (Srinivasan 1993, Appendix I) an expanded version of the Fel'dman Mahalanobis model with *two* commodities in each sector, with the commodities differing in their capital-output ratios. As long as both consumer goods and capital are demanded in positive amounts, under autarky all four goods will be produced in positive amounts. Suppose this economy has the opportunity to trade with the rest of the world at fixed relative prices. If it opens the economy to free trade only in consumer goods, it will specialize in the consumer goods sector in producing that good in which it has comparative advantage. However, as long as the share of investment devoted to the capital goods sector is unchanged, and that sector is closed to foreign trade, even though the welfare of the economy will rise relative to autarky, *the long-run growth rate of the economy would be unchanged.* In contrast, if the capital goods sector is opened to free trade (again at fixed world relative prices) while the consumer goods sector is kept closed, there will be a *positive long-run growth effect and a welfare effect relative to autarky.* The implication is that, from a growth perspective, keeping the growth-inducing sector (which is the capital goods sector in this model) closed to international competition is costlier than closing the consumer goods sector. But, of course, keeping neither closed would be even better since, for this small economy, there is no market power to be exploited through a tariff policy or any dynamic externalities due to learning effects to be internalized in the model.

To sum up this section, the starting point of some, though not all, of the recent contributions to growth theory, is a misleading characterization of neoclassical growth theory of the 1960s and earlier as implying that a steady-state growth path always exists along which output grows at a rate equal to the exogenously specified rate of growth of the labor force in efficiency units. Thus in the absence of labor augmenting technical progress, per capita income does not grow along the steady-state path. Policies that affect savings (investment) rates have only transient effects on the growth rate of per capita output, although its steady-state *level* is affected. Even a cursory reading of the literature is enough to convince a reader that neoclassical growth theorists were fully aware that a steady state need not exist and per capita output can grow indefinitely even in the absence of technical progress provided that the marginal product of capital is bounded away from zero by a sufficiently high positive number. Moreover, they showed that once one departs from the assumption that the marginal product of capital *monotonically* declines to zero as the capital-labor ratio increases indefinitely, multiple steady-state growth paths are likely (only some of which are stable) and that the steady state to which a transition path converges would depend on initial conditions. Attempts at endogenizing technical progress were also made by theorists of the era.

It was argued above that the perceived problems of neoclassical growth theory are not inherent features of all the growth models of the era but only of those which assumed that the marginal product of capital (or more generally of any reproducible factor) diminishes to *zero* as the input of capital (or that factor) is increased indefinitely relative to other inputs. Instead of directly relaxing this assumption about production technology the 'new' growth theorists in effect make assumptions that ensure that the marginal product of capital is bounded away from zero. In some of the models this is achieved by introducing a factor other than physical capital (for example, human capital, stock of knowledge) whose marginal product does diminish to zero. In doing so, some authors end up with an aggregate production function that exhibits increasing scale economies. Unsurprisingly, in such models multiple equilibria are possible. Be that as it may, new growth theorists have gone beyond their primary goal of specifying models in which there is a possibility that the long-run growth rate of per worker income is positive. By endogenizing the growth rate and allowing policy variables to influence it, they have opened up avenues for the analysis of policies that could promote long-run growth.

3 INSTITUTIONS IN DEVELOPMENT: STATE, MARKETS AND NONMARKET PRIVATE INSTITUTIONS

3.1 The Development Process from a Transactions Perspective

At early stages of development, most households are largely self-sufficient and the few transactions they engage in consist of sporadic exchanges through barter of a few goods and services. As development proceeds, exchanges (using money as a medium of exchange) of an enormous number of goods and services take place, regularly and repeatedly, through markets in which the original producers (that is, sellers) and the ultimate users (that is, buyers) may not be, and often will not be, known to each other and with the *quid* and *quo* of exchange being separated widely in time and space. With the separation of production and use, an important role for intermediation arises so that a class of traders and financial intermediaries emerges who buy goods and services only to sell them at a different time or place, rather than use them. Once intermediaries, whose sole interest is in the return from price arbitrage, that is, profits from buying low and selling high, emerge, speculative activities also arise. I must hasten to add, first, that it is not the existence of markets *per se* — after all, markets have existed since antiquity — but it is their scope, size and sophistication that characterizes successful development. In particular, efficient financial and capital markets, that is, markets in which intertemporal transactions involving saving, investing, borrowing and lending take place and insurance markets for transactions across uncertain states of nature are common in developed economies. Second, the relationship between markets and development runs both ways – as Adam Smith noted long ago, increased specialization through division of labor, which is a dominant characteristic of development, is limited by the size of the market.

Exchanges in which the *quid* and the *quo* are widely separated in time or space will not take place unless property rights are well defined and contracts are enforced. Availability of reliable and inexpensively acquired information, in particular about future conditions, facilitates such exchanges. It is a cliché to say that the three branches of the state (executive, judiciary and legislative) are crucial for determining what property rights (and more broadly, which laws) get enacted and what contracts are admissible, how well laws and contracts are enforced, and how efficiently disputes are settled and so on. The two fundamental theorems of neoclassical welfare economics, that establish the Pareto optimality of a competitive market equilibrium and the feasibility of achieving desired distributional objectives through lump-sum transfers, assume the existence of a complete set of markets for intertemporal and insurance transactions, far-sighted and rational behavior by agents and costless and certain enforcement of contracts. There are no problems of governance in public and private institutions in this idealized neo-classical world.

3.2 State and Markets in the Development Process

The pioneers of development economics believed that crucial markets (such as capital and insurance markets) did not exist (or functioned very imperfectly if they existed) and externalities and scale economies were pervasive in less-developed countries. For them the optimality asserted by the two fundamental theorems was irrelevant in the context of development. Given their premise of non-existence and failure of markets, it is not surprising that they saw a need for the state to intervene in the markets or assume the role of markets if they did not exist, to remedy the failures of markets in 'coordinating resource mobilization, allocating investment, and promoting technological catch-up at the developmental stage' (Aoki et al. 1997a, p. xv). Some later adherents of this view

argue that strong states in the East Asian economies succeeded in fulfilling these objectives by deliberately 'getting the prices wrong' (Amsden 1989) in order to boost industries that would not otherwise have thrived (see Johnson 1982 for Japan, Amsden 1989 for Korea, Wade 1990 for Taiwan). This view has been relatively more popular among political scientists and in public forums, but has never become the mainstream view in economics. (ibid., p. xv)

In contrast to the 'market failure' view of the early development economists and their latter day followers, World Bank (1991) propounded a 'market-friendly' view, according to which

> most economic coordination can be achieved through the market mechanism and that when markets alone are insufficient, other private-sector organization, such as intra-firm coordination, will suffice. The role of government in this view is limited to providing a legal infrastructure for market transactions and providing goods subject to extreme market failure (for example, when markets are missing for public goods such as a clean environment). (Aoki et al. 1997b, p. 1)

The three authors suggest that

> Both views look to markets as the initial basis for organization and recognize that markets alone are imperfect. Where they differ significantly is in the mechanism by which market imperfections are resolved. The market-friendly view expects that most market imperfections can be resolved by private-sector institutions, whereas the developmental-state view looks to government intervention as the solution. In this sense, these two views consider the role of government and that of the market (or, more broadly, market-based institutions) as substitutes, with competing roles for the resolution of market failures. (ibid., p. 1)

Aoki et al. (1997b) propose a third view, which they call the market enhancing view. Thus

> Instead of viewing government and the market as the only alternatives, and as mutually exclusive substitutes, we examine the role of government policy to facilitate or complement private-sector coordination. We start from the premise that private-sector institutions have important comparative advantages *vis-à-vis* the government, in particular in their ability to provide appropriate incentives and to process locally available information. We also recognize that private-sector institutions do not solve all important market imperfections and that this is particularly true for economies in a low state of development. The capabilities of the private sector are more limited in developing economies. The market-enhancing view thus stresses the mechanisms whereby government policy is directed at improving the ability of the private sector to solve coordination problems and overcome other market imperfections. (ibid., pp. 1-2)

I would argue that all three views implicitly assume what Dixit (1996) calls a 'crude but effective caricature', namely that policies are to be 'made by an omnipotent, omniscient, and benevolent dictator' (ibid., p. 8).[6] Dixit suggests that with the development of 'second best' theory, which recognized that the policy maker may be constrained from adopting first-best policies, his or her 'omnipotence' was removed. Once it is recognized that he or she may not have, and may not even be able to acquire, the information needed to design and implement optimal policies, 'omniscience' was removed. Yet most normative policy analysis continues to assume that the policy-maker is a benevolent dictator. Indeed, as Dixit argues,

> The implicit assumption is that once a policy that maximizes or improves social welfare has been found and recommended, it will be implemented as designed and the desired effects will follow.
>
> In reality, a policy proposal is merely the beginning of a process that is *political* at every stage ... The political process of policy making is constantly influenced by the legislature, the executive and its agencies, the courts, various special interest lobbies, the media and so on. The legislature may fail to enact the economist's desired policies; the administrative process may fail to implement the legislated policies in the intended manner. The outcomes may fail to correct market failures, and may instead new costs of their own. (ibid., pp. 8-9)

Anne Krueger (1990) perceptively noted that while it is tempting to look for 'government failures' as analogues of 'market failures', there is no clear norm the failure to attain which could be deemed a failure of the government. There is no analogue of the norm of Pareto optimality of resource allocation, the failure to achieve which, in a market equilibrium, constitutes market failure. Nonetheless, the phenomena that failures of the market and the political process portray can be viewed as arising from 'opportunistic behavior'.

3.3 Opportunism and its Mitigation

Opportunistic behavior arises in many contexts. Phenomena such as 'moral hazard', adverse selection, free riding and so on are instances of opportunistic behavior. In all these instances, parties to an agreement or contract have incentives to deviate, *ex post,* from what they have agreed or contracted to do. Unless the parties can credibly pre-commit not to deviate *ex post* or an inexpensive and sure third party enforcement (through the legal system, for example) is available, contracts will have to be incentive compatible and self-enforcing.

Opportunism is not confined to contracts between private agents. The problem of credibility of announced public policies is also a reflection of opportunism.[7] For example, if a government offers inducements for private investors to invest in some activity, and if capital once invested in that activity cannot be put to alternative uses, investors would not invest unless the government can credibly pre-commit not to tax the profits from the activity or expropriate the capital invested.

Once the possibility of opportunism is recognized, not only the assumption of 'benevolent dictatorship' underlying much normative policy analysis becomes moot, but the focus of comparative institutional analyses changes. As Williamson points out

> the main lesson of opportunism, for purposes of economic organization, is not the Machiavellian message to breach agreements with impunity because that is what others will do ... Instead, far sighted economic agents will ask what they can do to mitigate the hazards of opportunism. Because it is in their mutual interests to avoid *ex post* opportunism, far-sighted parties to a contract will give and receive credible commitments ex ante. (Williamson 1994, p. 183)

The essential point of organization of transactions through incentive compatible, self enforcing contracts is that it will involve real costs relative to the ideal where a relatively cheap and effective third party enforcement mechanism exists. But ideals are just that: they do not correspond to reality in which

> all feasible forms of organization are flawed ... and accordingly, the appropriate test of failures of all kinds – markets, bureaucracies, redistribution is remediableness: *an outcome for which no feasible superior alternative can be described and implemented with net gains is presumed to be efficient.* (ibid., p. 185, emphasis in original)

The transactions framework analyzed by Williamson in the context of economic organization is also applicable to the analysis of alternative forms of political organization. After all, constitutions are quintessentially incomplete contracts that do not envisage all potential contingencies and spell out actions to be taken by various actors in each one of them, let alone ensure that the specified actions will be taken.[8] The problem of opportunistic behavior is a serious one in politics as well. Weingast (1993, 1995) has addressed the issues in depth. He argues that 'the political institutions of society create a "governance structure" that at once allows the society to deal with on-going problems as they arise ... and yet provides a degree of durability to economic and political rights. Importantly these help limit the ability of the state to act opportunistically' (Weingast 1993, p. 288), and

> The main lesson ... for development and economic reform is ... that the benevolent attitude of government cannot be taken for granted. Markets require protection and thus a government strong enough to resist responding to the inevitable political forces advocating encroachments on markets for private gain. The fundamental dilemma of an economic system is that a government strong enough to protect private markets is strong enough to confiscate the wealth of its citizens.
>
> Put simply, the political foundations of markets are as essential to their success as the details and specification of the market itself. This conclusion implies that markets and limited government are complementary aspects of economic development and reform, each enhances the value of the other. Political development must therefore be placed simultaneously with economic development. (Weingast 1995, pp. 24-5)

3.4 Culture, Social Capital and All That!

Fukuyama (1993) emphasizes that 'culture affects economic behavior in certain critical ways just as it affects the ability of a people to sustain stable democracy' (p. 224). In a later work (Fukuyama 1995) he argues that the

> liberal policy and economic institutions depend on a healthy and dynamic civil society for their vitality ... A thriving civil society depends on a people's habits, customs, and ethics – attributes that can be shaped only indirectly through conscious political action and must otherwise be nourished through an increased awareness and respect for culture. (pp. 4-5)
>
> We can think of neoclassical economics as being, say, eighty percent correct ... But there is a missing twenty percent of human behavior about which neoclassical economics can give only a poor account. As Adam Smith well understood, economic life is deeply embedded in social life, and it cannot be understood apart from the customs, morals, and habits of the society in which it occurs. In short, it cannot be divorced from culture. (p. 13)

Fukuyama is certainly right in saying that the basic postulate, that is, rational behavior, of neoclassical economics is a powerful analytical tool and that because of its analytical power, neoclassical economics has triumphed over all other paradigms. Not only does he exaggerate the contribution of cultural differences in explaining differences in economic performance, but he does not seem to be aware that tools of neoclassical economics have been very fruitfully applied to analyze social norms and habits and nonmarket institutions. (For a survey of the so-called New Institutional Economics in the context of development, see Lin and

Nugent 1995.) In this connection, I cannot resist recounting the evaluation in 1903 of Japanese habits and customs by an Australian expert invited by the Japanese imperial government:

> My impression as to your cheap labor was soon disillusioned when I saw your people at work. No doubt they are lowly paid, but the return is equally so; to see your men at work made me feel that you are a very satisfied *easy-going race* who reckon time is no object. When I spoke to some managers they informed me that it was impossible to change the *habits of national heritage*.[9] (emphasis added)

I believe that given appropriate incentives, cultural traits that are deemed inimical to development somehow tend to disappear. Besides, within the same cultural milieu there is considerable heterogeneity among individuals in their attitudes toward work, risk and so on. It is a well-known fact that those individuals from a culture who emigrate to a more hospitable economic environment often do far better than those they leave behind and sometimes better than otherwise similar individuals in the country of their immigration, as Chinese and Indian emigrants have done all over the world. This reflects both the importance of incentives as well as the operation of self-selection, that is, in a heterogeneous population it is the more enterprising that are likely to emigrate and take their chances in a different cultural and economic environment.

Whether or not one agrees with the importance Fukuyama attaches to culture, one will agree with him that the efficiency of market exchange and the sustainability of liberal democracy both depend on aspects of social organization, such as trust, norms and networks. The sociologist James Coleman christened these features 'social capital' in analogy to human and physical capital. Social capital is not entirely culture determined – networks, such as 'rotating credit associations' which are based on trust, are found in most societies. But their adequacy is another matter. Robert Putnam (1993), in his comparative study of regions of Italy, found that the absence of social capital in southern Italy led to lawlessness, ineffective government and economic stagnation rather than to successful democratization and economic development. In contrast, in northern Italy where social capital in the form of norms of reciprocity and networks of civic engagement has existed for centuries, economic and institutional performance have been much better than in the south. Putnam concludes from this history that both states and markets operate more efficiently in areas endowed with higher social capital. While Putnam may well be right in his observation that building social capital is the key to making democracy work, neither he nor Fukuyama offer any operational guidelines as to how to accumulate it!

3.5 State Interventions in East Asia

Although the so-called 'gang of four' East Asian economies of Hong Kong, Korea, Singapore and Taiwan are often lumped together, it must be remembered that they vary in size, from a population in mid-1995 of about 3 million in Singapore at one end of the spectrum, to 45 million in Korea at the other end; in form of government, ranging from a past colonial, and a future totalitarian government in Hong Kong, to, until recently, authoritarian military governments in Korea, with 'guided' democracies of Singapore and Taiwan in between; and in economic policy, from almost complete *laissez-faire* in Hong Kong to varying degrees of intervention in others. The variation is even greater if one considers the larger group of 'high performing Asian economies' (HPAEs) as defined by the World Bank (1993), including China, Indonesia, Malaysia and Thailand, in addition to the 'gang of four'.

Leaving aside *laissez-faire* Hong Kong, the interventions in other HPAEs are claimed to have been in the form of contests whose ruler and rewards were transparent, whose referees impartially enforced the rules, and whose rewards accrued to those who met non-manipulable international market performance tests (ibid.) Further, they are said to have adopted 'specific institutional mechanisms such as wealth-sharing programs designed to include non-elites in economic growth, a cadre of economic technocrats insulated from narrow political pressures, and institutions and mechanisms to share information and win the support of business elites' (ibid., pp. 157-8).

The above characterization of interventions and institutions in HPAEs is based on an *ex post* rationalization, rather than *ex ante* causal explanation of the factors that led to high performance. Indeed, I would go further and suggest that the World Bank (1993) is an illustration of the logical fallacy of *post hoc ergo propter hoc.* After all, many governments, which are not high performers, also engaged in interventions similar to those of the HPAEs, and their institutions had similar features, at least for a considerable period of time. Although more could be cited, let me give one example with which I am more familiar, namely that of India.

In 1950, when India embarked on its planning for economic development, there was a broad consensus across the political spectrum on planning, a visionary and incorruptible political leadership (at the center and in the states) committed to development, as well as a very competent and honest bureaucracy at the decision-making levels. While the 'generalist' elite bureaucracy that was recruited through rigorous competitive examinations remained powerful, specialist or technical services such as the Indian Economic Service, Indian Statistical Service and so on were also created. Indeed, the bureaucracy was considered so insulated from politics that its nominal masters, namely the politicians, complained that it thwarted their directives. Unfortunately, the happy circumstance of an honest and visionary political leadership with very competent and incorruptible bureaucracy at its command did not last very long. To some extent this was inevitable. To a larger extent the dirigiste development strategy contributed to it.

The lesson from the Indian experience is that it is simply not enough to assert that, given a framework of appropriate rules, rewards and their impartial enforcement that the HPAEs allegedly had, rapid growth will come about. It is also necessary to show that the incentives to deviate from the specified rules, for the referee to collude in condoning such deviation, and so on, were absent. In fact, the range of government assistance in the form of subsidies, access to rationed credits and foreign exchanges, tax exemptions and so on was provided to exporters in many developed countries besides HPAEs. But such assistance did not result in export performance similar to that of HPAEs. The point is that without a deeper political-economy analysis to back it up, in particular whether or not an authoritarian framework *committed to development* is at the root of the impartiality of the referees, the three Rs (Rules, Referees, Reward) are no more than catchy slogans. Indeed, why the authoritarian leaders of HPAEs seemed to have been committed to development, while those of Nigeria, the Philippines and Zaire were apparently not, needs to be analyzed. As recent revelations demonstrate, it is not as if there was no corruption in HPAEs, or for that matter in industrialized countries, in contrast to the rampant corruption in the Philippines, Nigeria and Zaire.

The argument that East Asian economies had an unusually good macroeconomic management and relatively stable political regimes, both of which encouraged private domestic investment, needs to be qualified.[10] Once again, India's macro policies (until the 1980s) had the stability of a graveyard and there was no political instability at the center. In fact, in the 1980s when macro prudence was abandoned with rising fiscal deficits financed by domestic and external borrowing, and political instability seemed to threaten the center, growth was relatively rapid. Of course, it was a debt-led, unsustainable growth because there was no change in the 'fundamentals' as compared to the pre-1980s' period. It came to an inevitable end as a severe macroeconomic and balance of payments crisis hit the economy in 1991 following the Gulf War.

Turning to 'shared growth' in East Asia, it is too much of an *ex post* attribution to claim that the leadership promised *ex ante* that the fruits of growth would be shared to elicit appropriate responses from the citizenry. It is hard to argue that egalitarianism was the objective of either President

Chiang or President Park. Mao and his Communist Party certainly forced egalitarianism (outside of the leadership) but until the explicit move away from egalitarianism in the Deng era there was no spectacular growth. I would argue that the *character* of East Asian growth led to its fruits being shared widely rather than that a preannounced *objective* of 'sharing' the fruits led to rapid growth as an outcome. The argument that 'very explicit mechanisms were used to demonstrate that all would have a share of future wealth' has no basis in fact. Korean and Taiwanese land reforms were carried by 'outsiders' (in the Korean case before the growth strategy was adopted). Fertilizer price subsidies, preferential treatment of minorities and the underprivileged, encouragement of small-scale industries and so on, through distortionary policies are not signals of shared growth but of stifling potential growth. Ample experience with similar distortionary policies elsewhere supports this conclusion.

Finally, Lau and Kim (1994) and Young (1995) have shown that the contribution of total factor productivity growth in the spectacular growth of the 'gang of four' is not large. The contribution of the growth of physical and human capital is much larger. Whether their high savings and investment rates and their emphasis on human capital should be deemed miraculous is debatable. But there is likely to be more or less universal agreement on one thing (and perhaps one thing only): the policy framework of East Asia, in particular its emphasis on outward orientation and *external market* performance, and on the accumulation of *human capital* provided the incentives not only for rapid accumulation of *physical* capital but also, more importantly, for its *efficient* use. Thus, one does not have to look beyond the neoclassical explanations based on *fundamentals* (that is, rapid accumulation of factors and a framework for their efficient use) to understand East Asian growth.[11] There is no mystery or miracle.

4 CORRELATES AND DETERMINANTS OF DEVELOPMENT[12]

The recent empirical literature on growth across countries interestingly 'has not received its main inspiration from new theories', and in fact finds strong support for the neoclassical model's central idea of 'conditional convergence ... poorer countries grow faster per capita once one holds constant measures of government policy, initial levels of human capital, and so on' (Barro 1996b, p. 1). While stressing that 'the great strength of the cross-country approach is that it provides the breadth of experience needed to assess government policies and other determinants of long-term economic growth', Barro notes that 'At the same time, the use of these data creates problems related to measurement and estimation. Many critics of cross-country empirical work focus on these difficulties' (Barro 1996a, p. 70). I count myself among the critics and find that Barro's view that 'informational benefits override these objections' is more an article of faith, rather than an established fact. I remain sensitive to the serious problems of measurement and estimation, some of which were elaborated in Srinivasan (1994b) and other papers of the Symposium on the Data Base for Development Analysis in the *Journal of Development Economics*. But I do agree that there is suggestive and useful information in the findings of cross-country analyses, particularly since they include, in a common *empirical framework*, economic, political and social factors that in theory could influence growth. However, the link between theory and the estimated equations is suggestive, rather than definitive. Let me turn to a few of the important empirical findings.

4.1 Openness

It might seem odd in the context of contemporary trends towards global integration that once economists debated whether openness to foreign trade in goods and inflows of technology and capital was an 'engine of growth', as Dennis Robertson (1940) called it, or was an outcome or 'handmaiden of growth', as Irving Kravis (1970) put it. As is now well-known, the experience with the collapse of the world trading and payments during the interwar period, and the perception that there was a secular trend downward in the *terms of trade* of developing countries exporting primary products led to the adoption of an inward-orientated import-substituting industrialization strategy by most developing countries after the Second World War. The phenomenal success of the few who departed from such a strategy from the early 1960s on, namely the East Asian economies, has been attributed to their outward orientation.[13]

The recent empirical literature has examined the role of openness in promoting growth in a cross-section of countries. However, there are a number of serious problems with this empirical analysis: the choice of indicators for openness is somewhat arbitrary; whether to reduce barriers to trade and capital flows is an endogenous choice and the direction of causation of the relation between growth and openness can go both ways, so that growth and openness have to be treated as jointly determined endogenous variables, and virtually no study has done so; there are biasses and measurement errors in the data used which vitiate the consistency of the estimates of parameters. Nonetheless, the fact that a number of studies using different data sets, countries and methodologies happened to arrive at similar conclusions that are also consistent with a priori reasoning, suggests that they deserve serious consideration, with due allowances being made for their conceptual and statistical deficiencies. Let me cite a few.

Sachs and Warner (1995) find

> a strong association between openness and growth, both within the group of developing and the group of developed countries. Within the group of developing countries, the open economies grew at 4.49 percent per year, and the closed economies grew at 0.69 percent per year. Within the group of developed economies, the open economies grew at 2.29 percent per year, and the closed economies grew at 0.74 percent per year. (pp. 35-6)

By cross-classifying developing countries according to growth and openness, they reject 'the null hypothesis of no difference in growth rates between closed and open economies' (p. 36).

Their regressions explaining growth between 1970 and 1989 of 117 countries showed the following variables to be statistically insignificant: population density, primary and secondary school enrollment rates and the political variables, namely, average number of revolutions and coups per year and average number of assassinations per million of population, both during 1970-85.[14] While it is comforting that all the statistically significant variables have coefficients with expected signs, since some of the explanatory variables (for example, investment rate, relative price of investment goods) including the all-important dummy variable on openness could be endogenous, the estimated coefficients might be biased, though it is impossible to assess the seriousness of the bias.

Sachs and Warner also relate openness and the occurrence of severe macroeconomic crises (defined as the occurrence of any one of rescheduling of debt by official or private donors, arrears of external payments as reported by the International Monetary Fund or an inflation rate in excess of 100 percent). They offer several plausible reasons (greater dependence on debt, greater orientation of investment toward non-traded goods and a higher level of state involvement in the economy) as to why closed economies are more likely to experience severe macroeconomic crises. Out of 17 (respectively 73) economies that they classify as open (respectively closed) in the 1970s, as few as one (respectively as many as 59) experience macroeconomic crises in the 1980s.

Sachs and Warner are aware of the pitfalls in their analysis and properly cautious in distinguishing between various components of economic policy and their growth effects. They are certainly right in viewing their 'measure of trade policy [as serving] as a proxy for an entire array of policy actions' and that

> open trade has tended to be correlated with other features of a healthy economy, such as macroeconomic balance and reliance on the private sector as the main engine of growth. To some extent, opening the economy has helped to promote governmental responsibility in other areas. To that extent, trade policy should be viewed as the primary instrument of reform. (p. 63)

Sachs reports from yet another cross-country study that 'openness was decisive for rapid growth. Open economies grew 1.2 percent per year faster than closed economies, controlling for everything else' (Sachs 1997, p. 20).

Baldwin and Seghezza (1996) estimate two basic relationships: the first, between the rate of growth and its determinants, and the second, between trade barriers and investment, a possible channel through which trade could affect growth. They find that domestic *and* foreign trade barriers significantly depress investment. Clearly domestic trade barriers on the one hand raise domestic rental rate on capital, but on the other, they raise the cost of capital goods by raising the price of imported inputs used in their production. The latter effect, which makes investment less attractive, seems to dominate the former effect which makes investment more attractive. Their result on the deleterious effect of foreign barriers is apparently new – however, foreign barriers turn out to be less deleterious than domestic barriers. That both domestic and foreign barriers depress investment may be due to the fact that, in a multi-sector world, domestic and foreign barriers are very likely to apply to different sectors.[15]

Coe and Helpman (1995) test the impact of openness on the transmission of technical knowledge, and hence on the growth of total factor productivity (TFP). The basic idea is that technical knowledge is acquired both from domestic research and development (R&D) expenditures, and from imports, which convey information on the state of technological knowledge in the exporting country. A country that has a larger share of its imports originating in more advanced countries with higher technical knowledge will therefore experience faster TFP growth than one which imports more from less technically advanced countries. For their sample of 21 OECD countries and Israel for the period 1971-90, the results indicate a statistically significant, and similar, quantitative impact of domestic and foreign knowledge stocks on TFP growth.

Coe et al. (1997) apply the analysis of Coe and Helpman (1995) to a set of 77 developing countries for the period 1971-90. Since few developing countries undertake R&D, domestic R&D is not relevant for them. In addition to foreign knowledge stock, they include in their regression the secondary school enrollment rate, the share of imports from industrial countries, dummies for time periods 1971-75, 1975-80, 1980-85 and 1985-90, and their interaction with foreign knowledge stock. Simulations from their regression equation suggest that such spillovers from the North to the South are substantial and in 1990 'may have boosted output in the developing countries by 25 billion U.S. dollars. To put this figure in perspective, total official development aid from multilateral and bilateral sources in 1990 amounted to 50 billion U.S. dollars' (Coe et al. 1997, p. 148).

4.2 Savings, Investment and Growth

I noted that early development economists emphasized the importance of raising savings and investment. Arthur Lewis (1954, p. 155) went so far as to assert that the

> central problem of economic development is to understand the process by which a community which was previously saving and investing 4 or 5 percent of its national income or less converts itself into an economy where voluntary saving is running at about 12 to 15 percent of national income or more. This is the central problem because the central fact of economic development is rapid capital accumulation (including knowledge and skills with capital).

East Asian economies have succeeded in raising their saving and investment rates to very high levels. On the other hand, while most developing economies succeed in raising their savings about the threshold of 12-15 percent of national income set up by Arthur Lewis, few could be said to have solved the central problem of economic development!

Clearly, the direction of causation between growth and savings and investment goes both ways. Lewis and his contemporaries emphasized the causation going from exogenous investment to growth. The other line of causation is between growth opportunities and investment. Barro suggests that the latter

> is especially likely to apply for open economies. Even if cross-country differences in saving ratios are exogenous with respect to growth, the decision to invest domestically rather than abroad would reflect the domestic prospects for returns on investment, which would relate to the domestic opportunities for growth. (Barro 1996b, p. 22)

His statistical analyses 'suggest that much of the positive estimated effect of the investment ratio on growth in typical cross-country regressions reflects the reverse relation between growth and investment' (ibid., p. 23).

The cross-country study reported by Sachs (1997) found that 'prudent fiscal policy is crucial. Fast-growing countries tend to have governments with high rates of saving and low spending relative to GDP. Each rise of ten percentage points of GDP in government saving was found to raise the overall GDP growth by one percentage point' (Sachs 1997, p. 20). However it is not clear whether this study accounted properly for the possible two-way relationship between public savings and growth.

4.3 Democracy, Authoritarianism and Development

In his very readable and vividly illustrated (with photographs!) book on development economics, Jagdish Bhagwati (1966, p. 204) noted that the 'political economy of development ... poses a cruel choice between rapid (self-sustained) expansion and democratic processes', while adding in the very next sentence, 'The choice between them, however, is not necessarily unique; and rightly so'.[16] Nearly three decades later, Bhagwati concluded that the 'cruel choice' is by no means a compelling necessity ... either democracy does not handicap development or in the best of circumstances, it even promotes it' (Bhagwati 1995, p. 3). After reviewing the development experience in the last several decades he concluded that the 'cruel choice' thesis 'was too simpleminded, [and] the relationship between the two is far more structured, and less unfavorable to democracy, than we thought then ... [and] the chief lesson may then well be that democracy and markets are the twin pillars on which to build prosperity' (pp. 29-32).

In looking back with the perfect vision of hindsight, the 'cruel choice' thesis does indeed look simpleminded! It was driven in large part by the then dominant, and now discredited, paradigm of development that assigned a central role to the state and the public sector in bringing about development through capital-intensive, import-substituting, industrialization. It emphasized physical capital accumulation, financed almost entirely by domestic savings (public and private), as the crucial factor for growth. Democracies, in contrast to authoritarian regimes, were thought to be incapable of resisting pressures to redistribute income away from savers (the relatively well-off) to consumers[17] (the poor) and of raising taxes and saving a significant proportion of tax revenues. Yet in practice many developing countries, democratic and authoritarian, managed to raise savings and tax revenues. However, except in East Asia, higher savings and tax revenues did not result in rapid growth because of other dysfunctional policies.

A number of studies (Barro 1996a, 1996b, Londregan and Poole 1996, Przeworski and Limongi 1994) have used the cross-country regression framework to examine the relationship between democracy and development. Przeworski and Limongi (1994) classified a regime as a democracy if its chief executive *and* legislature are elected *and* if there was more than one party *and* it passes an incumbency condition (its precise definition is not of great interest for the purposes of this chapter). A regime which violated any one of the four conditions was classified as authoritarian. Over the period 1951-90, in all 229 regimes (101 democratic and 128 authoritarian) were observed in 139 countries. In terms of regime-years, 1731 were democracies and 2981 were authoritarian.

A commonly used crude comparison of annual average of PPP corrected GDP per capita growth rates yielded a rate of 2.44 percent for democracies and 1.88 percent for authoritarian regimes, the difference being statistically significant. Przeworski and Limongi rightly reject this comparison on the ground that whether or not a country is observed to be democratic or authoritarian in any period is endogenous, in part determined by economic growth itself. They find that a democracy that experienced positive growth in a year will change to an authoritarian regime in the next year with a probability of about 1/60, whereas if it had a negative growth, the transition probably trebles to about 1/20. On the other hand, an authoritarian regime will become a democracy in the next year with a probability of about 1/50 if it experienced positive growth this year and with a probability of about 1/40 if it experienced negative growth. It is thus clear that the probability of transition to a different regime or equivalently the probability of survival of the same regime, depends on the rate of growth experienced.

Once they allow for the endogeneity of regime change, Przeworski and Limongi find that the difference between regime types in their investment/GDP ratios is no longer significant, although a crude comparison yields an investment rate of 15 percent for authoritarian regimes and 23 percent for democracies.[18] Their analysis suggests that population grows faster in authoritarian regimes and this difference does not disappear even if correction for selection is made. If population is treated as *exogenous,* authoritarian regimes have a selection corrected per capita GDP growth rate of 2.50 percent per year on average while democracies have a significantly lower growth rate of 1.96 percent. However, if population growth rate is treated as *endogenous* to the regime type, there is no difference in per capita GDP growth rates between regimes.

Londregan and Poole (1996) attempt to discriminate statistically between conflicting hypotheses, such as 'democracy is simply an entailment of the high level of social and economic development' versus 'democratic political culture depends more on the institutional and historical context than on the level of economic development' (p. 1). Constructing and estimating 'a statistical model that allows for joint endogeneity of the change of leaders and the character of regime type' (p. 2), they find

> that even after (1) correcting for various measures of the political context, (2) allowing for the simultaneity of leadership change and regime type, and (3) correcting for country-specific fixed effects, income has a small but statistically significant effect ... Even a permanent doubling of income levels leads to a modest improvement toward democracy. (pp. 2-3)

While Londregan and Poole (1996) concentrate on *levels* of income, Barro (1996a, 1996b) uses his pioneering empirical framework of cross-country endogenous growth regressions to study the determinants of growth, democracy and the interrelationship between the two. Barro (1996a) concludes that

> the interplay between democracy and economic development involves the effect of political freedom on growth and the influence of standard of living on the extent of democracy. With respect to the determination of growth, the cross-country analysis brings out favourable effects from maintenance of the rule of law, free markets, small government consumption,[19] and high human capital. Once these kinds of variables and the initial level of GDP are held constant, the *overall effect of democracy on growth is weakly negative.* There is some indication of a nonlinear relation in which more democracy enhances growth at low levels of political freedom but depresses growth when a moderate level of freedom has already been attained.
>
> With respect to the effects of economic development on democracy, the analysis shows that improvements in the standard of living ... substantially raise the probability that political institutions will become more democratic over time. Hence, political freedom emerges as a sort of luxury good. (Barro 1996a, p. 98, emphasis added)

Barro (1996b) is more ambitious than Barro (1996a) in that it examines, using a common framework, the growth convergence hypotheses, the interplay between economic and political development and inflation (an indicator of macroeconomic instability) and growth. The study also accounts for endogeneity arising from two-way causation among some of the variables by estimating the relationships using instrumental variables.

This study confirms the nonlinear relationship found in Barro (1996a) between democracy and growth, so that '*one cannot conclude from this evidence that more or less democracy is a critical element for economic growth*' (Barro 1996b, p. 38, emphasis added).

Barro finds from 'inspection of the cross-country data ... that countries at low level of economic development do not sustain democracy ... conversely, nondemocratic places that experience substantial economic development tend to become more democratic' (ibid., pp. 38-9). Estimating a regression in which the indicator of democracy at any t is explained by its own lagged value (Barro uses a lag of five years) as well as other variables, he finds that 'the estimated coefficient on lagged democracy is 0.67 (s.e. 0.03). Thus, democracy is highly persistent over time, but roughly one-third of the adjustment to a target position (determined by other variables) occurs over five years' (ibid., p. 41). Other findings from this regression were: 'target level of democracy is increasing in ... indicators of standards of living ... once GDP and life expectancy are held constant ... the level of schooling does not help explain democracy ... the general link between democracy and the standard of living is firmly established' (ibid., pp. 41-3).

Among other determinants, Barro's regressions suggest that the inequality in income distribution is unimportant for democracy, although he concedes that this 'finding ... may reflect the poor quality of the data on income distribution, rather than the irrelevance of inequality for democracy' (ibid., p. 44). Degree of heterogeneity with respect to ethnicity, language and cultures has no significant effect on democracy. There is not much evidence that economic rights as measured by an index of rule of law promote political freedom, nor is there evidence that political freedom stimulates the rule of law. Past colonial status is insignificant for democracy once the standard of living is held constant. When dummies for religious affiliation of the population are included, the only statistically significant affiliation that *promotes* democracy is Hindu, while non-religion and Muslim applications significantly reduce the prospects for democracy! However, Barro points out that much of the significance of the religious affiliations is influenced by outliers (democracies of India and Mauritius as Hindu nations, China as a non-religious nation). If these outliers are omitted, the Hindu and nonreligion dummies lose their statistical significance.

Given the problems with the data and the fact that there is no well-founded theory of political economy on the basis of which the direction of causation between political and economic variables can be inferred, these results should not be treated as anything more than suggestive. After all, as is well-known, and is expressed clearly by Lal (1996, p. 300), 'there is no necessary empirical relationship between the form of government and successful development ... whilst democracy promotes liberty, it may not promote opulence, which depends upon an efficient market economy, and which in turn does not require a democratic form of government for its maintenance'.

5 CONCLUSIONS

The recent theoretical literature on endogenous growth has certainly advanced the frontiers of our knowledge of growth theory. But for analyzing the actual growth experience since the Second World War of a large cross-section of countries, developed and developing, conventional neoclassical growth theory is more than adequate. I am sure that this robustness of conventional growth theory would have pleased John Fei.

Let me now turn to the questions I raised in the introduction on the determinants of growth. From the empirical analysis of development experience, some lessons stand out: economic fundamentals matter. These are: openness to foreign trade, technology and capital flows; macroeconomic stability; incentives to accumulate human and physical capital; and economic environment that did not unduly distort the incentives such as those between consuming and saving, producing for home and foreign markets, investing at home and abroad, using resources productively and using them to seek policy created rents. The evidence is not conclusive on whether state interventions should go beyond being 'fundamentals friendly' and take on a proactive role (for example, pursuing an industrial policy of promoting specific industries) in furthering development.

Turning to the political framework, the conjuncture of the processes of democratization, economic liberalization and globalization has led some to pronounce

> the century that began full of self-confidence in the ultimate triumph of Western liberal democracy seems at its close to be returning full circle to where it started: not to an 'end of ideology' or a convergence between capitalism and socialism, as earlier predicted, but to an unabashed victory of economic and political liberalism. (Fukuyama 1989, p. 3)

and to argue the case for 'a coherent and directional history of mankind that will eventually lead the greater part of humanity to liberal democracy' (Fukuyama 1993, p. xii).

There is no doubt that many developing countries are moving toward greater dependence on the market for the management of the economy and on some form of representative government for managing the polity. However, they have a long way to go before it can be said that they are not only democracies but also unlikely to cease being democratic. As yet there are few solidly democratic developing countries. It is too early to say that the trend toward democracy is all encompassing and irreversible. Fukuyama's assertions are premature.

Whatever be the *intrinsic* value of representative democracy as a form of political organization, the empirical evidence is ambiguous on its *instrumental* role in either promoting or retarding development. Indeed, as Bardhan (1997) concludes, political democracy is neither a necessary nor a sufficient condition for promoting development. Let me conclude with a few remarks based on his contribution.

Does democracy provide what is deemed a basic pre-condition of development, namely, well-defined property rights, a transparent legal structure for contracts and enforcement of both, and is it the only political system that provides it? The answer is 'no' to both questions in the real world. Authoritarian regimes (such as Taiwan and Korea) have provided a stable, predictable, albeit corrupt, contractual environment for private business to thrive, without the procedural formalities of democracy. On the other hand, in India with all the procedural trappings of democracy, and a well-defined contract law, the legal machinery is far too slow to be a credible force for contract enforcement. Besides, Bardhan correctly points out that while democracy may be conducive to the enforcement of laws, the process of enactment of such laws may be far less predictable and transparent, influenced as it often is by the compulsions of fund-raising for election campaigns: 'When policies are up for sale to the highest contributor to the campaign fund, development prospects may not win out ... it is not much consolation to be told that the policies thus legislated will be implemented well by the bureaucracy and the count under a democracy' (Bardhan 1997, p. 4).

Does public participation and pressure in a democracy facilitate development? Again, not necessarily. 'Democracies may be particularly susceptible to populist pressures for immediate consumption, unproductive subsidies, autarchic trade policies and other particularistic demands that may hamper long-run investment and growth' (ibid., p. 5). Indian democracy is a prime illustration of such populism. On the other hand, in authoritarian East Asia, it has been claimed that development policy-making has been insulated from such pressures. Yet the authoritarianism of the Marcos regime in the Philippines did not provide such insulation.

Is democracy a requirement for states to pre-commit credibly to the pursuit of development-orientated policies? Again the answer is 'no': democracy is neither necessary nor sufficient for effective pre-commitment. The Korean government credibly pre-committed to applying the market test for its assistance to infant industries – it credibly threatened to withdraw protection if the protected industries did not become competitive in world markets. In India there was no credibility – 'infant' industry protection, once granted, became impossible to remove even when its objective was not achieved. It eventually became senile industry protection!

ACKNOWLEDGMENT

This chapter was written while I was a Visiting Scholar at the Center of Economic Development and Policy Reform (CEDPR), Stanford University. I thank the CEDPR and the Ford Foundation under Grant 950-1341 to Yale University for financial support. For their valuable comments on an earlier version, I thank Anne Krueger, Wan-Wen Chu, and the participants of the conference in memory of John C.H. Fei, 'The Economics and the Political Economy of Development at the Turn of the Century', Taipei, Taiwan, August 1-2, 1997.

NOTES

1. John's enthusiasm for Chinese opera was well known to his friends. Alas, if news reports are to be believed, Chinese operatic art is dying. This surely would have saddened John's heart.
2. The Symposium on New Growth Theory in the *Journal of Economic Perspectives* 8 (1), Winter 1994, is a good summary of the evolution of the new growth theory and its antecedents in, as well as contrasts with, conventional growth theory. I have drawn on Srinivasan (1995, 1997a) in this section.
3. I agree with the comment of Wan-Wen Chu, the discussant of this paper at the conference, that accumulation of human capital need not necessarily trigger growth. He cites as an example a phase in Taiwanese history in which, as in other developing countries, investment in human capital in the form of higher education led to brain drain rather than to growth.
4. Strictly speaking, only Harrod's 'warranted equilibrium path', along which available savings are continually absorbed into investment without changing the capital-output ratio, corresponds to this model.
5. There will be gain in intertemporal welfare but no change in growth rate in moving to free trade if the home output is the investment good in which the economy has a comparative advantage. With trade it will be able to transform one unit of output for more than one unit of consumption (that is, $\pi < 1$).

Equation (1.5) will then be rewritten as $\pi c_t = \beta K_t = (\dot{K} + \delta K_t)$. The free-trade steady-state growth rate of consumption and capital stock is $\tilde{g} = (\beta - \delta - \rho)/\sigma$ which is the same as its autarky value. The free-trade growth path of capital is $K_0 e^{\tilde{g}t}$ which is the same as its autarky path, while that of consumption is. $[\{(\beta - \delta)(\sigma - 1) + \rho\}/\pi\sigma]\, K_0 e^{\tilde{g}t}$. With $\pi < 1$, the free state consumption path is above that under autarky at all t.

6. Wan-Wen Chu suggests in his comments that this is an unfair characterization and that the adherents of the market-failure view do not necessarily assume that the state is omnipotent but only that it has the potential to, but not necessarily will, act developmentally. He questions what he calls the 'neo-utilitarian' approach to state behavior. I am not persuaded by either criticism. Once deviation from potentially beneficial behaviour by the state is admitted as possible, then simply pointing out that a potential for beneficial action by the state exists is not enough if the objective is to correct market failure. Also the crucial postulate of most economists in analyzing the state is rational behavior which is far more encompassing than utilitarianism.
7. An anonymous referee pointed out that corrupt behavior of public officials is also opportunism and suggested that I address the relationship between corruption and economic development. It would take me too long to delve deep into this issue. Let me just note that in those cross-country-growth regressions in which a corruption index is included as yet another explanatory variable, it is found to have a statistically significant negative coefficient. Thus greater corruption seems to be associated with lower growth. But, as in any regression, a causal interpretation of this impact is hazardous. In any case, the literature on corruption and development is largely anecdotal and superficial.
8. Persson et al. (1997) motivate checks and balances as in the US constitution as devices to contain opportunism. They quote the following particularly illuminating passage from James Madison:
   'If men were angels, no government would be necessary. If angels were to govern men, neither external nor internal controls on government would be necessary. In framing a government which is to be administered by men over men, the great difficulty lies in this: you must first enable the government to control the governed; and in the next place oblige it to control itself. A dependence on the people is, no doubt, the primary control on the government; but experience has taught mankind the necessity of auxiliary precautions' (James Madison, *The Federalist,* No. LI).
9. As quoted by Jagdish Bhagwati (1983).
10. Wan-Wen Chu, while agreeing that getting the fundamentals right is not sufficient for rapid growth, concludes from his study of Taiwanese growth that one of the sufficient conditions for rapid growth is that the government intervenes at the crucial setting up stage of some key industries to socialize investment risks. I am not entirely persuaded by this argument since there is no presumption that the government is good at picking winners, that is, the key industries, and intervening to help them grow.
11. As I was revising this paper for publication (in early December 1997), the turbulence in East Asian financial markets of November 1997 had led to several

bail-outs orchestrated by the IMF including a massive one of over $55 billion for South Korea. It would take too much space for me to analyze the bail-outs properly. But I am not convinced that the likely externalities from further declines in the financial markets of East Asia warranted a bail-out. In any case, the hand-wringing in the Western press about miracles turning to myths is silly. Given their sound real economies, the countries of East Asia can ride out the financial froth with appropriate policies and resume their growth.

12. I have drawn on Srinivasan (1997a, 1997b) in writing this section.
13. Wan-Wen Chu pointed out in his comments that Taiwan did not liberalize its imports until the 1980s or later even though it began promoting exports from the early 1960s. While this is true, its implications for the relationship between openness and growth is not clear. The reason is that in the case of Korea the variance in effective protection rates of the import regime was rather small and in any case protection was often conditioned on meeting a market competitiveness test in the near future.
14. Revolutions and coups are indicators of political instability. There are other indicators, such as the frequency of changes in regimes, which also have been used in growth regressions. There is a large literature on political business cycles as well as on economic growth and political instability. It would take too much space here to review this literature. The interested reader might wish to consult Alesina et al. (1996) and Alesina and Roubini (1997) and the references therein.
15. I owe this observation to Gary Saxonhouse.
16. Many political scientists shared the 'cruel choice' perception. Przeworski and Limongi (1994) quote several of them: La Palombara (1963, p. 57) thought that 'if economic development is the all-embracing goal, the logic of experience dictates that not too much attention can be paid to the trappings of democracy'. De Schweinitz (1959) argued that if the less-developed countries 'are to grow economically, they must limit democratic participation in political affairs'.

    Dictatorships are needed to generate development: as Huntington and Nelson (1976, p. 23) put it, 'political participation must be held down, at least temporarily, in order to promote economic development'.
17. Przeworski and Limongi (1994) provide several examples of this claim: Galenson (1959, p. 3) claimed that 'The more democratic a government is, ... the greater the diversion of resources from investment to consumption'. This was also the belief of Huntington and Dominguez (1975, p. 60): 'The interest of the voters generally lead parties to give the expansion of personal consumption a higher priority *vis-à-vis* investment than it would receive in a non-democratic system. In the Soviet Union, for instance, the percentage of GDP devoted to consumption was driven down from 65 percent in 1928 to 52 percent in 1937. It is most unlikely that a competitive party system would have sustained a revolution from above like this'.
18. The investment model includes several explanatory variables including one-period-lagged investment rate, lagged value of per capita GDP, world GDP growth rate of the year, relative price of investment goods and the US prime rate.
19. Sachs (1997) also finds that the rule of law and government savings promote

growth. He finds that 'Each rise of ten percentage points of GDP in government savings raises the overall GDP growth rate by 1 percentage point' (Sachs 1997, p. 20).

REFERENCES

Ahmad, Syed (1966), 'On the Theory of Induced Innovation', *Economic Journal,* 76, 344-57.

Alesina, Alberto, Sule Ozler and Philip Swagel (1996), 'Political Instability and Economic Growth', *Journal of Economic Growth*, 1 (2), 189-211.

Alesina, Alberto and Nouriel Roubini (1997), *Political Cycles and the Macroeconomy*, Cambridge, MA: MIT Press.

Amsden, A. (1989), *Asia's New Giant: South Korea and Late Industrialization*, New York: Oxford University Press.

Aoki, M., H. Kim and M. Okuno-Fujiwara (eds) (1997a), *The Role of Government in East Asian Development*, Oxford: Clarendon Press.

Aoki, M., K. Murdock and M. Okuno-Fujiwara (1997b), 'Beyond the East Asian Miracle: Introducing the Market-Enhancing View', Chapter 1 in M. Aoki, H. Kim and M. Okuno-Fujiwara (eds), *The Role of Government in East Asian Development*, Oxford: Clarendon Press, 1-37.

Arrow, K.J. (1962), 'The Economic Implications of Learning by Doing', *Review of Economic Studies*, 29, 155-73.

Baldwin, R.E. and E. Seghezza (1996), 'Testing for Trade-Induced Investment Growth', *Discussion Paper* 1331, London: Center for Economic Policy Research.

Bardhan, P. (1997), 'Democracy and Development', Berkeley, University of California (processed).

Barro, R. (1991), 'Economic Growth in a Cross Section of Countries', *Quarterly Journal of Economics*, 106 (2), 407-33.

Barro, R. (1996a), 'Democracy: A Recipe for Growth?' in M.G. Quibria and J. Malcolm Dowling (eds), *Current Issues in Economic Development*, Oxford and New York: Oxford University Press, 67-104.

Barro, R. (1996b), 'Determinants of Economic Growth: A Cross-Country Empirical Study', *Working Paper* No.5698, Cambridge, MA: National Bureau of Economic Research.

Baumol, W.J. (1986), 'Productivity Growth, Convergence and Welfare: What the Long Run Data Show?', *American Economic Review*, 76, December, 1072-85.

Bhagwati, Jagdish (1966), *The Economics of Underdeveloped Countries*,

World University Library Series, London: Weidenfeld Nicholson.

Bhagwati, Jagdish (1983), 'Development Economics: What Have We Learnt?', Distinguished Speakers, Lecture, Manila, Asian Development Bank, October.

Bhagwati, Jagdish (1995), 'Democracy and Development: New Thinking on an Old Question', Rajiv Gandhi Memorial Lecture, New Delhi, Rajiv Gandhi Foundation.

Boserup, E. (1965), *The Conditions of Agricultural Growth*, Chicago: Aldine.

Cass, D. (1965), 'Optimum Growth in an Aggregative Model of Capital Accumulation', *Review of Economic Studies*, 32, 233-40.

Coe, D.T. and E. Helpman (1995), 'International R&D Spillovers', *European Economic Review*, 39, 859-87.

Coe, D.T., E. Helpman and A.W. Hoffmaister (1997), 'North-South R&D Spillovers', *Economic Journal*, 107, January, 134-49.

Commons, John R. (1934), *Institutional Economics, Its Place in Political Economy*, Maddison: University of Wisconsin Press.

de Schweinitz, Karl Jr. (1959), 'Industrialization, Labor Controls and Democracy', *Economic Development and Cultural Change*, 7, 385-404.

Dixit, A. (1996), *The Making of Policy: A Transaction-cost Politics Perspective,* Cambridge, MA: MIT Press.

Domar, E. (1957), *Essays in the Theory of Economic Growth*, London: Oxford University Press.

Fel'dman, G.A. (1928), 'K teorii tempov narodnogo dokhoda', *Planovoe Khoziaistvo*, 11, 146-70 and 12, 152-78.

Fukuyama, Francis (1989), 'The End of History?', *The National Interest*, Summer, 3-30.

Fukuyama, Francis (1993), *The End of History and the Last Man*, New York: Avon Books.

Fukuyama, Francis (1995), *Trust*, New York: The Free Press.

Galenson, Walter (1959), 'Introduction' to Walter Galenson (ed.), *Labor and Economic Development*, New York: Wiley.

Grossman, G. and E. Helpman, (1991), *Innovation and Growth in the Global Economy*, Cambridge, MA: MIT Press.

Huntington, Samuel P. and Jorge I. Dominguez (1975), 'Political Development', in F.I. Greenstein and N.W. Polsby (eds), *Handbook of Political Science*, Vol. 3, Reading: Addison-Wesley, 1-114

Huntington, Samuel P. and Nelson (1976), *Socio-economic Change and Political Participation*, Cambridge, MA: Harvard University Press.

Jorgenson, D.W. and Z. Griliches (1966), 'Sources of Measured Productivity Change', *American Economic Review*, 56, 50-61.

Kaldor, N. and J. Mirrlees, (1962), 'A New Model of Economic Growth', *Review of Economic Studies*, 29 (3), 174-92.

Kennedy, C. (1964), 'Induced Bias in Innovation and the Theory of Distribution', *Economic Journal*, 74 (298), 541-47.

Koopmans, T.C. (1965), 'On the Concept of Optimal Economic Growth', in *The Econometric Approach to Development Planning* Amsterdam: North-Holland for Pontificia Academic Science, 225-300.

Kravis, I. (1970), 'Trade as a Handmaiden of Growth: Similarities Between the Nineteenth and Twentieth Centuries', *Economic Journal*, 80 (320), 850-72.

Krueger, A. (1990), 'Government Failures in Development', *Journal of Economic Perspectives*, 4 (3), Summer, 9-24.

Lal, Deepak (1996), 'Participation, Markets and Democracy', in M. Lundahl and B.J. Ndlu (eds), *New Directions in Development*, London: Routledge.

LaPalombara, J. (ed.) (1963), *Bureaucracy and Political Development*, Princeton, NJ.: Princeton University Press.

Lau, L.J. and J. Kim (1994), 'The Sources of Economic Growth of the East Asian Newly Industrializing Countries', *Journal of Japanese and International Economies*, VIII, 235-71.

Lewis, Arthur (1954), 'Economic Development with Unlimited Supplies of Labor', *The Manchester School*, 22, 139-91.

Lin, Justin Yifu and Jeffrey Nugent (1995), 'Institutions and Economic Development', in Jere Behrman and T.N. Srinivasan (eds), *Handbook of Development Economics*, Vol. 3B, Amsterdam: North-Holland, 2301-70.

Londregan, J.P. and K.T. Poole (1996), 'Does High Income Promote Democracy?', *World Politics*, 49 (1), 1-30.

Lucas, R.E. (1988), 'On the Mechanics of Economic Development', *Journal of Monetary Economics*, 22, 3-42.

Lucas, R.E. (1993), 'Making a Miracle', *Econometrica*, 62 (2), 251-72.

Mahalanobis, P.C. (1955), 'The Approach of Operational Research to Planning in India', *Sankhya: The Indian Journal of Statistics*, 16 (1-2), 3-62.

Milgrom, P. and J. Roberts (1992), *Economics, Organization and Management*, Englewood Cliffs, NJ: Prentice Hall.

North, D. (1990a), *Institutions, Institutional Change and Economic Performance*, New York: Cambridge University Press.

North, D. (1990b), 'A Transaction Cost Theory of Politics', *Journal of Theoretical Politics*, 2 (4), 355-67.

Olson, M. (1982), *The Rise and Decline of Nations: Economic Growth, Stagflation and Social Rigidities*, New Haven: Yale University Press.

Persson, T., G. Roland, and G. Tabellini (1997), 'Separation of Powers and Political Accountability', Institute of International Studies, Harvard University (processed).

Przeworski, Adam and Fernando Limongi (1994) 'Democracy and Development', paper presented at the Nobel Symposium, Uppsala, August 27-30.

Putnam, Robert (1993), *Making Democracy Work: Civic Tradition in Modern Italy*, Princeton, NJ: Princeton University Press.

Ramsey, F.P. (1928), 'A Mathematical Theory of Saving', *Economic Journal*, 38 (152), 543-59.

Robertson, D. (1940), *Essays in Monetary Theory*, London: P.S. King & Son.

Romer, P.M. (1986), 'Increasing Returns and Long-run Growth', *Journal of Political Economy*, 94 (5), 1002-37.

Sachs, J. (1997), 'The Limits of Convergence', *The Economist,* 343 (8021), June 14, 19-22.

Sachs, J.D. and A. Warner (1995), 'Economic Reforms and the Process of Global Integration', *Brookings Papers on Economic Activity*, 1-118.

Schumpeter, J. (1942), *Capitalism, Socialism and Democracy*, New York, Harper & Brothers.

Solow, R.M. (1956), 'A Contribution to the Theory of Economic Growth', *Quarterly Journal of Economics*, 70, 65-94.

Solow, R.M. (1957), 'Technical Change and the Aggregate Production Function', *Review of Economics and Statistics*, 39, 312-20.

Srinivasan, T.N. (1962), 'Investment Criteria and Choice of Techniques of Production', *Yale Economic Essays*, 32, 59-115.

Srinivasan, T.N. (1964), 'Optimal Savings in a Two-sector Model of Growth', *Econometrica*, 2, 358-73.

Srinivasan, T.N. (1993), Comments on Paul Romer, 'Two Strategies for Economic Development: Using Ideas vs. Producing Ideas', in Proceedings of the World Bank Conference on Development Economics, 1992, *World Bank Economic Review*, Supplement, 103-9.

Srinivasan, T.N. (1994a), *Agriculture and Trade in China and India: Policies and Performance Since 1950* (with contributions from Justin Y. Lin and Yun-Wing Sung), San Francisco: ICS Press.

Srinivasan, T.N. (1994b), 'Data Base for Development Analysis: An Overview', *Journal of Development Economics*, 44 (1), 3-28.

Srinivasan, T.N. (1995), 'Long-run Growth Theories and Empirics: Anything New?', in Takatoshi Ito and Anne Krueger (eds), *Growth Theories in Light of the East Asian Experience*, Chicago: University of Chicago Press, 37-70

Srinivasan, T.N. (1997a), 'Trade Orientation, Trade Liberalization and

Economic Growth', in Gary Saxonhouse and T.N. Srinivasan (eds), *Development, Duality and the International Economic Regime*, Ann Arbor: University of Michigan Press (forthcoming).

Srinivasan, T.N. (1997b), 'Democracy, Markets, Governance and Development', Yale University, processed.

Stiglitz, J. (1990), 'Comments: Some Retrospective Views on Growth Theory', in P. Diamond (ed.), *Growth/Productivity/Unemployment*, Cambridge, MA: MIT Press.

Summers, Robert and Alan Heston (1988), 'A New Set of International Comparisons of Real Product and Price Levels: Estimates for 130 Countries', *Review of Income and Wealth*, 34, 1-25.

Summers, Robert and Alan Heston (1991), 'The Penn World Table (Mark V): An Extended Set of International Comparisons, 1950-88', *Quarterly Journal of Economics*, 106, 327-36.

Tirole, J. (1994), 'The Internal Organization of Government', *Oxford Economic Papers*, 46 (1), 1-29.

Uzawa, H. (1964), 'Optimum Growth in a Two-Sector Model of Capital Accumulation', *Review of Economic Studies*, 31, 1-24.

Uzawa, H. (1965), 'Optimum Technical Change in an Aggregative Model of Economic Growth', *International Economic Review*, 6, 18-31.

von Neumann, J. (1945), 'A Model of General Equilibrium', *Review of Economic Studies*, 13, 1-9.

Weingast, B. (1993), 'Constitutions as Governance Structures', *Journal of Law and Economics*, 22, 233-61.

Weingast, B. (1995), 'The Economic Role of Political Institutions, Market-preserving Federalism and Economic Development', *The Journal of Law, Economics and Organization*, VIII, i, 1-3.

Williamson, O. (1994), 'The Institutions and Governance of Economic Development and Reform', Proceedings of Annual Conference on Development Economics 1994, Supplement to the *World Bank Economic Review*.

World Bank (1991), *World Development Report*, New York: Oxford University Press.

World Bank (1993), *The East Asian Miracle: Economic Growth and Public Policy*, New York: Oxford University Press.

Young, A. (1995), 'The Tyranny of Numbers: Confronting the Statistical Realities of the East Asian Growth Experience', *Quarterly Journal of Economics*, 110 (3), 641-80.

Part II Sources of Development

2. The Sources of East Asian Economic Growth

Lawrence J. Lau*

1 INTRODUCTION

The East Asian Newly Industrialized Economies (NIEs) – Hong Kong (HON), South Korea (KOR), Singapore (SIN) and Taiwan (TWN) – have been among the fastest growing economies in the world in the postwar period, achieving long-term annual rates of growth of between 8 and 9 percent. What are the sources of this economic growth? Is the growth in output in these economies mostly the consequence of the growth in inputs, or is it mostly the result of technical progress, that is, improvements in technology and efficiency (or equivalently, of growth in 'total factor productivity')?

The recent interest in the sources of growth of East Asian NIEs was stimulated by a study by Kim and Lau (1992, 1994a), the results of which were first presented at the Conference on the Economic Development of ROC and the Pacific Rim in the 1990s and Beyond, held in Taipei in May, 1992.[1] Kim and Lau (1992, 1994a, 1994b), in their analysis of a combined sample of the Group-of-Five (G-5) countries – France (FRA), West Germany (GER), Japan (JPN), the United Kingdom (UK) and the United States (USA) – and the four East Asian NIEs for the postwar period, obtain the initially surprising empirical finding that there has been no technical progress (or increase in efficiency) in the East Asian NIEs, despite the very rapid growth of their outputs. Young (1992) has initially argued that there has been technical progress (or equivalently, growth in total factor productivity) in Hong Kong but not in Singapore. Subsequently, Young (1995) also reaches a similar conclusion to Kim and Lau, namely, that there has been no technical progress in the East Asian

*The author is grateful for discussions with Michael Boskin, Yujiro Hayami, Jong-Il Kim, Paul Krugman, Jung-Soo Park and Anthony Tang. Responsibility for any errors remains with the author.

NIEs. These empirical findings have been used by Krugman (1994) to support his celebrated but provocative thesis that the rapid economic growth of the East Asian NIEs cannot be sustained.

The objective of this chapter is several fold. First, we examine the empirical evidence on the sources of economic growth in the postwar period for a group of economies that include both industrialized and developing ones. We compare the relative importance of the different sources of economic growth of the East Asian economies — Hong Kong, Japan, Singapore, South Korea and Taiwan — against the experience of the non-Asian industrialized economies (IEs) — France, West Germany, United Kingdom and United States. Second, we analyze and interpret the results of the comparison in the light of the global experience of economic growth. Third, we assess the prospects for continued economic growth of the East Asian newly NIEs on the basis of both the past experience of the IEs, including Japan, and future trends in the global economic environment.

In order to analyze the sources of economic growth of the East Asian NIEs, we introduce the concept of a production function.

Definition: A production function is a rule that gives the quantity of output, Y, for a given quantity of input, X. It is denoted:

$$Y = F(X). \tag{2.1}$$

Note that the quantity of output is measured in terms of *value added* rather than *gross output*. Thus, for example, the value added in the manufacture of a notebook computer is the value of the notebook computer less the value of the microprocessor, the liquid crystal display, and the software of the operating system, as well as other parts such as disk drives and memory chips to the extent that they are purchased from outside suppliers. For a notebook computer with a market price of US$2000, the value added may be no more than US$200.

A production function may change over time. Thus, output, Y, may also depend on t, chronological time, in addition to X, the quantity of input, with the production function denoted as:

$$Y = F(X,t). \tag{2.2}$$

A shift in the production function between two periods is identified by economists as technical progress.

Definition: There is *technical progress* between period 0 and period 1 if given the *same* quantity of input, X_0, the quantity of output in period 1, Y_l, is greater than the quantity of output in period 0, Y_0, that is,

$F(X_0,1) \geq F(X_0,0)$.

Thus, technical progress has a very precise meaning: it is the growth of output holding measured inputs constant. There is true technical progress if and only if one is able to produce more output with the *same measured inputs* or the same output with fewer measured inputs.

In Figures 2.1 and 2.2, we illustrate the concepts of a production function and technical progress graphically in the context of a single-output, single-input aggregate production function. Figure 2.1 presents a single-output, single-input production function and shows how output varies with input. Figure 2.2 shows that if there is technical progress

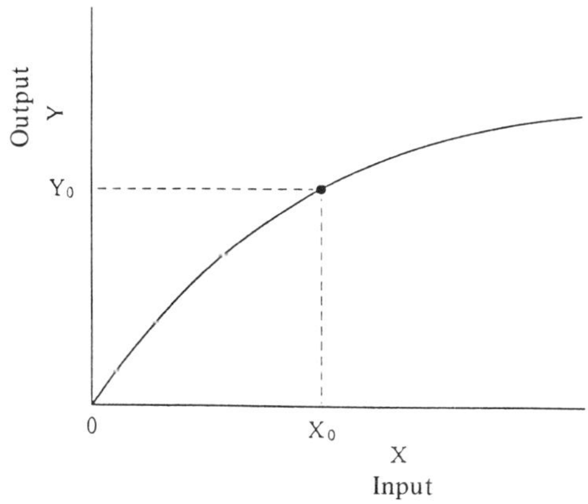

Figure 2.1 The concept of a production function – the single-output, single-input case

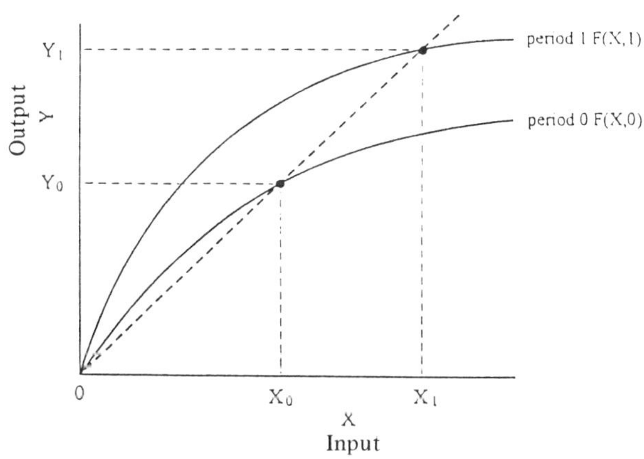

Figure 2.2 The concept of technical progress – the single-output, single-input case

between period 0 and period 1, the production function will have shifted upward between the two periods. The input-output combinations of the two periods, (Y_0, X_0) and (Y_1, X_1) will lie on different curves (the production functions represented by solid lines). If there is no technical progress between period 0 and period 1, the production function will not have changed between the two periods. The input-output combinations of the two periods will lie on the same curve (the production function represented by the broken line).[2]

If the production function, $F(X,t)$, is known, the growth of output can be decomposed into two components: the growth of output due to the growth of input (movement along a production function), and technical progress (shift in the production function). We illustrate the decomposition of the growth of output in Figure 2.3. Let the production functions of period 0 and period 1 be represented by the two solid lines marked $F(X,0)$ and $F(X,1)$ respectively. Then the growth of output between the two periods can be decomposed into two components, with the first component representing the growth due to the growth in input, and the second component the growth due to technical progress, that is, due to a shift in the production function between the two periods.

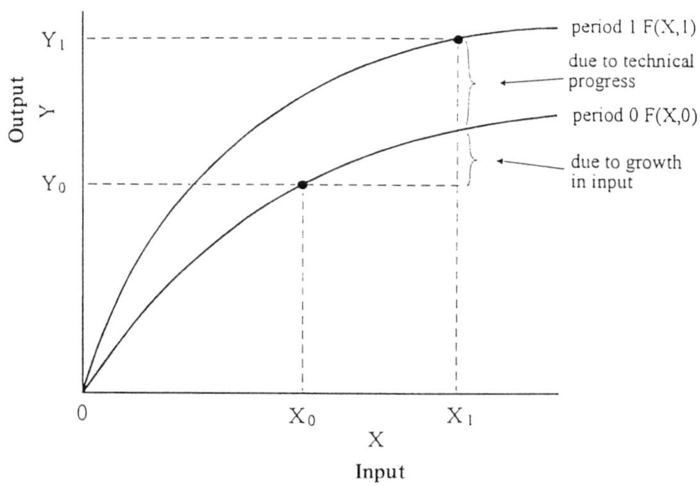

Figure 2.3 Decomposition of the sources of economic growth

Our interpretation of technical progress is that it is *not* 'manna from heaven', but that it mostly reflects the effects of changes in omitted or unmeasured variables on the aggregate production function, such as land or more generally the natural endowment of resources (to the extent that they increase or decrease over time) and the environment, and 'investments' in what may broadly be referred to as 'intangible capital', including human capital, R&D capital, goodwill (including advertising and market development), organizational innovation and restructuring, software development and implementation, and information system development and implementation, which are customarily listed as expenses and hence not reflected in the balance sheets as 'capital', but which have an effect on output beyond the period in which the expenditures are made. Given that the natural endowment of land and resources is generally fixed, measured technical progress in this study may be regarded as principally capturing the effects of investments in intangible forms of capital, including human capital and R&D capital. It is the growth in output that cannot be explained by or attributed to the growth in the measured inputs. That is why it is sometimes also referred to as the 'residual' or a measure of our ignorance.

In this study, we present growth accounts that distinguish explicitly the two primary factory of production – tangible or physical capital (K), and labor (L), in addition to technical progress, represented by t, as sources of economic growth. The aggregate production function may therefore be written as:

$$Y = F(K, L, t). \tag{2.3}$$

Given knowledge of the aggregate production function, the growth of output between any two periods can be decomposed into the growth of output due to the growth of measured inputs and the growth of output due to technical progress. The growth of output due to the growth of measured inputs can be further decomposed into the growth of output due separately to capital and labor. The interesting questions are: 'What is the relative importance of each of the factors for each economy?' and 'How much of the economic growth is due to the growth of the measured inputs, capital and labor, and how much to technical progress?'.

In order to facilitate our discussion of growth accounting, we introduce the concept of a production elasticity of an input. Starting with the production function, $Y = F(K, L, t)$, a change in output, ΔY, may be decomposed into three components:

$$\Delta Y = \frac{\Delta Y}{\Delta K} \cdot \Delta K + \frac{\Delta Y}{\Delta L} \cdot \Delta L + \frac{\Delta Y}{\Delta t} \cdot \Delta t \tag{2.4}$$

where ΔK, ΔL, and Δt are the changes in capital, labor and time respectively. Dividing the above equation through by Y, we have:

$$\frac{\Delta Y}{Y}=\left[\frac{\Delta Y}{Y}\Big/\frac{\Delta K}{K}\right]\cdot\frac{\Delta K}{K}+\left[\frac{\Delta Y}{Y}\Big/\frac{\Delta L}{L}\right]\cdot\frac{\Delta L}{L}+\left[\frac{\Delta Y}{Y}\Big/\Delta t\right]\cdot\Delta t \qquad \text{or}$$

$$\frac{\Delta Y}{Y}=\varepsilon_K\cdot\frac{\Delta K}{K}+\varepsilon_L\cdot\frac{\Delta L}{L}+\gamma\cdot\Delta t \tag{2.5}$$

where $\varepsilon_K \equiv [(\Delta Y/Y)/(\Delta K/K)]$ is the percentage change in output in response to a one-percent change in capital alone (it is the answer to the question: suppose all other inputs are held constant, and just capital is increased by one percent, how much additional output, in percentage terms, will be produced?) — it is also called the elasticity of output with respect to capital; $\varepsilon_L \equiv [(\Delta Y/Y)/(\Delta L/L)]$ is the percentage change in output in response to a one-percent change in labor alone, or equivalently, the elasticity of output with respect to labor; $\gamma \equiv [(\Delta Y/Y)/\Delta t)]$, is the instantaneous percentage rate of change in output with respect to time, holding all inputs constant, or equivalently, the instantaneous rate of technical progress.

Equation (2.5) may be rewritten, with annual data, as:

$$\%\Delta Y=\varepsilon_K\,\%\Delta K+\varepsilon_L\,\%\Delta L+\gamma \tag{2.6}$$

where Δt is set equal to one. Equation (2.6) is the fundamental equation of growth accounting. It expresses the rate of growth of output as the sum of three components that may be identified as the contributions of physical capital, labor and time (representing technical progress), respectively. The first term on the right-hand side of equation (2.6) is the product of the elasticity of capital and the percentage change in the capital stock; it is therefore the growth in output due to the growth in capital. Similarly, the second term is the growth in output due to growth in labor, and the final term is the growth in output due to technical progress. Note that the contribution of each input depends on both its elasticity and its percentage change. An input with a large elasticity but a small percentage change, as well as an input with a small elasticity but a large percentage change, will both make relatively small contributions to the rate of growth of output.

The potential importance of tangible capital and technical progress can be illustrated with a little simple arithmetic. The contribution of the growth of labor to the growth of aggregate output is approximately given by the product of the elasticity of output with respect to labor and the rate of growth of the labor input. The typical values of the elasticity of output with respect to labor may be taken to be 0.6 for industrialized economies and between 0.3 and 0.4 for developing economies. The rate of growth of labor is typically less than 2 percent per annum for industrialized economies and less than 5 percent per annum for developing economies. Thus, the contribution of the growth of labor to the growth of output is bounded by 1.2 percent for industrialized economies and 2.0 percent for developing economies, respectively. Any time the growth of output of an economy significantly exceeds 2 percent per annum, it must be due to the growth of tangible capital, or technical progress (which includes the effects of human capital, R&D capital and other forms of intangible capital).

2 THE SOURCES OF ECONOMIC GROWTH

2.1 Growth of Outputs and Inputs

Before presenting the growth accounts, it is instructive to examine the underlying data on the growth of outputs and measured inputs. They are summarized in Table 2.1. Tangible capital is measured as utilized capital – the total nonresidential tangible capital stock at the beginning of the year multiplied by the rate of capacity utilization. Labor is measured as the number of personhours worked. For future reference, we also include in Table 2.1 two of the most important forms of measurable intangible capital – human capital and R&D capital. The human capital variable is defined as the average number of years of education per person of the working age (15-64, inclusive) population at the beginning of the

Table 2.1 Average annual rates of growth of output and measured inputs (percent)

Economy	Period	GDP	Capital stock	Utilized capital	Employ-ment	Labor hours	Human capital	R&D capital
Hong Kong	66-90	7.8	9.0	8.7	2.9	2.6	2.3	NA
Singapore	65-90	9.0	10.4	11.3	4.4	4.3	3.4	15.9
S. Korea	64-90	9.0	13.0	13.0	3.2	3.8	3.7	14.6
Taiwan	64-90	9.0	12.1	12.2	3.2	2.9	2.4	14.5
Japan	64-92	5.5	8.0	8.1	1.2	0.5	0.8	8.9
France	64-91	3.2	5.2	5.2	0.5	0.3	1.3	5.0
W. Germany	65-91	3.0	4.4	4.4	0.0	−0.6	1.1	5.7
UK	65-91	2.1	3.8	3.7	0.3	−0.3	0.9	2.1
US	49-92	3.0	3.1	3.2	1.6	1.5	0.8	6.1

year.[3] R&D capital is measured as the cumulative expenditures in constant prices on R&D less a 'depreciation' of 10 percent per annum.[4]

It is apparent from Table 2.1 that the East Asian NIEs have had much higher rates of growth of aggregate real output than the industrialized G-5 countries (only Japan, among the IEs, has achieved a rate of growth close to those achieved by the East Asian NIEs). It is also apparent, however, that the rates of growth of all the measured inputs, tangible and intangible, are systematically higher in the East Asian NIEs than in the IEs, so that one should not be surprised that the rates of growth of output are also higher (again, Japan is intermediate between the East Asian NIEs and the non-Asian IEs).

2.2 Accounts of Economic Growth

Based on the data on outputs and inputs presented in Table 2.1, Kim and Lau (1992, 1994a, 1994b) undertake to account for the sources of growth of the nine economies by estimating the aggregate meta-production function for this group of economies. They find that there has been no measured technical progress in the East Asian NIEs in the postwar period, despite their high rates of economic growth. Since the contribution of the labor input to economic growth is constrained by the rate of growth of the labor force, by far the most important source of economic growth of the East Asian NIEs is tangible capital accumulation. By contrast, Kim and Lau find statistically significant positive technical progress in every one of the industrialized G-5 countries. Moreover, technical progress is found to have played the most important role in the economic growth of these IEs, except for Japan. Because of the absence of technical progress, the East Asian NIEs have actually experienced a significant decline in measured productive efficiency relative to the IEs as a group.

The growth accounting of Kim and Lau is summarized and presented in Table 2.2. Table 2.2 shows that for the East Asian NIEs, tangible capital is overwhelmingly important, accounting for between 68 (Singapore) and 85 (Taiwan) percent of economic growth: labor accounts for the remainder. Technical progress is found to be statistically insignificant for the growth of output in the East Asian NIEs. In contrast, technical progress is found to be the most important source of growth for the non-Asian IEs, accounting for approximately 60 percent of its economic growth, followed by capital (approximately 35 percent),with labor playing a relatively minor role (approximately 5 percent). The experience of Japan lies in between those of the East Asian NIEs and the non-Asian IEs. Like the East Asian NIEs, tangible capital is the most important source of growth in Japan, accounting for more than 50 percent. Unlike the East Asian

Table 2.2 Relative contributions of the sources of economic growth (percent)

Economy	Tangible capital	Labor	Technical progress
Hong Kong	74	26	0
Singapore	68	32	0
S. Korea	80	20	0
Taiwan	85	15	0
Japan	56	5	39
Non-Asian G-5	36	6	59

NIEs, technical progress is statistically significant and a major source of growth, accounting for almost 40 percent, comparable in order of magnitude to the contribution of tangible capital.

We conclude that while technical progress is the most important source of growth of aggregate real output for the IEs (except Japan), it is, however, at least up to the present time, still not an important source of growth for the East Asian economies except Japan.

As a byproduct of their analysis, Kim and Lau have also confirmed the finding of Boskin and Lau (1990) that technical progress is tangible capital-augmenting. In other words, tangible or physical capital and technical progress, which also reflects the effects of intangible capital, are complementary. Complementarity implies that the more tangible capital there is, the more productive is intangible capital. It also implies that if there is very little tangible capital, investment in intangible capital may not be that productive.

3 REASONS FOR THE ABSENCE OF MEASURED TECHNICAL PROGRESS

Why is there is no *measured* technical progress in the East Asian NIEs, in contrast to the IEs, including Japan? There are several important reasons.

3.1 Low Level of Investment in Intangible Capital

First, since technical progress mostly reflects the effects of omitted and unmeasured inputs, including different forms of intangible capital, it is more likely to be found in economies where the quantities of such inputs are significant. Until recently, there has been little investment not in only

R&D,[5] especially basic research, but also in such activities as organizational innovation, software development, market development, advertising and on-the-job training, which have long-term effects on output, in the East Asian NIEs.[6] In Figure 2.4, R&D expenditures as a percentage of GDP are plotted for the East Asian NIEs and the G-5 countries. It is evident that the IEs have been investing a much greater percentage of their GDPs than the East Asian NIEs and for a much longer period.[7] The percentages have been rising for the East Asian NIES in recent years but given the long gestation period for R&D investment it will take some time before any effects on the aggregate GDPs become noticeable. And while the rates of growth of human capital have been high in the East Asian NIEs, the levels of human capital stocks still lag behind those of the IEs by a wide margin. However, for both human capital and R&D capital, there is evidence at both the microeconomic and the macroeconomic levels of threshold effects, that is, critical levels are required before they have significant effects, as well as complementarity with tangible or physical capital. Thus, the growth in the value added attributable to technical progress, or the growth in omitted and unmeasured inputs, is likely to be small in the East Asian NIEs. By contrast, the IEs invest a significant percentage of their GDPs in human capital and R&D and perhaps equally large amounts in other forms of

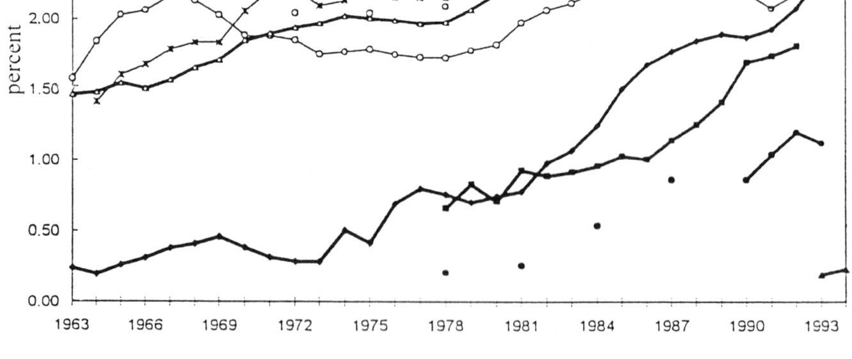

Figure 2.4 Percentage of total R&D expenditure in GDP(current prices)

'intangible capital' and productivity-enhancing activities. Thus, it should not be surprising that measured technical progress, or the 'residual', is found to be much larger and more significant in the IEs than in the East Asian NIEs.

It is of some interest to compare the levels of the omitted but measurable intangible capital (human capital and R&D capital) stocks across the East Asian NIEs and the IEs. They are presented in Figures 2.5 and 2.6 respectively. It is apparent from Figure 2.5 that the United States has always had the highest level of human capital and still does. However, the other economies, including the East Asian NIEs, have been narrowing the gap in human capital significantly over the past four decades. Nevertheless, the levels of human capital in the East Asian NIEs are still significantly below those of the IEs. Figure 2.6 also indicates that the United States has always had the highest level of R&D capital and still does. The East Asian NIEs lag behind the United States and the other G-5 countries significantly in terms of R&D capital. However, the rates of growth of both human capital and R&D capital in the East Asian NIEs are significantly higher than those in the G-5 countries.

The complementarity between technical progress (intangible capital) and tangible capital is one reason why investment in intangible capital has been relatively scarce until recently in the East Asian NIEs. At the prevailing levels of tangible capital (relative to labor), it has not yet become profitable, until recently, for many of the East Asian NIEs to invest in R&D and other forms of intangible capital. In time, with rising levels of tangible capital, the marginal productivity of intangible capital is enhanced while the marginal productivity of tangible capital diminishes, and the attractiveness of investments in R&D and in other forms of intangible capital will increase relative to traditional investments in tangible capital. That point has probably just been reached in the East Asian NIEs within the last few years. So it is quite possible that we should find higher levels of investments in intangible capital and hence more technical progress in the East Asian NIEs in the future.

3.2 Problems of Measurement of Capital

Second, the measurement of technical progress, or total factor productivity, depends critically on the measurement of the quantity of the capital input. Two principal problems may be identified in the present context: (1) the effect of depreciation of tangible capital; and (2) the differential accounting treatment of intangible capital between innovators and adopters.

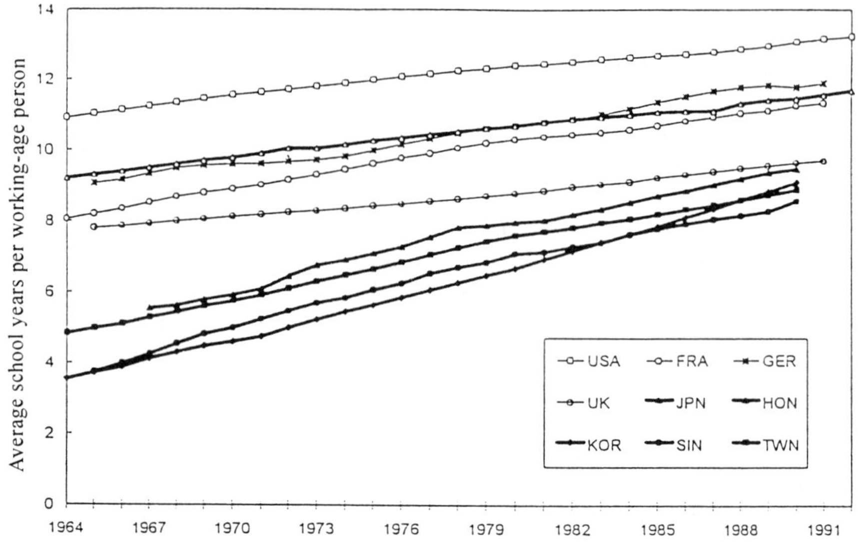

Figure 2.5 Human capital

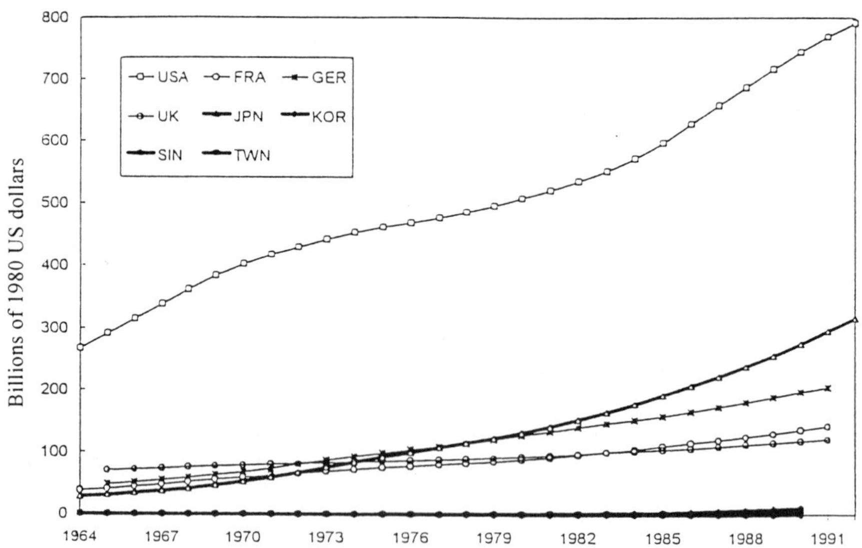

Figure 2.6 R&D capital

1. *The effect of depreciation of tangible capital* It may be argued that the use of gross capital stock, rather than the net capital stock, as a factor input in the estimation of the aggregate production function by Kim and Lau (1992, 1994a), makes allowance for only retirement of capital, but not physical depreciation. To the extent that physical depreciation is significant, the measured capital stock will overstate the 'true' capital stock (and hence the contribution of capital to output), and the estimated rate of capital-augmenting technical progress may be an underestimate of the 'true' rate of technical progress. Thus, an estimated rate of capital-augmenting technical progress of zero may not necessarily imply a zero 'true' rate. However, since the same concept of the gross capital stock is also used for the IEs, the above argument cannot explain why the estimated rates of capital-augmenting technical progress are positive and statistically significant for the IEs (including Japan) but low or negative and statistically insignificant for the East Asian NIEs. That is, unless one were to assume, in addition, that the 'true' depreciation rate is higher in the developing economies than in the IEs because of various factors, such as the differences in the composition of outputs (for example, a higher proportion of light industrial products). However, we may also note that Japan, which is supposed to have a high 'depreciation' rate, also has a high estimated rates of capital-augmenting technical progress. In any case, given the magnitudes of the estimated rates of capital-augmenting technical progress of the IEs, the implied 'true' depreciation rates in the East Asian NIEs would have to be implausibly high to be consistent with our empirical findings.
2. *The differential accounting treatment of intangible capital between innovators and adopters* Another measurement problem that may arise is the difference in the 'pricing' or 'costing' of capital equipment between the innovator and the adopter. For example, a corporation in an industrialized country, such as IBM, values all of its own fixed investments without taking into account its associated intangible investments. However, its actual revenue includes 'innovation rents' – that is, the returns to its investment in intangible capital. Thus, for IBM, one would expect to find a positive residual unaccounted for by the measured inputs or, equivalently, measured technical progress. But a corporation in a developing country, even if it has the same *measured* inputs as IBM, will not be able to produce the same value-added as IBM because it lacks the complementary intangible capital. It can, of course, try to purchase the necessary know-how, but that will result in a higher cost and lower value added than for IBM and hence a reduction or even elimination of the positive measured residual compared to IMB.

What makes things worse for the corporation in the developing country is that the capital equipment it purchases may, in fact, cost more to it than is carried on the books of IBM because it has been priced to include the 'innovation rents'. In short, IBM values its fixed investments at its cost without regard to intangible investments, whereas a corporation in a developing country has to value its fixed investments at market price, which is likely to include innovation rents and the former may be much lower than the latter if intangible capital is a significant input in the production process. Measured value added will therefore be higher at IBM than at a corporation in a developing country, holding all *measured inputs* constant.

3.3 The Distribution of Innovation Rents

Third, an important reason why there is no measured technical progress in the East Asian NIEs in the postwar period, despite their rapid economic growth and their apparently massive adoption of new 'technology' imported from abroad, has to do with the way the returns to innovation—innovation rents—are distributed between innovators and adopters: they may be biassed in favor of the innovators in the IEs, which have been and still remain the principal source of new technology in the world. The capital goods and technology used in developing economies are typically imported from the IEs and may have been fully priced (that is, the acquisition as well as royalty costs fully reflect the possible efficiency gains by the importing economy as well as the amortization of R&D and other developmental costs incurred by the exporting economy) in the international market, so that there is little or no *net increase in value-added, over and above the normal returns to the factor inputs*. In other words, the innovation rents have been largely captured by the foreign inventors, manufacturers and distributors of the new technology, equipment or intermediate inputs of the IEs in markets that are only very imperfectly competitive. New technology is not in general freely available to the East Asian NIEs.

The innovation rents can take the forms of higher than competitive and possibly discriminatory prices for the capital equipment (including maintenance contracts) and/or royalties and fees paid to the technology licensers of the IEs by the East Asian NIEs, which, for some sectors, can constitute a rising share of the output produced, correspondingly reducing the real value added of the importing developing economy. The fact that technical progress has been found to be mostly embodied in new tangible capital goods rather than disembodied also makes it easier for the inventors of new technologies to appropriate the rents through their monopolistic power in the capital equipment market.

While foreign direct investments from the IEs can also be a vehicle for the transfer of new technology to the developing economies, they should have a similar effect as the use of imported new equipment and subject to the same pricing problem. In addition, intra-firm transfer pricing of both outputs and intermediate inputs is yet another way in which 'innovation rents' (as well as other rents) can be shifted between a foreign direct investor in a developing host economy and its parent firm in the industrialized home economy, thus possibly lowering the measured GDP of the developing economy and raising the measured GDP of the industrialized economy.[8]

Still another way in which there may be little or no net increase in value added, controlling for the measured inputs, even with the adoption of new equipment and technology, is if the supply of 'critical components' that are needed as intermediate inputs are controlled by monopolistic suppliers in the IEs and can be imported by the developing economies from the IEs only at high monopolistic prices. Thus, the benefits of the new technology may be largely appropriated by the foreign manufacturers and suppliers of the critical components in IEs. Examples of such critical components include microprocessors, liquid crystal displays, and 'DOS' and 'Windows' operating-system softwares for notebook computers, plastic lenses for cameras, recording heads for video-camera recorders, and compressors for air-conditioners and refrigerators. Original equipment manufacturers (OEM), that is, producers in developing economies that enter into contracts with firms in IEs to supply goods designed and specified by the latter, which often provide the technological know-how as well, have razor-thin margins because the distribution and marketing of these goods are completely controlled by the firms in the IEs.[9] Consequently, even if a new technology were adopted by a developing economy, its effect might not be reflected in the form of a higher real (domestic) value added, holding measured factor inputs constant.[10] Moreover, to the extent that the enterprises in the IEs have monopolistic or monopsonistic power, even if there were genuine technical progress in the developing economies (for example, one cannot deny that there must have been learning by doing in at least some industries in the developing economies), it is not always the case that all or even most of the benefits accrue to the developing economies. It depends on the relative bargaining power between enterprises in the IEs and the developing economics. For example, while it is entirely likely that producers of notebook computers in developing economies have been lowering their costs through learning by doing, it is also possible that the bulk of their potential gains (in terms of profits) may be appropriated by the suppliers of critical components, or by branded distributors in the IEs. In fact, it is possible that the more the developing economies learn, the higher the profits for the critical component manufacturers in the IEs (and the higher their measured GDPs).

Furthermore, it is also well established that imported technology frequently is not very effective in the absence of indigenous R&D. In other words, indigenous R&D capital is complementary to imported knowledge or R&D capital. For example, the new rice varieties developed by the International Rice Research Institute in the Philippines must be further improved through indigenous R&D in each adopting country before their maximum yield potential can be realized. Thus, to the extent that there is little or no indigenous R&D, there will also be little or no measured spillover effect from technical progress in the rest of the world.

3.4 Aggregation

Fourth, it should be emphasized that our finding of no measured technical progress in the East Asian NIEs is for the aggregate economy as a whole. It is entirely consistent with the possibility of the simultaneous existence of significant positive technical progress in certain industries and sectors and negative technical progress (rising inefficiency) in other industries and sectors in the East Asian NIEs. Thus, positive technical progress in these industries may be offset by rising inefficiency in certain other industries, especially those in the nontradable sectors, such as construction, which are often also the most monopolistic and tradition-bound as well as the least competitive, so that the economy as a whole exhibits no measured technical progress. (This is less likely to be true for an open and competitive economy such as Hong Kong.) Rising inefficiency can persist only in protected markets under monopolistic or oligopolistic conditions. Moreover, the inefficient industries and sectors may actually be able to appropriate and transfer all or part of the gains from technical progress in the efficient industries through rising land prices, construction costs, space rents, internal transportation costs and distribution margins. For example, South Korea and Taiwan and even Japan have well-known inefficient nontradable sectors.

3.5 The Omission of the Value of the Quality of Life

Finally, it is also possible that improvements in the quality of life, such as a reduction in air pollution or traffic congestion, brought about by increased inputs of capital and labor, may not be fully reflected in measured real GDP. In other words, not all of the outputs resulting from the measured inputs and their growth over time are captured by measured real GDP, and hence in the efficiency and productivity measurements. It is necessary either to impute a value to the improvements in the quality of life, or to net out the measured inputs used specifically for such improvements, in order to arrive at a correct measurement of technical progress. If such imputation or netting out is not done, measured technical progress will be biassed downward.[11]

4 THE GLOBAL EXPERIENCE

4.1 The East Asian Experience in the Global Context

The finding that technical progress plays no role in the postwar economic growth of the East Asian NIEs, but the dominant role in the postwar economic growth of the IEs, may, at first glance, appear quite surprising. However, it has been independently confirmed by other studies using different methodologies, for example, Tsao (1985) and Young (1992) for Singapore, and Young (1995) for the four East Asian NIEs. Kim and Lau (1996) extend their sample of developing economies to include, in addition to the four East Asian NIEs, China, Indonesia, Malaysia, the Philippines and Thailand and again reach the same conclusion: there is no measured technical progress in the Asian Pacific developing economies. While there are studies, such as the World Bank (1993), that find technical progress in some East Asian economies, most of them are flawed because of the restrictive assumptions that are maintained, namely: constant returns to scale, neutrality of technical progress, and instantaneous competitive profit maximization.

It is also worth pointing out that similar findings have been made for the IEs in an earlier era. That the growth of measured output can be entirely explained by the growth of measured inputs is by no means unique to East Asian developing countries. Abramovitz and David (1973) have found that economic growth in the 19th-century United States can be largely attributed to the growth of measured inputs rather than to technical progress. Tostlebee (1956) has found the same for US agriculture in the 19th century – in fact he reports a negative rate of growth of total factor productivity. Hayami and Ogasawara (1996) have found that the growth of the Japanese economy between the Meiji Restoration and the First World War can be largely explained by the growth of measured inputs, principally tangible capital accumulation.

Whether there has actually been zero or some technical progress in the East Asian NIEs is in fact not that important. What is important is that tangible capital accumulation has been absolutely critical to the economic growth of the East Asian NIEs, as it was for Japan and the United States in an earlier era. No one would argue that between the growth of labor and technical progress the East Asian NIEs could have achieved their rapid rates of growth. The centrality of the accumulation of tangible capital and its efficient allocation to economic growth at an early stage of economic development is reaffirmed by the East Asian experience.

What the historical experience of economic growth suggests is that at different stages of economic development, the different types of measured inputs play different roles. For example, for economies starting out with a low level of tangible capital, the marginal efficiency of investment in human capital (and R&D capital), may be very low. It is only after tangible capital accumulation has proceeded to a certain stage that investment in human capital begins to be productive, and still later for investment in R&D and other forms of intangible capital to be so. It is therefore really a matter of the complementarity between tangible and intangible capital and among the different types of intangible capital, as well as their relative marginal productivities at different stages of the process of economic development and growth.

However, while tangible capital accumulation is necessary for economic growth, it alone is not sufficient. Some economies that had rapid rates of growth in their capital stocks, such as the former Soviet Union and the Chinese economy before it began its economic reform in 1979, did not experience rapid growth in their output. What is needed is thus not just capital accumulation, but efficient capital accumulation. This the East Asian NIEs have mostly achieved. They have grown rapidly not only because they have high savings and investment rates, but also because they have allocated their investments to sectors in which they are the most productive. The accumulation of capital, as well as its efficient allocation, over a long period of time, are genuinely impressive accomplishments of the East Asian NIEs.

Why have the East Asian NIEs been able to allocate their investment efficiently while other developing economies have not? We believe that it is because on the whole the market forces are allowed to direct the flow of investments. The export orientation of the East Asian NIEs makes it difficult if not impossible for their respective governments to intervene excessively on behalf of their producers, since they are essentially powerless to affect the world markets. Thus, in order to compete effectively on the world markets, the producers in the East Asian NIEs, at least those which export, must deploy their resources efficiently. Moreover, these export-orientated producers, out of their own self-interest, are likely to oppose anti-competitive and protectionist economic policies in their respective home countries that raise the costs of their inputs of producer goods and intermediate goods and affect adversely their ability to compete on the world markets, or that may lead to retaliation from other countries. Thus export orientation also tends to create a domestic constituency for competition and liberalization. Finally, the fact that most enterprises in the East Asian NIEs are privately owned and managed means that they have the incentives for prompt self-correction if mistakes are made, in contrast to public enterprises. Managers of private enterprises are not necessarily more intelligent than the managers of public enterprises. However, managers of private enterprises have to meet the market test – they therefore cannot afford to be wrong for very long. This is probably the principal reason why private enterprise is likely to result in a more efficient allocation of capital in the long run.

4.2 Sustainability of East Asian Economic Growth

Finally, if the past economic growth of the East Asian NIEs has been based on the growth of measured inputs, can it be sustained in the long run? Or is there a risk that diminishing marginal productivity of tangible capital will eventually limit their economic growth and their prosperity? This is essentially the question posed by Krugman (1994).

This question can be addressed in two parts. First, it should be recognized that there is still plenty of room even for exclusively input-based growth. If we compare the input intensities across the East Asian NIEs and the G-5 countries, we would discover that the East Asian NIEs are still far behind the IEs. In Figure 2.7 the tangible capital stocks per labor hour of both the industrialized and the newly industrialized economies are presented. It shows, as one expects, that the tangible capital-labor ratio is still much higher in the IEs than in the East Asian NIEs, with Japan again being intermediate between the two groups. In Figure 2.8, the total numbers of school years per labor hour of the two groups of economies are presented. Here, while the rates of growth are higher in the East Asian NIEs, the levels are still much higher in the IEs. In Figure 2.9, the R&D capital stocks per labor hour are presented. It shows that the United States has had and continues to have the highest quantity of R&D capital stock relative to its labor in the world. The East Asian NIEs, despite their much higher rates of growth, still have a long way to go before they catch up to the levels of R&D capital stocks of the IEs. We conclude that overall there is still a large gap for the East Asian NIEs to close before their tangible capital, human capital and R&D capital *per unit labor* reach the levels prevailing in the IEs. Economic growth based on the growth of measured inputs, as opposed to technical

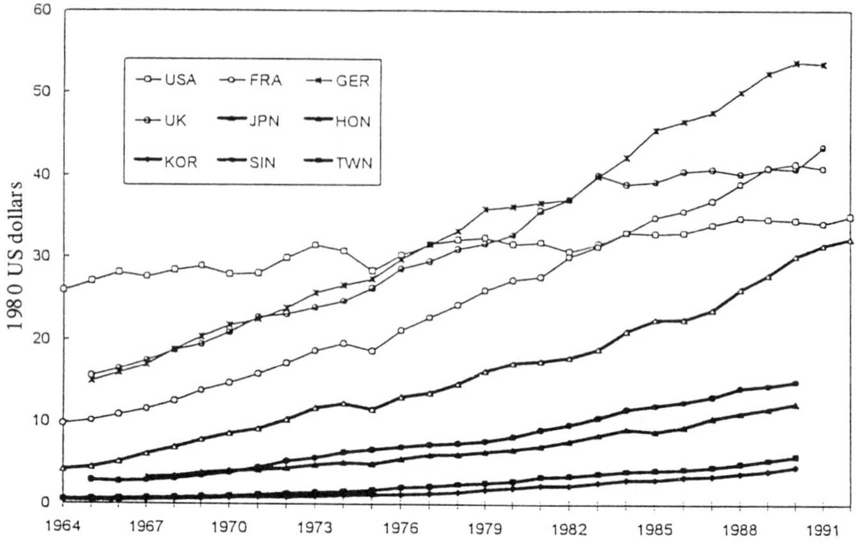

Figure 2.7 Tangible capital stock per labor hour

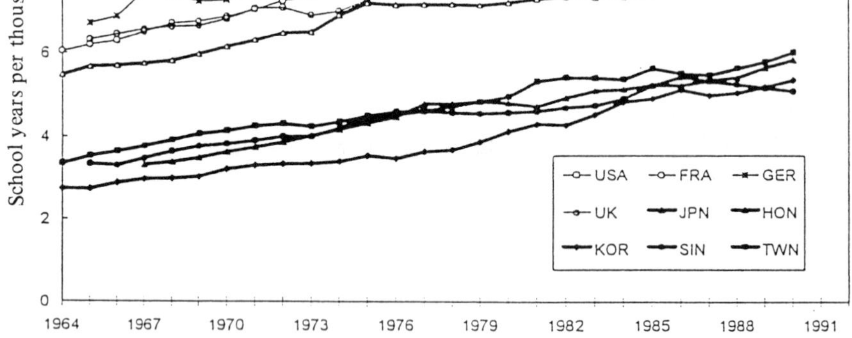

Figure 2.8 School years per labor hour

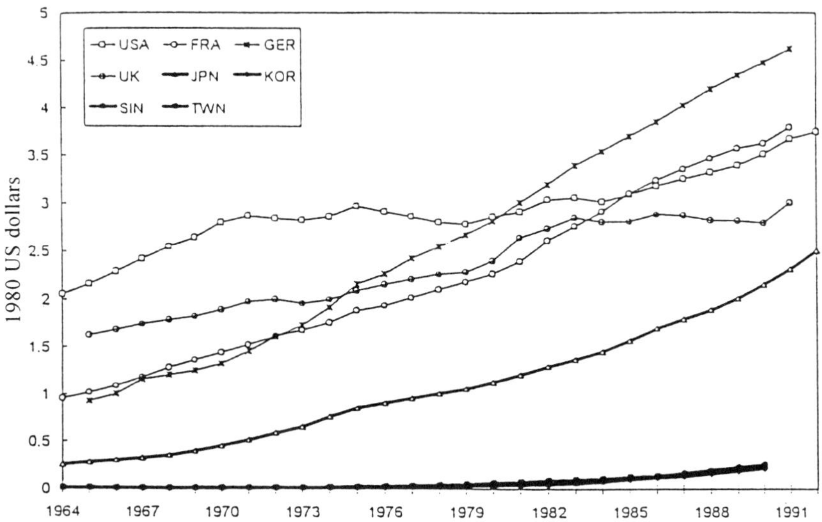

Figure 2.9 R&D capital stock per labor hour

progress, can therefore be expected to continue for quite some time, even though it is true that eventually measured-inputs-based growth will reach its limits.

Second, based on the experience of current IEs such as Japan and the United States, we may reasonably draw the conclusion that physical, or tangible, capital accumulation is the most important source of growth for countries at an early stage of economic development. After a certain level of tangible capital intensity (tangible capital per unit labor) has been reached, diminishing marginal productivity of tangible capital will inevitably set in, given that land and natural resources are fixed and the labor input can only grow slowly in the long run if at all. (Even human capital can only grow slowly.) When that happens, the desirability of intangible capital will increase relative to that of tangible capital. This advantage of intangible capital will be further reinforced by the complementarity between tangible and intangible capital,[17] (and among human capital, R&D capital, and technical progress). Because of this complementarity, investments in intangible capital can retard the decline in the marginal productivity of tangible capital even as the latter increases. Intangible capital can therefore be expected to assume increasing importance as an economy is transformed from developing to developed status. And this is the likely path for the East Asian NIEs. Japan, in fact, has shown by its own example how this transformation can be accomplished.

There is thus a time sequence – stages of economic growth, if you will – with tangible capital accumulation being the most important source of economic growth in the early stage and technical progress (intangible capital) assuming an increasingly significant role in the mature stage, after sufficient tangible capital accumulation has taken place.[13] Among investments in the different forms of intangible capital, investment in human capital is likely to take off first, to be followed by investments in R&D capital and other intangible forms of capital. The historical experiences of economic growth of the IEs, especially that of Japan and the United States, suggest that investment in intangible capital, even with its longer gestation period, will pay off handsomely.

5 IMPLICATIONS FOR EAST ASIAN NEWLY INDUSTRIALIZED ECONOMIES

Our empirical findings have important policy implications for the East Asian NIEs. In the long run, as their tangible capital stocks continue to grow, their marginal productivities of tangible capital will continue to decline, and increases in the tangible capital inputs alone will not be sufficient for the NIEs to maintain their current rates of economic growth. Simply having high levels of saving and tangible investment and allocating the tangible investment efficiently will no longer be enough. It will be necessary for the more advanced East Asian NIEs to devote greater proportions of their resources to investment in human capital and in R&D, and more generally in intangible capital. Otherwise it is unlikely that they will be able to catch up with the IEs in terms of productive efficiency and hence standard of living. However, our findings for Japan also show that sustained investments in intangible capital can lead to higher productive efficiency over time and thus narrow the gap between the technological levels of the leading and the lagging economies.

The globalization of markets, and the trends toward deregulation, liberalization and privatization suggest that the world is likely to become much more competitive in the future. It also means that national governments will become less and less effective in protecting or subsidizing their firms. The allocation of resources will therefore become more and more market directed.[14] Investment in intangible capital is an essential way to augment and transform an economy's comparative advantage.

In order to promote the investment and accumulation of intangible capital, the East Asian NIEs must continue to protect intellectual property rights, both domestic and foreign, vigilantly. Otherwise, it will inhibit indigenous innovation as well as international transfer of technology. Fortunately, the East Asian NIEs have already moved significantly to strengthen the enforcement and protection of intellectual property rights.

The East Asian NIEs must also try to enhance the efficiency of their non-tradable sectors by promoting more competition there. With sufficient monopolistic and/or monopsonistic power, inefficient industries and sectors in an economy may actually be able to appropriate all or part of the gains from technical progress in the efficient industries and sectors. Increasing efficiency in the nontradable sectors is necessary in an increasingly global market because the inefficiency of the non-tradable sectors will adversely affect the competitiveness of the tradable sectors. Liberalization and deregulation of markets, both domestic and international, are important strategies in forcing the nontradable sectors to become competitive and efficient and in so doing to realize measured technical progress.

5.1 The Case for Investment in R&D

It has already been pointed out that indigenous R&D and innovation are necessary for the successful exploitation of imported technology and imitation alone is not enough.[15] The distribution of gains from technology trade and transfer is biassed in favor of the innovators and the owners of intangible capital (for example, brand names) and against the imitators. This is because the former possess market power, derived through and protected by patents and other investments in intangible capital. Moreover, strategic R&D can be used by developing economies under some conditions to acquire technology from IEs either through cross-licensing or through credible threats of competing indigenous investment. The experience of developed economies, especially that of Japan, suggests that investment in R&D capital and other forms of intangible capital pays off.

However, it is well known that R&D projects are characterized by a high degree of risk, a long gestation period, 'lumpiness' – that is, a 'critical mass' investment is required – and possible nonappropriability of benefits by the R&D investors themselves. The relatively small sizes of firms in Hong Kong, Singapore and Taiwan (compared to Japan and South Korea) imply that they are less likely to have the resources and the long-term staying power to undertake substantive R&D projects on an individual basis. The non-appropriability of the benefits of many R&D

projects, especially those in basic research, which implies that the social rate of return on R&D will in many instances be greater than the private rate of return, and the lack of well-developed venture capital market in these economies, suggest that direct or indirect government support for R&D may be necessary. R&D and science and technology policy may also be viewed as instruments of a more general industrial policy.

5.2 Investment in Intangible Capital

The East Asian economies have already been making significant investments in human capital. Secondary education is almost universal in the four East Asian NIEs.[16] Tertiary enrollment rates in South Korea and Taiwan are among the highest in the world, somewhere between 35 and 40 percent and are rising fast in Hong Kong and Singapore. Japan has been investing an increasing percentage of its GDP in R&D since the late 1950s and has made big strides in the development of new processes as well as new products. Both South Korea and Taiwan began to make significant investments in R&D in the 1980s. In South Korea, the *chaebols* (large conglomerates) with 'deep pockets', such as Samsung and Hyundai, also invest heavily in R&D. The personal computer and the semi-conductor industries in Taiwan provide successful examples of government-financed R&D as an instrument of industrial policy. In Hong Kong, Singapore and Taiwan, the government and quasi-public institutions support as well as conduct R&D (for example, the Industrial Technology Research Institute in Taiwan and the Nanyang Technological University in Singapore). Among the four East Asian NIEs, Hong Kong lags behind the others in R&D expenditures as a percentage of GDP because of the relatively small sizes of its enterprises, the more service-orientated industrial composition, and the noninterventionist nature of its government.

As the East Asian NIEs step up their investment in intangible capital, they will gradually become innovators in addition to being adopters, as Japan did. They will be able to create, and enjoy, their own innovation rents. As these rents become meaningful in the future, we should be able to see positive measured technical progress.

5.3 Implications for East Asian NIEs

From our analysis of the experience of economic growth of the G-5 countries and the East Asian NIEs, we may reach the conclusion that the continued economic growth of the East Asian NIEs in the future depends on the fulfillment of three conditions: (1) maintaining the growth in tangible capital; (2) assuring the efficiency of tangible capital; and (3) closing the gap on intangible capital. We discuss each of them in turn.

1. *Maintaining the growth in tangible capital* This implies that the government must continue to adopt policies that encourage and promote savings and investment, which include the preservation of a low-tax environment, controlling inflation, maintaining free flows of capital, labor and goods, upholding the exchange value of the currency, providing needed infrastructure, and avoiding open-ended social welfare programs.
2. *Assuring the efficiency of tangible capital* This implies that tangible capital must be allowed to flow freely to whichever sectors yield the highest market returns. To ensure that the allocation of tangible capital will be market directed, the East Asian NIEs must maintain steadfastly their commitment to free trade, and to continued liberalization and deregulation. They must preserve open competition in all markets, maintain the rule of law, and eschew intervention except in cases of clear market failures.
3. *Closing the gap on intangible capital* The government must promote the investment in intangible capital, for example, by providing R&D investment tax credits, so that over time the East Asian NIEs can catch up to the level of intangible capital per labor hour of the IEs. Where non-appropriability is a real problem, as for example, in the investment of human capital,[17] the governments must step forward to provide the necessary financial support for different forms of education (formal, technical, on-the-job training, and re-training), as they have done in the past. Investment in other forms of intangible capital (design, goodwill, knowhow, market development, information systems and software, and so on) should also be encouraged. Intellectual property rights should be strictly enforced in order to promote indigenous efforts for its creation. The competitive advantage of the East Asian NIEs *vis-à-vis* China and other Asian Pacific developing economies depends not on cheap labor, and not on low-cost capital, but on the intangible capital that the East Asian NIEs manage to accumulate and continually renew.

5.4 The Possible Role of the Government in R&D

For the East Asian NIEs, with their economies increasingly more service-orientated, any investment in R&D should be focussed on development rather than basic or applied research. A consortium approach, which was adopted in Taiwan in the development of the notebook computer, may work. Hong Kong and Singapore are somewhat disadvantaged relative to

Taiwan and South Korea in not having an extensive network of their former citizens and residents in the high-technology industries in the United States. Many of these former Taiwanese and South Korean citizens and residents have returned to their respective home countries and are responsible for the phenomenal success of the high-technology industries there. Given the rapid expansion of the manufacturing subsidiaries of the East Asian NIEs in China, R&D efforts in design and in manufacturing engineering may make sense. The governments may also promote research efforts in the areas of standardization and quality assurance.

5.5 Prospects for the Future

The prospects for continued rapid economic growth of the East Asian NIEs are good, as long as they continue their high investment rates in tangible capital, maintain its efficient allocation, and gradually increase their investment rates in intangible capital. Increasing the stock of intangible capital helps to counter the decline in the marginal productivity of tangible capital as the latter keeps rising. However, intangible capital typically has long gestation periods, which means that the sooner they step up their investment in intangible capital, the better.

What are the prospects of the other East Asian developing economies, such as Indonesia, Malaysia, the Philippines and Thailand? Kim and Lau (1996) have found that during the postwar period, there has been no technical progress in these East Asian developing economies either. In other words, the accumulation of tangible capital is still by far the most important source of economic growth of these economies. Their experiences are thus quite similar to those of the four East Asian NIEs, which are perhaps between one and two decades ahead of them. However, there are also two differences that may turn out to be significant in the longer run.

First of all, the savings rates in the four East Asian developing economies, while they must be considered high by the standards of developing countries, in the high 20s or the low 30s, are also significantly lower than the savings rates in the four East Asian NIEs at a comparable stage of development. A lower savings rate in turn implies a lower investment rate and therefore a lower rate of capital accumulation, which in turn implies a lower rate of economic growth. And while it is true that domestic savings can be supplemented with foreign investment (both direct and portfolio) and loans, the latter cannot last forever. Moreover, to the extent the foreign capital inflows are of the short-term kind (either portfolio investment or short-term loans), the capital-importing country remains vulnerable, and too much capital inflow can make the exchange rate overvalued and encourage imports of consumption goods which may further reduce the domestic savings rate.

Second, the human resources bases in the four East Asian developing economies are weak relatively to those of the four East Asian NIEs,[18] and will eventual constrain the speed of upgrading of industries as the domestic wage rates rise. Insufficient human capital can affect adversely the marginal productivities of both tangible and intangible capital because of its complementarity.

Finally, the globalization of markets have made them much more competitive and unpredictable than before. The advent of the World Trade Organization (WTO) means that many protective trade barriers, including voluntary textile quotas, will eventually disappear. It is not clear that a simple export-orientated strategy, which worked so well for the East Asian NIEs, will be sufficient for the East Asian developing economies today. For sustained economic growth, they will have to return to the tried and true formula of heavy investment in both tangible and human capital.

China faces the same difficulties in terms of human resources as the East Asian developing economies. However, it has the advantages of a very high domestic savings rate and a huge domestic market. It also has the ability to attract both the resources and the entrepreneurial talents of the Chinese Diaspora. It may therefore do better in the long run.

NOTES

1. Kim and Lau and their collaborators employ the 'Meta-production function' approach which does not require the assumptions of constant returns to scale, neutrality of technical progress, and profit maximization in competitive output and input markets, assumptions that are maintained by the users of the total factor productivity formula approach. In fact, these maintained assumptions have been consistently rejected whenever they are statistically tested.
2. We note that it is not always possible to identify whether the production function has shifted using data from a single country, especially if the output and the measured inputs of the country have all been growing steadily over time. That is one of the principal reasons for the introduction of the meta-production function approach by Boskin, Lau, Yotopoulos and their collaborators.
3. This definition of human capital does not include many other forms of investment in human capital, for example, on the job training provided by firms. To the extent that such omitted investments in human capital are significant, their effects will be captured by the time trend variable, that is, technical progress.
4. The 10 percent rate of depreciation of R&D capital has been adopted by many researchers. For basic research, the rate of depreciation is lower, say 5 percent; for applied R&D, the rate of depreciation is higher, say 20 percent. Ten percent

represents an approximate average of the two rates.

5. Bear in mind that investments in R&D typically have long gestation periods and their effects on real output will be apparent only after a lag of quite a few years.
6. For example, in the early phase of the economic development of the East Asian NIEs, the international marketing is, with some exceptions, mostly handled by large Japanese trading firms and buyers from Europe and the United States.
7. For Hong Kong, the data include only R&D expenditures at academic institutions.
8. Complicating the matter of transfer pricing is the practice of profit shifting for tax avoidance purposes. For example, a foreign direct investor in a host country may be granted a tax holiday for a fixed period. During this period, it is beneficial to attribute all of the profit, including innovation rents, to the subsidiary in the host country. After the expiration of the tax holiday, it may be more beneficial to attribute all of the profit, including that which properly should be attributed to the subsidiary in the host country, to the parent. If this happens, the measured value added of the foreign direct investor in the host country will be over-stated in the initial years and understated in the subsequent years, resulting in a downward bias in its rate of growth and hence in any estimate of technical progress or rate of growth of total factor productivity.
9. This phenomenon is not unrelated to the theory of product cycles, which implies that the price (and hence value added) per unit output of a new product declines over time.
10. In extreme cases of inefficiency, the real value-added may actually be lower or even turn negative after adoption of the new technology, as, for example, when a country insists on investing in industries against its own long-term comparative advantage.

    Of course, to the extent that there is intellectual piracy in the developing economies, that is, nonpayment of royalties and fees that should have been paid, the real value added in the developing economies will be higher than otherwise and there will appear to be measured technical progress. Empirically, this effect does not seem to be important for the aggregate real output of the entire economy in the East Asian NIEs.
11. Singapore arguably partially fits this case.
12. Note that if there is little or no tangible capital, the return to any investment in intangible capital is also likely to be low. This is a manifestation of the complementarity between tangible and intangible capital.
13. Thus, it is possible that there may be own and cross-threshold effects for tangible capital, human capital, as well as R&D capital.
14. The protection of the environment is an exception.
15. For example, Japan, although widely known as an excellent imitator, has invested heavily in R&D and has been responsible for many significant innovations in process and product technologies.
16. Compulsory education is up to at least nine years in the East Asian NIEs.
17. For example, a private firm will have little or no incentive in investing in generalized human capital for its employees because of the mobility of the latter. However, for society as a whole, investment in human capital is beneficial. This provides the case for public funding of some types of education. The public

funding can, however, take many forms. For example, at the tertiary level, it may take the form of loans rather than grants to the students, who will clearly benefit from the education personally.

18. For example, Thailand has a relatively underdeveloped system of secondary education and Indonesia lags even further behind.

REFERENCES

Abramovitz, M. (1990), 'The Catch-Up Factor in Postwar Economic Growth', *Economic Inquiry*, 1, 1-18.

Abramovitz, M. and P.A. David (1973), 'Reinterpreting Economic Growth: Parables and Realities', *American Economic Review*, 63, 428-39.

Barro, R.J. (1991), 'Economic Growth in a Cross Section of Countries', *Quarterly Journal of Economics*, 106, 407-43.

Boskin, M.J., and L.J. Lau (1990), 'Post-War Economic Growth of the Group-of-Five Countries: A New Analysis', Technical Paper No. 217, Stanford, CA: Center for Economic Policy Research, Stanford University (mimeograph).

Boskin, M.J., and L.J. Lau (1991), 'Capital Formation and Economic Growth', in *Technology and Economics: A Volume Commemorating Ralph Landau's Service to the National Academy of Engineering*, Washington, DC: National Academy Press, 47-56.

Boskin, M.J. and L.J. Lau (1992a), 'Capital, Technology, and Economic Growth', in N. Rosenberg, R. Landau and D. Mowery (eds), *Technology and the Wealth of Nations*, Stanford: Stanford University Press, pp. 17-55.

Boskin, M.J., and L.J. Lau (1992b), 'International and Intertemporal Comparison of Productive Efficiency: An Application of the Meta-production Function Approach to the Group-of-Five (G-7) Countries', *Economic Studies Quarterly*, 43, 298-312.

Boskin, M.J., and L.J. Lau (1996), 'The Contribution of R&D to Economic Growth: Some Issues and Observations', in B. L. R. Smith and C.E. Barfield, (eds), *Technology, R&D and the Economy*, Washington, DC: The Brookings Institution and American Enterprise Institute, 75-107.

Boskin, M.J. and L.J. Lau (1998), *Post-War Economic Growth of the Group-of-Seven Countries*, forthcoming.

Christensen, L.R., D.W. Jorgenson and L.J. Lau (1973), 'Transcendental Logarithmic Production Frontiers', *Review of Economics and Statistics*, 55, 28-45.

Griliches, Z., and D.W. Jorgenson (1966), 'Sources of Measured

Productivity Change: Capital Input', *American Economic Review*, 56, 50-61.

Hall, R.E. (1968), 'Technical Change and Capital from the Point of View of the Dual', *Review of Economic Studies*, 35, 35-46.

Hayami, Y. and J. Ogasawara (1996), 'Changes in the Sources of Modern Economic Growth: Asian NIEs in Japan's Historical Perspective', paper presented at the Department of Economics, Stanford University, March (mimeograph).

Hayami, Y. and V.W. Ruttan (1970), 'Agricultural Productivity Differences Among Countries', *American Economic Review*, 60, 895-911.

Hayami, Y. and V.W. Ruttan (1985), *Agricultural Development: An International Perspective*, revised and expanded ed, Baltimore: Johns Hopkins University Press.

Jorgenson, D.W. and B.M. Fraumeni (1989a), 'The Accumulation of Human and Nonhuman Capital, 1948-1984', in R.E. Lipsey and H.S. Tice eds, *The Measurement of Saving, Investment and Wealth*, Vol. 52, Chicago: University of Chicago Press, 227-82.

Jorgenson, D.W. and B.M. Fraumeni (1989), 'Investment in Education', *Educational Researcher*, 18, 35-44.

Jorgenson, D.W., F.M. Gollop and B.M. Fraumeni (1987), *Productivity and U.S. Economic Growth*, Cambridge, MA: Harvard University Press.

Kim, J.-I., and L.J. Lau (1992), 'The Sources of Economic Growth of the Newly Industrialized Countries on the Pacific Rim', paper presented at the Conference on the Economic Development of ROC and the Pacific Rim in the 1990s and Beyond, Taipei, May.

Kim J.-I., and L.J. Lau (1993), 'The Role of Capital in the Economic Growth of the East Asian Newly Industrialized Countries', Working Paper, Stanford, CA: Department of Economics, Stanford University, June (mimeograph).

Kim, J.-I., and L.J. Lau (1994a), 'The Sources of Economic Growth of the Newly Industrialized Countries on the Pacific Rim', in L.R. Klein and C.-T. Yu (eds), *The Economic Development of ROC and the Pacific Rim in the 1990s and Beyond*, Singapore: World Scientific Publishing Co., 65-102.

Kim, J.-I., and L.J. Lau (1994b), 'The Sources of Economic Growth in the East Asian Newly Industrialized Countries', *Journal of the Japanese and International Economies*, 8, 235-271.

Kim, J.-I., and L.J. Lau (1996), 'The Sources of Asian Pacific Economic Growth', *Canadian Journal of Economics*, 29, Special Issue, S448-S454.

Krugman, P. (1994), 'The Myth of Asia's Miracle', *Foreign Affairs*, 73, 62-78.

Lau, L.J., D.T. Jamison, S.-C. Liu and S. Rivkin (1993), 'Education and Economic Growth: Some Cross-sectional Evidence from Brazil', *Journal of Development Economics*, 41, 45-70.

Lau, L.J., and P.A. Yotopoulos (1989), 'The Meta-production Function Approach to Technological Change in World Agriculture', *Journal of Development Economics*, 31, 241-69.

Levine, R. and D. Renelt (1992), 'A Sensitivity Analysis of Cross-Country Growth Regressions', *American Economic Review*, 82, 942-63.

Romer, P.M. (1986), 'Increasing Returns and Long-Run Growth', *Journal of Political Economy*, 94, 1002-1937.

Solow, R.M. (1956), 'A Contribution to the Theory of Economic Growth', *Quarterly Journal of Economics*, 70, 65-94.

Solow, R.M. (1957), 'Technical Change and the Aggregate Production Function', *Review of Economics and Statistics*, 39, 312-320.

Tostlebee, A. (1956), *On U.S. Agricultural Growth – Sources of Productivity*, New York: National Bureau of Economic Research.

Tsao, Y. (1985), 'Growth without Productivity: Singapore Manufacturing in the 1970s', *Journal of Development Studies*, 18, 25-38.

The World Bank (1993), *The East Asian Miracle: Economic Growth and Public Policy*, Oxford: Oxford University Press.

Young, A. (1992), 'A Tale of Two Cities: Factor Accumulation and Technical Change in Hong Kong and Singapore', in O.J. Blanchard and S. Fischer (eds), *National Bureau of Economic Research Macroeconomics Annual*, Cambridge, MA: The MIT Press, 13-54.

Young, A. (1995), 'The Tyranny of Numbers: Confronting the Statistical Realities of the East Asian Growth Experience', *Quarterly Journal of Economics*, 110, 641-80.

3. Can Capital Fundamentalism be Revived? A General Equilibrium Approach to Growth Accounting

Kenneth S. Lin and Hsiu-Yun Lee*

1 INTRODUCTION

In the view of capital fundamentalism, the best way to promote economic growth is simply increasing investment. Differences in national stocks of capital were the major determinants of differences in the levels of national income. A straightforward piece of advice on the development problem is that public policies must be designed to speed up a nation's physical capital accumulation. However, the neoclassical growth model and growth accounting research in the 1950s and 1960s indicated that differences in the patterns of investment were not the factors behind cross-country differences in living standards in the long run.

Recent explosions of research in growth accounting have reinstated capital fundamentalism at the forefront of economic analysis and policy discussions. For example, Jorgenson et al. (1987) found that capital accumulation is the most important source of economic growth, while productivity growth is the least important source in the US economy. King and Levine (1994) found that capital-output ratio is systematically related to the level of development. Kim and Lau (1994, 1995) concluded that capital accumulation remains the most important source of economic growth, followed by labor in the East Asian newly industrialized

*This is the revised version of the paper originally titled 'What New Growth Theory Teaches Us About Economic Growth Dynamics', presented at Economics and Political Economy of Development at the Turn of the Century: Conference in Memory of John C.H. Fei, August 1-2, 1997, Taipei, Taiwan. We thank Professor Chao-hsi Huang and participants in the conference and in the Macro Workshop at National Taiwan University for helpful comments and suggestions. All remaining errors are ours.

countries (NICs). In DeLong and Summers (1992), international comparisons suggested a very special role for equipment investment as a trigger for productivity growth, which led them to make a policy prescription that equipment investment should receive special incentives.

The purpose of this chapter is to evaluate econometrically the role of physical capital accumulation in economic growth and development. Such an exploration is essential to understanding whether capital fundamentalism should guide public policy recommendations and research strategies. Unlike previous studies, we provided the growth accounting exercises in a general equilibrium framework. We first characterize different sets of restrictions on a transitional path implied by old and new growth theories, which allow us to explore how transitional dynamics depend on parameters of preference, production technology and exogenous shocks. To achieve this, we propose a solution procedure which yields the explicit Autoregressive Moving Average (ARMA) representation of output growth rate in various growth models. A growth model is to be used as a description of actual growth experience, and its ARMA representation must be consistent with the ARMA counterpart in actual growth path. We employ this research strategy by presenting the time-series 'facts' about GDP growth rates, and then check whether there is a model that likewise delivers the ARMA representation of the data.

To achieve the identification of the model, the value of capital share in production function must be given a priori. We estimate structural parameters for various growth models under the pre-specified values of capital share. In addition to statistical evaluation of the model performance, we vary the value of capital share to trace its dynamic effects on output growth as growth accounting exercises, focussing on the fraction of long-run growth that can plausibly be attributed to physical capital accumulation. The estimation and hypothesis testing also help us answer the question whether there are enough time-series characteristics in the data to discriminate various growth models.

New growth theory enhances the importance of capital accumulation either through the introduction of an additional reproducible input factor such as human capital or through externalities. For example, Mankiw et al. (1992) included human capital in a neoclassical growth model and found the cross-country evidence in favor of the neoclassical models: while maintaining the assumption of decreasing returns to capital, physical capital accumulation generates larger effects on growth. The explanatory power in their cross-country regression comes from the steady state. Recently, King and Rebelo (1993) conducted dynamic simulations to learn about the quantitative transitional dynamics in various neoclassical growth models with intertemporally optimizing households. They found that lengthy transitions occur only with very low intertemporal substitution, but then the model has predictions inconsistent with observed variation in interest rates, asset prices and factor shares over time and across countries. They all adopted the neoclassical classical models with decreasing returns to capital. Romer (1986) emphasized the external effects of capital accumulation through the following channel: when firms accumulate capital, they inadvertently contribute to the productivity of capital held by others.

Another strand of development is endogenous growth models which focussed on the formulation of technical progress. It has been motivated by two empirical regularities: first, many countries have experienced the sustained growth in per capita output. Second, there has been a significant cross-country disparity of growth paths for a long period of time. The accumulation of additional reproducible factors such as human capital or knowledge requires intermediate input factors. For example, Romer (1990) used the number of intermediate inputs to model the accumulation of another reproducible input factor. Grossman and Helpman (1991) emphasized the importance of the quantity of the fixed number of intermediate inputs.

As argued in Romer (1990), the production function in the above type of model has the feature of increasing returns to scale. The increasing returns provide a role for government policy in enhancing social welfare. Permanent changes in variables that are potentially affected by government policy induce permanent changes in growth rates. Also, the advice offered by endogenous growth models on development policies is very different form that offered by capital fundamentalism. For example, Kocherlakota and Yi (1996) found that government policy variables such as marginal tax rates and money supply (M2) growth rate have permanent effects on GNP growth rates. This result stands in marked contrast to the neoclassical growth model in which the long-run growth rate is determined by the exogenous technical progress. In general, the endogenous growth model has shifted its focus from the specification of production function to the formulation of technical progress. If this type of model provides a better characterization of economic growth dynamics, then the possibility of resuscitating capital fundamentalism will decrease.

The organization of the chapter is as follows. Section 2 reviews three types of growth models commonly used in the growth literature. In Section 3, we derive the time-series representation of transitional dynamics in those models presented in Section 2. We emphasize that different specifications of exogenous shocks in the model imply different ARMA representations of transitional paths. In Section 4, we first present the time series evidence on per capita real output growth in Japan, South

Korea, Taiwan and the United States. Then we take these models to the time-seres data in the above four countries and test the time-series implications of the models. Results from the growth-accounting exercises suggested a much smaller role for physical capital accumulation in economic development and growth than that advocated by capital fundamentalism. Section 5 concludes.

2 THE MODELS

In this section, we present exogenous and endogenous growth models. The first of these is the neoclassical model of exogenous growth in which the engine of growth is the exogenous technical progess. The second class of growth models include the stochastic versions of the Ak model and the intermediate-goods-based model without externality. In specifying preferences and technology, we set the specification criterion that makes it possible to uniquely solve in closed form for output growth dynamics.

A representative consumer ranks a sequence of current and future consumptions according to the expected present value of current and future utilities:

$$E_0 \sum_{t=0}^{\infty} \beta^t \frac{c_t^{1-\sigma} - 1}{1 - \sigma},$$

in which c_t is consumption at time t, $E_0 x \equiv E[x|\Omega_0]$ denotes the conditional expectation of x given information available at time 0, Ω_0, parameter β is the constant discount factor between 0 and 1, and σ is the relative risk averse measure which is positive. The value of σ determines the elasticity of intertemporal substitution. It is a crucial factor in consumption growth.

Consider a constant returns to scale production technology which at least uses the reproducible factor k_t and labor $1 - l_t$ as inputs:

$$y_t = a_t k_t^{\alpha} \left[h_t (1 - l_t)\right]^{1-\alpha}, \tag{3.1}$$

in which y_t is output at time t, α is the capital share, and a_t is the stationary exogenous productivity shock.

2.1 Neoclassical Models of Exogenous Growth

In the neoclassical growth model, h_t is an exogenous technical progress:

$$\log h_t = g_h + \log h_{t-1} + \varepsilon_{ht}, \tag{3.2}$$

in which ε_{ht} is a white noise with mean zero and variance σ_h^2. Hence g_h is the expected growth rate of h_t. Here h_t can be interpreted in many ways: as improvements in knowledge such as organization routines, better management of inventory, or other changes that do not require knowledge to be embodied in new equipment. When $\sigma_h^2 = 0$, equation (3.2) can be solved as $\log h_t = \log h_0 + g_h t$, which states that $\log h_t$ exhibits a deterministic linear time trend.

Under the specfication in equation (3.2), equation (3.1) is a standard production function with Harrod-neutral technical progress. Since $1 - l_t$ is not a decision variable in this neoclassical growth model, let $l_t = 0$ for simplicity. The resource constraint at time t is given by

$$y_t = c_t + k_{t+1} - (1-\delta)k_t,$$

in which δ is the constant rate of depreciation for all reproducible factors.

According to the production technology in equation (3.1), trends in y_t and k_t are completely determined by the Harrod-neutral labor-augmenting technical progress, h_t. The resource constraint imposes the equality between the consumption growth rate and the output and capital stock growth rates in steady states. The balanced growth conditions simply state the stationarity of the following variables: y_t/h_t, c_t/h_t, and k_t/h_t. Hence, for the phenomenal sustained growth in per capita output, the explanation offered by this model is exogenous technical progress. It is silent on the cross-country difference in economic growth rate in the long run.

2.2 *Ak* Models of Endogenous Growth

The first wave of endogenous growth models focussed on constant returns to a sufficiently broad definition of capital as the device for generating endogenous growth. Its essence is reflected in the equation $y = Ak$.

In order for equation (3.1) to match the Ak specification, h_t becomes another reproducible factor. The laws of motion for these two reproducible factors are:

$$k_{t+1} = i_{kt} y_t - (1-\delta)k_t,$$

$$h_{t+1} = i_{ht} y_t - (1-\delta)h_t,$$

here the fixed factor such as labor does not enter the production of reproducible factors. This capital accumulation technology was used in Mankiw et al. (1992) augmented Solow model. The resource constraint is given by $c_t=(1-i_{kt}-i_{ht})y_t$. Although this model allows the second input factor h_t to accumulate endogenously, the two types of capital must accumulate in lockup. We can rewrite equation (3.1) in terms of a new form of production function:

$$y_t = \tilde{a}_t k_t, \tag{3.3}$$

in which $\tilde{a}_t \equiv a_t i^{1-\alpha}$ with $i=(1-\alpha)/\alpha$. Here i is the steady-state value of h_t/k_t. Equation (3.3) looks exactly like the standard *Ak* production function in which the parameter multiplying k_t is a stationary productivity shock.

As argued in Jones (1995), the formulation of the two reproducible factors production technology is more appealing intuitively than the common *Ak* structure because it explicitly recognizes the role of human capital (or knowledge) in production. Even though the two types of accumulable factors move together, the specification of production technology is likely to be robust to a number of changes and interpretations of the two-factors models. The non-stochastic steady-state growth rate of output denoted g_y is determined by

$$g_y = -\delta + \tilde{a} i_k,$$

in which $\tilde{a} = a \cdot i$ and i_k is the steady-state value of investment rate for k_t. Like the neoclassical growth model, the steady-state ratio of output to capital (y_t/k_t) is constant in the *Ak* model. However, the investment rate (i_k) is the determinant of output growth rate in the *Ak* model. It also implies that the investment rate and growth rate must have similar statistical properties in the steady states.[1]

Recently, Jones and Manuelli (1990) studied a convex model of equilibrium growth. To generate sustained growth in per capita income, they simply impose a lower bound on marginal product of capital so that the marginal product must stay above the discount rate for investment to remain profitable. One example under their consideration is $Ak_t+g(k_t)$ with $\beta(A+1-\delta)>1$ and $g(k_t)>0$, and clearly the *Ak* model is the simplest example. They also show that the presence of increasing returns to scale is neither necessary nor sufficient to generate sustained growth. Because of the convex structure of their model and the lack of externalities, competitive equilibrium is Pareto optimal. Unlike models with increasing returns/externalities, the distortionary policies are not optimal in the convex model of growth. For example, in the presence of externalities generated by capital stock, it is likely that optimal policy requires subsidizing investment. Even though the *Ak* model also emphasizes the importance of government policy in determining g_y through its permanent effect on i_k, this policy will increase the output growth rate to a suboptimal (too high) level. In other words, the capital fundamentalism should be revived in the *Ak* model, but its policy prescription on promoting investment cannot be optimal.

As documented in Jones (1995), US and other OECD countries' growth rates do not exhibit large persistent changes. Since the investment rate exhibits large persistent changes, he concluded that the *Ak* growth model is not consistent with time-series evidence.

2.3 The Intermediate-goods-based Model of Endogenous Growth

Another strand of development of endogenous growth models shifted from the specification of production function to the formulation of technical progress. More specifically, the determinants of g_h is left unexplained within the neoclassical growth model. This new growth model seeks to remedy this omission.

Unlike the *Ak* model, the accumulation of reproducible factor h_t requires labor engagement (l_t):

$$h_{t+1} = (1 + \rho_h l_t)h_t, \tag{3.4}$$

in which ρ_h is the technology parameter. ρ_h can be interpreted as the maximal growth rate of h_t, and the actual growth rate of h_t is determined by the labor engaged in R&D or in human capital accumulation, l_t: $\rho_h l_t$. The balanced growth condition implies the stationarity of y_t/h_t, c_t/h_t and i_t/h_t. One policy implication is that subsidies to the R&D activities or human capital accumulation can increase l_t and therefore the balanced growth rates are raised.

Here h_t can be interpreted either as the number of intermediate inputs (Romer 1990) or as the quantity of the fixed number of intermediate inputs (Grossman and Helpman 1991) or as human capital (Lucas 1988). Here we cast h_t as the engine of economic growth. Labor can be used in the production of final output or in the search for innovation or in human capital accumulation. Since leisure is not a decision variable for the representative household, labor is an intermediate good in production. The resource constraint at time t is identical to that in the neoclassical model of exogenous growth. As argued in Romer (1990), the production function now has the feature of increasing returns to scale: given h_t, doubling k_t and $1-l_t$ to production is sufficient to double final output; doubling h_t as well would lead to more than a doubling of final output.

Given the specification of h_t in (3.4), the accumulation of h_t does not require any use of final goods. It is not a required specification of the accumulation technology for h_t. Suppose that k_t is another input factor in the accumulation of h_t. As long as the accumulation technology of h_t is constant returns to scale with respect to all reproducible factors, we can still cast h_t as the engine of growth. One such specification is:

$$h_{t+1} = \rho_h k_t^{\phi} (l_t h_t)^{1-\phi} + (1-\delta) h_t .$$

When $\phi = 0$ and $\delta = 0$, this specification simply reduces to the original one. Evidently, alternative specifications can affect the steady-state output growth rate.

Another specification emphasizes the role of learning by doing in human capital accumulation: work effort accelerates human capital accumulation.[2] Total time endowment is allocated either to leisure activities or to work efforts. Hence, labor is not an intermediate good. For example, the effect of providing a PC to a secretary accustomed to working with a typewriter. Marginal product of labor and final output all increase right away. Once the secretary rapidly accumulates skill while working with a PC, her future expected earnings will also increase as the result of human capital accumulation. This consideration could offset the wealth effect on leisure. However, as shown in Ladron-de-Guevara et al. (1997), when leisure enters a utility function and $\rho_h > 0$, one may encounter the multiple steady-states problem. We believe that labor employment decisions are important in the study of aggregate fluctuations, and will not consider this specification simply for this reason.

Recently, Jones (1995) used the prediction of long-run growth effects to design time-series tests for endogenous growth models. More specifically, when the R&D-based model holds in steady states, the implied growth rate must have a positive trend as the total amount of labor devoted to the R&D activities increases over time. He found evidence against the R&D-based model.

3 TIME-SERIES REPRESENTATION OF TRANSITIONAL PATH

We derive the time-series representations of transitional paths for both the neoclassical growth model and the intermediate-goods-based growth model. First, we solve for dynamic competitive equilibrium, and transform the associated necessary first-order conditions to alternative stationary representations. Since the stationary representations are highly nonlinear functions of relevant variables, the log-linear approximation of these representations is implemented around the nonstochastic steady states. Once the log-linear approximations are expressed as linear expectational difference equations, it is straightforward to obtain the closed-form solution of output growth rate using the conventional solution procedure in rational expectations literature.

In the absence of increasing returns/externality, dynamic competitive equilibrium can be characterized by exploiting the equivalence between competitive equilibrium and Pareto-optimal allocation. The intertemporal allocation problem faced by the social planner is to choose a contingency plan, c_t, k_{t+1}, and l_t, to maximize the expected present value of current and future utilities subject to resource constraint and the laws of motion for accumulable factors.

For example, for the intermediate-goods-based growth model, a social planner chooses $(c_t, l_t, h_{t+1}, k_{t+1}, t \geq 0)$ to maximize

$$E_0 \sum_{t=0}^{\infty} \beta^t \frac{c_t^{1-\sigma} - 1}{1-\sigma},$$

subject to

$$a_t k_t^{\alpha} \left[(1-l_t)h_t\right]^{1-\alpha} = c_t + k_{t+1} - (1-\delta)k_t,$$

$$h_{t+1} = (1 + \rho_h l_t)h_t.$$

Here we assume that log a_t has an AR(1) representation:

$$\log a_t = (1-\gamma_a)\log a + \gamma_a \log a_{t-1} + \varepsilon_{at},$$

in which $|\gamma_a| < 1$, and ε_{at} is a white noise with mean zero and variance σ_a^2. The Pareto optimal allocation of k_{t+1}, h_{t+1}, c_t and l_t must satisfy the necessary first-order conditions for any realization of a_t:

$$c_t^{-\sigma} a_t k_t^{\alpha} \left[(1-l_t)h_t\right]^{-\alpha} = \beta(1+\rho_h)E_t\left\{c_{t+1}^{-\sigma} a_{t+1} k_{t+1}^{\alpha} \left[(1-l_{t+1})h_{t+1}\right]^{-\alpha}\right\},$$

$$c_t^{-\sigma} = \beta E_t\left(c_{t+1}^{-\sigma}\left\{\alpha a_{t+1} k_{t+1}^{\alpha-1} \left[(1-l_{t+1})h_{t+1}\right]^{1-\alpha} + 1 - \delta\right\}\right),$$

$$a_t k_t^{\alpha}\left[(1-l_t)h_t\right]^{1-\alpha} = c_t + k_{t+1} - (1-\delta)k_t.$$

Since both c_t and k_t contain an upward trend induced by h_t, we transform the above conditions in an alternative stationary form. Let $\widetilde{x}_t \equiv x_t / h_t$, for any random variable x_t. Then we have the following stationary representations:

$$\widetilde{c}_t^{-\sigma} = \beta E_t\{[\widetilde{c}_{t+1}(1+\rho_h l_t)]^{-\sigma}[\alpha a_{t+1}\widetilde{k}_{t+1}^{\alpha-1}(1-l_{t+1})^{1-\alpha} + 1 - \delta]\}, \qquad (3.5)$$

$$\widetilde{c}_t^{-\sigma} a_t \widetilde{k}_t^{\alpha}(1-l_t)^{-\alpha} = \beta(1+\rho_h)E_t\{[\widetilde{c}_{t+1}(1+\rho_h l_t)]^{-\sigma} a_{t+1}\widetilde{k}_{t+1}^{\alpha}(1-l_{t+1})^{-\alpha}\}, \quad (3.6)$$

$$(1+\rho_h l_t)\widetilde{k}_{t+1} = a_t\widetilde{k}_t^{\alpha}(1-l_t)^{1-\alpha} - \widetilde{c}_t + (1-\delta)\widetilde{k}_t. \qquad (3.7)$$

Imposing $\sigma_a^2 = 0$, then $a_t = a$ and equations (3.5)-(3.7) imply a set of restrictions on the non-stochastic steady state values of l_t, $\widetilde{c}_t$ and $\widetilde{k}_t$ denoted l, $\widetilde{c}$ and $\widetilde{k}$, respectively:

$$\beta(1+\rho_h l)^{-\sigma}\left[a\alpha\widetilde{k}^{\alpha-1}(1-l)^{1-\alpha} + 1 - \delta\right] = 1, \qquad (3.8)$$

$$\beta(1+\rho_h)(1+\rho_h l)^{-\sigma} = 1, \qquad (3.9)$$

$$(1+\rho_h l)\widetilde{k} - a\widetilde{k}^{\alpha}(1-l)^{1-\alpha} + \widetilde{c} - (1-\delta)\widetilde{k} = 0. \qquad (3.10)$$

From equations (3.8)-(3.10), we can determine unique values of l, $\widetilde{k}$, and $\widetilde{c}$ in terms of structural parameters in preferences and technology. First, from equation (3.9), we have l in terms of β, ρ_h and σ:

$$l = \frac{\left[\beta(1+\rho_h)\right]^{1/\sigma} - 1}{\rho_h}.$$

Once we have the value of l, the non-stochastic steady state growth rate of output can be obtained from the specification of h_t in equation (3.4):

$$g_h = \left[\beta(1+\rho_h)\right]^{1/\sigma} - 1.$$

Unlike the neoclassical growth model, the value of g_h is determined by the structural parameters in the representative household's preferences, σ, β and ρ_h. It remains to determine the value of $\widetilde{k}$ and $\widetilde{c}$. Note that the non-stochastic steady-state real interest rate denoted r is given by

$$r = \left[a\alpha\widetilde{k}^{\alpha-1}(1-l)^{1-\alpha} + 1 - \delta\right] - 1.$$

It is clear from equations (3.8) and (3.9) that r must satisfy $r = \rho_h$. Then the above expression of r yields $\widetilde{k}$ in terms of structural parameters in preferences and technology. Finally, we substitute the resulting expressions of l and $\widetilde{k}$ into equation (3.10) and have the value of $\widetilde{c}$.

According to Jones and Manuelli (1990), one sufficient condition for the sustained long-run growth in per capita output is

$$\beta\left[a\alpha\widetilde{k}^{\alpha-1}(1-l)^{1-\alpha} + 1 - \delta\right] > 1.$$

It is clear from equations (3.8) and (3.9) that the sufficient condition is satisfied as long as $\beta(1+\rho_h) > 1$.

Define $c_t^* \equiv \log\widetilde{c}_t - \log\widetilde{c}$, $k_t^* \equiv \log\widetilde{k}_t - \log\widetilde{k}$, $l_t^* \equiv \log l_t - \log l$, and $a_t^* \equiv \log a_t - \log a$. Then we apply the certainty equivalence principle to obtain the log-linear approximation of equations (3.5)-(3.7) around c_t^*, k_t^*, l_t^* and a_t^*:

$$\begin{aligned}\sigma(E_t c_{t+1}^* - c_t^*) + (1-\alpha)\phi_0 k_{t+1}^* + \frac{(1-\alpha)l}{1-l}\phi_0 E_t l_{t+1}^* \\ + \frac{\sigma\rho_h l}{1+\rho_h l} l_t^* - \phi_0 E_t a_{t+1}^* = 0,\end{aligned} \tag{3.11}$$

$$\begin{aligned}\sigma(E_t c_{t+1}^* - c_t^*) - \alpha(k_{t+1}^* - k_t^*) - \frac{bl}{1-l}(E_t l_{t+1}^* - l_t^*) \\ + \frac{\sigma\rho_h l}{1+\rho_h l} l_t^* - E_t a_{t+1}^* + a_t^* = 0,\end{aligned} \tag{3.12}$$

$$\phi_1 c_t^* + \phi_2 k_{t+1}^* - (\alpha+\phi_3)k_t^* + \left[\phi_4 + \frac{(1-\alpha)l}{1-l}\right] l_t^* - a_t^* = 0, \tag{3.13}$$

in which coefficients, $\phi_0,\dots,\phi_4$, are non-linear functions of structural parameters in preferences and technology:

$$\phi_0 = \frac{\rho_h + \delta}{1+\rho_h},$$

$$\phi_1 = 1 - \frac{\alpha(\delta + \rho_h l)}{\rho_h + \delta},$$

$$\phi_2 = \frac{\alpha(1 + \rho_h l)}{\rho_h + \delta},$$

$$\phi_3 = \frac{\alpha(1 - \delta)}{\rho_h + \delta},$$

$$\phi_4 = \frac{\alpha \rho_h l}{\rho_h + \delta}.$$

Equations (3.11)-(3.13) are the system of expectational linear difference equations of c_t^*, k_t^* and l_t^*. We substitute out c_t^* and l_t^* in equations (3.11)-(3.13) to yield the following third-order linear expectational difference equation of k_t^*:

$$E_t\left[(1 - m_1 L)(L^{-1} - m_2)(L^{-1} - m_3)k_{t+1}^*\right] = m_4 a_t^*,$$

in which $m_1,\ldots,m_4$ are non-linear functions of structural parameters and L is the lag operator with $L^j k_t^* \equiv k_{t-j}^*$. In particular, we have $m_1 = \alpha(1+\rho_h)/[\alpha + \rho_h + \delta(1-\alpha)]$, $m_2 = 1 + \tilde{c} / [(1 + \rho_h l)\tilde{k}]$, and $m_3 = (1+\rho_h)/(1+\rho_h l)$. It is straightforward to show that $0 < m_1 < 1$, $m_2 > 1$ and $m_3 > 1$. The stationarity requirement of k_t^* forces us to solve the two unstable roots, m_2 and m_3, forwards, and the stable root, m_1, backwards. After some algebra, we have the closed-form solution of k_{t+1}^*:

$$k_{t+1}^* = m_1 k_t^* + E_t\left[\frac{m_4 a_t^*}{m_2 m_3 (1 - m_2^{-1} L^{-1})(1 - m_3^{-1} L^{-1})}\right].$$

$$= m_1 k_t^* + \frac{m_4}{(m_2 - \gamma_a)(m_3 - \gamma_a)} a_t^*.$$

Using the fact that $\log l_t = \log l + l^{-1}(l_t - l)$, the log-linear approximation of production function in equation (3.1) gives the following expression of demeaned output growth rate denoted z_t:

$$z_t \equiv \log y_t - \log y_{t-1} - g_h$$
$$= a_t^* - a_{t-1}^* + \alpha\left[k_t^* - k_{t-1}^*\right] - \frac{(1-\alpha)l}{1-l}\left[l_t^* - l_{t-1}^*\right] + \rho_h l_{t-1} - g_h.$$

Finally, from equations (3.11)-(3.13) and the closed-form solution of k_{t+1}^*, the transitional path of z_t can be solved as

$$z_t - \mu_1 z_{t-1} - \mu_2 z_{t-2} = \mu_3 \varepsilon_{at} + \mu_4 \varepsilon_{a,t-1} + \mu_5 \varepsilon_{a,t-2}, \qquad (3.14)$$

in which

$$\mu_1 = m_1 + \gamma_a,$$

$$\mu_2 = -m_1 \gamma_a,$$

μ_3, μ_4 and μ_5 are non-linear functions of structural parameters.[3] It is clear from (3.14) that m_1 and γ_a represent the characteristic roots of the AR component in the ARMA(2,2) representation. m_1 characterizes endogenous dynamics in the endogenous growth model, while γ_a represents the exogenous dynamics induced by the AR(1) representation of a_t. Since m_1 depends on the value of capital share (α), we can evaluate the transitional dynamic effects of physical capital accumulation by varying the value of α.

One salient feature of this solution procedure is that dynamic properties of output growth rate can be explored fully without relying on the observability assumption of h_t. That is, the time-series representation of the transitional path encompasses various interpretations of h_t as long as h_t satisfies the specification in (3.4). Finally, the time-series representation of the transitional path depends on the specification of exogenous stochastic shocks. For example, if a_t is white noise $(\gamma_a = 0)$, then the time-series representation of z_t becomes an ARMA(1,2) representation. In general, when the exogenous productivity shock (a_t) is an AR(p) representation with $p \geq 1$, the time-series representation of z_t is an ARMA ($p+1, p+1$) representation.

For the neoclassical growth model, we apply the similar solution procedure to obtain the following time-series representation of k_{t+1}^*:

$$k_{t+1}^* = s_1 k_t^* + s_0 a_t^* - e^{-g_h} \varepsilon_{h,t+1}.$$

Here s_1 represents the stable characteristic root in the AR component in the neolassical growth model, and s_0 is a non-linear function of structural parameters. Taking the natural logrithm of both sides in (3.1) gives

$$\log y_t - \log h_t = \log a_t + \alpha(\log k_t - \log h_t),$$

and then substituting the closed-form solution of k^*_{t+1} into the above equation yields the growth rate of demeaned output:

$$\begin{aligned} & z_t - \theta_1 z_{t-1} - \theta_2 z_{t-2} \\ & = \varepsilon_{at} + w_1 \varepsilon_{a,t-1} + w_2 \varepsilon_{a,t-2} + w'_0 \varepsilon_{ht} + w'_1 \varepsilon_{h,t-1} + w'_2 \varepsilon_{h,t-2}, \end{aligned} \tag{3.15}$$

in which

$$\theta_1 = s_1 + \gamma_a,$$

$$\theta_2 = -s_1 \gamma_a,$$

$$w_1 = (\alpha s_0 - s_1) - 1,$$

$$w_2 = -(\alpha s_0 - s_1),$$

and w'_i, for $i = 0,1,2$, are nonlinear functions of structural parameters. Both ε_{at} and ε_{ht} enter (3.15) as innovations in the time-series representation of transitional dynamics. Since they are serially uncorrelated random variables, the time-series representation in (3.15) also implies an ARMA (2,2) representation for z_t.

As in the intermediate-goods-based models of endogenous growth, the time-series representation of z_t is also an ARMA ($p+1$, $p+1$) model when the exogenous productivity shock (a_t) is an AR (p) process with $p \geq 1$. However, from the coefficients in the AR components of z_t in (3.14) and (3.15), it is clear that even though the neoclassical growth model and the intermediate-goods-based growth model have the same exogenous dynamics characterized by γ_a, they have different endogenous dynamics characterized by m_1 and s_1, respectively. If a growth model is used to characterize actual growth experience, the theoretical ARMA representation of transitional path must be consistent with the ARMA counterpart implied by the actual growth path. The above results suggest that the time-series facts may discriminate between these two growth models due to different sets of restrictions.

Finally, suppose that the exogenous technical progress follows a linear deterministic trend, that is, $\varepsilon_{ht} = 0$, for all t. Equation (3.15) becomes

$$z_t - \theta_1 z_{t-1} - \theta_2 z_{t-2} = \varepsilon_{at} + w_1 \varepsilon_{a,t-1} + w_2 \varepsilon_{a,t-2}.$$

As displayed in the expressions of w_1 and w_2 , there is a unit root in the MA component: $1 + w_1 + w_2 = 0$. Then equation (3.15) is further collapsed to an ARMA(2,1) representation:

$$y_t^* - \theta_1 y_{t-1}^* - \theta_2 y_{t-2}^* = \varepsilon_{at} + w_2 \varepsilon_{a,t-1},$$

in which $y_t^* = \log y_t - \log h_t - \log \tilde{y}$ and $\tilde{y}$ is the steady state value of $\tilde{y}_t$. This model has been studied by King and Rebelo (1993). Since $\log h_t$ exhibits a linear deterministic trend, the appropriate stationarity inducing procedure is to remove the trend component: $\log h_0 + g_h t$ from $\log y_t$. Note that the characteristic roots in the AR component are identical across different trend specifications of technical progress. That is, physical capital accumulation in the neoclassical model generates the same endogenous dynamics both for z_t with the random-walk specification of h_t and for y_t^* with the linear deterministic trend specification of h_t. However, the two trend specifications of h_t imply different stationarity-inducing procedure and have different ARMA representations.

It is clear from the solution procedure that the time-series representation of output growth rate depends on the specification of either technical progress or the reproducible factor in equation (3.1). Growth in the two types of growth model can arise for the following two reasons. First, there is the nonstochastic steady-state growth associated with the technical progress in the neoclassical growth model or the reproducible factor in the endogenous growth model. Second, there is transitional growth associated with movement from an initial capital stock toward the steady-state growth path. Here the transitional path is determined by the exogenous productivity shock (a_t) and physical capital accumulation. Hence, the discussion of properties of transitional growth can be misleading when we ignore information contained in the nonstochastic steady-state growth in the derivation of the time-series representation of transitional growth.

4 THE ROLE OF CAPITAL ACCUMULATION IN ECONOMIC GROWTH

In this section, we present evidence on the empirical significance of exogenous and endogenous growth models in Japan, South Korea, Taiwan and the United States and provide growth-accounting exercises in the general equilibrium framework. More precisely, we evaluate the role of physical capital accumulation in economic growth and development by varying the value of capital share in estimation. Such an exploration can help us understand whether capital fundamentalism should guide public policy recommendations and research strategies.

A growth model is to be used as a description of actual growth and development experiences, and the theoretical ARMA representation of transitional path must be consistent with its estimated counterpart. Here we use the statistical selection criterion to choose the optimal lag length in the ARMA representation of output growth rate, and verify if the theoretical lag lengths in various exogenous and endogenous growth models can be consistent with the selected ones.

In Section 3, we derived that different growth models imply different sets of restrictions on structural parameters. To evaluate the statistical significance of various models, we use the exact maximum likelihood method to estimate structural parameters in various growth models and test whether or not the set of restrictions implied by growth models holds. This also allows us to answer the question if there are rich enough time-series characteristics to discriminate between new and old growth models.

To achieve identification, the value of capital share must be given a priori. It in turns justifies our growth-accounting exercises in the general equilibrium framework. Suppose that growth models hold. If the impact on the statistical performance of models is not significant by varying the value of capital share, then the physical capital accumulation cannot play an important role in accounting for transitional paths under current specifications. Therefore, capital fundamentalism should not be revived as the guideline of research and policy prescription.

4.1 Time-series Evidence on Output Growth Rates

The countries involved are Japan, South Korea, Taiwan and the USA. South Korea and the US real GDP and Japanese real GNP series were taken from *International Financial Statistics*, while Taiwanese real GDP series were taken from *Natioanl Income Accounts, Taiwan.* We divide real total output by total population to construct the per capita real output. All data are annual series. The sample period is 1952-95 for Taiwan, 1953-94 for Japan, 1949-95 for the US, and 1954-94 for South Korea.

Figures 3.1-3.2 display the graphic description of the logarithm of per capita real output series for the four countries. We also plot the growth rate of per capita real output and the per capita real output with linear time trend removed. When technical progress exhibits a linear deterministic trend, removing the linear deterministic trend from the log

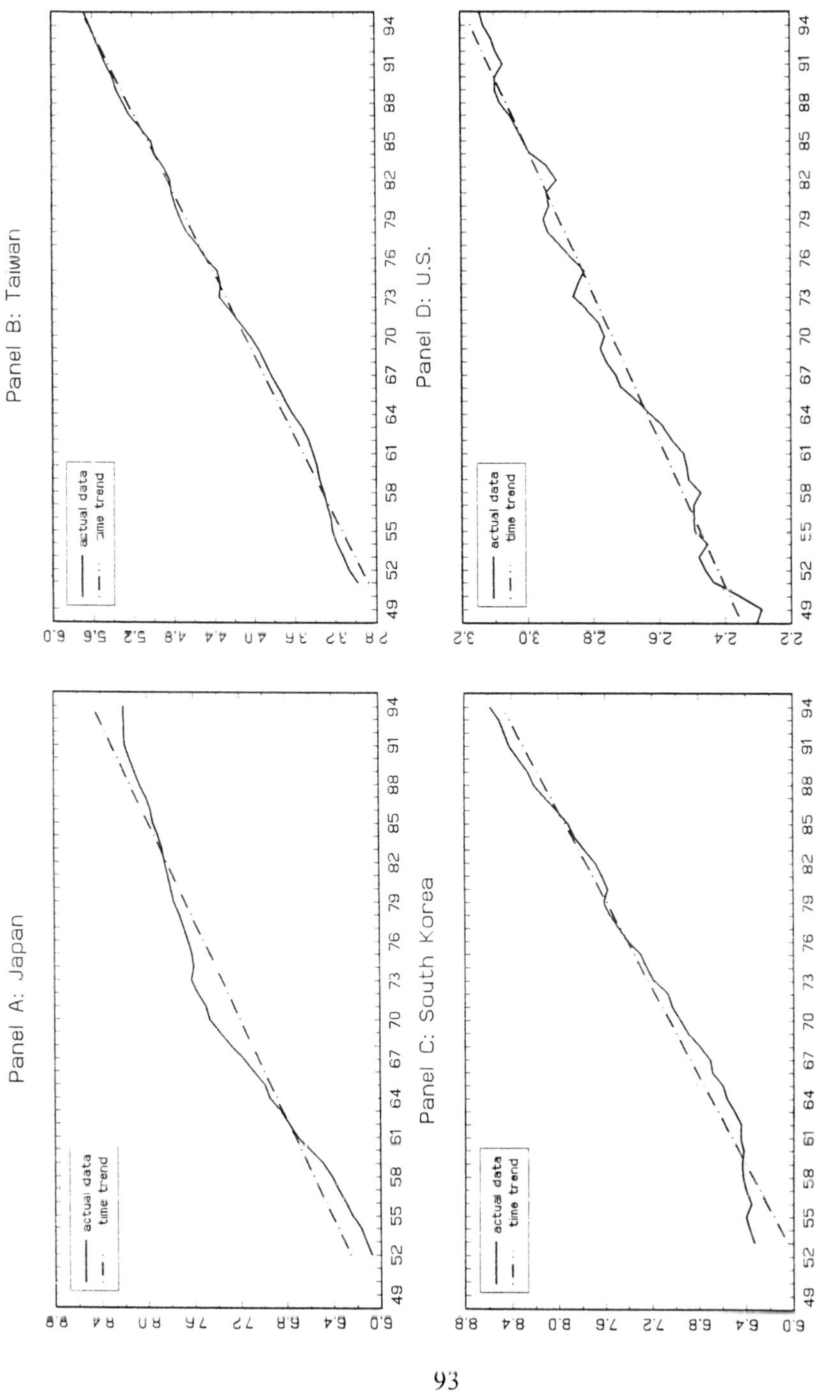

Figure 3.1 Per capita real output and its linear time trend

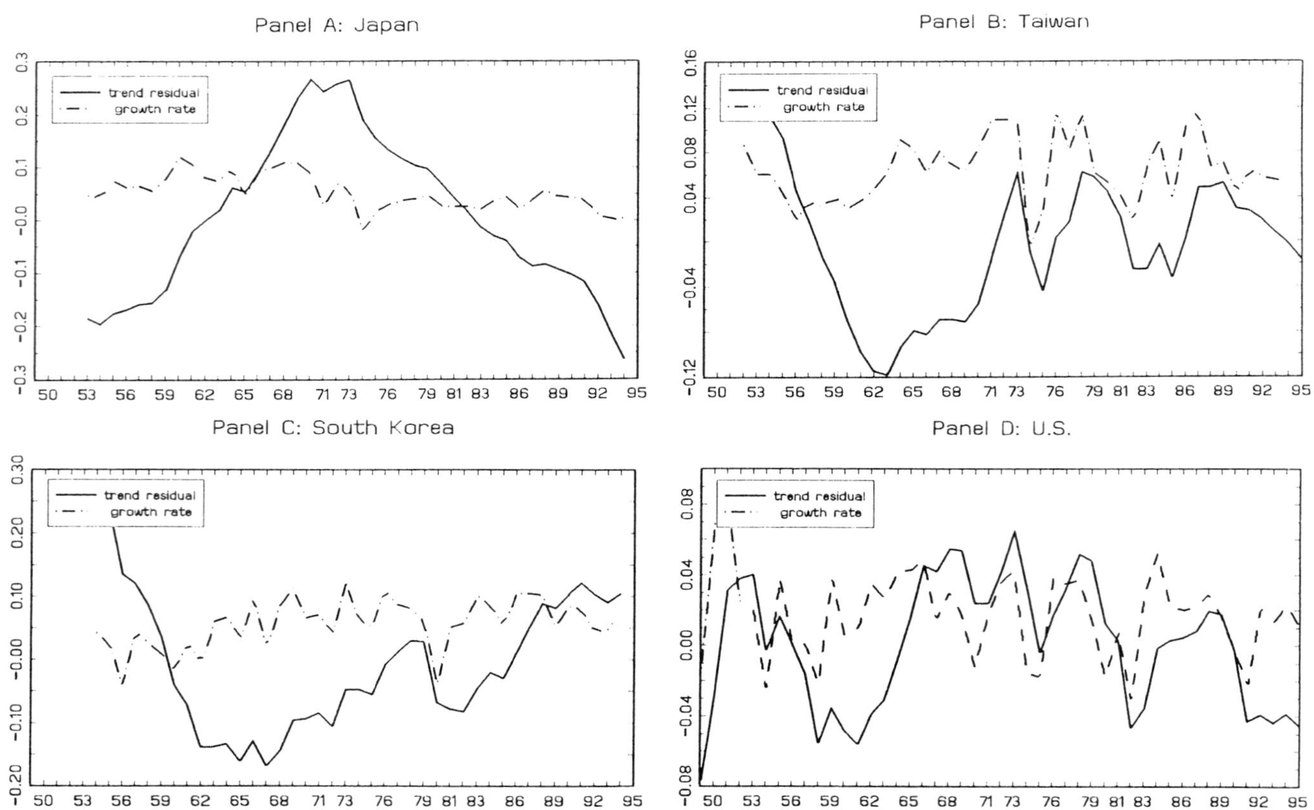

Figure 3.2 Linear time trend residual versus annual growth rate

of per capita real output before estimation is the required stationarity-inducing procedure. As discussed in Section 3, the physical capital accumulation in the neoclassical growth model implies similar endogenous dynamics for both the per capita real output growth rate (z_t) and the logarithm of per capita real output series with linear trend removed (y_t^*). Another dynamics is induced by the AR(1) representation of a_t in the productivity shock. When z_t and y_t^* have similar dynamics, then we say that the neoclassical growth model is consistent with actual output growth experience. Visual inspections of Figure 3.2 reveal that the neoclassical growth model receives only some support from the US data series. For the other three countries, we need very different exogenous dynamics induced by a_t to account for very different dynamics between z_t and y_t^*.

For the Japanese and South Korean output series, both linear time-trend residuals and annual growth rates display different time-series characteristics. There was a structural break in the mean of annual growth rate around 1962 as clearly revealed in panels A and C of Figure 3.2. The mean shift also occurred around 1970 in Taiwan. On the other hand, the US growth rates appear to fluctuate around a constant mean for the entire sample period. Formal testing results for a single endogenously chosen mean shift in growth rates are reported in Table 3.1. Testing results support the null hypothesis that US growth rates are well described by a stochastic process with a constant mean and little persistence. However, there was significant evidence against the null hypothesis in Japan, South Korea and Taiwan. Output growth rates fluctuate around two different

Table 3.1 The statistical properties of growth rates

	Japan	South Korea	Taiwan	USA
	I. Endogenous mean shift			
1. Mean shift date	1962	1962	1970	1973
2. Coefficient	2.454	5.699	-4.963	-0.976
3. F test statistic	6.611*	22.702*	52.481*	1.885
	(0.014)	(0.000)	(0.000)	(0.177)
	II. Unit root tests			
ADF test statistic	-1.217	-2.252	-3.475**	-3.831**

Notes:
The mean shift is taken from Bai et al.(1991). The following equation is estimated:
$z_t = \alpha + \beta I_{(t>T^*)} + \varepsilon_t$,
in which I is an indicator that takes the value one for $t > T^*$.
* Significant at the 5% level for the F-ratios.
** Rejects the null hypothesis that there is a unit root at the 5% significant level.

means in the entire sample period for these three countries. It will be difficult to test the steady-state properties of growth models using the per capita real output series in these three countries.

According to steady-state properties in endogenous growth models, one testable implication is that the economic variables highlighted by endogenous models as the determinant of the steady-state growth rate must have the similar time-series properties of per capita output growth rates. For example, Jones (1995) found that the persistence of economic variables is not consistent with that of real output growth rates, and concluded that many *Ak* and R&D-based growth models are rejected. When the sample period is extended from 1987 back to 1870, the US growth rates still fluctuate around a constant mean for an extended period. However, Japanese output growth rates apparently fluctuated around a constant mean until the Second World War but after the war they jumped upward and then declined slowly over subsequent years. The above evidence indicates that the time-series properties of output growth rates sensitively depend on the sample period chosen. Hence, the statistical rejection in Jones (1995) only suggested that it is not appropriate to test the steady-state implications of growth models directly. The ARMA representation of the per capita real output growth obtained in Section 3 characterizes the transitional paths. Hence, it is more appropriate to be used in the evaluation of various models along the transitional paths.

To select the optimal lag length for the AR and MA components in the ARMA representation of the transitional path, we apply the Akaike information criterion (AIC) to the per capita real output series in the four countries. For the annual growth rate of per capita real output (z_t), we concluded from Table 3.2 that (i) both the Japanese and Taiwanese data series admit a parsimonious ARMA(1,1) model; (ii) the South Korean data series is well represented by an ARMA(1,2) model; and (iii) the US data series can be represented by an ARMA(2,1) model. Results in Section 3 show that different specifications of exogenous stochastic shocks (a_t) give different time-series representations of transitional paths. If the theoretical ARMA representation of growth rates describes the time-series facts, then a useful growth model is the one that likewise delivers an ARMA representation of the data. Given the above results on lag length, we cannot find any specifications of a_t so that the theoretical ARMA representations of transitional paths are consistent with the growth and development experiences in Japan, Taiwan and the USA. However, for South Korea both neoclassical and endogenous growth models can deliver a consistent implication for the ARMA representation when a_t is assumed to follow a white noise process.

For the per capita output series with linear time trend removed, the

Table 3.2 The empirical results for reduced-form ARMA models

ARMA (p, q)	Japan	South Korea	Taiwan	USA
I. The selection of lag length (p, q) in ARMA models (using AIC)				
1. Annual growth rate of per capita output (z_t)				
ARMA (1, 1)	−188.75*	−145.90	−190.96*	−211.60
ARMA (1, 2)	−187.42	−148.40*	−189.55	−214.13
ARMA (2, 1)	−187.17	−148.36	−189.69	−214.75*
ARMA (2, 2)	−186.90	−147.98	−187.70	−212.76
2. Residuals with linear time trend removed (y_t*)				
ARMA (1, 1)	−184.92	−150.71	−199.34*	−224.43
ARMA (1, 2)	−185.50	−151.02	−197.69	−224.49*
ARMA (2, 1)	−193.33	−157.96*	−199.26	−223.45
ARMA (2, 2)	−196.24*	−156.03	−198.46	−222.50
II. Estimates of ARMA (2, 2) model: $z_t - \alpha_1 z_{t-1} - \alpha_2 z_{t-2} = e_t + \beta_1 e_{t-1} + \beta_2 e_{t-2}$				
α_1	0.006 (0.238)	1.877 (0.049)	0.419 (0.139)	1.020 (0.383)
α_2	0.715 (0.124)	−0.972 (0.042)	0.484 (0.139)	−0.288 (0.333)
β_1	0.640 (0.289)	−1.863 (0.135)	0.000 (0.100)	−0.960 (0.408)
β_2	−0.360 (0.279)	1.000 (0.141)	−1.000 (0.099)	−0.040 (0.399)

Notes:
The Akaike Information Criterion (AIC) selects the model for which AIC = $-2\log L + 2(p+q+1)$ is a minimum. Here L is the value of likelihood function.
We estimate the ARMA model using the maximum exact likelihood estimation.
* means the minimal AIC.
Numbers in parentheses are the standard deviations of coefficient estimates.
Data Sources: See Section 4.1 for description.

AIC results can be summarized as follows; (i) the ARMA(1,1) model is a good description of the Taiwanese series; (ii) the South Korean series is well represented by an ARMA(2,1) model; (iii) the ARMA(2,2) model well describes the Japanese data series, (iv) the ARMA(1,2) model well describes the US data series. Apparently, when the technical progress is assumed to be a linear deterministic time trend, the neoclassical growth model receives support in Taiwan and South Korea.

Straightforward comparisons of the theoretical lag length and its empirical counterpart indicated that growth model specifications cannot obtain the lag length observed in the actual growth experience. These comparisons offer only informal evaluation of the model performance. Since different growth models also impose different sets of restrictions, we need to explore these restrictions and formally evaluate the model performance. To do this, notice that most of the dynamic characteristics of output growth rates seem to be satisfactorily represented by relatively low-order ARMA models, and that different stationarity-inducing procedures imply different ARMA representations. We take these findings to be the facts of transitional paths in formal evaluations.

4.2 Estimating Structural Parameters in Growth Models

Here we use the exact likelihood function in estimation. Even though the time-domain and frequency-domain approximations of the likelihood function have been widely used in the estimation of ARMA models, we shall use the computationally burdensome exact likelihood function in estimation for the following reasons. First, Newbold (1974) argued that when either the AR component or the MA component has a root near one, or the sample period is not long enough, the estimation results cannot be accurate. Second, Phadke and Kedem (1978) also argued that when the MA component has a root near one, parameter estimates using the exact likelihood function have smaller mean square errors than those obtained using the approximation methods.

Given a set of structural parameters denoted Θ, we first obtain the theoretical covariance matrix for z_t denoted $\Sigma(\Theta)$. Here $\Sigma(\Theta)$ is a $T \times T$ symmetric matrix in which T is the number of observations in z_t series. Let $Z_T = (z_1, z_2, \ldots, z_T)$ be the $T \times 1$ column vector of T observations of z_t. Then the exact likelihood function can be expressed as

$$-\frac{T}{2}\log 2\pi - \frac{1}{2}\log\det[\Sigma(\Theta)] - \frac{1}{2}Z_T'\Sigma(\Theta)^{-1}Z_T.$$

Here the dimension of $\Sigma(\Theta)$ increases with the sample size. We find a maximum likelihood estimate of Θ to maximize the exact likelihood function. Given the AR(1) specification of a_t and the random walk with drifts specification of h_t, both exogenous and endogenous growth models imply the ARMA(2,2) representation of z_t. For the identification, we impose the values of the following structural parameters a priori: the constant discount rate (β), the constant depreciation rate (δ), the capital share (α), and the maximal growth rate of h_t in the endogenous growth model (ρ_h) and the expected growth rate of h_t in the neoclassical growth model (g_h). Hence the set of structural parameters under consideration is $\Theta_1 = \{\sigma, \gamma_a, \sigma_a^2\}$, and $\Theta_2 = \{\sigma, \gamma_a, \sigma_a^2, \sigma_h^2\}$, for the endogenous growth model and the neoclassical growth model, respectively.

Let L_u be the value of the log-likelihood function as its maximum for the unrestricted ARMA(2,2) model of per capita output growth rate and L_r the maximum value of the log likelihood function for the ARMA(2,2) under alternative sets of restrictions incorporated in (3.14) for the endogenous growth model or in (3.15) for the neoclassical growth model. Then $-2(L_r - L_u)$ is asymptotically distributed as $\chi^2(n)$, where n is the number of restrictions imposed by the model. High values of the likelihood ratio lead to rejecting the restrictions.

Before estimating structural parameters and conducting growth accounting exercises, we estimate the unrestricted ARMA(2,2) model for the per capita real output growth rate. For the annual output growth rate in each of the four countries, we present in panel 3 of Table 3.2 coefficient estimates of the unrestricted ARMA(2,2) model. The similarities and differences of the four series are apparent here. The ARMA(2,2) representation of Japanese and US per capita growth rate has an insignificant moving average coefficient at the lag two. On the other hand, the ARMA(2,2) representation of South Korean and Taiwanese per capita growth rate has significant MA coefficients.

Now we conduct the likelihood ratio test for the restricted ARMA(2,2) model against the unrestricted counterpart in the four countries. Two general findings from Table 3.3 are worth mentioning. First, the implied value of the stable (characteristic) root in the AR component (m_1 in the endogenous growth model and s_1 in the neoclassical growth model) increases with the assigned value of α. As shown in Section 3, the empirical importance of physical capital accumulation in transitional growth can be characterized by the stable root. Second, the value of the χ^2 statistic declines slightly as the assigned value of capital share increases in the two types of growth models for Japan, South Korea and Taiwan. These results suggest a much smaller role for physical capital accumulation in growth than that advocated by capital fundamentalism. On the other hand, with regard to the US data, the χ^2 statistic decreases with an increase in α in the neoclassical growth model, but it increases with an increase in α in the endogenous growth model. This suggests that the role of physical capital accumulation even diminishes when we allow for the additional reproducible factor in the production function. Hence, if our discussion is restricted on the empirical significance of physical capital accumulation along transitional growth in the framework of the neoclassical growth model, then the resulting implications could be misleading.

According to the χ^2 statistic reported in Table 3.3, several country-specific findings are apparent. First, the set of cross-equation restrictions implied by the neoclassical growth model is rejected at the 5 percent significance level in Japan. Second, we did not have any significant evidence against the set of cross-equation restrictions imposed either by the endogenous growth model or by the neoclassical growth model in the three other countries. Third, for Japan and South Korea, the empirical evidence yields more support for the intermediate-goods-based endogenous growth model than for the neoclassical growth model. Fourth, in the US data series, the neoclassical growth model receives more support than the endogenous growth model does. Fifth and finally, for Taiwan, there is an almost identical statistical performance between the two models.

4.3 Growth Accounting in the General Equilibrium Framework

In this subsection, we conduct the growth accounting exercises in a general equilibrium framework. The ARMA representation of output growth rate allows us to explore how transitional dynamics depend on parameters of preference, production technology and exogenous shocks. As noted above, the value of the capital share in production function must be given a priori as an identifying assumption. Hence, we can vary the value to trace its dynamic effects on output growth as growth-accounting exercises.

We propose to use L/L' as a measure of the empirical significance of physical capital accumulation in accounting for the transitional path of output growth rate. Here L (L') denotes the maximum value of likelihood function with either $\rho_h \neq (=) 0$ in the endogenous growth model or $g_h \neq (=) 0$ in the neoclassical growth model. The value of L' measures the model performance without either the technical progress or the additional reproducible factor. Therefore, it measures the empirical significance of physical capital accumulation along transitional dynamics. We expect that L/L' is greater than or equals one. When $L/L' = 1$, the exogenous technical progress in the neoclassical growth model or the accumulation of reproducible factor did not play any significant role in transitional dynamics.

According to Table 3.3 as the value of capital share increases, the value of L/L' decreases only slightly in the four countries. That is, physical

Table 3.3 Estimates in various growth models

α	σ	γ_a	σ_a^2	σ_h^2	Stable root	χ^2	L/L'
			I. Japan				
			1. Neoclassical growth model				
0.35	0.010	0.998	0.001	3e-5	0.242	10.490*	1.293
0.40	0.010	0.997	0.001	0.000	0.285	8.604*	1.259
0.45	0.014	0.996	0.001	0.000	0.384	7.034*	1.229
			2. Endogenous growth model				
0.35	0.091	0.948	5e-4		0.798	2.062	1.346
0.40	0.092	0.938	5e-4		0.830	1.906	1.303
0.45	0.091	0.926	5e-4		0.857	1.818	1.262
			II. South Korea				
			1. Neoclassical growth model				
0.35	0.123	0.982	0.001	3e-5	0.645	2.568	1.241
0.40	0.142	0.979	0.001	7e-6	0.700	2.162	1.212
0.45	0.172	0.976	0.001	4e-5	0.754	1.848	1.184
			2. Endogenous growth model				
0.35	0.200	0.938	0.001		0.798	1.532	1.249
0.40	0.208	0.930	0.001		0.830	1.384	1.218
0.45	0.212	0.922	0.001		0.857	1.288	1.188
			III. Taiwan				
			1. Neoclassical growth model				
0.35	0.010	0.907	0.001	3e-6	0.246	3.800	1.396
0.40	0.010	0.881	0.001	0.000	0.285	3.680	1.353
0.45	0.010	0.869	0.001	4e-6	0.330	3.680	1.312
			2. Endogenous growth model				
0.35	0.019	0.427	7e-4		0.798	4.106	1.394
0.40	0.010	0.321	7e-4		0.830	3.854	1.352
0.45	0.010	0.342	7e-4		0.857	3.742	1.312
			IV. USA				
			1. Neoclassical growth model				
0.35	0.012	0.722	4e-4	3e-6	0.267	0.760	1.078
0.40	0.011	0.704	4e-4	6e-6	0.307	0.652	1.076
0.45	0.010	0.681	4e-4	1e-5	0.332	0.568	1.075
			2. Endogenous growth model				
0.35	0.010	0.239	5e-4		0.798	1.188	1.076
0.40	0.010	0.260	5e-4		0.830	1.742	1.070
0.45	0.010	0.281	5e-4		0.857	2.310	1.066

Notes:

In estimation, we set the values of following parameters as follows: $\beta = 0.96$, $\delta = 0.1$, $\rho_h = 0.042$ and $g_h = 0.025$, and assign α to 0.35, 0.40 and 0.45.

* Significant at the 5% level for χ^2 test.

L denotes the value of likelihood function with $\rho_h \neq 0$ or $g_h \neq 0$ and L' denotes the value of likelihood function with $\rho_h = 0$ or $g_h = 0$.

capital accumulation takes a slightly more important role in the transitional growth when neither technical progress nor the additional reproducible factor are allowed in the model. Generally, it is a much smaller role than that is required by capital fundamentalism.

We found that the physical capital accumulation plays a significant role in the US transitional path of output growth. The model performance did not greatly improve even with the exogenous technical progress or the additional reproducible factor added to the model. This finding is consistent with that in Jorgenson et al. (1987). Comparisons of estimates of γ_a between the two types of growth model indicate that the additional reproducible factor enhances the role of physical capital accumulation. More precisely, the role of exogenous productivity shock (a_t) reduces significantly once we incorporate the additional reproducible factor into the growth model. On the other hand, the technical progress or the additional reproducible factor play an more important role in accounting for transitional growth in Japan as the value of *L/L'* varies between 1.346 and 1.229. Generally, the additional reproducible factor enhances the empirical significance of physical capital accumulation in transitional growth in Japan. For example, the estimated stable root increased from 0.242 to 0.798 when the value of α is pre-specified at 0.35 in Japan. This finding is consistent with Mankiw et al. (1992), who showed that the introduction of human capital in production can enhance the role of physical capital accumulation.

As revealed by the value of *L/L'* in Table 3.3, both the technical progress and the reproducible factor played a significant role in the development process of Taiwan and South Korea. Our findings are contrary to results in recent research. Young (1995) emphasized the fundamental role of factor accumulation in explaining the extraordinary postwar growth of four East Asian NICs. The region's growth was largely achieved through heavy investment and a big shift of labor from farms into factories rather than through technical progress or organizational changes. Kim and Lau (1994, 1995) also found that capital accumulation is the most important source of economic growth in the East Asian NICs.

The intertemporal substitution elasticity ($1/\sigma$) is another crucial determinant in transitional dynamics. Estimates of σ became significantly larger in the endogenous growth model than in the neoclassical growth model in both Japan and South Korea. With less intertemporal substitution in preference, agents choose smoother consumption profiles and hence smaller investment. As a result, output grows much more slowly. Since the technical progress did not enhance the role of physical capital accumulation in transitional dynamics, the persistence of transitional growth did not leave much room for the stable root (s_1) to capture, and therefore the estimate of σ must stay at a low value. On the other hand, the endogenous and exogenous dynamics characterized by m_1 (or s_1) and γ_a switched their relative importance between the two types of growth model in both Taiwan and the US. Hence, we found that the estimate of σ stays relatively constant between the two types of model. Nevertheless, we did not find lengthy transitional paths in the four countries.

Recently, King and Rebelo (1993) conducted dynamic simulations to learn about the quantitative transitional dynamics in various neoclassical growth models with intertemporally optimizing households. They parameterize the model parameters and generate the 'time-series data' from the closed-form solution, and compare a selective set of second-moment properties of the generated data with those of actual series with the trend removed in evaluating the performance of the model. They found that very low intertemporal substitution is preferred in order to generate the 'time-series facts', which is not consistent with our findings.

5 CONCLUSIONS

Recent research in growth accounting has reinstated capital fundamentalism at the forefront of economic analysis and policy discussions. The development of new growth theory suggests that the importance of capital accumulation can be enhanced either by the introduction of additional reproducible input factor such as human capital or by externalities. However, based on the growth accounting conducted in this chapter, we found a much smaller role for physical capital accumulation in growth than that advocated by capital fundamentalism. There is little support for the view that capital fundamentalism should guide the research agenda and policy advice, at least in the four countries studied. Moreover, there is little reason to believe that our empirical findings could provide any positive evidence that increasing investment will cause faster growth.

Since the additional reproducible factor can enhance the role of physical capital accumulation in transitional growth, we hope that future research into the economic, institutional determinants underlying this factor will improve our ability to design policies that promote sustained economic growth.

NOTES

1. One major weakness is that this model lacks transitional dynamics. One way to generate the transitional path requires that a_t be a stationary stochastic process,

and then the transitional path is solely driven by stationary exogenous productivity shock. Or one can incorporate the adjustment costs into the models. As noted in Turnovsky (1996), the model with adjustment costs may have multiple steady states. However, he showed that the stable steady states may violate the transversality conditions, while the unstable ones do not have meaningful transitional dynamics.

2. One example is Christiano and Eichenbaum (1988).
3. The complete description of the solution procedure can be obtained on request from the authors.

REFERENCES

Bai, J., R. Lumsdaime and J. Stock (1991), 'Testing for and Dating Breaks in Integrated and Cointegrated Times Series', working paper.

Christiano, L.J. and M. Eichenbaum (1988), 'Human Capital, Endogenous Growth and Aggregate Fluctuations', Federal Reserve Bank of Minneapolis, Working Paper No. 430.

DeLong, J. Bradford and L.H. Summers (1992), 'Macroeconomic Policy and Long-Run Growth', Federal Reserve Bank of Kansas City, *Review Economic*, 4th Quarter, 1-29.

Evans, P. (1996), 'Growth and the Neutrality of Money', *Empirical Economics*, 21, 187-202.

Grossman, G. and E. Helpman (1991), *Innovation and Growth in the World Economy*, Cambridge, MA: MIT Press.

Jones, C.I. (1995), 'Time Series Tests of Endogenous Growth Models', *Quarterly Journal of Economics*, 110, 495-525.

Jones, L.E. and R.E. Manuelli (1990), 'A Convex Model of Equilibrium Growth: Theory and Policy Implications', *Journal of Political Economy*, 98, 1008-38.

Jorgenson, D.W., F.M. Gollop and B.M. Fraumeni (1987), *Productivity and U.S. Economic Growth*, Harvard Economic Studies, Vol. 159, Cambridge, MA: Harvard University Press.

Kim, J. and L. Lau (1994), 'The Sources of Economic Growth of the East Asian Newly Industrialized Countries', *Journal of the Japanese and International Economies*, 8, 235-71.

Kim, J. and L. Lau (1995), 'The Role of Human Capital in the Economic Growth of the East Asian Newly Industrialized Countries', *Asia-Pacific Economic Review*, 1, 3-22.

King, R.G. and R. Levine (1994), 'Capital Fundamentalism, Economic Development, and Economic Growth', *Carnegie Rochester Conference Series on Public Policy*, 40, 259-92.

King, R.G. and S. Rebelo (1993), 'Transitional Dynamics and Economic

Growth in the Neoclassical Model', *American Economic Review*, 83, 908-31.

King, R.G. and S. Rebelo (1994), 'Explaining Business Cycles: A Multiple-Shock Approach', *Journal of Monetary Economics*, 34, 415-28.

Kocherlakota, N.R. and K. Yi (1996), 'A Simple Time Series Test of Endogenous vs. Exogenous Growth Models: An Application to the United States', *Review of Economics and Statistics*, 78, 126-34.

Ladron-de-Guevara, A., S. Ortigueira and M.S. Santos (1997), 'Equilibrium Dynamics in Two-Sector Models of Endogenous Growth', *Journal of Economic Dynamics and Control*, 21, 115-43.

Levine, R, and D. Edinelt (1992), 'A Sensitivity Analysis of Cross-Country Growth Regerssions', *American Economic Review*, 82, 942-63.

Lucas, Robert E., Jr. (1988), 'On the Mechanics of Economic Development', *Journal of Monetary Economics*, 22, 3-24.

Mankiw, N.G., D. Romer and D.N. Weil (1992), 'A Contribution to the Empirics of Economic Growth', *Quarterly Journal of Economics*, 107, 407-37.

Neusser, K. (1991), 'Testing The Long-run Implications of the Neoclassical Growth Model', *Journal of Monetary Economics*, 27, 3-27.

Newbold, Paul (1974), 'The Exact Likelihood Function for a Mixed Autoregressive-moving Average Process', *Biometrika*, 61: 3, 423-26.

Phadke, M.S. and G. Kedem (1978), 'Computation of the Exact Likelihood Function of Multivariate Moving Average Models', *Biometrika*, 65, 511-19.

Robelo, Sergio (1991), 'Long Run Policy Analysis and Long Run Growth', *Journal of Political Economy*, 99, 500-21.

Romer, P.M. (1986), 'Increasing Returns and Long-Run Growth', *Journal of Political Economy*, 94, 1002-37.

Romer, P.M. (1990), 'Endogenous Technological Change', *Journal of Political Economy*, 98, S71-102.

Turnovsky, S.J. (1996), 'Fiscal Policy, Growth, and Macroeconomic Performance in a Small Open Economy', *Journal of International Economics* 40, 41-66.

Young, A. (1995) 'The Tyranny of Numbers. Confronting the Statistical Realities of the East Asian Growth Experience', *Quarterly Journal of Economics*, 110, 641-78.

4. Incomplete Currency Markets and Growth: Some Evidence from Southeast Asia and the Lessons from Japan and Taiwan

Pan A. Yotopoulos*

1 INTRODUCTION

State intervention in the business of development has been the hallmark in many countries in the Asia-Pacific region. Where development has failed, the outcome is squarely blamed on such intervention. The considerable cases of success, on the other hand, are usually dismissed by the 'revisionist' conventional wisdom as unique events,[1] or else they are cast in a rational expectations framework as having occurred despite the existence of proactive governments, rather than because of them.

This chapter proposes a systematic economic interpretation of development success which rests on selectively overriding certain incomplete markets, that is, on imposing 'quantity closure' (rationing). This becomes necessary especially in developing countries (DCs) where certain markets are missing and others fail to clear at any observed price. The market for insurance is an example of the former condition; the rationing of credit and the unemployment of labor are examples of the latter. I shall argue below that the market for foreign exchange in developing countries is also incomplete and that competition in free-currency markets becomes 'bad competition' and leads to a 'race for the bottom' in terms of development outcomes.

Section 2 develops the proposition of asymmetric reputation that leads to substitution away from the soft currency in free-currency markets. The

---

* This chapter draws on Pan A. Yotopoulos, *Exchange Rate Parity for Trade and Development: Theory, Tests, and Case Studies* (London and New York: Cambridge University Press, 1996). I would like to acknowledge support from the Center of East Asian Studies, Stanford University.

empirical implication of currency substitution, systematic devaluations that are contractionary, is formulated operationally. It is tested in an endogenous growth model in Section 3, and the policy implications of the tests are discussed. Good governance becomes the conditional variable for success in economic development when intervention becomes requisite. The case studies in Section 4 serve to illustrate the two components of good governance, competence and integrity. In the case of Taiwan, the market-supporting interventions in the financial sector are detailed; they led to a strong currency and in due process they allowed for the successful integration of the country into the global economy. In the case of Japan, the appropriate interventions in the real sector that complemented the mild financial repression of the foreign exchange market are discussed. Moreover, the component of integrity in government, relating to the process of plowing the economic rents of intervention back into the process of development, is made operational through pluralistic economic development, which leads to broadly-based increases in incomes. Thus the domestic demand became the real locomotive of growth of Japanese economic development. Section 5 presents the conclusions of the study. The systematic component of the argument implies that these policies can have full transference to other developing countries, especially the emerging economies.

2 THE HYPOTHESIS: ASYMMETRIC REPUTATION AS A SOURCE OF INCOMPLETENESS IN CURRENCY MARKETS

The basic hypothesis is that there exists an inherent distortion in free-currency markets that makes developing countries systematically misallocate resources.

The specific distortion relates to asymmetric reputation, which in free-currency markets validates the distinction between hard and soft currencies.[2] While there is a continuum in the real world between hard and soft currencies, there is only a handful of currencies in which central banks hold their reserve positions. These reserve currencies are treated as a store of value internationally and as a safe haven for capital. The international appeal of reserve currencies is based on ‘reputation’, which means that there is a credible commitment to the stability of relative hard-currency prices (toward other hard currencies or, say, gold). The soft currency, in contrast, is expected to devalue in a free currency market since it lacks reputation as a safe haven. Under these conditions, and with international financial intermediation present, there is an asymmetric demand from Mexicans to hold dollars as a store of value – a demand not offset by Americans holding pesos as an asset. This asymmetry tends to increase the price of the dollar in Mexico – to depreciate the peso. This will encourage currency substitution, with Mexicans fleeing the peso in exchange for dollars, which will precipitate further depreciation. Expectations of devaluation feed unto themselves to become a self-fulfilling prophecy. The fault is not with the peso as such. In free-currency markets, without restrictions on foreign exchange, devaluation of the soft currency is inevitable and it becomes a political economy bubble: a set of reinforcing expectations.

The systematic and endemic devaluation of soft currencies is likely to occur in a regime of free-currency markets whether the soft currency is fixed, pegged, or floating freely. The empirical implication of the proposition of asymmetric reputation is that while hard currencies tend to fluctuate (possibly with a mean-reversion property), soft currencies tend to depreciate systematically. The policy implication of the proposition of asymmetric reputation is that foreign exchange markets need to be 'mildly repressed'. It is, therefore, symmetrical to the case of incomplete markets on the grounds of asymmetric information (Jaffe and Russel 1976; Stiglitz and Weiss 1981; Floro and Yotopoulos 1991).

Should the proposition of currency substitution, taken as a postulate so far, be correct, the question arises how is it transmitted from the financial markets to the real economy? Moreover, would not the devaluation of the soft currency translate into improved prospects for growth?

In answering this question it helps to make the distinction between tradables and nontradables. Tradables can be defined as those commodities that enter a country's current account as exports or imports and their respective values can be used as weights in constructing a commodity-specific index of tradability (Yotopoulos 1996). Nontradables are defined accordingly as commodities that do not enter to a significant degree a country's international trade. Tradability, therefore, is not a binary issue but a question of degree. And the degree, at least in part, is determined by what a country can afford to pay for in foreign exchange, most often in reserve currency.

One way of understanding the coupling of the distinction between hard and soft currency with that of tradables and nontradables is to compare two economics along the continuum of possibilities for transforming nontradable output, or the resources that produce it, into tradables. To enhance the intuition, suppose both countries are overindebted, for example, the United States and Mexico. With the peso being a soft currency and the Mexican debt being denominated in dollars (because the peso is soft currency), Mexico cannot service its foreign debt from the proceeds of producing nontradables. These are traded in pesos. It has instead to shift resources away from the nontradable sector to produce tradable output in order to procure the dollars for servicing the debt. In the United States, on the other hand, the debt is serviced in dollars. Then all output produced, whether it consists of more aircraft or more haircuts, serves directly to service the dollar-denominated debt.

A parable can help enhance understanding of how the process of shifting resources from the production of nontradables to that of tradables, when fuelled by currency substitution and systematic devaluations, can create a negative feedback loop that leads to resource misallocation in developing countries. Consider an equilibrium allocation where a bundle of resources produces tradables (T) and nontradables (N), measured so that one unit of each is worth $1. Entrepreneurs should normally be indifferent between producing one unit of the former or one of the latter. But in the case of Mexico, T trade in dollars while N trade in pesos. Since the soft currency may be devalued it becomes risky for entrepreneurs to produce (or hold) one unit of N that could not be converted for later spending into $1. Expressed in another way, entrepreneurs see the future price of tradables increasing relative to the price of nontradables and they are attracted to producing T because that is the cheapest way they can acquire $1 from their bundle of resources in the future. This dilemma does not exist with the developed countries that have hard currency. For their entrepreneurs, $1 of T will always be worth $1 of N in hard currency, contrary to the soft-currency case where the expectation of devaluation becomes a self-fulfilling prophecy. In the latter case, production becomes biassed excessively toward T, despite the fact that the relative productivities of the bundle of resources have remained unchanged *ex hypothesi*. This shift of resources represents misallocation and produces inefficiency and output losses. It originated in free-currency markets setting prices wrong, not right, for the soft peso.[3]

The misallocation of resources is not the result of a factor specificity. Instead, it is the result of bad competition in the currency market with good competition in the factor market. The situation then arises when the prices of T are 'high' relative to those of N, with resources moving 'excessively' from the latter to the former. The case is a mirror image of the Dutch disease (Corden and Neary 1982), except that the origin is depreciation, as opposed to appreciation of the domestic currency, and the result is not deindustrialization but contraction in the N sector with detrimental outcomes for growth.

The intuition behind the parable is simple. Distortions inherent in free-currency markets lead to systematic depreciation of soft currencies of developing countries — to 'high' nominal exchange rates. Devaluation of the exchange rate means increasing prices of tradables and leads to increased exports. But not all exports are a bargain to produce compared to the alternative of producing nontradables. For instance, some countries without a climatic or resource advantage in producing grapes are known to export wine. Other countries graduate from being exporters of sugar and copra to exporting their teak forests, and on to systematically exporting nurses and doctors, while they remain underdeveloped all the same. If this happens, it may represent competitive-devaluation trade as opposed to comparative-advantage trade. Competitive-devaluation trade is misallocating resources against nontradables at great cost to growth and to the detriment of development.

3 EMPIRICAL IMPLEMENTATION: ENDOGENOUS GROWTH ANALYSIS

The maintained hypothesis is that competitive price-setting of foreign exchange rates in soft-currency countries is detrimental to growth. In submitting the hypothesis to an empirical test we note that the nominal exchange rate (*NER*) is the intermediate variable. Currency-substitution-induced high *NER*s lead to high prices of tradables, and the expectation of further devaluation in the future gives the signal to producers for shifting resources away from nontradables.

For the test of the hypothesis an index of the relative price of tradables to nontradables, the real exchange rate (*RER*, with prices of tradables in the numerator) is required. For that purpose, the operational framework of the research utilizes purchasing power parity (PPP) data. Micro-ICP (International Comparisons Project, Kravis et al. 1982) data provide prices for a complete set of outputs of an economy, appropriately normalized by the international prices of the same commodities. Data from international trade statistics are used to define T ('traded') and N ('nontraded') on a country-by-country basis. The ratio of the prices of the two is an index of the real exchange rate (*RER*, with prices of T in the numerator). An example appears in Table 4.1, which ranks 33 countries by the value of their *RER* index in 1985.[4]

The meaning of 'setting the prices right' is setting the *RER* precisely at its equilibrium value. And although the index cannot be used to measure the deviation of the *RER* from its equilibrium value, it can indicate clearly whether one country has higher prices of tradables relative to nontradables than another – that is, it has a more undervalued *RER*, always in relative terms. Moreover, the proposition of reputation asymmetry of the previous section constitutes the link between the *RER*

Table 4.1 Countries ranked by the value of the RER *index, 1985*

Country	*RER*	Country	*RER*
Ethiopia	1.967	Kenya	1.070
Rwanda	1.962	Morocco	1.069
Pakistan	1.747	Norway	1.013
Malawi	1.713	Netherlands	1.009
Sri Lanka	1.546	Turkey	0.998
Yugoslavia	1.542	Denmark	0.980
Greece	1.417	Australia	0.969
Ivory Coast	1.329	Belgium	0.963
Portugal	1.230	Jamaica	0.949
New Zealand	1.208	Sweden	0.933
Nigeria	1.196	Canada	0.928
Thailand	1.193	Japan	0.923
Hungary	1.192	Ireland	0.918
Egypt	1.186	Finland	0.879
India	1.178	Italy	0.831
Germany	1.155	Poland	0.829
France	1.095		

Source: Yotopoulos (1996, chapter 1, Table 1.1) by permission of the publisher.

and the *NER*. Examined within an international cross-section, high values of the index (which mean high prices of tradables) are more likely to be associated with high *NER* than are low values. 'High' exchange rates, or devaluations, lead initially to high prices of tradables, until the effect of devaluation is eventually offset by price increases in the nontradable sector.

The *RER* is related to the record of growth in an endogenous growth analysis. The objective of the endogenous growth literature is to go beyond the Solow-type decomposition that defines technological change as the residual, after accounting for the contribution of the neoclassical factors of production. Instead, growth is viewed as the endogenous outcome of the economic system. Accordingly, the empirical branch of the endogenous growth literature casts a broad net in identifying variables that represent private choices, public sector policies and institutional factors that could explain the intercountry variance in rates of growth.

Two observations have been gleaned from the large number of

empirical studies on the macroeconomics of endogenous growth. It is not hard to devise econometric specifications in which sundry variables measuring economic policy are significantly correlated with economic growth. It is almost impossible, however, to discover explanatory variables that are robust enough so that their estimated coefficients do not depend importantly on the conditioning set of information (Solow 1994; Pack 1994). Levine and Renelt (1992) reviewed 41 studies and found more than 50 variables that correlated significantly with growth in various studies, But only one, the ratio of investment in GDP, had a robust coefficient in an 'extreme bounds' analysis (Leamer 1983, 1985).

In the tradition of the endogenous growth literature this chapter introduces factors that relate to public sector choices (*GOVCONS, GINFL, SECENROL, GPOP*), private sector policies (*INV*), and institutional factors that capture a country's exposure to international trade (*OPEN, DIR*).[5] The innovation in this chapter is the introduction of the *RER* as a variable which varies directly with the *NER*, high values of which denote competitive price-setting of the foreign exchange rate. A free-currency market, in turn, is associated with low growth outcomes in developing countries. The motivation behind the analytical framework is to control for the effect of the stylized endogenous growth variables while measuring the impact that *RER* has on measures of development performance.

The reduced form of the estimating equation is:[6]

$$G_t = f\,(RER,\ DUM,\ OPEN,\ DIR,\ INV,\ GINFL,\ GOVCONS,\ SECENRL,\ GPOP)$$

where G_t is the rate of growth of real GDP per capita. The test of the hypothesis consists of explaining the intercountry variance in G_t by the variance in *RER*, subject to the other conditioning variables. The purpose of the *DUM* variables is to account for differences in initial per capita incomes by including as a variable the value of the real GDP per capita, *RGDPC*, or else a dummy, *DumL/M*, which distinguishes between low/middle-income countries and DCs. The classification of countries as low/middle-high income is from the World Bank (1992). The second problem relates to the general slowdown in growth since the 1980s. A dummy variable, *Dum80/85* (with the value of 1 for the observations of 1980 and 1985) is also used. In both cases the pooled data have also been partitioned so that the influence of these two factors has been excluded from the analysis.

Since Adam Smith first formulated the traditional trade-growth nexus the extent of the market has been considered a determinant of efficiency.

This is usually captured by the openness of an economy, *OPEN*, which is a measure of the ratio of trade to GDP. More recently a second effect, the direction of trade, *DIR*, has become a prominent variable. Controlling for the volume of trade, the direction-of-trade variable may capture the technological spillovers from trading with more developed partners. One advantage of such trade is that the innovation-producing skilled labor of DCs is extended to less-developed countries (LDCs) through technological diffusion (Grossman and Helpman 1990, 1992). Investment, *INV* (as opposed to the accumulated stock of capital), becomes an important vehicle for technological diffusion because of the vintage effect of new capital. The two conventional variables intended to capture the crowding out of private investment that may occur as a result of public sector policies are *GOVCONS,* which represents (unproductive) government consumption expenditure, and *GINFL*, the average rate of change in inflation that depresses the level of savings. Finally, an education variable, commonly *SECENRL*, secondary school enrollment, and a demographic variable, *GPOP*, the rate of growth of population, often appear in endogenous growth equations.

The results in Tables 4.2 and 4.3, respectively, refer to the international cross-section model of the parent study, and to the subset of the Southeast Asian countries. The presentation is organized into five models that group variables so as to provide an immediate indicator of the robustness of the maintained hypothesis. The logic of the testing procedure is to regress *GRGDPC* on *RER*, the main variable of interest, and successively on a greater number of variables. Comparison of the parameter values across models gives an idea of the robustness of the functional form employed.

The first test reported (Table 4.2) is the longitudinal analysis for the sample of 123 observations (62 countries) for the years 1970, 1975, 1980 and 1985. In Model I, *RER* appears as the single variable. The simple regression of *GRGDPC* on *RER* has the expected negative sign and is consistently significant. Moreover, the coefficient of *RER* is robust, as evidenced from the fact that it varies within a very narrow range (from −0.020 to −0.024) as other conditioning variables are added seriatim in the other models reported in the table. The maintained hypothesis construes the inverse relationship between *RER* and *GRGDPC* as evidence that intervention in an incomplete foreign exchange market can lead to better developmental outcomes.

The empirical results reported in Models II to V are in general in accord with expectations and consistent with the parallel studies on endogenous growth. The coefficient of *Dum80/85* is robust and captures the slowdown of growth. The *INV* variable is also significant with coefficient values ranging from 0.089 to 0.104, which is very close to the

Table 4.2 Cross-section/time-series regressions on growth, all countries, 1970, 1975, 1980 and 1985

Explanatory variables	Model				
	I	II	III	IV	V
Constant	0.040	0.056	0.068	0.043	0.044
RER	−0.021 (−2.708)	−0.022 (−2.774)	−0.024 (−2.947)	−0.020 (−2.450)	−0.022 (−2.683)
Dummy low/middle (*DumL/M*=1)		−0.003 (−0.668)	−0.003 (−0.601)	−0.004 (−0.824)	0.004 (0.493)
Dummy 1980/1985 (*Dum80/85*=1)		−0.017 (−3.652)	−0.017 (−3.474)	−0.016 (−3.439)	−0.016 (−3.346)
Openness (*OPEN*)			−0.010 (−1.127)	−0.012 (−1.352)	−0.017 (−1.731)
Dir. of trade (share of OECD) (*DIR*)			0.015 (0.904)	0.023 (1.410)	0.022 (1.341)
Investment in GDP (*INV*)				0.104 (2.812)	0.089 (2.277)
Rate of inflation (change) (*GINFL*)					−0.023 (−1.960)
Gov. consumption in GDP (*GOVCONS*)					−0.000 (−0.178)
Secondary enrolment (*SECENRL*)					0.012 (0.880)
Population Growth (*GPOP*)					−0.048 (−0.460)
Sample size	123	123	123	123	123
Adjusted R^2	0.049	0.0142	0.139	0.187	0.193
Standard error	0.025	0.024	0.024	0.023	0.023
F-statistic (zero slopes)	7.333	7.754	4.944	5.682	3.923

Notes:
The dependent variable is annual rate of growth of real per capita GDP, GRGDPC, for the five-year period centered on the year of observation.
For definition of independent variables see text.
Numbers in parentheses are t-statistics.

Source: Yotopoulos (1996, Ch. 7, Table 7.1), by perulssion of the publics les.

Table 4.3 Cross-section/time-series regressions on growth, Southeast Asian countries, 1970, 1975, 1980 and 1985

Explanatory variables	Model I	II	III	IV	V
Constant	0.098	0.097	0.117	0.062	0.056
RER	−0.050	−0.044	−0.056	−0.046	−0.031
	(−3.369)	(−3.227)	(−3.490)	(−3.660)	(−1.948)
Dummy 1980/1985		−0.017	−0.012	−0.009	−0.011
(*Dum80/85*=1)		(−1.992)	(−1.237)	(−1.239)	(−1.510)
Openness (*OPEN*)			0.020	0.022	0.011
			(0.701)	(0.993)	(0.511)
Direction Of trade			−0.035	−0.065	−0.084
(share of OECD) (*DIR*)			(−1.021)	(−2.296)	(−2.854)
Investment in GDP (*INV*)				0.194	0.235
				(2.746)	(3.280)
Rate of inflation (change)					−0.125
(*GINFL*)					(−1.472)
Sample size	14	14	14	14	14
Adjusted R^2	0.486	0.622	0.695	0.843	0.880
Standard error	0.018	0.016	0.016	0.012	0.011

Notes:
The dependent variable is annual rate of growth of real per capita GDP, GRGDPC, for the five-year period centered on the year of observation.
For definition of independent variables see text.
Numbers in parentheses are t-statistics.

Source: Yotopoulos data bank.

modal values reported in other studies for the same variable. This coefficient presents a strong link with the celebrated and most significant result that other studies of endogenous growth have established (Levine and Renelt 1992). The negative coefficient of *OPEN*, reported also in other studies and considered an aberration (Edwards 1993; Rodrik 1995), is totally expected within the confines of the maintained hypothesis. Countries that control the level of *NER*, have low *RER*, and grow fast, are expected to have a lower volume of trade than would have obtained under free foreign exchange markets. The more open the economy is, as a result, the lower the rate of growth. The *DIR*, on the other hand, has a positive but nonsignificant coefficient (which, however, improves in other specifications in the parent study). The sign indicates that, controlling for

RER and *OPEN*, the benefit of trade arises from the technological spillover of having more developed trading partners (proxied by *OECD* member countries). The remaining variables appear as commonly in the literature.

The results in Table 4.3 for the Southeast Asian countries are in general consistent with those for the international panel data of the parent study, but they are distinctly weaker because of the small size of the sample. Looking across models, the coefficient of the *RER* is consistently negative and significant, although not as robust as in the longitudinal analysis with the full sample. The income dummy was omitted in this test since Japan would have been the only country accounting for the variance in this variable. The coefficient of the dummy for the slowdown of growth is negative, as it is in Table 4.2. The coefficients of *OPEN* and *DIR* are not significant, and the latter has the wrong sign. Next to *RER* the variable *INV* is the star performer with positive, significant and robust coefficients, as it is also in Table 4.2. Finally, *GINFL* has the expected negative coefficient, but it is nonsignificant. The rest of the variables were tested and omitted in this application because of the few degrees of freedom remaining.

The grand theme that emerges from the analysis (and is further documented in the parent study) has as its foundation the negative relationship between the *RER* and *GRGDPC*, the rate of growth of real GDP per capita. The relationship is consistently significant and robust to changes in the other conditioning variables. Is it also a causal relationship?

Causality in economics is not a heuristic attribute that is established merely by mechanistic tests.[7] It is, rather, an empirical implication of a model of mind – a hypothesis that is grounded on extant theory. Given the link that currency substitution establishes between *RER* and *NER*, the results are consistent with causality going from high *NER* to low *GRGDPC* and favor policies that would reduce *RER* as leading to a better allocation of resources.

Why should some countries, specifically LDCs, tend to have high *NER*s that lead to high *RER*s? The explanation, as already mentioned, is substitution of the hard currency for the soft in free-currency markets. It is triggered by the reputation asymmetry and the expectation that the soft currency will devalue – an expectation that is validated by the absence of restrictions in hedging soft-currency asset-holdings by converting them to hard currency. The implications of substitution in financial holdings extend also to the real world through the bias in the allocation of resources in favor of tradables. This misallocation is captured by the negative sign of the relationship between *GRGDPC* and *RER*.

Under these conditions policies that would reduce the *RER* would achieve a better allocation of resources. One such set of policies is increasing the productivity in tradables, that is, reducing their peso prices. Another policy reaction which has been largely ignored (or, worse, passionately dismissed) both in the literature and in operations so far is intervention in the foreign exchange market to reduce the *NER* by rationing or protection. Intervention contains the increase in *RER* and the premature shift of resources away from nontradables.

The policy of maintaining a 'mildly repressed' exchange rate is totally symmetrical with, and a logical consequence of, the finding in the literature on credit in favor of mildly repressed interest rates and financial markets (Stiglitz and Weiss 1981; World Bank 1993). In the latter case, some restrictions of free entry into banking and setting interest rate ceilings help keep banks profitable and eliminate adverse selection of risk (Caprio and Summers 1993). By analogy, restricting competition in dealing in foreign exchange, for example, by limiting it to authorized banks only, will increase the spread between the two sides of currency substitution and will limit the exposure of a soft currency to it. Conceptually, the precise meaning of 'mildly repressed' exchange rates is easy to define. It consists of setting the ceiling for the exchange rate closer to the range determined by the transactions demand for foreign exchange, the balance between imports and exports, plus the capital account balance in the investment account. On the other hand, short-term capital inflow and asymmetric demand for currency substitution should be restricted and 'sterilized' from impacting on the exchange rate.[8]

Fixed exchange rates, let alone 'mildly repressed' markets, have their disadvantages and require skill and resources to be managed properly. Would not currency substitution taken to its extreme through 'dollarization' of the economy directly, or in the form of a currency board, indirectly, remedy the distortion in free-currency markets and solve the problem of reputation asymmetry and its contractionary effects on the economy?

The costs of dollarization are substantial and may offset its benefits of reducing uncertainly and limiting foreign exchange risk. The cost of seigniorage is trivial and can be handled readily as in the case of Argentina where the peso is still the legal tender. More importantly, currency substitution, or in the extreme case dollarization, is predicated on a country's success in attracting the requisite foreign exchange. In the process of luring foreign financial capital, higher interest rates, not lower, become necessary. Next, foreign exchange, once attracted, has an opportunity cost in being productively used for the growth of the real economy. Holding it as reserves in a currency board system or as a store of value for asset-holders represents an inefficient use of a valuable resource. Finally, dollarization amounts to adopting the international rate of inflation. While this is appropriate for the tradable sector of the economy, it is totally gratuitous and unnecessarily contractionary for the nontradable sector (Yotopoulos 1996, ch. 12). This may be one reason why a quasi-currency-board system has worked well in city-states, like Singapore and Hong Kong, where the bulk of the economy consists of the tradable sector.

The systematic nature of the relationship between *RER* and *NER* at different levels of income implies that market incompleteness, and thus the need for rationing, abates as development occurs. The same two factors, the real and the financial, that account for the incomplete market are at play in remedying the situation. As development occurs the prices of N increase relative to those of T, thus reducing the *RER* (the Ricardo principle). At the same time, self-sustained growth breeds reputation and the soft currency 'hardens', thus inducing less currency substitution and dampening expectations of devaluation. This reduces the *NER*. As the divergence between the allocation of resources that obtains under the equilibrium *RER* and the one under the equilibrium *NER* decreases, that is, as the two equilibria tend to converge, eventually free-market, free-trade, laissez-faire policies can be allowed to determine the *NER*. Empirically, this stage has been reached when a currency operates in a free market as hard currency: its exchange rate fluctuates instead of depreciating systematically.

In an environment of incomplete foreign exchange markets free-market, free-trade, *laissez-faire* is not likely to lead LDCs to the primrose paths of development. Government intervention is required. Yet there is no presumption that intervention will succeed. The success of intervention ultimately depends on the agent of intervention, the government. And government failure is as frequent as market failure.

Intervention always raises a host of issues that make the task of governance more complex. How can policy-makers distinguish between markets that require intervention and those that are best left to their own devices? What specific form should intervention take? How are various interventions to be sequenced? Competence in government cuts through the thicket of all possible forms of intervention, most of which could be wanton and many downright injurious. Competence is one constituent component of good governance.

Distortions create economic rents. In Krueger's (1974) formulation rent-seeking accounts for the resources wasted in the attempt of expropriating and capturing economic rents. Quantity rationing in the foreign exchange market, for example, creates scarcity rents and resources are wasted in an attempt to capture them. Overvaluation of the *NER* creates black market activities and a competition to appropriate the black-market premia. By the same token, smuggling, underinvoicing and overinvoicing are rewarded.

The existence of economic rents is inevitable, whether they are created by market failure, market incompleteness or by government intervention. The important issue, however, becomes who captures the economic rents and how are they used. At one extreme, thieving elites capture the rents which end up in bank accounts in Zurich or Miami, or in financing imposing schemes of import-substitution industrialization that cater to the needs of the middle-income classes and of the wealthy. At the other extreme an honest government or far-sighted entrepreneurs collect the economic rents and reinvest them in economic development. Integrity thus becomes the second constituent component of good governance.

The balance of this chapter relates to the mechanics and outcomes of intervention. Instances of failed intervention abound, and so do the shipwrecks among development outcomes. Relatively rare are the cases where intervention was appropriate in the sense that it was targetted where it was essential because of a specific market defect or market distortion; and even more infrequent are the cases where intervention was carried out with competence and integrity. Teleologically, one can always tell such interventions by successful development outcomes. But this *ex post* prediction is circular. By making the pluralistic spread of development the operational discriminant of successful intervention the etiology changes and the likely success of intervention can be judged *ex ante*. It becomes easier to evaluate policy consequences by asking the question whether their outcome is likely to spread the dividends of growth broadly as opposed to rewarding exclusively some privileged segment of the population.

4 MILD FINANCIAL REPRESSION AND GOOD GOVERNANCE

The focus of the case studies is the control of the foreign exchange market and the various interventions this requires in other sectors of the economy. The case study of Taiwan demonstrates how mild financial repression is imposed at early stages of development in order to offset the inherent distortion in free-currency markets. As development proceeds, on the other hand, sequential liberalization leads gradually to the complete liberalization of the financial sector. The broader issue of how the various interventions in the economy are successfully sequenced, plus the operational content of good governance, will be illustrated with reference to the case of Japan.

4.1 Strong Currency and the Sequencing of Financial Integration in Taiwan

By the early 1980s the free-market approach to economic development had totally supplanted the paradigm of import-substitution industrialization that had held since the Second World War. The new mainstream view to development advocates free markets and strong currency (Krugman 1995). Devaluation and liberalization of the foreign exchange market are expected to strengthen a soft currency by putting it on head-to-head competition with the world's reserve currencies. Financial integration in the global economy becomes the ultimate objective of the complete monetary package of the free-market reforms in LDCs.

Financial integration is predicated on opening the foreign account. As a minimum, it entails abolishing restrictions on capital movements and on exchange transactions. It often also involves eliminating controls on interest rates and improving the competitive environment of financial institutions by deregulation and by facilitating the establishment of foreign banks. The objective of financial integration is to use the external sector as an anchor for stabilizing the economy, for setting the prices right, and for increasing efficiency. Additionally, the monetary and exchange rate policies of liberalization are expected to lure foreign capital, thus further contributing to the improvement of the fundamentals of the economy. In this scenario the external account and the financial sector play a crucial role in the rehabilitation of the real economy.

The preceding conceptual and empirical analysis has definite implications that militate against attempting financial integration in the face of macroeconomic instability — which is the automatic outcome of a free market in currencies with asymmetric reputation. Asymmetric financial integration involves heavy contraction costs for an LDC economy. Symmetric integration, on the other hand, is properly sequenced only after the real economy has been stabilized and is launched into self-sustained growth. The case study of Taiwan illustrates the mechanics of gradual and appropriate financial integration.

Stung from the experience of hyperinflation in the 1950s, the authorities in Taiwan starting in 1960 resorted to Draconian measures to combat inflation and secure price stability. The policy instruments used were fiscal, monetary, and an exchange rate that was pegged and stable through the 1970s (Table 4.4).[9] The NT$ was considered generally overvalued for most of the period (Kuo 1983, chs 10, 14). The fiscal policy was premised on curtailing government consumption expenditure while favoring savings and capital formation in the private and in the public sector. On the revenue side income taxes were moderate, except for agriculture in the earlier period, which was assigned the role of financing the industrialization drive. The fiscal side produced a consistent surplus in the operating budget averaging over the period at above 1 percent of GNP.

The three components of monetary policy that will be examined here are interest rates, money supply, and the intersection of the two as it relates to the balance of payments and the net foreign assets.[10] The criterion for evaluating the outcomes of monetary policy is the extent to which the growth of real GDP was accommodated and the rate of inflation was controlled.

The interest rate policy became early on the foundation of the monetary policy. The 'preferential interest rate deposit scheme' that has been in existence for more than 40 years intended to lure out of the private sector a continuous increase in monetary savings. The incentive was high interest rates that were consistently positive, turning to high when inflationary risks lurched (Table 4.4). The rate of personal savings rose from 3 percent of the disposable income in 1952 to 21 percent in 1980 and has remained at that high level since then. Real interest rates averaging 6 percent through the mid-1970s are very high in comparison to the negative real interest rates that are stylized facts in comparable growth histories. Still, the average productivity of capital was high enough so that the high interest-rate policy did not choke off investment and growth.[11]

The second component of monetary policy was based on the stable growth of the money supply to finance the vertiginal growth in real GDP, bordering on an average of 8 percent per year (Table 4.4). The annual increase in the transactions demand for money for accommodating the rate of growth alone was 16 percent per year.[12] In addition, the requirements of financing foreign trade transactions, and those imposed by a significant increase in net foreign assets, resulted in a vigorous growth in the money supply throughout the period.[13] Nevertheless, with the combination of interest-rate policies and fiscal policies, along with the overvalued exchange rate that accounted for cheap imports of raw materials and intermediate products, inflation was tamed. With the exception of an interlude of double-digit rates around the years of the oil crisis, inflation stabilized below 5 percent for most of the period (Table 4.4).

Real interest rates in Taiwan were higher than in the United States. In an open economy the inflow of capital would have driven interest rates down. Similarly in the textbook case the overvalued currency would

Table 4.4 Taiwan rate of growth of GNP and financial statistics, 1953-91

Year	Growth rate of real GNP (percent)	Inflation rate (percent)	Growth in money supply (percent)	Interest rate (percent per annum)	Exchange rate (NT$ per US$)
1953-56	7.7				
1957-63	7.5				
1964-68	10.0				
1969-74	10.2				
1974-79	10.1				
1980-89	8.5				
1970	11.3	3.6	23.30	9.80	40.00
1971	13.1	2.8	27.20	9.25	40.00
1972	13.4	3.0	33.50	8.50	40.00
1973	12.8	8.2	45.40	10.75	37.90
1974	1.2	47.5	11.80	12.00	37.95
1975	4.4	5.2	24.70	10.75	37.95
1976	13.7	2.5	21.90	9.50	37.95
1977	10.3	7.0	34.40	8.25	37.95
1978	14.0	5.8	35.30	8.25	35.95
1979	8.5	9.7	10.20	11.00	35.98
1980	7.1	19.0	19.10	11.00	35.96
1981	5.8	16.3	13.80	11.75	37.79
1982	4.1	3.0	14.60	7.75	39.86
1983	8.6	1.4	18.40	7.25	40.22
1984	11.6	0.0	9.30	6.75	39.42
1985	5.6	−0.2	12.20	5.25	39.80
1986	12.6	0.7	51.40	4.50	35.45
1987	12.3	0.5	37.80	4.50	28.50
1988	8.3	1.3	24.40	4.50	28.12
1989	8.0	4.4	6.10	7.75	26.12
1990	5.5	4.1	−6.60	7.75	27.11
1991	7.6	3.6	12.10	6.25	25.75

Note: Interest rate is the rediscount rate of the Central Bank of China.

Sources: The Central Bank of China, *Financial Statistics*, Monthly and Annual issues; Council for Economic Planning and Development, Republic of China, *Taiwan Statistical Data Book 1990, 1997*. Yotopoulos (1996, Ch. 11, Table 11.3) by permission of the publisher.

have contributed to capital outflow. In Taiwan, foreign exchange controls were used to insulate the domestic interest rates from external influences, whether during the period of the current account deficits, prior to 1976, or afterwards when the inflow of foreign assets was increasing. The exception was the financing of foreign trade that had from the beginning free access to foreign capital at interest rates that were lower than domestic interest rates. Other inflows of capital were strictly controlled, and so were, of course, capital outflows. In the period of persistent current account surpluses interest rates were nudged downwards, and some capital outflows were countenanced, but both remained strictly controlled.

Despite the success that Taiwan had experienced in stabilizing the domestic sector and in enjoying a consistent record of self-sustained growth, it approached liberalization and financial integration gingerly, cautiously, and late. Copious effort went into building and diversifying the institutional structure for financial intermediation and for integration into the global economy. A security market had been started in the 1960s. A bond market was established in 1974, and a money market in 1976. Both these markets were exempted from interest ceiling regulations and they were intended to pave the way for interest rate deregulation and to contribute to capital deepening by channeling financial savings from the informal market to capital formation. The success of the policies is best gauged by the doubling of the value of money market instruments outstanding to the total banking loans, from 8.6 percent to 15.6 percent, in a period of only 18 months in late 1970s (Kuo 1983, p. 321).[14]

With the preconditions met and the institutional structure established, a managed floating exchange rate was introduced in 1978 and the liberalization of the capital market followed in 1983.[15] Foreign capital transactions, however, continued to be closely monitored[16] and strict oversight of the foreign exchange rate was maintained at least until 1989, when a 'liberalized' floating exchange rate system was introduced. At the same time interest rates became fully liberalized.

In conclusion, the mild financial repression was evidenced by the stability and relative overvaluation of the nominal exchange rate, by strict restrictions in capital flows and total control of financial capital inflows, by positive interest rates that encouraged savings, while lending rates were narrowly targetted and heavily subsidized at times.

4.2 Operational Implications of Incomplete Markets: The Lessons from Japan

By the early 1950s, Japan shared the vital characteristics of all underdeveloped economies. With cheap labor and expensive capital it had comparative advantage in labor-intensive, low value-added manufactures. Its exports became notorious for their shabby quality and cheap price. However, the next stage in development was reached soon thereafter and was characterized by expensive labor and relatively cheap capital. It fostered specialization in capital- and technology-intensive exports with high value added and significant technological rents associated with products that have high income elasticity of demand and conceivably low price elasticity. High wages and high living standards followed.

This swift graduation owes much to what we have called 'good governance'. The component of competence relates to aiding the market, instead of supplanting it. It consisted of fostering the market where it failed and of introducing the appropriate interventions where the market was incomplete. The component of integrity relates exclusively to the utilization of the economic rents that accrue when markets are not perfect and when intervention becomes requisite. Integrity denotes that the economic rents are plowed back into the process of development in a way that achieves a broadly-based increase in incomes early on in the process. Investing the dividend of growth into increasing wages and achieving pluralistic economic development is not viewed as a self-rewarding aim of the welfare state. It is, instead, the means towards the aim of creating the foundation of sustained effective domestic demand that can propel the manufacturing sector past the threshold of economies of scale and into the exports that have high value added and capture important technological rents.[17] Furthermore, in the case of Japan, the large domestic demand provided the advantage of 'learning by using', in the sense that it allowed infant industries to test their products in a protected market before facing international competition. In this sense, the 'Japanese miracle' was domestic-demand driven, as opposed to export driven.

Competence

Japan ranks in Table 4.1 among the countries with the lowest *RER*. The ranking is similar for the other years (1970, 1975, 1980) of the panel micro-PPP data in the parent study (Yotopoulos 1996, pp. 114-15, Table 6.1). According to the underlying hypothesis, relatively low prices of tradables in the international cross-section is evidence of overvalued nominal exchange rates. Other studies have reached the same conclusion on the historical overvaluation of the yen. Komiya has inferred overvaluation, especially in the period 1955-67 (Komiya and Itoh 1988, p. 176). Hamada and Patrick (1988, p. 122) have calculated (via *CPI, WPI* proxies) overvaluation for the period 1970-87.

The finding of an overvalued yen is not new. What is new, however, is the thesis of this chapter that a mild financial repression with an overvalued domestic currency is a necessary condition for success in economic development. But it is not a sufficient condition, since appropriate trade and industrial policies have to complement it. On this count the Japanese experience is quite revealing. An overvalued domestic currency provides the impetus for selective intervention, as opposed to indiscriminate protection of all exports that undervaluation affords. Overvaluation makes inevitable the exercise of trade and industrial policy. The panoply of such policies is featured in a careful study of the Japanese experience.

The control and husbanding of foreign exchange becomes a crucial component in a regime of overvaluation. Japan had a long history of public expertise in managing scarce foreign exchange resources. In view of the fact that the country had been deprived (until 1911) of tariff autonomy, the Meiji government required of all the agencies to prepare a foreign exchange budget, along with their yen budget. Such a requirement lasted in one form or another until 1964 when it was abolished in the early round of trade liberalization (Johnson 1982, p. 25).

The foreign exchange budget facilitated the purpose of husbanding scarce foreign currency and coping with the chronic deficits in the current account (which persisted until 1968). Moreover, in an era of high growth with increasing demand for imported raw materials, control of the foreign exchange budget meant control of the economy. Foreign exchange thus became an important tool of industrial policy in the hands of MITI (Ministry of International Trade and Industry). Overvaluation also provided a simple mechanism of matching subsidies to imports with those to exports in a self-liquidating operation, without burdening the public budget. The foreign exchange proceeds were targetted on imports of raw materials and machinery essential for domestic production, which, as a result, were made cheap in terms of yen. The imported intermediate products were in turn targetted to the growth sectors of industrial policy, according them with implicit protection that offset the detrimental impact of overvalued exchange rates on exports. This type of targetting required fine-tuning of import, export, and industrial policies.

Import policies severely restricted importation of final products and especially of consumer goods. The whole arsenal of tools for import restrictions was used very effectively: discriminatory tariffs, quotas and nontariff barriers, variable levies and minimum price systems. The list of commodities under import restrictions was large. In combination with low or no tariffs for the preferential imports of raw materials, the system yielded in 1961 as low a ratio of tariff revenues to imports as that of the United States, Germany, France or Italy (Komiya and Itoh 1988, p. 193). The difference is that in Japan, low tariff revenues were the outcome of total control of imports; in the other countries they were due to reasonably free trade at low tariff rates.

The barriers to trade erected at the Japanese borders started coming down rapidly in the mid-1960s, after the Kennedy Round was completed. At that time, the importance of the distribution system as a nontransparent barrier to imports increased. The wholesale distribution system was dominated by few well-established trading companies and it was designed to provide industry with the raw materials and components it needed and to secure domestic outlets for the industry's output. Few consumer goods imports would trickle through that system, and where they did they were effectively blocked at the retail level. The retail distribution system was built around the 'papa-mama' (family-operated small) stores and was too fragmented and unsophisticated for handling foreign merchandise. The system plowed back into pluralistic economic development the economic rents of currency overvaluation instead of leaking them out to consumer imports benefitting the elites.

Early Japanese exports concentrated on labor intensity and cheapness: textiles, light industry products, inexpensive cameras and so on. Those achieved notoriety in the 'dollar-blouse' trade war with the United States in the late 1950s. It is less well known, however, that in the early 1950s, and while unemployment was still high, Japan had already made the decision to extricate itself from labor-intensive, low value-added exports. The criteria for 'heavy and chemical industrialization' laid down by MITI favored the development of dynamic comparative advantage down the road: capital intensive, high-technology, high value-added industries which were facing high income elasticity of demand for their products (and possibly low price elasticity) and had the potential of accruing high economic rents. The 'Okano Plan' was formally adopted in 1954.

The main scope of industrial policy was to sequence the leading sectors in the economy according to the requirements of the broadly growing domestic demand. In the process, domestic production was geared to reaching an early threshold of economies of scale so that each sector, in sequence, was launched into the export market. This was the basic component of the 'shifting band of protection' of the Japanese industry (Krugman 1987).

In discussing Japanese industrial policy it is helpful to distinguish three broad groups of industries.

First, industrial policy mildly but successfully discouraged tourist development, supermarkets, shopping centers or fast-food restaurants. One can think of ex post ratiocinations for such disfavor, including the high leakage through imports that those industries have and their negative impact on the marginal propensity to save. Although the initial rationale for such policy is unclear, the effect was still visible to the casual observer in the early 1990s.

The second group includes some industries that came into prominence in the 1950s, before the industrial policy was fully articulated: sewing machines, cameras, bicycles, motorcycles, pianos, zippers and transistor radios. These industries were treated with benign neglect on the grounds that they were no longer infant industries and they could continue to rely on strong domestic demand to prosper. Another group was added in the mid-1960s, presumably also on the grounds that the strong domestic demand emanating from the overall industrial policy was already providing sufficient stimulus. It included color televisions, tape recorders, magnetic recording tape, audio equipment, fishing gear, watches and clocks, calculators, electric wire, machine tools, numerically controlled machine tools, textile machinery, agricultural machinery, insulators, communications equipment, ceramics and robots.

Finally, the third group belonged squarely to the 'heavy and chemical industry' classification and became by commission the main beneficiary of the industrial policy. It included electricity, iron and steel, shipbuilding, merchant marine, machine industries in general, heavy electrical equipment, and chemicals; to which later were added automotives, petrochemicals, nuclear power, computers, semiconductors and related industries. The famed shifting band of protection applied fully to these industries, focussing on one at a time, bringing it up to the level of world competition, and moving on to the next.

Both general policies and specifically targetted policies were used to achieve cost reduction in the heavy and chemical industry, the priority industrial group. The fiscal measures included accelerated depreciation and tariff exemptions for 'important' machinery, exemptions from import and other taxes for important raw materials and property tax exemptions for facilities that were 'modernized'. These exemptions were substantial, totaling 5.7 percent of corporate tax receipts in fiscal year 1955 (Kosai 1988, p. 35).

Government financing of priority industries came to 28.3 percent of the total credit to industry extended in the period 1952-55, excluding loans from the World Bank and foreign currency lending by the Bank of Japan. Government credit was extended at preferential rates, although the extent of the subsidy involved was not always clear. Shipbuilding was probably the exception where important interest subsidies were involved, amounting to yen 10.3 billion in the period 1953-57 (ibid., p. 36).

Industrial policy focussed on 'industrial rationalization', which had as major components guarding against insufficient scale and preventing excessive competition. In industries with many suppliers and low market concentration, industrial policy attempted to coordinate the division of products among firms, to foster a system of specialized producers and to develop cooperation in production. Control of imports was a most important component in preventing excessive competition. Given an environment of restricted imports, licensing of foreign capital (including foreign borrowing), purchases of foreign technology, and imports of foreign machinery became control instruments of industrial policy. The policy of permitting initial but not subsequent items to be imported was beneficial to the development of domestic industry through imitation (ibid., p. 43).

Integrity

Emphasis on domestic demand flies in the face of the conventional 'thaumatological' explanations of Japan that pivot around export growth. This conventional interpretation of the Japanese experience often disregards the facts. The share of exports in GNP was 10.5 percent in 1965 and rose to 13.5 percent in 1986, which in either case is much lower than that of other industrialized countries with the exception of the United States which has a share of 5.1 percent. In comparison, the share of exports in GNP was one-third in pre-war Japan (Johnson 1982, p. 16).

The role of domestic demand received full recognition first in the early 1950s, when the Okano Plan saw 'heavy and chemical industrialization' as the means of extricating Japan from recurring balance-of-payments constraints. The intent was to have MITI promote exports and domestic demand countercyclically. Exports were to gain importance during the period in the cycle when current account account deficits increased as a result of importing raw materials and intermediate products to satisfy the growing domestic demand (ibid., p. 229).

An effect of learning by using can be hypothesized to explain how the development of domestic demand could provide a testing ground for Japanese manufactures before they were launched into export markets (Rosenberg 1982, ch. 6). This seems to be consistent with the Japanese experience where the growth of such industries as automobiles, household electric appliances, pianos and integrated circuits (for example, calculators) was heavily leveraged on domestic demand, and the products that developed in the process reflected the tastes of Japanese consumers. However, I know of no existing formal test of the hypothesis, although Figure 4.1 provides some circumstantial evidence at a level of high

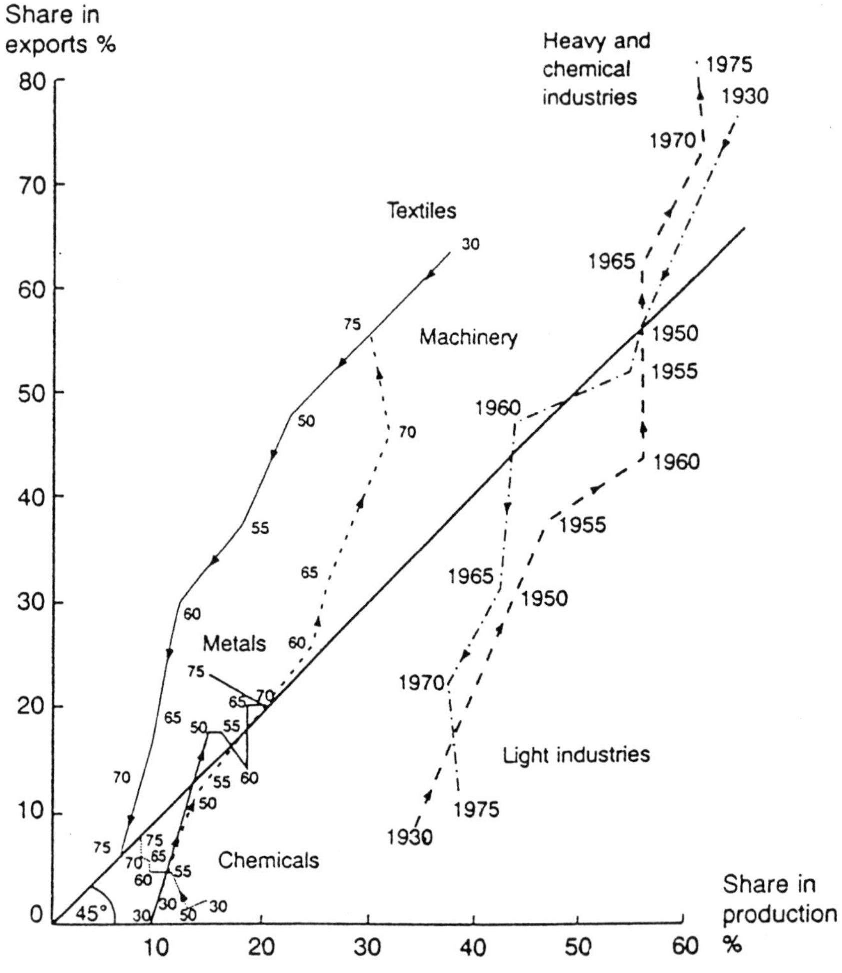

Source: Itoh and Kiyono (1988, p. 156), by permission of the publisher.

Figure 4.1 Shifts in Japanese industrial structure and patterns of trade, 1930-75

aggregation (Itoh and Kiyono 1988, p. 156). One can consider observations above the 45° line as export driven, while those below are domestic-demand induced. The entire phase of textile manufacturing (including the period before the war) was export driven, and the same is true for the early phase of light industries (among others, transistor radios and cameras), which, however, became domestic-demand driven in the 1960s. The heavy and chemical industries, on the other hand, and machinery, started with a high proportion of their output absorbed by the domestic market in order to mature in the 1960s into important export industries.

Industrial policy played a direct role in ushering along the consumer revolution. The sectoral sequencing was coordinated with the income elasticities of demand of increasingly affluent consumers, and the Ministry of Finance managed to adjust excise taxes on specific domestic goods at the opportune times to induce a wave of purchases. This gave rise to the particularly Japanese phenomenon of synchronous acquisition of the same good by the majority of households: 'the three sacred treasures',[18] television, washing machine and refrigerator in the early 1960s, or the 'three c's', car, cooler and color TV in the late 1960s. Table 4.5 adds perspective to the purchasing power of 120 million consumers who shared in the benefits of pluralistic economic development. The profile of consumer demand would have been totally different if intervention had bred rent-seeking activities that concentrated the economic rents of development in the hands of the elites.

Table 4.5 Ownership of consumer durables, 1957-80 (percent)

	1957	1960	1965	1970	1975	1980
Electric washing machine	20.0	45.4	68.5	88.3	97.6	98.8
Electric refrigerator	2.8	15.7	51.4	84.6	96.7	99.1
Black and white TV	7.8	54.5	90.0	90.2	48.7	22.8
Color TV	–	–	–	26.3	90.3	98.2
Automobile	–	1.2	–	22.1	41.2	57.2

Source: Yasuba, (1991), by permission of the publisher.

In addition to the industrial policies, wage and income policies were also used to stoke development by fanning domestic demand broadly among the population. Not unlike all other (developing) countries, Japan faced the problem of keeping surplus and subqualified labor from driving wages down (which would drive the prices of tradables up in relation to nontradables) and thus lowering incomes to levels that depress effective domestic demand and trigger pressures for setting up a welfare state. Agricultural protection is one conventional mechanism for this goal. Another unconventional Japanese solution was the retail trade.

The distribution network

In 1980, wholesale and retail trade provided 40 percent of the total nonprimary sector employment. Almost all (99.5 percent) of the distribution establishments are categorized as small and medium (fewer than 300 employees). The small establishments, with four workers or less, constitute 84.1 percent of the distribution outlets, had 32.8 percent of the sales, and provided 47.9 percent of the employment of the sector (Yokokura 1988, pp. 516, 519-20). In contrast, only 3 percent of the establishments in the United States are 'papa-and-mama' family stores.

There are some good economic reasons for the preponderance of small retail outlets in a country where storage space is small and taste for freshness is strong (fish, tofu, vegetables, even rice) requiring frequent trips to the neighborhood store. There are social reasons also in a country where consumers are fastidious and they expect a pleasant mien and plenty of service. However, by far the most convincing rationale for the proliferation of small retail outlets in the Japanese cities and countryside was the employment they provided to 6.2 million people, almost 17 percent of the nonprimary sector employment. Moreover, the small stores became the residual sector that kept the marginal and the subqualified workers at work, among others the elderly and the infirm, thus weakening the pressures for a welfare state. The government, on its part, through regulatory and small business assistance policies strove to maintain incomes and to curtail excessive competition in the sector.[19]

Agriculture

Japanese agricultural policy has been remarkably pragmatic, displaying great flexibility as the economic environment was changing. During the period of 'food crisis' (1937 to early 1950s) strict rationing and price controls of agricultural commodities were practiced. During the 'food problem period' (1950s to early 1960s) of low income levels and high Engel coefficients of demand, the escalation of food prices was contained in order to protect the real incomes of the working classes. Of the two available mechanisms for doing that job, food subsidies at the consumption level, and price controls at the production level, Japan opted for the latter mechanism, instituting a guaranteed 'parity price' which actually amounted to compulsory delivery of rice by producers at prices below the market equilibrium level (Hayami 1988, p. 43).

Japan's graduation into the 'farm problem' was swift. At higher income levels a combination of factors contributes to a huge transfer of income and of resources out of agriculture: lower Engel coefficients, slowing population growth rate, increasing (absolute) agricultural productivity that accounts for an elastic supply of food. They all lead to declining prices, reflected in the shift of the domestic terms of trade against agriculture. The disparity between agricultural and nonagriculturral incomes sets in motion huge transfers of resources out of agriculture.

Table 4.6 indicates that this stage occurred in Japan sometime in the 1960s, but the process of 'agricultural adjustment' was gradual. With the onset of the farm problem one would have expected the agriculture/ manufacturing terms of trade to decline, reflecting lower agricultural prices. Instead they were relatively stable (and in favor of agriculture) in 1955 and 1960 and they improved by another 75 percent by 1970. The analysis of these trends provides a useful insight into the role that agriculture played in fomenting the Japanese Miracle.

Besides social and political considerations, there exist solid economic reasons that explain Japanese 'agricultural protectionism': to advance the 'turning point', where wages start increasing, by prematurely exhausting the unlimited supplies of labor (Fei and Ranis 1964). This safeguards pluralistic economic development and the industrial demand linkages that follow. Unless surplus labor is contained, increases in agricultural productivity, and conceivably in incomes, will not be forthcoming. Moreover, pressure from rural-urban migration will thwart increases in productivity, wages and incomes in the industrial sector. While this is rather commonsensical with conventional wisdom, the exclusive reliance on the absorptive capacity of the industrial sector for exhausting the unlimited supplies of labor is naive and dangerous. Development is not promoted by substituting labor-intensive industry for labor-intensive agriculture. Japan has demonstrated that there is a combination of policies that can do the job better: modernizing agriculture; providing ample agricultural infrastructure, moving the factories closer to the farms, so that agricultural incomes are augmented by non-farm wage earnings; and, especially, by providing protection and price support to agriculture. Agricultural protection amounts to increasing the value of the marginal product of agricultural labor, although its physical product might not have increased commensurately. All that matters for the turning point to occur is that marginal productivity in agriculture increases. It helps if this is done through increasing yields, although in the face of the 'farm problem' this cornucopia may be uncomfortable. But it can also be done through agricultural protection, that is, by taxing the consumers at large.

Careful examination of Table 4.6 shows the results of agricultural protection in terms of relative incomes, and reveals indirectly an additional rationale for income policies favoring agriculture: providing employment to subqualified labor. The disparity between income from agriculture and income from wage employment (off-farm) per farm household started from a ratio of 1:1.4 in 1955 and widened to a ratio of 1:5 in 1985. Since income from agriculture reflects the effects of price supports, protection alone has not been intended to stem the flow of resources out of agriculture. Instead, the importance of off-farm income for the farm household, which rises from 28 percent of the total in 1955 to 85 percent in 1985, indicates that protection had an important effect in lengthening and smoothing out the adjustment process. Moreover, considering both agricultural and off-farm income, income parity with the urban worker household, on a per member basis, was achieved and exceeded some time after 1970.

The bottom panel of Table 4.6 shows that full-time farm households have lower agricultural income than part-time I households, defined as farms with farm income larger than off-farm income. This seeming paradox is explained by the high proportion of full-time agricultural households that have no member below 65 years old – 38 percent the total number of full-time farms (Hayami 1988, p.91). Full-time agriculture thus served the purpose of keeping off the welfare rolls subqualified workers who were too old to work hard on the farm, let alone to accept off-farm employment. Among agricultural commodities, rice was the crop ideally suited for 'old-age farming'. It was a high-value crop (at Japanese prices). Its marketing was handled exclusively by the government and thus required little managerial input. With huge public inputs in research and extension it had become highly standardized to the point that there was little difference in productivity between part-time, full-time, young or elderly farmers (Hayami 1988, p. 90).

Postscript

To many Western observers Japanese industrialization seemed counterintuitive in the period before the Second World War. As an example, the noted American demographer Warren S. Thompson (1929) posed the question whether Japan could ever become a great manufacturing nation and answered it with a resounding 'No!' After the devastation of the war, a Japanese miracle seemed even more improbable. Again Thompson (1950), as an example, repeated his earlier prediction based on pessimism about labor relations, industrial prospects and trade

Table 4.6 Comparisons of income levels between farm households and urban worker households in Japan

Year	Farm household income (000 yen)[1]: Per household[2]: Agriculture (1)	Farm household income: Per household: Off-farm[3] (2)	Farm household income: Per household: Total (3)	Farm household income: Per household member (4)	Urban worker household income (000 yen): Per household (5)	Urban worker household income: Per household member (6)	Relative income: Per household (3/5) (7)	Relative income: Per household member (4/6) (8)
1955	256	102	358	57	350	74	102	77
	(72)	(28)	(100)					
1960	225	224	449	78	502	115	89	68
	(50)	(50)	(100)					
1965	356	470	835	157	797	194	105	81
	(44)	(56)	(100)					
1970	508	1084	1592	326	1390	358	115	91
	(32)	(68)	(100)					
1975	1146	2815	3961	867	2897	760	137	114
	(29)	(71)	(100)					
1980	952	4651	5603	1273	4254	1111	132	115
	(17)	(83)	(100)					
1985	1065	5860	6926	1596	5388	1422	128	112
	(15)	(85)	(100)					
1985								
Full-time	2520	1969	4489	1207	5388	1422	83	85
	(56)	(44)	(100)					
Part-time I[3]	4124	3275	7399	1465	5388	1422	137	103
	(56)	(44)	(100)					
Part-time II[4]	495	6971	7466	1682	5388	1422	39	118
	(7)	(93)	(100)					

Notes

[1] Off-farm income includes private grants and government transfer payments.

[2] Percentage shares are shown in parentheses.

[3] Farms with farm income greater than off-farm income.

[4] Farms with farm income less than off-farm income

Source. Hayami (1988, pp. 92-3), with permission of the publisher.

opportunities. *Ex post,* the same episodic approach and special traits have been used to rationalize the emergence of Japan into top economic prominence in the world. The 'revisionist' approach amounts to discounting any lessons that could have been derived from Japan's economic development because its citizens are either 'superhuman' (cultural homogeneity, high savings rates, and so on), or 'subhuman' (misers, low consumption rates, and so on).

The sympathetic interpretation in this paper suggests that the Japanese Miracle was indeed impressive, especially because its traditional ingredients were unremarkable. The initial conditions in Japan after the War were none too dissimilar from those faced by other developing countries; the initial constraints were often more binding. Export policies, in comparison with other countries, were tame; exports did not drive development in the early period, contrary to the conventional wisdom.

The unorthodox components of the Japanese development success – and ditto for the Taiwanese – are, however, noteworthy. In our analytical framework a distortion inherent in free-currency markets makes developing countries systematically misallocate resources. The need for state intervention was fostered upon Japan in an attempt to avoid 'trade bias' and the misallocation of resources that entails. State intervention in the process of development is widespread, and therefore unremarkable. The remarkable feature of Japanese industrial policy was that it picked the winners – the industries which had dynamic comparative advantage down the road. This is due less to an uncanny instinct possessed by Japanese bureaucrats; it is more related to the paramount role that domestic demand played in Japanese economic development. The sequence of industrialization went in tandem with the increasing levels of consumption enjoyed by the majority of the population through an economic strategy that spread broadly the rents of economic development. In the model of state-led capitalism that Japan exemplifies, pluralistic development may well have been the cause, as opposed to the result, of the Japanese Miracle.

5 CONCLUSIONS

This chapter is of the incomplete-market variety, and it is cast within an endogenous growth framework. The strong empirical link between overriding foreign exchange (and trade) markets and the rate of growth of real GDP is remarkable, and to some extent preternatural. While intervention is necessary in incomplete markets, the success of intervention is conditional on the agent of intervention, the government. Despite that, an adequate variable for good governance has not been introduced in the endogenous growth model. The case studies of the management of Japanese and Taiwanese economic development under incomplete markets were intended to make amends for that omission by focussing on the two components of good governance. Competence in government consists of identifying the markets that require intervention and those that do not, and intervening in the former for supporting, as opposed to supplanting the market. Integrity consists of capturing the economic rents of market incompleteness and plowing them back into the process of development, as opposed to using them for self-serving purposes. The broadly-based increase in incomes that follows makes domestic demand the powerful locomotive of growth.

The diagnosis of market incompleteness in foreign exchange (and trade) and the policy prescription of intervention – the need for which systematically decreases with the level of development – is unorthodox. Nevertheless, it is grounded on pragmatism, and it has been consonant with development policy since the beginning of the new development era, and long before the sea-change happened in the mainstream view toward the indiscriminate liberalization and globalization of the process of development. All the same, the preconditions of good governance are strict; and many a country that loses sight of that fact faces the risk of moving back into the future with intervention. The second objective, therefore, of the two case studies of development success is learning from Japan and Taiwan.

NOTES

1. Revisionism basically rejects the view that capitalism and democracy are fundamentally the same everywhere and suggests that Japan, as well as the other success cases in Southeast Asia, operated along a different set of cultural, economic and political imperatives. Revisionism originated with Japan and is usually attributed to Johnson (1982) – which is a trifle unjust. The crop of this genre of literature is considerable and it includes, among others, Prestowitz (1988), van Wolferen (1989) and Fallows (1989). More recently it appears that bashing Japan* has been turned on its head by certain Asian politicians who needed a moral high chair to gloat about economic success.
2. Asymmetric reputation in this context is different from credibility that entered the literature on foreign exchange management following the seminal article of Barro and Gordon (1983). In this literature, reputation is related to time inconsistency with policy-makers reneging on their commitment to target one of the two alternative targets, the inflation rate or the balance of payments. For examples of this literature, see Agènor (1994) and references therein.
3. Would the process not make N relatively scarce and help restore equilibrium? This is the classical textbook case. But the answer is 'no' in incomplete markets where there is 'bad competition' that sets off a race for the exit of currency

substitution.

4. For detailed methodology of constructing the *RER* index see Yotopoulos (1996, ch. 6).
5. For a definition of variables see immediately below, and Table 4.2.
6. For the complete specification of the model and the derivation of the reduced form equation, see Yotopoulos (1996, ch. 7).
7. Such tests were performed and are reported in the parent study. The assumption that the right-hand-side variables of the model are truly exogenous was tested explicitly. Moreover, a simultaneous equation model was formulated with G_t, *RER*, and *INV* determined endogenously. The results of the reported formulation were proven extremely robust (Yotopoulos 1996, ch. 7).
8. In any event, a case can be made that the last two are causally related and by imposing restrictions on both currency substitution and short-term capital the instability in exchange rates (and in interest rates) plus some incremental weakness in the fundamentals through higher current account deficits, can be alleviated.
9. There was a small appreciation of the NT$ in 1973, and a general appreciating trend after the introduction of the (guided) float in 1978.
10. For a detailed account of the monetary policy of Taiwan, see Chiu (1992) and Liu (1992).
11. It is estimated that the net productivity of capital was 25 percent in the 1960s, 20 percent in the 1970s, and 15 percent in the 1980s (Fry 1989).
12. The estimated long-run GNP elasticity of the real demand for money is 1.7 (Chiu 1992).
13. The ratio of M2 (currency, quasi-money and deposits) to GNP was 9 percent in 1955 and 56 percent in 1975, thus approaching that of Japan in just two decades (Lundberg 1979). By 1990 that ratio was 141 percent (Republic of China 1997).
14. With the exception of treasury bills, all other money market instruments, including bankers' acceptances, certificates of deposits and commercial paper, increased by multiple factors for a few years in a row, in comparison to total loans that were increasing at the rate of 20 percent (Kuo 1983, ch. 15).
15. For a detailed chronology of the policy interventions in the Taiwan economy, see Li (1988).
16. For instance, there still remains an overall limit in foreign investment in Taiwan's stock exchange (effectively at about 7 percent of the market's capitalization); no more than one-tenth of a company's stock can be owned by foreigners; and the Central Bank drags its feet in processing investment applications from foreigners (US$4 billion worth are still pending in mid-1994).
17. The importance of domestic demand for self-sustained economic growth has also been emphasized by various writers, from the big-push theorists (Rosenstein-Rodan 1943) to the demand-linkage practitioners (Hirschman 1958; Yotopoulos and Nugent 1976, ch. 15). For more recent interest in the role of demand growth in economic development, see Eswaren and Kotwal (1993) and Rodrik (1996).
18. The analogy refers to the three sacred treasures possessed by the Emperor, the mirror, the bowl and the sword, that confirm his divine origins according to the Shinto religion.

19. Entry in the distribution sector is tightly controlled, with the paperwork at times requiring up to ten years. For other details see Yokoyura (1988), Yotopoulos (1996), and Upham (1993).

REFERENCES

Agènor, Pierre-Richard (1994), 'Credibility and Exchange Rate Management in Developing Countries', *Journal of Development Economics,* 45, October, 1-16.

Barro, Robert J. and David B. Gordon (1983), 'Rules, Discretion and Reputation in a Model of Monetary Policy', *Journal of Monetary Economics,* 12, July, 101-21.

Caprio, Gerard and Lawrence Summers (1993), 'Finance and its Reform: Beyond Laissez-Faire', *The World Bank: Policy Research Working Paper*, WPS 1171.

Chiu, Paul C.H. (1992), 'Money and Financial Markets: The Domestic Perspective', in Gustav Ranis (ed.), *Taiwan: From Developing to Mature Economy*, Boulder, CO: Westview Press, 121-93.

Corden, Warner M. and J. Peter Neary (1982), 'Booming Sector and De-industrialization in a Small Open Economy', *Economic Journal*, 92, December, 825-48.

Edwards, Sebastian (1993), 'Openness, Trade Liberalization, and Growth in Developing Countries', *Journal of Economic Literature*, 31, September, 1358-93.

Eswaren, Mukesh and Ashok Kotwal (1993), 'A Theory of Real Wage Growth in LDCs', *Journal of Development Economics*, 42, December, 243-69.

Fallows, James (1989), 'Containing Japan', *The Atlantic Monthly,* May, 40-54.

Fei, John C.H. and Gustav Ranis (1964), *Development of the Surplus Labor Economy: Theory and Policy,* Homewood, IL: Irwin.

Floro, Sagrario L. and Pan A. Yotopoulos (1991), *Informal Credit Markets and the New Institutional Economics: The Case of Philippine Agriculture*, Boulder, CO: Westview Press.

Fry, Maxwell J. (1989), 'The Rate of Return to Taiwan's Capital Stock, 1961-1987', *Hong Kong Economic Papers*, 20, 17-30.

Grossman, Gene M. and Elhanan Helpman (1990), 'Comparative Advantage and Long-run Growth', *American Economic Review*, 80, September, 796-815.

Grossman, Gene M. and Elhanan Helpman (1992), *Innovation and Growth in the Global Economy*, Cambridge, MA: MIT Press.

Hamada, Koichi and Hugh T. Patrick (1988), 'Japan and the International Monetary Regime', in Takashi Inoguchi and Daniel I. Okimoto (eds), *The Political Economy of Japan*, Vol. II, Stanford, CA: Stanford University Press. 108-37.

Hayami, Yujiro (1988), *Japanese Agriculture under Siege: The Political Economy of Agricultural Policies*, London: Macmillan.

Hirschman, Albert O. (1958), *The Strategy of Economic Development*, New Haven, CT: Yale University Press.

Itoh, Motoshige and Kazuaru Kiyono (1988), 'Foreign Trade and Direct Investment', in Ryutaro Komiya, Masahiro Okuno and Kotaro Suzumura (eds), *Industrial Policy of Japan*, New York, NY: Academic Press, pp. 155-81.

Jaffe, Dwight M. and Thomas Russel (1976), 'Imperfect Information and Credit Rationing', *Quarterly Journal of Economics*, 90, November, 651-66.

Johnson, Chalmers (1982), *MITI and the Japanese Miracle: The Growth of Industrial Policy, 1925-1975*, Stanford, CA: Stanford University Press.

Komiya, Ryutaro and Motoshige Itoh (1988), 'Japan's International Trade and Trade Policy, 1955-1984', in Takashi Inoguchi and Daniel I. Okimoto (eds), *The Political Economy of Japan*, Vol. II, Stanford, CA: Stanford University Press, 173-224.

Kosai, Yutaka (1988), 'The Reconstruction Period', in Ryutaro Komiya, Masahiro Okuno and Kotaro Suzumura (eds), *Industrial Policy of Japan*, New York, NY: Academic Press, 25-48.

Kravis, Irving B., A. Heston and R. Summers (1982), *World Product and Income: International Comparisons of Real Gross Product*, Baltimore, MD: Johns Hopkins University Press.

Krueger, Anne O. (1974), 'The Political Economy of the Rent-Seeking Society', *American Economic Review*, 64, June, 291-303.

Krugman, Paul (1987), 'The Narrow Moving Band, the Dutch Disease, and the Competitive Consequences of Mrs. Thatcher: Notes on Trade in the Presence of Dynamic Economies of Scale', *Journal of Development Economics*, 27, October, 41-55.

Krugman, Paul (1995), 'Dutch Tulips and Emerging Markets', *Foreign Affairs*, 74, July/August, 28-44.

Kuo, Shirley W.Y. (1983), *The Taiwan Economy in Transition*, Boulder, CO: Westview Press.

Leamer, Edward F. (1983), 'Let's Take the Con out of Econometrics', *American Economic Review*, 73, March, 31-43.

Leamer, Edward F. (1985), 'Sensitivity Analyses Would Help', *American Economic Review*, 75, June, 308-13.

Levine, Ross and David Renelt (1992), 'A Sensitivity Analysis of Cross-Country Growth Regressions', *American Economic Review*, 82, September, 942-63.

Li, K.T. (1988), *The Evolution of Policy behind Taiwan's Development Success*, New Haven, CT: Yale University Press.

Liu, Christina Y. (1992), 'Money and Financial Markets: The International Prespective', in Gustav Ranis (ed.), *Taiwan: From Developing to Mature Economy*, Boulder, CO: Westview Press, 195-221.

Lundberg, Erik (1979), 'Fiscal and Monetary Policies', in Walter Galenson (ed.), *Economic Growth and Structural Change in Taiwan*, Ithaca, NY: Cornell University Press, 263-307.

Pack, Howard (1994), 'Endogenous Growth Theory: Intellectual Appeal and Empirical Shortcomings', *Journal of Economic Perspectives*, 8, Winter, 55-72.

Prestowitz, Clyde V., Jr. (1988), *Trading Places*, New York, NY: Basic Books.

Rodrik, Dani (1995), 'Trade and Industrial Policy Reform', in Jere Behrman and T.N. Srinivasan (eds), *Handbook of Development Economics*, Vol. III B, Amsterdam: North-Holland, 2925-82.

Rodrik, Dani (1996), 'Coordination Failures and Government Policy: A Model with Applications to East Asia and Eastern Europe', *Journal of International Economics*, 40, February, 1-22.

Rosenberg, Nathan (1982), *Inside the Black Box*, New York: Cambridge University Press.

Rosenstein-Rodan, Paul N. (1943), 'Problems of Industrialization in Eastern and Southeastern Europe', *Economic Journal*, 53, June/September, 202-12.

Solow, Robert M. (1994), 'Perspectives on Growth Theory', *Journal of Economic Perspectives*, 8, Winter, 45-54.

Stiglitz, Joseph E. and Andrew Weiss (1981), 'Credit Rationing in Markets with Imperfect Information', *American Economic Review*, 71, June, 393-410.

Thompson, Warren S. (1929), *Danger Spots in World Population*, New York, NY : A.A. Knopf.

Thompson, Warren S. (1950), 'Future Adjustments of Population to Resources in Japan', *Modernization Programs in Relation to Human Resources and Population Problems*, Milbank Memorial Fund, New York, NY, 142-53; reprinted in *Population and Development Review*, 7, March 1981, 111-17.

Upham, Frank K. (1993), 'Privatizing Regulation: The Implementation of the Large Scale Retail Stores Law', in Gary D. Allinson and Yasunori

Sone (eds), *Political Dynamics in Contemporary Japan*, Ithaca, NY: Cornell University Press, 264-94.

van Wolferen, Karel (1989), *The Enigma of Japanese Power*, New York, NY: Random House.

World Bank (1992), *World Development Report 1992*, New York, NY: Oxford University Press.

World Bank (1993), *The Asian Miracle: Economic Growth and Public Policy*, New York, NY: Oxford University Press.

Yasubu, Yasukichi (1991), 'Japan's Post-war Growth is Historical Perspective', *Japan Forum*, 3 April, 57-70.

Yokoyura, Takashi (1988), 'Small and Medium Enterprises', in Ryutaro Komiya, Masahiro Okuno and Kotaro Suzumura (eds), *Industrial Policy of Japan*, New York, NY: Academic Press, 513-39.

Yotopoulos, Pan A. (1996), *Exchange Rate Parity for Trade and Development: Theory, Tests, and Case Studies*, London and New York, NY: Cambridge University Press.

Yotopoulos, Pan A. and Jeffrey B. Nugent (1976), *Economics of Development: Empirical Investigations*, New York, NY: Harper & Row.

5. Initial Pre-takeoff Conditions and Stages of Growth

Anthony Y.C. Koo*

1 INTRODUCTION

After a period of quiescence in the 1960s and 1970s, development and growth economics have again become an active area of inquiry in theoretical as well as empirical approaches. Two factors may have been responsible for the resurgence of interest. The spectacular success of the East Asian economies, notably, the four tigers (Hong Kong, Korea, Singapore and Taiwan) has focussed the attention of growth and development analysts on the lessons of what we can or cannot infer. The emergence of endogenous growth theory by Romer (1986) and Lucas (1988) is in answer to the challenge of the neoclassical growth theory of Ramsey (1928) and Solow (1956) which states that growth is necessarily subject to diminishing returns and except for (exogenous) technical change determined outside the model, is independent of preference, most aspects of production function and policy behavior, and that there is a tendency for convergence to a steady state of constant per capita income worldwide. On that interpretation, poor and developing countries would undergo a period of rapid growth and would eventually decelerate as the income gap closes.

In reality, different nations have maintained different per capita growth rates over long periods of time and these rates seem to be systematically related to various national features. For instance, the middle-income countries tended to grow more rapidly than low-income countries – an empirical regularity that seems to contradict the catchup or convergence hypothesis. In fact, in the original growth-accounting literature, Solow's residuals were a puzzle in that they represented portions of growth that

* I wish to thank Professors Henry Y. Wan Jr. of Cornell University and John A. Strauss of Michigan State University for their comments and suggestions. Needless to add, I am alone responsible for any errors and shortcomings that remain.

his model cannot explain, whatever interpretation one may invoke. Do large residuals show a deficiency of assumptions (such as constant returns) that underlie the regression? Sophisticated models have since been created to account for technical changes embodied in capital or in labor. If the unit of manhours for 'labor input' produces large residuals, then the researcher may want to improve the labor input variable by including 'education', 'years of experience', and so on, to take into account the quality of labor.

The kernel of endogenous growth theory is that the accumulation of knowledge or externality is not subject to diminishing returns. Once growth starts, there are factors that will contribute to its perpetuation.

The availability of the UN cross-section data covering most members has inspired cross-section regression to test, among others, the relevance of endogenous growth theory versus neoclassical growth theory. A number of researchers have found a significant relationship between a variety of variables such as average share of investment and average of exports of GNP and growth rates. But cross-country comparisons of growth rates are always complicated by the difficulty of controlling political and social variables that appear to influence growth rates strongly. Krager also points out that the investment shares and trade export/import shares of GDP are not policy variables and that quantification of policy variables across countries is difficult and external events may have different impacts on different countries as countries' initial conditions can be significantly different (Krager 1995 p. 25). As an example, one should distinguish between growth and development. Growth theory applies more appropriately to industrialized countries where income changes are the main concern, while development theory attempts to explain and elucidate the process of qualitative change from an agrarian society to a modern industrial economy. In the course, the economy will take off, to be followed by sustained growth. There will be a change in the components of exports and imports as industrialization proceeds. Savings rates will also increase as growth rates accelerate.

Thus Krager aptly raised the question whether one might not better undertake analysis in individual countries, especially since one's focus is not on international differences in income level but in a model designed to provide understanding about growth and development.

This chapter begins by emphasizing the importance of initial conditions and the social cultural milieu within which the economy operates.[1] In Section 3, I argue that the prevailing growth contributions left out or pay insufficient attention to the old-fashioned idea of stages of growth (Rostow) because the latter, I believe, gives one deeper insight into the growth process by uncovering the relative role of new and growing versus old and declining sectors. In Section 4, I attempt to show two possible growth contours, one by the stages of growth and the other by aggregate income, and to show that one complements the other.

2 INITIAL CONDITIONS

The importance of initial conditions for economic take-off and growth can be supported on both theoretical and empirical grounds. Actual equilibrium in theoretical models where multiple equilibria exist depends upon initial conditions as illustrated by Krugman in a simple but ingenious model in which the relative importance of the past and expected future will determine the final outcome (Krugman 1991). In an empirical investigation, Rodrik traced the average growth of income per person in 44 countries during 1960-85 back to the initial conditions in 1960 and found that countries that were poor but had good primary education systems and less inequality of income and wealth distribution around 1960 grew faster than others during the following period (Rodrik 1994).[2] Undoubtedly, Rodrik's findings are significant but upon closer examination they are the derivatives of even more basic conditions or alternatively represent the result of prior institutional arrangements in the country and the social and cultural background of its people. The role of government policy in achieving relative equitable income and wealth distribution is obvious. Even the level of education achievement is the result of the supply by government of schooling and the demand for education by its citizens. To quote an adage, one can lead a horse to water but one cannot make it drink. Thus the initial conditions as found by Rodrik should be explored further to include more basic factors such as political stability and the cultural values of the people. I shall look at these in the following subsections.

2.1 Political Stability

The link between political stability and economic takeoff and growth is obvious and close. We face uncertainty in human interaction. To reduce such uncertainty, we have to structure human interaction in an institutional framework that reduces that uncertainty. An institutional framework is made up of formal rules such as constitutions, statute law, common law, and so on. Equally important are norms of behavior, conventions and codes of conduct for informal constraints (cultural value). There are also ways whereby rules are enforced. After all, an institution is no more effective than the degree to which the members of the society either live up to and live by that rule, or are forced to live by it. Regardless of the political system political stability implies all these: the transparency of formal rules, the informal norms of behavior and the degree to which they are enforced. No economy will have sustained growth until it has a stable political structure. After political stability comes macroeconomic stability meaning, at the very least, no runaway inflation or constant threat of inflation. More generally, the government must establish as a policy of priority, basic social overhead infrastructure, be capable of organizing the nation so that there exist unified factor and product markets, and develop, create and maintain a tax and fiscal system which directs resources from waste into productive uses. It must lead the way through the whole system of national policy from education to public health.

2.2 Cultural Value

In light of the economic success of the four tigers in East Asia, we will look at a common feature in their traditional culture – that is Confucianism. Confucianism attaches a high value to human dignity which is strengthened by dedication to education and the self-imposed moral discipline of diligence and frugality. In his book *Why Has Japan 'Succeeded'? Western Technology and the Japanese Ethos,* Michio Morishima defines cultural role in these terms. 'Confucianism had spread widely and deeply among Japanese people. Confucianism was understood in Japan as an ethical system rather than a religion and it directly taught Japanese people that frugal behavior was noble behavior, (Morishina 1992, p. 86). Without these values among people, there is little a government can accomplish in raising the level of education, or encouraging a propensity to save and a proclivity to diligence and hard work. Why, then, was it that the modern epoch based on science and technology did not first occur in China? – a logical question raised by John Fei (1995). He answered that people in the West were curious about the outside (physical) world, but in the case of China, the outside world was believed to be fully embodied in one's mind, that is, in the inside world. A lack of interest in, and the foundations of, natural science were the missing links that accounted for the late arrival of the modern epoch in China.

3 STAGES OF GROWTH

There are at least two methodical approaches to the study of economic growth. One is to measure growth in terms of broad aggregates (such as GNP and the proportion of income invested) or one links these aggregates to movements in sectors within which new technologies are absorbed and generate a rise in output and income. In his study *Modern Economic Growth*, Kuznets abandoned the earlier approach which he had expounded in *Secular Movements in Production and Prices*. In *Modern Economic Growth*, he offered a variety of reasons, the main one being that he knew he could not establish the links between the arrival of new technologies and the growth process. It is a relationship that depends on whether the institutions of the society respond to potential spreading effects. The comparable data for a full and systematic statistical analysis on an international basis were not there. As a statistician, he chose to use the data available in which he had confidence.

The stages-of-growth as adopted by Rostow are a judgmental way of dramatizing not merely the uniformity of the sequence of economic changes but also the uniqueness of the sequence of each nation's experience.

Kuznets was once a proponent of this stages-of-growth theory:

> Some nations seem to have led the world at one time, others at another. Some industries were developing most rapidly at the beginning of the century, others at the end. Within single countries or within single branches of industries (on a world scale) there has not been uniform unretarded growth. The main reason for the shift seems to be that a rapidly developing industry does not continue its vigorous growth indefinitely, but slackens its pace after a time, and is overtaken by industries whose period of rapid development comes later. (Kuznets 1930, pp. 3-4, 10; as quoted in Rostow 1971, pp. x-xi)

We all agree that modern growth is rooted in the sequential diffusion of new technologies of two broad types, incremental and discontinuous, although one cannot generate data at this level of disaggregation to form a statistical base that permits elegant international cross-country comparison. Thus all development and growth economists are ardent users of the aggregate data as suggested by Kuznets. An analytic advantage of using the aggregate income approach means that the growth path can be treated as a continuous process which is amenable to characterization by differential equations. Unfortunately, although the approach details the incremental type of inventions and innovations yet it covers poorly the impact of technical change involving major breaks and discontinuities. While following stages of growth, the rise and decline of new and old industries cannot be expected to follow a continuous path. In short, there are elements automatically built into the nature of the growth process, such as a continuous stream of innumerable minor adjustments, modifications and adaptations by skilled technicians or treating growth as an incremental consequence of widening the market or learning by doing, but there is also a succession of challenges which must be met successfully in order to continue and prolong the growth where successful solutions are by no means automatic, as attested by the irregularities of growth. For example, for initial takeoff, a transition from predominantly traditional and agricultural society is a matter of enhancing agricultural productivity so that it will make three distinct contributions to the transition. Agricultural productivity will supply more food for domestic consumption as well as for exports. Expansion of the agricultural sector, through linkage, will enlarge demand for farm machinery, chemical fertilizer, pumps, and so on. Rising rural income will broaden a tax base for government taxes which are necessary to finance social overheads such as railways, ports, roads, public health and education. Social overhead investment is generally lumpy, has a long period of gestation and payoff and provides through indirect channels, such as a large external economy, rather than to individual investors. But in subsequent takeoffs for continued growth, investments have and will assume many different forms. There is no single pattern. The rate and productivity of investment and the consequences of its rise can be spread into several reinforcing routes by many different technical and economic conditions within different political, social and cultural settings, all driven along by a wide variety of human motivation. It is true that although economic changes have political and social consequences, economic change in itself can be viewed as the consequence of political, social and economic forces, as Keynes once remarked: 'If human nature felt no temptation to take a chance, no satisfaction (profit apart) in constructing a factory, a railway, a mine or a farm there might not be much investment merely as a result of cold calculation' (Keynes 1936, p. 50). Alternatively, social and political milieu should also be an argument of aggregate production as suggested by Adelman and Morris, Major breaks in technology will bring about impacts in the productivities of capital, labor and natural resources individually if not in the functional form of the production function.

4 CONTOUR OF HISTORICAL GROWTH

Theories about long-run growth at a constant exponential rate can be expressed by an equation, as dcseribed by Romer

$$\frac{dX}{dt} = X(t)$$

According to Romer, many theories are variations of the expression that fills in the blank and the name attached to the variable *X*. For example, in a model with exogenous technological change, *X*(*t*) is the level of technology at *t*, and a constant fills the blank. Thus the difference between endogenous and exogenous growth can easily be identified. Exogenous growth models fill in the blank with a constant while endogenous growth models fill it in with an expression that is a function of other basic parameters of the model, including parameters that are the result of policy change such as ideas and knowledge which have spillovers and external effects. We shall not get embroiled in the debate on the issue of whether there is anything really new in the recent contributions to the long-run growth process (Srinivasan). However, these concepts are helpful to those who are mainly interested in explaining the stylized facts of long-run growth in industrialized countries — or the historical sequence of growth. In Great Britain, the textile industries, which rose so spectacularly toward the end of the 18th and the beginning of the 19th centuries, ceded to pig iron, then to steel which in turn gave way to the electrical industries that assumed leadership in the 1880s and 1890s. The occurrence of these major industrial breakthroughs is hard to predict, notwithstanding considerable investment in research and development and accumulation. Leading sectors are determined not merely by the changing flow of technology but also by the changing willingness of entrepreneurs to accept the available innovation. These transitions from one major industry to another come in spurts which change the level of income but at the same time there is nothing one can infer about the rate of growth. Each country must engage in an endless struggle against deceleration and must repeat the creative reins of actually introducing a new production function. In this sense, sustained growth requires the repetition of the takeoff process. It requires the organization around new technology of new and competent management, new types of workers, new types of financing and marketing arrangements. It also requires a struggle against constraints in the previous generation for the benefit of previous leading sectors which are now defunct. These transitions are sufficiently powerful for an effective takeoff to make growth an ongoing process in the long run. Human behavior must be seen not as an act of maximization but as an act of balancing alternatives of often conflicting human objectives in the face of a range of choices which people perceive to be open which is, of course, more complex and difficult from a single maximization proposition.

Another way of assessing the contribution of successive major new industries to British growth from 1750-1990 is through the different products which dominated British exports: first woollens, then cotton, while metals and engineering products grew steadily in importance and finally with coal, chemicals and other exports outstripping textiles, as shown in Table 5.1.

In Figure 5.1, the export percentage data from Table 5.1 is plotted on the vertical axis and the years are plotted on the horizontal axis, and we see the ups and downs of various dominant British exports throughout the last two and a half centuries. What has been the contribution of leading sectors to exports over time and by inference to the growth of the whole economy? One temptation is to derive an 'envelope' curve encompassing all relevant segments of sector curves or to fit a contour by a polynomial. Since an 'envelope' curve has been used by economists in connection with a family of average cost curves, we shall avoid the term. Instead, for convenience of reference, I name it the Rostow contour. Although no simple equation can be derived to represent the contour, it shows a historical course representing what actually happened – the rise and fall of the leading sectors, the role of entrepreneurs, and the constantly changing social and economic background of social the respective deceleration of the old and take-off of the new. (See Appecdix 5A for an example based on experience in Taiwan.)

With the inspiration of the Rostow contour, in Figure 5.2 time (t) is plotted on the horizontal axis and GNP is indicated by line 1. Suppose there was a spike of growth path, say, at t, that is a shift in the level of GNP, the height of which depends on the strength of the new sector. If the spike has impacted favorably on inputs, that is, the labor supply, capital and natural resources, productivity and social and cultural milieu, then the growth path will continue at path 2. According to Solow, 'It is no mean achievement to shift the steady-state growth path upward, parallel to itself ... There is no reason in theory or practice why such temporary bursts of investment have to be reversed'. (J.S. Fuhrer and J.S. Little (eds) (1996), Technology and Growth, Federal Reserve Bank of Boston, p. 300)

What has been the overall growth of the economy over time? Again, fit a polynomial including points located on growth path at t_1, t_2, t_3 and t_4. For convenience, I name it the Kuznets contour in contrast to the Rostow sectoral contour. It is difficult to project the shape of the contour unless successive waves of new sectors occur just in time to achieve a smooth growth path. Generally, an economy will suffer a decline or downturn from time to time, due to the slowing down of technical progress, the damping effect of slower growth of complementary industries, limitation of finance to achieve large-scale operation and competition from the same industry in a younger country (with

Table 5.1 Orders of magnitude of major components of the British economy

Year	GDP (at constant price) 1800=100	Exports as % of GDP	1750-90:Proportion of total exports (%)				
			Woollens	Cottons	Metals and engineering	Coal	Other
1750	50	9	75	5	14	2	1
1800	100	8	43	32	17	3	1
1850	460	12	16	55	20	2	7
1880	810	15	12	48	25	5	10
1890	1180	15	12	40	28	9	11
1913	1930	15	9	41	22	16	12
1937	2780	13	9	22	47	12	10
1965	4860	16	3	6	47	1	43
1990	7950	17	1	1	42	1	55

Source: Robinson (1991, p. 106).

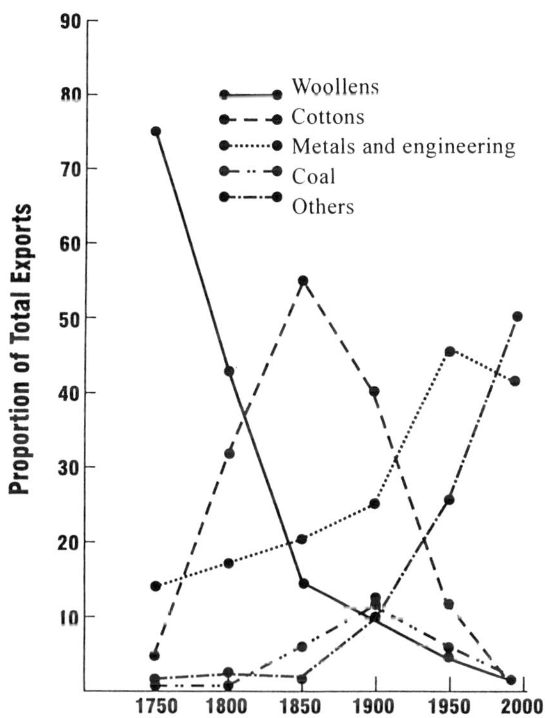

Figure 5.1 A Rostow contour

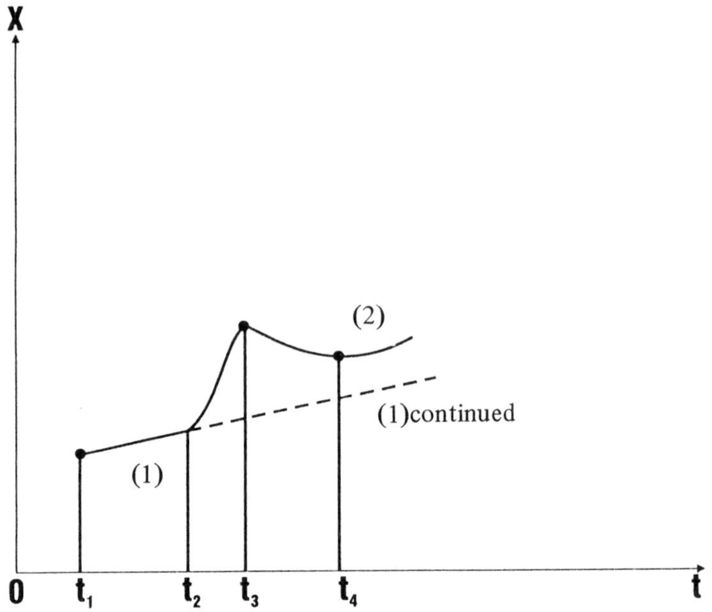

Figure 5.2 A Kuznets contour

presumably lower money cost). As a consequence, the contour will drop downward to the line 1 level or even lower. By observing the curvature of the contour between a pair of neighboring points, we can determine whether public policy intervention in the economy is called for from the perspective of influencing the growth process and, if so, what the characteristics of such an intervention should be. These are issues in which historical facts of what actually happened can provide valuable insights. Specifically, if the contribution of endogenous factor accumulation is small and an overwhelming share of observed growth is due to exogenous technical progress, then there is little that public policy can do to affect the growth process significantly. In contrast, if most growth can be attributed to factor accumulation (physical and human) then public policy can have an influence. This is not to say that the experience between two points on the contour is likely to be repeated in the future or in the developing world. In short, one needs a flexible guideline which changes with time and the political, social and economic environment such as the one proclaimed by Lincoln.[3]

Through contributions of growth-accounting, neoclassical and new growth theories, we know much about what makes a society productive and we can ask what determines the rate of growth and how to speed up the rates. From a historical perspective, we are not too clear what determines the long-term direction and speed of change of an economy or how to create sequentially the conditions contributing to growth and put them in place because here we are concerned not so much with allocative efficiency – a much-developed branch of economics – but adaptive efficiency. One is searching for the means to create a political, economic and institutional framework which over time will continue to structure the rules of the game so that we may adapt to the shocks and unexpected changes that growth inevitably involves.

Inquiry into the cause of economic growth has been an area of major concern to economists and economic historians alike. On the theoretical side of research, growth is most amenable to being expressed in differential or difference equations. Because of the mathematical framework, such models tend to view growth as a result of incremental advances in technology and the expansion of markets. On the other hand, historians generally focus their research on the revolutionary development of technology which is usually unexpected and discontinuous in nature and embedded in the social and cultural tradition of each nation. At the risk of gross oversimplification, the neoclassical and new growth theories seem to belong to the first group while the stages of growth are closer to the second approach.

5 CONCLUSIONS

This chapter attempts to find a common ground for the two alternative ways of viewing the problem by means of graphic representation. One uses the percentage of exports in total exports over time as a proxy for the rise and fall of industrial sector(s). The other relies on national income changes over time, noting occasional spikes of income which bring about the possible consequent changes in the level and rate of growth. By contrasting the two ways of looking at the issue of growth in graphic form, we can, by superimposing one contour (Rostow) on top of the other (Kuznets) with matching years, measure the leads and lags of sectoral rise and fall as compared with the income levels and rates of change. After all, they are two sides of the same coin. Additionally, by superimposing the Rostow contour of one country on top of that of another with matching years, we can measure the speed of transfer of technology between them. If we have enough of the Rostow contours of different countries, we can get some idea of the rate of diffusion of technology worldwide. Finally, the varying social and cultural milieu among nations can be related to the mathematical growth models by attributing the differences to the initial or boundary conditions.

NOTES

1. Irma Adelman and Cynthia T. Morris have pioneered and applied statistical analysis to testing the association between economic growth and a wide range of social and political variables (see Adelman and Morris 1971 and 1973).
2. Initial conditions in terms of income, education and equality levels alone can explain more than 50 percent of the variation in subsequent growth rates in the sample. The sample is restricted to countries for which distributional indicators are available. The number of observations was 41 in all regressions except one, where it was 49 (Rodrik 1998).
3. 'The legitimate object of government is to do for a community of people, whatever they need to have done, but can not do, *at all* or can not, *so well do*, for themselves – in their separate, and individual capacities' (Bresler (ed.) 1953, p. 220; emphases are in the original quotation).

REFERENCES

Adelman, Irma and C.T. Morris (1971), *Society, Politics and Economic Development,* rev. edition, Baltimore, MD: Johns Hopkins University Press.

Adelman, Irma and C.T. Morris (1973), *Economic Growth and Social Equity in Developing Countries*, Stanford, CA: Stanford University Press, New Brusswick, N.J.

Bresler, Roy P. (ed.) (1953), *Collected Works of Abraham Lincoln*, Vol. II, Rutgers University Press.

Fei, J.C.H. (1995), 'China's Cultural Value and Industrial Capitalism', in Tzong-shian Yu and Joseph Lee (eds), *Confucianism and Economic Development*, Taipei Chung-Hua Institution for Economic Research.

Fuhrer, J.C. and J.S. Little (1996), *Technology and Growth*, Conference Proceedings, Federal Reserve Bank of Boston.

Keynes, J.M. (1936), *The General Theory of Employment, Interest and Money*, New York: Harcourt, Brace & Co.

Krager, A.O. (1995), 'East Asian Experience and Endogenous Growth Theory', in T. Ito and A.O. Krager (eds), *Growth Theories in Light of the East Asian Experience*, Chicago: University of Chicago Press, 9-30.

Krugman, Paul (1991), 'History versus Expectations', *Quarterly Journal of Economics*, CVI, 651-67.

Kuznets, Simon (1930), *Secular Movements in Production and Prices*, Boston and New York: Houghton Mifflin.

Kuznets, Simon (1966), *Modern Economic Growth: Rate Structure and Spread,* New Haven, CT: Yale University Press,.

Lucas, R.E. (1988), 'On the Mechanism of Economic Development', *Journal of Monetary Economics*, 22, 8-42.

Morishima, Michio (1982), *Why Has Japan 'Succeeded'? – Western Technology and Japanese Ethos*, London: Cambridge University Press.

Ramsey, E.P. (1928), 'A Mathematical Theory of Savings', *Economic Journal*, 38, 543-59.

Robinson, Austin (1991), 'The Economics of Next Century', *Economic Journal*, 101, 94-106.

Rodrik, Dani (1994), 'King Kong Meets Godzilla: The World Bank and the East Asian Miracle', in Albert Fishlow et al. (eds), *Miracle or Design? Lessons from the East Asian Experience*, Washington, DC: Overseas Development Council, 13-53.

Romer, Paul M. (1986), 'Increasing Returns and Long-run Growth', *Journal of Political Economy*, 94(5), 1002-37.

Romer, Paul M. (1995), 'Comments', in T. Ito and A.O. Krager (eds) *Growth Theories in Light of East Asian Experience*, Chicago: University of Chicago Press, 66-70.

Rostow, W.W. (1971), *The Stages of Economic Growth*, 2nd edn, Cambridge: Cambridge University Press.

Solow, R.M. (1956), 'A Contribution to the Theory of Economic Growth', *Quarterly Journal of Economics*, 70, 65-74.

Srinivasan, T.N. (1995), 'Long-term Growth Theories and Empirics: Anything New?' in T. Ito and A.O. Krager (eds), *Growth Theories in Light of the East Asian Experience*, Chicago: University of Chicago Press, 32-66.

APPENDIX 5A

In Figure 5A.1 for a short span of Taiwan development (1949-88), we plot the percentage of two broad categories of exports: agricultural and processed agricultural goods; and industrial goods. We see that the dominance of the first category of agricultural-related goods up to the mid-1960s is followed by the spectacular rise and dominance of industrial goods.

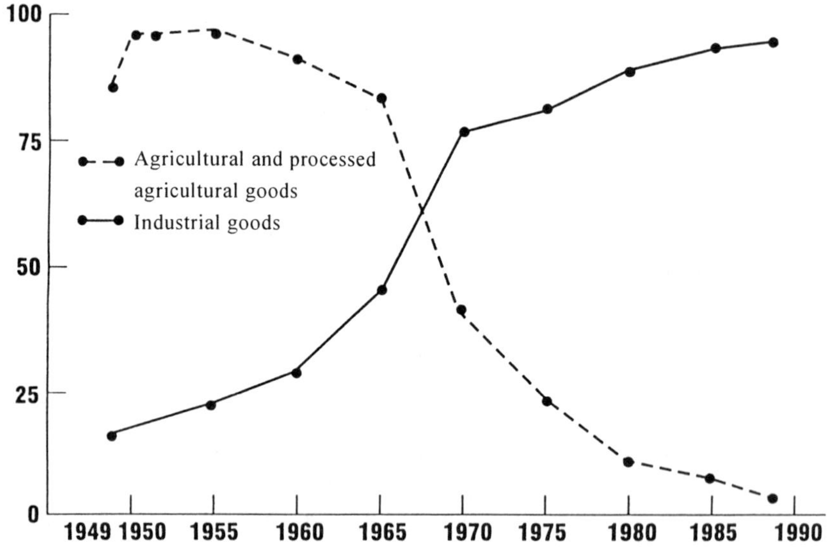

Sources: Y.F. Chen (1956), *Finance and Foreign Trade of Taiwan 1895-1955* (in Chinese) Taipei, Taiwan: San Sun Publisher, p. 179; Gustav Ranis (ed.) (1992), *Taiwan—From Developing to Mature Economy*, Figure: Commodity Composition of Exports 1952-1988 (percentages), Boulder, CO: Westview Press, p. 261.

Figure 5A.1 Taiwan's export pattern, 1949-88

6. A Dual-Dual Framework to Analyze Intersectoral Relationships throughout the Development Process

Erik Thorbecke

1 INTRODUCTION

John Fei was one of the fathers and main architects of dual models. These models yielded new and fundamental insights into the dynamics of the process of economic development. At the same time these two-sector models could not distinguish between different aspects of dualism that are endemic to developing countries. This chapter expands the analytical framework by proposing a 'dual-dual' framework that distinguishes different forms of dualism such as the rural-urban dichotomy; the agriculture-nonagriculture dichotomy; and the dichotomy between traditional technologies and forms of organization (family enterprises and self-employment) and modern technologies and forms of organization (for example, incorporation).

The dual-dual framework is used in this chapter to illustrate two different applications. In Section 2 this framework provides the basis for exploring intersectoral issues in the process of development. In Section 3 it is used to describe and identify different phases in the evolution of the secular pattern of exchange. Three prototypical development phases are identified, that is, an early (essentially agrarian) phase; a middle development phase often characterized by a pronounced dualism between rural and urban areas and between traditional and modern technologies; and a mature development phase. Different historical patterns of development followed by different countries over time can be observed based on the extent to which the various forms of dualism could be alleviated by appropriate strategies in the middle development phase.

2 THE DUAL-DUAL FRAMEWORK TO EXPLORE INTERSECTORAL ISSUES

John Fei together with Gustav Ranis (1964) made a fundamental contribution to a better understanding of the development process by focussing on dualism and formulating corresponding two-sector models. Whereas the development doctrine of the 1950s implicitly recognized the existence of the backward part of the economy complementing the modern sector, it lacked the dualistic framework to explain the reciprocal roles of the two sectors in the development process. The naive two-sector models *à la* Lewis (1954) continued to assign to subsistence agriculture an essentially passive role as a potential source of 'unlimited labor' and 'agricultural surplus' for the modern sector. It was assumed that the farmers could be released from subsistence agriculture in large numbers without a consequent reduction in agricultural output while simultaneously carrying their own bundles of food (that is, capital) on their backs or at least having access to it.

As the dual-economy models became more sophisticated the interdependence between the functions which the modern industrial and backward agricultural sectors must perform during the growth process was increasingly recognized. The backward sector had to release resources for the industrial sector, which in turn had to be capable of absorbing them. However, neither the release of resources nor the absorption of resources by and of themselves were sufficient for economic development to take place. Recognition of this active interdependence was a large step forward from the naive industrialization-first prescription because the above conceptual framework no longer identified either sector as leading or lagging.

At the same time these dual models assumed, at least implicitly, that the backward sector was rural and agricultural and the modern sector was urban and industrial. In fact, a clear understanding of dualism and its various forms is crucial to an understanding of the development process. The two most important manifestations of dualism in large parts of the developing world appear to be related, first, to the physical and locational environment, and, second, to the technology and form of organization adopted. The first manifestation captures the dichotomy between rural and urban areas and the second between traditional technologies and family farms or enterprises, on the one hand, and modern technologies adopted in more complex forms of organization, on the other. This yields a dual-dual framework as illustrated in Figure 6.1 which can be further modified by distinguishing between agricultural and nonagricultural activities in rural areas.[1]

			Technology and form of organization	
			Traditional labor-intensive technology and family enterprises	Relatively capital-intensive technology and large-scale enterprises
Physical and locational environment and type of production	Rural	Agriculture	Peasant agriculture and owner-cultivators and tenants	Estates, plantations and commercial, large-scale agriculture
		Nonagriculture	Informal-rural off-farm activities	Rural, modern industry and services
	Urban		Informal sector	Modern industry and services

Figure 6.1 Dual-dual framework according to technology and form of organization, and physical environment (location) and type of production

The resulting six-way classification identifies and delineates six broad sectors, that is, (i) subsistence (small-scale) agriculture applying traditional labor-intensive technologies on family farms and producing mainly, but certainly not exclusively, domestic food crops; (ii) commercial, large-scale (for example, plantation-type) agriculture using more capital-intensive technology and being orientated more toward export crops; (iii) informal rural nonfarm activities undertaken in very small, often one-person, enterprises using highly labor-intensive techniques; (iv) rural modern industry and services relying on incorporated enterprises and modern vintage technologies; (v) the informal urban sector; and (vi) urban modern industry and services. The standard models of dualism such as that of Fei and Ranis (1964) and Lewis (1954) tend to highlight the difference between modern (formal) industry and traditional (informal) agriculture. In contrast the dual-dual framework extends the standard dualistic model by incorporating regional dimensions. Such a framework thus allows one to analyze the distribution of modern and informal sector activities in both rural and urban areas. Through such a framework, therefore, one can incorporate the rural nonfarm sector as well as the urban informal sector into the discussion of dualism. These two sectors have been relatively ignored in standard discussions of dualism but are now widely recognized as being very important analytical categories to understand poverty.

The dual-dual framework is used first, to identify the major types of production activities and sectors in which the different categories of workers (particularly the poor) are employed. The emphasis in this section is to point out the characteristics of these sectors separately. The various linkages among these different sectors are discussed, next, in an attempt to understand the causes and pattern of poverty at a fairly general level. In particular, the impact of various development strategies on these intra- and-intersectoral linkages and hence on income distribution and migration are analyzed.

2.1 Regional and Locational Characteristics: Rural-urban Dichotomy

The dichotomy between rural and urban areas determines to a large extent the types of production and other opportunities open to the poor in these areas. In this respect, a major difference between rural and urban areas is related to the much greater seasonal and annual periodicity and synchronicity characterizing agricultural production and income variables, as opposed to nonagricultural production and income variables in urban areas. Seasonality and uncertainty thus are important characteristic features of rural poverty in contrast to urban poverty. These characteristics point to the need for off-season (nonagricultural) employment provision and some form of countercyclical intervention by the government to dampen the uncertainty associated with fluctuating agricultural output, both seasonally and annually.

A second difference between rural and urban areas relates to the greater accessibility in urban areas to social services (education and health) and infrastructure (transport, information, technical services, and banking). However, in spite of better access to these facilities, poor town dwellers often suffer more than rural households from certain aspects of poverty. The urban poor are typically housed in slums or squatter settlements, and often have to contend with appalling overcrowding, poor sanitation and contaminated water.

A third difference between rural and urban areas is the greater administrative ease of enforcing rules in urban areas. However, this does not necessarily mean that there is a higher prevalence of official as opposed to unofficial transactions in urban markets. Indeed, because of the size of these markets and the greater degree of policy intervention, unofficial and informal activities flourish in that environment. It is these informal (and often unofficial) activities that most of the urban poor are engaged in. The urban poor households who derive most of their incomes from working on informal activities constantly face the threat of forcible eviction and municipal regulations discriminating against them.

Still another way in which regional dualism manifests itself is a tendency in many developing countries to concentrate public and private investment projects around central urban metropolitan areas (typically the capital city). Such policies reduce significantly the employment opportunities in the periphery – particularly for the unskilled workers – and contribute thereby to high poverty levels. A relevant question, in this context, relates to the magnitudes of the interregional multipliers from projects originating in the periphery on value added and incomes in the center region and vice versa. This raises interesting implications regarding the location of industries. While there are obvious external and agglomeration economies from clustering industries and firms in urban areas, a key question relates to the impact on rural poverty of a process of rural industrial decentralization particularly concentrated on those industries intensive in unskilled labor.

2.2 Agriculture-nonagriculture Dichotomy Within Rural Sector

The fate of the poor is intimately linked to agriculture in the developing world. The bulk of the poor is located in rural areas and depends either directly or indirectly on agriculture for much of their incomes. The direct agricultural production effects operate through the incomes accruing to farmers and agricultural workers – much of it in the form of food produced and consumed by the farm households. The indirect production effects of agriculture on poverty alleviation are channeled through forward linkages creating jobs for the self-employed and hired workers engaged in agro-processing, trade, services and other marketing activities, and, to a lesser extent, through backward linkages creating a demand for intermediate inputs (for example, fertilizer, cement, and so on) required to produce food and cash crops. Other very important indirect effects of agricultural output are through the consumption linkages of farmers and agricultural workers who spend a significant share of their incremental incomes on non-agricultural commodities such as consumer goods (for example, radios, bicycles, clothing, leather products) and services, in turn, benefitting the rural and urban poor engaged in these activities.

Within agriculture the poor are those who either own no land or very small plots of land that is often unproductive and frequently lies outside the irrigated areas. The poor are usually unable to improve their plots since they lack access to formal credit and technology. An important question is thus regarding which form of investment (say investment in dairy cattle versus investment in irrigation, integrated rural development projects) has the greatest impact on poverty alleviation at the least output cost.

Nonfarm activities include all economic activities other than crop and livestock production, encompassing services, construction, mining, commerce and manufacturing. It also includes agro-industrial activities that store, process and market agricultural commodities. The nonfarm economy is crucial to the rural poor. Although those activities already occupy an important place in many rural economies, they have an even more important potential role to play throughout the developing world, particularly in Africa. While nonfarm activities account for only 14 percent of full-time employment in rural Africa, their share jumps to 26 percent in Asia and 28 percent in Latin America, respectively.

The rural nonfarm economy plays a valuable equity-enhancing function across countries. Landless and near landless households everywhere depend on nonfarm earnings; those with less than half a hectare typically earn over half their income from nonfarm sources. Moreover, the seasonality of nonfarm earnings runs countercyclically to agricultural income, so that the promotion of nonfarm activities can help dampen seasonal income fluctuations. Women, relatively more active than males, in nonfarm activities in Africa and Latin America, dominate many of the equity-enhancing nonfarm activities such as food processing, beverage preparation, weaving, gathering, selling of prepared snack foods and personal services. A major reason why women form the majority on such activities is because most of these activities can be carried out within the home together with taking care of children and doing other household chores.

Technological and organizational characteristics: modern-traditional, formal informal dichotomy

Technological dualism is a characteristic feature of developing countries.

Within the agricultural sector, this dualism manifests itself in the form of traditional, labor-intensive technology being used in family farms in contrast with more capital-intensive technology relying on hired labor on estates and plantations. Although the main reason for the choice of relatively capital-intensive techniques is to reduce labor-monitoring costs, in some instances, this technology is not appropriate given the underlying resource endowment. The prevalence of distorted prices such as subsidized access to credit, minimum wage legislation and an overvalued exchange rate, encouraged the adoption of an overly mechanized technology. Two important questions arise in this respect. The first is regarding the aggregate output and employment effects of traditional technologies versus the corresponding modern counterparts. The second is whether a tradeoff may, in fact, exist between output and efficiency objectives, on the one hand, and employment and poverty alleviation objectives, on the other.

In general it appears that the use of modern technology — across both rural and urban areas — tends to be highly associated with corporate structure and the use of traditional technologies with family farms and enterprises (Cornelisse and Thorbecke 1991). The type of technology and the form of organization that are adopted have differential impacts on product and labor markets. Thus, for example, in the labor market it is observed that large firms generally hire more skilled, often organized and unionized workers, while small firms in the informal sector rely more on family, self-employed labor. As pointed out earlier, the urban poor are highly dependent on the urban informal sector. The informal sector in developing countries is thus emerging as a potentially dynamic and transitional sector providing important income and employment sources for the poor. The World Bank (1990) points out that in Brazil in 1985, an estimated 75 percent of heads of poor families worked in the informal sector, compared with 35 percent of the population as a whole. Similarly, in Pakistan about half the urban poor are self-employed, mostly in trade and manufacturing. They are generally less skilled than the people who work for wages.

2.4 Intersectoral Linkages Under Various Development Strategies

A key issue relates to the proper role of agriculture and other sectors (industry and services) and the interaction among them during the development process. In the 1950s and 1960s, the prevailing view, and the preferred development strategy, was that of 'industrialization first' This strategy considered industry to be the active, dynamic sector while agriculture was viewed as a passive sector. Industry was the engine of growth pulling agriculture behind it. The resources needed for building the social overhead capital and the buildings, machinery and equipment required for an industrial takeoff were to be squeezed out of agriculture. The agricultural surplus was to be extracted largely through a form of taxation, that is, by turning the internal terms of trade (the relative prices of agricultural commodities *vis-à-vis* industrial commodities) against agriculture.

The experience of many developing countries during the 1950s and 1960s which adopted this industrialization-first strategy (prime examples were India and much of Latin America) taught some important lessons. First, the extraction of the agricultural surplus tended to be so large and so blunt that it led to agricultural output stagnation. Farmers lacked the incentives to adopt more productive technologies and supply response was extremely inelastic. The goose was killed before she could lay the golden egg. At the same time, much of the industrial growth occurred in heavily protected sectors through the process of import substitution. Production tended not only to be inefficient, but also overly capital intensive. Under those circumstances the rate at which agriculture was releasing labor was much higher than the very limited amount of labor that could be productively absorbed in the incipient modern industrial sector. This led to a massive rural-urban migration where most new migrants ended up almost residually looking for meager jobs in the urban informal sector. The incidence of poverty was increasing in both rural and urban areas. Squatter settlements started appearing around most of the large metropolitan centers.

The failure of the industrialization-first strategy led to an almost complete reversal in the conception of the appropriate roles of agriculture and industry, within the development process. Many economists and development practitioners started assigning an active and dynamic role to small-scale agriculture. The latter was envisaged to create gradually a derived demand and opportunity for industrial development through production linkages (backward and forward) and consumption linkages. It may only be a slight exaggeration to say that in some quarters small-scale agriculture was being viewed as the engine of growth pulling the development train behind it, while the industrial sector had become the caboose. In particular, starting in the 1970s, a *unimodal* strategy in agriculture was being promoted. This strategy emphasizes the growth of small-scale, subsistence agriculture. Under a *unimodal* strategy, resources and incentives are provided to small farmers. Development is to occur, as it were, from the bottom up. It contrasts with a bimodal strategy that favors the commercial, large-scale food sector, and plantations and large estates producing export crops. In the 1980s the pendulum swung even further with the advent of the so-called agricultural development-led industrialization (ADLI) strategy that incorporated the unimodal strategy as an integral component.

From the standpoint of poverty, it is very important to note the implications of these various development strategies on income distribution and the migration pattern. Figure 6.2 illustrates the changes in the migration pattern under a growth-orientated bimodal strategy and under a unimodal strategy. The *bimodal* structure shows a clear compartmentalization between modern and traditional agriculture. This structure is very typical of a large number of Central and Latin American countries characterized by minifundias and latifundias and of African countries where landholdings are sharply divided between small subsistence farming on customary village plots and large-scale crown lands and other excolonial holdings. Countries such as Taiwan, South Korea and Japan (during the Meiji period) followed consciously a unimodal strategy of agricultural development and, as a consequence, largely avoided the marked dualism in agriculture one finds in much of Latin America and Africa. In those East Asian countries a major land reform provided the foundation for a *unimodal* land distribution and structure. Under a *unimodal* strategy, the distinction between the sectors may disappear gradually (hence the deletion of the vertical line separating these two subsectors in the lower part of Figure 6.2) and the number of landless farmers will be reduced through land acquisition and increased employment. Rural nonfarm activities will also get a boost from the forward and backward linkages with agricultural development. Overall employment within the rural sector is thus expected to increase. Thus, in comparison to the industrialization-first strategy, the rural to urban flow of migrants is expected to be lower under the unimodal strategy. Also the probability that these migrants will get jobs is expected to increase given the reduction in their numbers over time.

The pattern of migration under a unimodal structure is sketched in the lower part of Figure 6.2. The few landless or marginal farmers remaining after the land redistribution will tend to migrate to rural off-farm activities and to the urban informal sector. Only a few of the latter will acquire the necessary skills and discipline to obtain jobs in the modern sector. In contrast, the offspring of landed farmers – who are likely to benefit from more education and human capital than the landless – might be more successful in finding urban modern sector jobs.

However, a number of problems that could arise in the implementation of the unimodal strategy need to be mentioned briefly here. The first problem is that of mounting a frontal attack in terms of a policy package consisting of a set of complementary measures such as land and structural

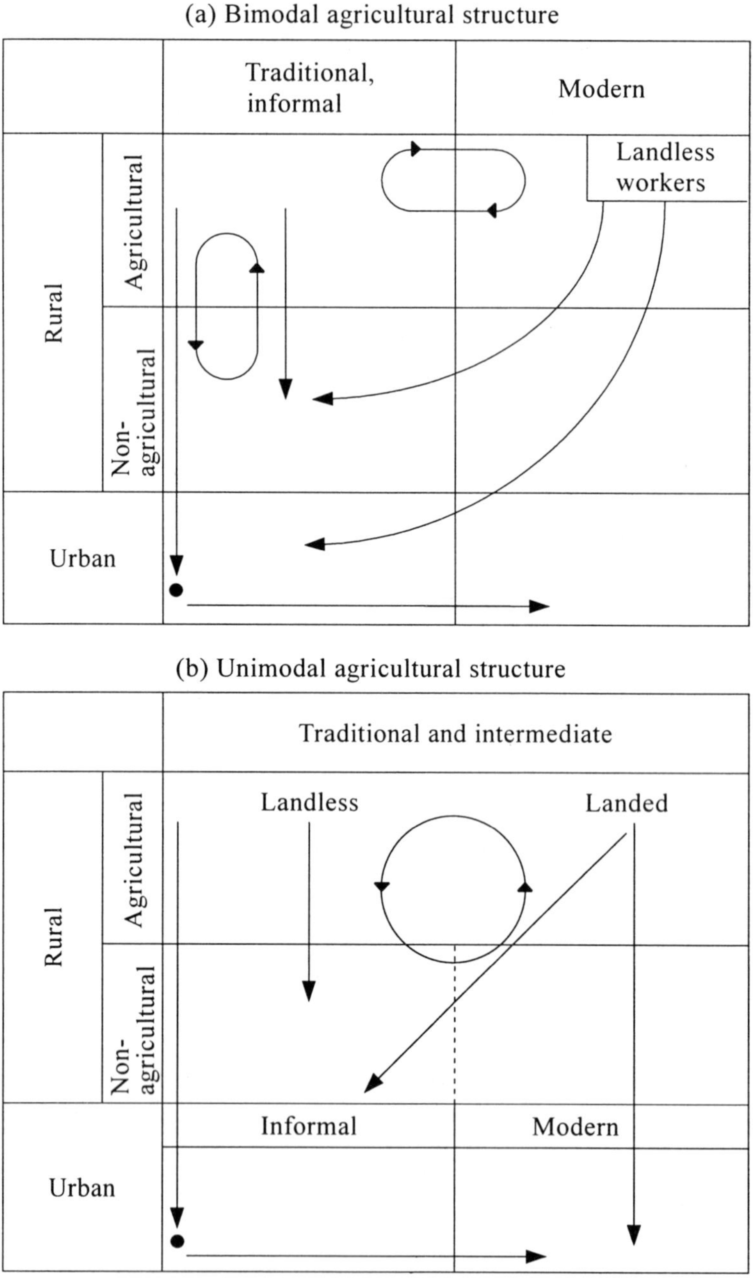

Figure 6.2 Migration pattern under a bimodal agricultural structure and an unimodal agricultural structure

reforms, institutional changes, price policies and research in a synchronized way. The political feasibility of such a policy package in many countries is questionable. The second problem is regarding the achievement of a mutually reinforcing relationship between agricultural and nonagricultural activities. This is a key element of a successful rural development policy particularly because of the limited potential that agricultural development alone may have in many developing countries.

It is thus essential that the off-farm activities be designed in such a way as to be seasonally complementary from an effective employment standpoint with the calendar of agricultural activities. Given the very high level of seasonal underemployment in traditional agriculture, it means identifying productive activities that can be turned on and off according to the seasonal employment and production pattern in agriculture. Activities which might be consistent with those criteria appear to be small-scale rural infrastructure projects, trade, transportation, personal services, and small-scale and cottage industries.

Agriculture and nonagriculture can best be viewed as coequal partners in the development process. Each has an active role to play within the strongly interdependent and interactive socioeconomic system prevailing in any given country at any point in time. Their roles will, of course, differ during, and evolve with, the different phases of economic development – a country passes through the structural transformation from an essentially agrarian economy to a mature industrial and service-orientated state. The evolution in the pattern of exchange is discussed in Section 3.

A multisectoral framework focussing on the linkages among various economic sectors and subsectors is essential in studying issues related to employment and income distribution. Take, for example, the case of rural industrialization, which has great potential for poverty alleviation. One cannot talk about rural industrialization in isolation, it has to be contextualized within the overall socioeconomic structure of the economy. This means that one has to identify its linkages with both the agricultural sector and the urban industrial sector and analyze its development in relation to the stage of development in these two sectors.

The link between the development of the urban industrial sector and rural industrialization is illustrated best by the experience of East Asian countries. In all these countries, the rural industrial demand benefitted from the export drive, through the role of subcontracting and the development of ancillaries. This type of linkage, which has developed most strongly in Japan, broke the demand-side contradiction between large- and small-scale (whether rural or urban) industries by structuring the two in a complementary mutually beneficial relationship.

Equitable and sustainable development requires a balanced and interactively reinforcing growth process between agriculture and industry. Conversely, in those instances where development was unbalanced, that is, where agriculture was not able to retain more than a modest portion of its surplus, overall growth has been much less impressive.

3 PHASES IN THE EVOLUTION OF EXCHANGE CONFIGURATIONS

Different forms of exchange relationships have evolved over time together with the process of economic development. The concept of exchange configuration is used in analyzing the evolution of exchange relationships (see Cornelisse and Thorbecke 1991). Transactions occur within given configurations which, in turn, can be of the market or non-market type. Exchange configurations are shaped by different specific combinations of three major sets of elements: (i) the object or *item* around which the exchange takes place; (ii) the actors engaged in the exchange; and (iii) the environment within which a transaction occurs. The various elements are used to identify *different combinations* of environmental settings, characteristics of items and attributes of actors that together yield relatively distinct and homogeneous transactions. In what follows, a number of examples of exchange configurations are given. In most discussions on patterns of economic development, the interrelationship between changes in the structure of the economy and changes in exchange relationships are not explicitly analyzed.[2]

For example, Simon Kuznets (1966) in his comparative study of the economic growth of nations describes the period since the mid-18th century to the present as the epoch of 'modern economic growth'. According to him, the epochal innovation that distinguishes this modern economic period is the extended application of science to the problems of economic production. His study characterized this epoch of modern economic growth by the sustained increase in per capita product, growth in population, increase in efficiency of inputs, sectoral shift of national product and labor force from agriculture to manufacturing and services, increase in the rate of capital formation, improvement in transport and communications, and the movement away from small enterprises to large enterprises. However, in his study, the changes in exchange relationships that occurred concurrently during this period are not explicitly analyzed. In terms of the configuration approach, developed here, the transformations that he described correspond to changes in the characteristics of the underlying elements. In this section, an attempt will be made to relate these changes to the evolution of exchange relationships.

To do this, the secular process of economic development can be broken down into three broad phases: an early development phase, a middle development phase and a mature development phase. Although it is true that history cannot be compressed into three phases and there is nothing sacrosanct about the number three, it can be claimed that a certain analytical logic underlies this division.[3] The early development phase is the period before the start of the process of modern economic growth and the purpose in delineating this phase is to capture the initial conditions that prevailed in different countries before they embarked on this process. The middle development phase describes the period when most of the structural changes pointed out by Kuznets took place and the late development phase characterizes the period after that. Thus, according to this classification, most of today's 'developing countries' are in the middle development phase and the 'developed countries' are in the late development phase.

Typically a number of exchange configurations characterize each phase. However, for analytical purposes one needs to focus on those configurations that are considered to be most representative of a particular phase. The dual-dual framework provides a useful tool in identifying key configurations in each phase. As a society and economy move from one phase to another, two changes occur simultaneously. First, the characteristics of elements within each configuration change and, second, the relative importance of each configuration within the overall structure is also altered. Thus, it will be shown that the family farm configuration is present in all the three phases, but its characteristics and relative importance undergo a major modification in the process of socioeconomic development.

3.1 Phase 1: The Early Development Phase

In Phase 1, traditional agriculture predominates and production and transactions are generally concentrated in the northwest quadrant of the dual-dual framework as shown in Figure 6.3. Food production constitutes the bulk of total output. During this phase, however, household and cottage enterprises start to appear in the form of various crop-processing units, carpentry, masonry, handicrafts and so on. The technology used is very traditional and the form of organization is informal. Urban activities are limited and relate primarily to various artisan crafts, trade and services, public administration, the military and education.[4]

<table>
<tr><td colspan="3"></td><td colspan="2">Technology and form of organization</td></tr>
<tr><td></td><td></td><td></td><td>Traditional labor-intensive technology and family or self-employed enterprises</td><td>More capital-intensive technology and large enterprises</td></tr>
<tr><td rowspan="3">Geographical location nature of product</td><td rowspan="2">Rural</td><td>Agri-cultural</td><td>Family farm configuration (for details refer to Figure 6.4)</td><td rowspan="2">Undeveloped</td></tr>
<tr><td>Non-agri-cultural</td><td>Beginnings of cottage enterprises handicrafts, textiles, masonry, carpentry</td></tr>
<tr><td>Urban</td><td colspan="3">Undeveloped</td></tr>
</table>

Figure 6.3 Early development phase (predominance of family farm configuration)

Traditional agriculture in this phase is characterized by certain distinct features that largely determine the kind of transactions likely to emerge.[5] First, agricultural production activities tend to be strongly interdependent due to ecological interdependence of biological processes. For example, diversion of irrigation water may result in water shortage for downstream farmers in a river valley. An individual farm is usually too small a production unit to internalize many of these production externalities. It thus becomes imperative for the village members to coordinate their production and exchange activities to reduce these conflicts. Customs or accumulated precedents rather than stipulations of formal laws tend to be more effective in governing exchange relationships (see Hayami 1989).

Second, traditional agriculture is subject to a lot of uncertainty. Vagaries of nature cause substantial variations in the food production of each household. Primitive technology does not allow the storage of output for more than one production period. Furthermore, in such societies where there is no centralized state, it is not possible to use regular taxes and bounties to affect the distribution of food among households. Binswanger and Rosenzweig (1986) point out that formal insurance markets are also impracticable as a consequence of moral hazard, covariant yield risks and lack of suitable collateral options. The nuclear household is too small for spreading the risks of harvest failure or animal disease, so the larger kinship unit or horizontally and/or vertically integrated families become the insurance collectivity in many such cases.

Third, information is costly and asymmetrically distributed. Thus incentive problems arise in all transactions that involve payment or deliveries of goods and services at a future time (that is, credit, insurance, labor or rentals of assets). In the case of agricultural products, marketable agricultural surplus of semi-subsistence peasants is usually small in volume and variable in quality. Therefore, as Hayami (1989) points out, 'It is impracticable to introduce modern marketing practices such as grading and brand names, aimed at reducing the uncertainty about product quality. A market tends to be inefficient or vanish altogether because of high transaction costs due to absence or asymmetry of such quality information'(p. 6).

The problem of quality uncertainty in traditional agriculture also makes it more difficult to monitor labor. In urban industries characterized by machine process, work is highly standardized and easy to monitor. The biological process of agricultural production is, however, subject to infinite variations in ecological conditions. It thus matters a great deal whether a laborer performs his or her work with careful attention and adjustments in response to variations in ecological conditions. Such work quality is extremely difficult to monitor. Moreover, agricultural operations are generally spread over a wide space and this adds to the problem of monitoring.

Because of the above-mentioned characteristics associated with traditional agriculture, such as production and quality uncertainty, costly and asymmetric information, incentive problems and small market size, it has been shown that transactions tend to be interlinked (see, for example, Bardham 1980 and 1989, and Basu 1983).[7] A widely studied example of such interlinked transactions is sharecropping tenancy where the tenant agrees to pay a certain proportion of the total product as rent. Such an arrangement, as opposed to a pure wage contract, helps to overcome the problem of incentives and monitoring and, as opposed to a pure rental contract, helps to overcome the problem of missing insurance markets. Usually the landlord also advances credit for production and consumption purposes. Braverman and Stiglitz (1982) point out that by altering the terms and the amount of the loan made available to the tenant, the landlord can induce the tenant to work harder or to undertake projects more to the liking of the landlord. This interlinking of credit with tenancy contracts helps in internalizing some of the externalities associated with traditional agriculture. Very often the landlord also patronizes his tenants in such ways as giving gifts at the birth of a child or using his connections to help solve the tenants' problems with other villagers. The tenant reciprocates by his or her loyal services to the landlord.

Due to the multistranded nature of exchange relationships in this phase, it does not make much sense to analyze land, labor and credit configurations separately. Most transactions are virtual, implicit and within the family. Thus the family farm configuration is the appropriate unit of analysis here, as shown in Figure 6.4 which lists the main characteristics of the elements (actors, item and environment). The *raison d'être* of the family farm configuration lies in the two forms of insurance that it provides. The first is an intergenerational form of 'old age' or social security insurance and the second is insurance against state contingent uncertainty (Thorbecke 1993).

In this phase, family farms tend to be very often horizontally linked with other family farms through a variety of patron-client, kinship and tribal relations (as in various parts of Asia, Africa and Latin America).

In Europe, the family farms formed part of the great medieval estates. According to Pirenne (1936, p. 60), these estates consisted, on average, of 300 farms (*mansi*), or about 10,000 acres, and many of them were undoubtedly considerably larger. The whole of the land was under the jurisdiction of a *cour* or a manor and was divided into three parts: the demesne, the tenants' holdings and the commons. The demesne constituted the seignorial reserve and consisted of all the lands set apart

Transaction type	• Personalized nonmonetary implicit interlinked. • Terms of contract governed by customary laws. • Governing principle behind exchange is that of reciprocity or redistribution rather than economic gain

↑

Elements

Actors	Item	Environment
Typical actors: • Family/community farms • Traditional artisans Number and density: • Low population density Occupation: • Traditional agriculture predominant • Artisans: smiths, masons, carpenters, weavers Form of employment: • Largely self-employed Behavioral characteristics: • Risk averse • Personal and custom bound value orientation Education: • Trained in traditional skills • Formal education not widespread Assets: • Largely in form of land, tools, precious metals	Product: • Narrow range of products produced • Food production constitutes bulk of production • Food can be stored only for a limited period • Most goods produced cater to consumption needs, not many investment goods Credit: • Collateral options limited because: (i) land has no sales value (ii) no major stocks of machines exist • Major collateral is therefore gold or other precious metals • Value of claim tends to be small • Generally short-term loans, paid back at harvest time • Purpose of loan is for consumption Labor: • Largely trained in traditional skills • Formal education rare	Infrastructure: • Transport and communications very primitive Level of urbanization • Very low Cultural: • Strong community feelings • Kinship ties very high Technology: • Traditional • Limited division of labor • Very labor intensive • Technical economies of scale in agriculture are unimportant • Almost no physical capital is used in production except simple hand tools, but farm animals are common Organizational: • Largely self-employed • Family enterprises/farms Legal: • Property rights not developed • Customary laws prevail Political: • Generally no central Government, local centers of power

Figure 6.4 Family farm configuration in early development phase

for the exclusive use of the lord. The size of the tenants' holdings was based on the minimal size of land required to support a family. The commons consisted of the natural meadows, marshes, heath or forests which surrounded the cultivated soil. The tenants had to work for one to three days a week on the lord's demesne and also had to pay various dues in kind, on certain customary dates. In turn, the lord provided them with protection. Thus the manor was not just an economic but also a social institution. It imposed itself on the whole life of its inhabitants. In this case, the family farm can be seen as an exchange configuration within the larger configuration of the manor.

Within the specific context of SubSaharan Africa (SSA), certain distinguishing characteristics have implications for the way exchange relations evolved in that region. These characteristics are low population density, land abundance and semi-arid climate. In terms of the configuration approach, these are characteristics of the environmental elements. In the discussion below, it is shown how these initial characteristics shaped the market and non-market exchange configurations that emerged over time. In particular, the lineage system is identified as an important exchange configuration.

In the case of SSA, because of the semi-arid climate and the absence of irrigation, there is just one short growing season. Seasonality in production is thus highly pronounced. Coupled with this is the high weather risk. Within small areas, crop yields tend to have high positive covariance. Furthermore, risks arising from this weather uncertainty cannot be mitigated by trade across different agro-climatic regions due to high transport and communications costs. Thus, the need for some form of insurance appears high.

Binswanger and Rosenzweig (1986) show that in this underdeveloped phase, crop insurance was infeasible as a consequence of moral hazard, covariant yield risks, geographical isolation and limited collateral options. Under such conditions, lineage relations based on kinship ties emerged as an organizational framework to afford its members maximum insurance against risks that could not be adequately self-insured. Besides insurance, Platteau (1991) points out that the lineage-based system served another major function. He argues that, 'In SSA problems of survival arise not because land is in short supply but because it can only be exploited through an effective human organization ... It is precisely one of the roles of the lineage to provide such an organizational framework' (p. 73)

The lineage-based system of land relations can be characterized as a system under which land is held under corporate tenure, implying that it is subject to strong communal regulations. The general principle underlying it is that each member of the group is entitled to be allocated a sufficient amount of land to support his or her family. Moreover, the allottee has possession and use of the land as long as it is being cultivated and the heirs would normally be given the land that was cultivated at the time of his or her death. Possession of land in tribal or lineage-based societies is thus personal and statutory in the sense that access to a portion of the communal resources is mediated through membership in a social group.

Lineage or social groups with surplus cultivable land can always accommodate land-hungry outsiders provided that the latter agree to enter the local network of personal interrelationships and accept the authority of the local chief. The new residents are expected to pay regular dues, usually in the form of labor services, a share of the harvest or other types of contributions.

In contrast to the case of Asia where land was scarce and hence was a symbol of economic prestige, in African societies the control of labor power proved far more important and constituted the real base of economic prosperity and social prestige.

3.2 Phase 2: The Middle Development Phase

Transition from self-sufficient to market-orientated units

In Phase 2 there is a movement away from self-sufficient units to market-orientated units. To understand the factors that lie behind this movement, we shall discuss here the model on market failures built by de Janvry et al. (1991). They argue that

> Typically when commodities such as food and labor can be bought and sold by a peasant household, their sales price is a fraction of the purchase price. The widths of the price bands depend on transportation costs to and from the market, mark-up by merchants, the opportunity costs of time involved in selling (search costs) and buying (recruitment and supervision costs) risks associated with uncertain prices and availabilities that determine perceived certainty equivalent prices that are lower than farm gate prices for items sold and higher for items bought, and a variety of other transaction costs that are largely household specific. (pp. 1401-2)

According to this model, then, whenever the shadow price of a product or a factor which the household produces and uses falls within this price band, trade will not occur. If the shadow price is above the price band, the household should buy the commodity until the shadow price that equates supply and residual demand for home production falls to the purchase price and vice versa. Thus the greater is the size of the price band the more likely it is that the household will remain self-sufficient. The poorer the infrastructure, the less the information that is available and the more risky the transactions; the greater is the size of the price band. Thus, it is a multiplicity of factors such as improved transport and communication facilities, improvement in storage and processing technology, and the spread of legal and financial institutions, which by reducing the size of the price band can ensure greater market participation by earlier self-sufficient units. Also factors like imposition of monetary tax and increased availability of manufactured goods, by raising the cash requirements and the incentives of the households, can have the same effect. Notice that all of these factors correspond to the various elements in the configuration approach.

Factors behind the transition

What led to the above outlined changes in the characteristics of elements? Many of these changes were triggered by exogenous forces such as wars, colonial rule and the appearance of new trade routes and new products. Other changes, particularly in the historical experience of Western Europe, were of an endogenous type. However, in almost all countries, two factors can be singled out as being essential in the evolution from self-sufficient units to market-orientated units. These are the increase in population and the opening up of internal and external trade.

Population growth In Boserup's (1965) analysis, population growth has eight principal effects: (i) it reduces the fallow period; (ii) it increases investment in land; (iii) it encourages the shift from hand hoe cultivation to animal traction; (iv) it encourages soil fertility maintenance via manuring; (v) it reduces the average cost of infrastructure; (vi) it permits more specialization in production; (vii) it induces a change from general to specific land rights; and (viii) it reduces the per capita availability of common-property resources.

Further, as Binswanger et al. (1989) point out, 'population growth mitigates the effects of person-specific risk in two ways. (1) It leads to markets for specialized crops and non-farm products, and allows greater diversification into them. (2) It reduces the average cost of infrastructure, thus allowing greater market expansion for some goods, and further diversification' (pp. 133-4).

By thus affecting various characteristics of the underlying elements, population growth has a major impact on the evolution of exchange configurations.

Opening of external trade The principal effect of the opening up of external trade is that the household or the village community is no longer constrained to remain self-sufficient. For example, in an earlier closed region, the availability of external markets breaks the prevailing demand and supply constraints and allows the usual gains from trade to be reaped. This immediately raises the marginal value of factors to their former levels of utilization.

The opening up of external trade also has important consequences on the risks facing an agrarian economy. If the export crop is a new or previously minor crop, a decline in covariant risks facing the villagers is likely. This is because the new crop often becomes a source of portfolio diversification. Furthermore, food can be imported in bad years, thus reducing the risks facing traditional agriculture. Since covariant risks decline, Binswanger et al. (1989) argue that there is less need for the vertical extension of households.

Evolution of specific markets

As the family farm configuration shrinks in importance, a variety of market and nonmarket exchange configurations emerge. Here again the key characteristics of these configurations can best be described within the dual-dual framework.

Let us start with the product market and nonmarket configurations. It is to be noted here that two changes are occurring simultaneously. First, a larger output is being produced and marketed, and second, new products start appearing. Accordingly four distinct product configurations can be distinguished within the dual-dual structure. These are:

1. family (or community) farm system which is gradually moving away from a purely subsistence orientation to a more market orientation;
2. commercial large-scale (often mechanized) agriculture which might comprise plantations and/or large scale production of food crops;
3. the informal rural and urban manufacturing and service market in which small firms are gradually replacing household and cottage enterprises; and
4. modern industry and the beginning of a modern service configuration.

Figure 6.5 presents these configurations within the dual-dual framework. A careful examination of this figure reveals that these four configurations can be identified fairly distinctly in terms of different specific combinations of characteristics of elements and the corresponding exchange relationships.

During this second phase, the informal sector continues to grow. Gradually, small firms replace household enterprises. As agricultural production expands together with the size of the marketable surplus and rural incomes, newly created and expanding markets for consumer goods and some capital goods (used as inputs into agriculture) appear. Because of the rudimentary nature of the infrastructure and the transportation network (in Figure 6.5 this is one of the characteristics of the underlying environment in the informal sector configuration), a highly fragmented pattern of production centered on small-scale units results. Products tend to be differentiated, subject to low-scale economies and covering small markets.

Perhaps of even greater importance during this phase is the increasing relative importance of modern technology and form of organization and of urban industrial production. This movement can be seen clearly when Figure 6.5 describing Phase 2 is compared with Phase 1 in Figure 6.3. The northwest configuration which was predominating in the early phase is being encroached on from the east (through the use and application of modern technology and form of organization and all other characteristics of elements related with the former) and from the south (through the increasing importance of urban production and associated characteristics).

Product markets are generally the fastest to develop. Markets for factors of production, particulary land, develop very slowly. The peculiarities of land as a commodity – its physical heterogeneity, the diversity of motives for its purchase and the relatively small volume of transactions – generally hinders the development of land markets (Morris and Adelman 1988, p. 65).

Monetization

Transactions can be expressed in monetary or non-monetary terms. As transactions grow and become more comparable, professional traders can start to play a role. With the introduction of metallic and later fudiciary money, the problems of storage, acceptability and transport of bullion can largely be overcome. Yet, there are specific situations, very common in rural areas of developing countries, where money is hardly needed. Again, the example of subsistence farming applies since the same actors (that is, the members of the farm household) produce the food and consume it. Another example concerns the labor market during the harvest season, when labor services can be traded directly for food since each party can supply the item that the other needs in a complementary and barter fashion.

Generally speaking, the first markets to be monetized are product markets.[6] Families or communities orientated toward subsistence production may find that they produce a surplus and offer it for sale. By so doing they run a relatively small risk as long as they retain a quantity considered adequate for survival. Labor markets tend to be monetized at

Geographical location nature of product		Technology and form of organization: Traditional technology and family or self-employed enterprises	Technology and form of organization: Modern technology incorporated or unincorporated enterprises
	Rural agricultural	Family farm configuration Actors • Family farms • Subsistence orientated • Risk averse • Personal and custom-bound value orientation Item • Generally food crops (some cash crops beginning to be grown) Environment • Traditional technology • Small-scale family orientated units • Land rights beginning to emerge	Large-scale farms/plantations Actors • Large-scale farms/plantations • Foreign dominated/domestic • Interested in profit maximization Item • Cash crops/plantation products Environment • Modern technology used • Large incorporated or unincorporated enterprises • Capital intensive technology • Hired labor used • Generally sheltered by government
	Rural agricultural	Transaction type • Personalized, interlinked, some monetization appears Market structure • Fragmented markets, low level of competition	Transaction type • Impersonal, monetized Market structure • Linked with foreign markets, labor markets emerge, banking, finance for trade, limited commercialization of land
	Rural & urban Nonagricultural	Nonagricultural informal Actors • Family and cottage enterprises • Traditional orientation • Risk averse Item • Textiles, blacksmithry, food-processing, construction, household services, transport and trade services Environment • Traditional technology • Small-scale enterprises • Labor-intensive units • Self-employment	Modern industrial sector Actors • Emergence of large factories • Beginnings of modern services sector • Interested in profit maximization Item • Capital goods • Some consumer goods – such as textiles, electrical goods Environment • Modern technology • Large-scale, capital intensive • Hired labor used • High degree of government intervention
	Rural & urban Nonagricultural	Transaction type • Generally monetize, often personal Market structure • Regional markets, limited linkages with formal sector, low competition	Transaction type • Monetized, impersonal Market structure • Product markets nationally linked • Labor markets emerge • Specialized banking institutions linked

Figure 6.5 Middle development phase – product exchange: emergence of four distinct configurations

a later stage. If the surplus production over own consumption continues and perhaps expands with the introduction of improved technologies, a tendency towards commercialization may begin. Other well-known causes for monetization are increased division of labor, the desire to buy consumer goods, the conscious introduction of cash crops by the government and the obligation to pay taxes.

After the introduction of money, the relations among individuals in a community will gradually become more impersonal. In a group that used to be self-supporting and self-sufficient, the possession of money allows consumption of goods produced by outsiders. Furthermore, as the surplus becomes an established part of total revenues, production decisions are likely to change when account is taken of opportunities in the product market. Motivations will become less inward-looking than before and traditional rules of distribution will be eroded. At the same time, increased monetization heightens sensitivity to inflation. This is the reason why the degree of monetization does not increase monotonically over time; in many cases a drop in the use of money in transactions has been observed as a reaction to high rates of inflation.

Development pattern in SubSaharan Africa (SSA) in Phase 2

In the case of SSA, the middle development phase can be subdivided into two periods: the colonial period and the period after independence. The focus here is to analyze the impact of exogenous forces in the nature of colonial rule and later the emergence of nationalist governments, on the evolution of exchange configurations. Since SSA, like most other developing countries today, has not really reached Phase 3, it is hoped that the analysis here would contribute to an understanding of the forces that hinder or foster the further development of markets.

The colonial period Colonial policy towards land was perhaps one of the most important triggering factor in breaking up the old lineage system. Therefore a logical starting point is to analyze how colonialism affected not only the evolution of land markets but also the evolution of labor, credit and agricultural product markets through its impact on the existing interlinkages.

IMPACT OF LAND POLICIES Platteau (1991) points out that one important objective of colonial land policies in SSA was the appropriation of land for commercial purposes whenever there were expatriate settlers willing to put land into cultivation or foreign concessionaries willing to set up plantations or explore mineral resources. In the British African colonies, the first step consisted of considering that only land under active and visible cultivation was really occupied. Unoccupied land was classed as Crown Land. Thus, in assessing African land-use patterns, the Western powers were led by conceptual categories that are only relevant to intensive forms of agricultural cultivation. They failed to see that fallow land areas have a critical role to play in extensive methods of land exploitation and in the social reproduction of indigenous societies.

Such a policy of expropriation of unoccupied land enabled the colonial powers to deprive indigenous societies of vast areas of land. Large estates were set up on some of these lands. Here authorities outside the community and household organized the structure and location of production and defined the rules of exchange. In most cases, especially in settler countries (like Kenya and Rhodesia) the appropriated land areas were the best lands available. The consequence was that a large number of African peasants were forced to draw their livelihoods from land of inferior quality or work as hired labor on these estates. Sahn and Sarris (1992) point out that

> In Mozambique, colonial policies forced many Africans to work as contract laborers rather than tend their farms, and those that remained on their land were often forced to produce cotton and rice intended for Portugal. Hence the labor markets developed not through population growth and external trade, as outlined by neoclassical theory of institutional change, but through coercion. (p. 7)

With respect to land occupied by the natives, the British colonial authorities adhered to the doctrine that all colonial land in SSA was held in communal tenure: individuals had only user rights to land and ownership of tribal lands was vested in the chiefs. Many studies have pointed out that the village political domain was traditionally 'plural'. The chief was not allowed to concentrate power and could often be removed if his rule was arbitrary. By strengthening the power of the chiefs, the British colonial policy often made them corrupt.

French colonial policy towards land rights was very different. Right from the beginning to their domination they generalized the adoption of formalized private property among indigenous populations with a view of creating inviolable rights that could be freely negotiated according to the willingness of the individual holders. Clearly this notion of individual property rights was quite alien to the African social system and led to the breakdown of the traditional system of land management and exchange relations associated with it.

In contrast to the SSA's case where land was abundant, in land-scarce countries like India, the creation of individual property rights during British colonial rule led not only to the breakdown of traditional systems of land management but also to massive land transfers, rising indebtedness and landlessness in the rural areas. On the other hand, the creation of land rights in most of the presently developed countries was an induced response to the changing characteristics of the underlying elements and hence was largely endogenous in nature.

IMPACT OF STATE INTERVENTION IN AGRICULTURAL MARKETING With respect to agricultural marketing, the dominant form of state intervention in SSA was the setting up of the various state marketing boards. Although the marketing boards themselves date mainly from the Great Depression and the Second World War, for export crops they were preceded by the private monopolistic trading companies, particularly in West Africa. The main goals of the state marketing boards were that they would reduce monopoly profits, lower price variability and increase marketing efficiency. Bates (1981) argues that extraction of surplus was, and is, the principal function of export marketing boards and that there is very little historical evidence of price stabilization in the face of fluctuating world prices.[7]

Period after independence

THE DIRECT IMPACT OF GOVERNMENT POLICIES Most of the nationalist governments that emerged after independence were rooted in the socialist paradigm. These new governments had to create resources for running the state apparatus and had to establish a political base of support particularly through the urban elite. Thus colonial institutions such as the export marketing boards that were quite efficient at surplus extraction from the peasants, were adopted and adapted by the newly independent countries. The leaders of the post-colonial period also had to come to terms with the legacy of the colonial period that had left these new nations dependent on international trade. The system of international trade was often perceived to be unfair and a source of vulnerability that in some cases led to the rejection of trade as a path of growth. Most governments followed a type of industrialization-first strategy based on import-substitution and strong dscrimination against agriculture – particularly traditional agriculture.

IMPACT OF POPULATION GROWTH A distinguishing characteristic of SSA in its middle development phase has been its extraordinarily high rate of population growth. Between 1970 and 1996, Africa's population grew by 2.7 percent per annum and very few SSA countries have yet entered the demographic transition. In contrast, during the 19th and early 20th centuries, when European nations were industrializing, Europe's rate of population growth seldom exceeded one percent a year. In other parts of the developing world, although population growth has been rapid, it has not been as rapid as in Africa

In an earlier section, the effects of population growth in the middle development phase have been touched upon. It was pointed out there that population growth led to an increasing pressure on land, some intensification of agriculture and a fall in the average cost of the infrastructure. This was also observed in the case of SSA. However, unlike the case in other regions, there has been very little increase in land productivity in SSA and agricultural production all over Africa has been largely stagnant. Per capita production of food grains in many African countries actually fell during the last quarter of a century.

Africa's urban areas have not been able to keep up with this rapid population growth and the accelerating influx of migrants from the rural areas. Above all, modern sector enterprises have not been able to absorb this flow of migrants. The result has been massive unemployment and underemployment in the urban areas. To optimize their survival strategy, migrants enlist themselves in the informal economy before some lucky ones get absorbed into the lower ranks of the city's formal sector. A large reverse migration from the urban areas back to the rural areas has also been observed recently.

GROWTH OF THE INFORMAL SECTOR The massive growth of the informal sector and the exchange configurations associated with it, are a characteristic feature of today's developing countries. In the context of SSA, the informal sector can be regarded as a positive response to the defects of the formal economy that have been outlined above. It was essentially a spontaneous adaptation on the part of the urban poor to the needs, structures and markets that are not adequately provided by the formal sector. Thus in the case of SSA, the dual-dual framework is particularly useful since it captures very well this dualism between formal and informal sectors on the one hand and the dualism between rural and urban areas on the other.

Sahn and Sarris (1992) point out that, in the rural areas,

> Important response to state control by the peasantry included the development of parallel markets, reliance on barter and inward looking strategies as revealed through high subsistence ratios. It was the emergence of these parallel markets and related coping mechanisms that sustained the producers and consumers during the years of disintegration and decline. And, in fact, evidence would suggest that the more pervasive state controls, the more vital and pervasive a role played by such indigenous institutions. (p. 16)

They further point out that in Tanzania, farmers withdrew from the cash economy and into barter. This is evidenced by the fact that the amount of real per capita currency holdings declined by 45 percent between 1979 and 1985, the period of the most acute crises. In fact, all over Africa, the growth of parallel retail food markets was a clear manifestation of the state's inability to administer its ill-conceived policies of pan-territorial, pan-seasonal pricing of agricultural products. Consequently, a parallel retail system emerged along with the official sales through the marketing board where normal seasonal price increases were observed. These parallel markets raised marketing costs because private traders required greater returns to undertake the risks associated with unofficial marketing

All this raises an important question as to whether increased monetization of exchange relations and greater integration of markets can be expected to take place, over time, with development, in the case of all countries. The above experience of SSA suggests that there may sometimes be a 'backward' movement in the sense of reverting back to barter and the emergence of greater market segmentation. This arises essentially as a response to the prevalent distortions in the economy. In terms of the configuration approach this illustrates the idea that there is a correlation between the evolution of exchange relationships and the underlying elements. Thus very different exchange configurations could emerge depending on the evolution of underlying elements.

3.3 Phase 3: Mature Development Phase

The mature development phase (Phase 3) is marked by the predominance of modern industry and service activities. Figure 6.6 which is, likewise, self-explanatory, captures the new situation. It can be seen that encroachment from the east (through the application of modern technology and related elements) has continued and that the traditional sector in both rural and urban areas is disappearing. Simultaneously, the increasing importance of urban production is reflected through the much larger area covered by the southeast quadrant which has become predominant. Improvements in the physical environment (such as an improved road network) lead to a much larger domestic market that now integrates previously smaller regional and subregional markets. This same element is partly responsible for the relative decline of small firms which are losing their previously held locational advantage. In addition, economies of scale with respect to plant, management and marketing play an increasingly important role in the choice of technology which, in turn, strongly favors large firms.[8] Specialized institutions evolve for

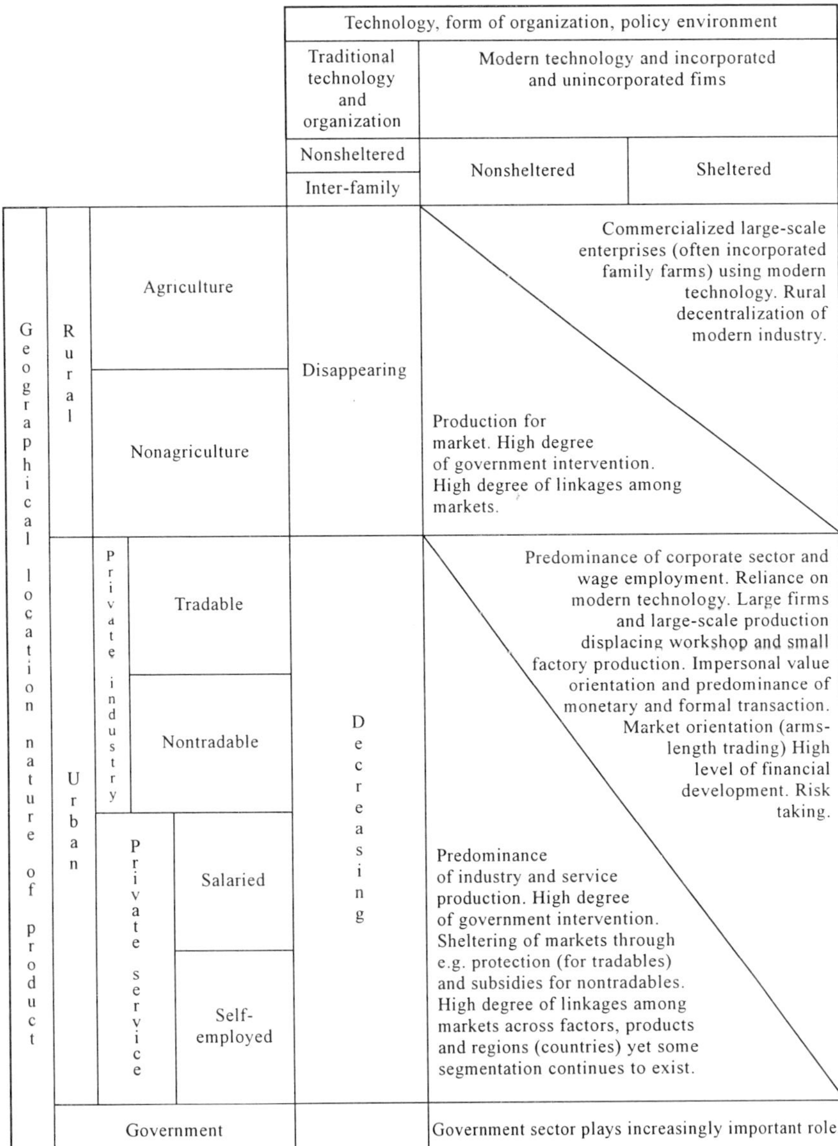

Figure 6.6 Phase 3. Mature development phase: predominance of industry and service sectors

commodity exchange and for mobilizing labor, land and capital, such as staple food exchanges, joint-stock companies and land mortage and investment banks.

NOTES

1. This section relies on Thorbecke (1994).
2. This section draws on Thorbecke and Mehra (1994).
3. For instance, according to Rostow (1961), the transition from underdevelopment to development, can be described in terms of five stages, through which all countries must proceed. These are the traditional society, the preconditions for takeoff into self-sustaining growth, takeoff into self-sustaining growth, the drive to maturity and the age of high mass-consumption.
4. For instance, according to Pirenne (1936, pp. 57-8) in the case of medieval Europe, 'the towns contained a minority, sometimes even a very small minority of the population. In the absence of statistical data prior to the fifteenth century no precise numerical estimate can, of course, be formed, but we shall probably not be far wrong in supposing that in the whole of Europe between the twelfth and the fifteenth centuries the urban population comprised never more than a tenth part of the total number of inhabitants ... It is an undoubted fact that from the demographic point of view, medieval society was essentially agricultural'. This was true in other parts of the world as well during this phase.
5. The discussion here is largely based on the recent literature on agrarian institutions and in particular the work by Hayami (1989).
6. For a more extensive discussion, see Chandavarkar (1977).
7. For a detailed discussion of commodity boards and other forms of state intervention, see Thorbecke (1993).
8. At this stage, it ought to be mentioned that Anderson has developed a three-phase explanation of changes in the size structure of industry over time for a large number of developing countries. Using the percentage shares of total manufacturing employment in respectively, (i) household and artisanal activities; (ii) small workshops and factories; and (iii) large factories, Anderson shows clearly that the former dominates in Phase 1, small workshops and factories increasingly replace household activities in Phase 2 and large firms become increasingly important in Phase 3 which also sees the gradual disappearance of household activities. Anderson's explanation of the factors which influenced these changes is generally consistent with the present analysis although focussed by design on the changing size and structure of firms throughout the development process. See Anderson (1982).

REFERENCES

Anderson, D. (1982), 'Small Industry in Developing Countries: A

Discussion of Issues', *World Development,* 10 (11), 913-48.

Bardhan, P. (1980), 'Interlocking Factor Markets and Agrarian Development: A Review of Issues', *Oxford Economic Papers*, 32, 82-98.

Bardhan, P. (ed.) (1989), *The Economic Theory of Agrarian Institutions*, Oxford: Clarendon Press.

Bardhan, P. (1993), 'Analytics of the Institutions of Informal Cooperation in Rural Development', *World Development*, 21 (4), 633.

Basu, K. (1983), 'The Emergence of Isolation and Interlinkage in Rural Markets', *Oxford Economic Papers*, 35, 262-80.

Bates, R.H. (1981), *Markets and States in Tropical Africa: The Political Basis of Agricultural Policies*, Berkeley: University of California Press.

Binswanger, H. and M.R. Rosenzweig (1986), 'Behavioral and Material Determinants of Production Relations in Agriculture', *Journal of Development Studies*, 20, 503-39.

Binswanger, H., J. McIntire and C. Udry (1989), 'Production Relations in Semi-arid African Agriculture', in P. Bardhan (ed.), *The Economic Theory of Agrarian Institutions*, Oxford: Clarendon Press, 122-44.

Boserup, E. (1965), *The Conditions of Agricultural Growth: The Economics of Agrarian Change Under Population Pressure*, London: George Allen & Unwin.

Chandavarkar, A.G. (1977), 'Monetization of Developing Economies', *IMF Staff Papers*, 24, 665-721.

Cornelisse, P. and E. Thorbecke (1991), 'Markets and Transactions in Developing Countries', Institute for Policy Reform, Working Paper Series, November.

de Janvry, A., M. Fafchamps and E. Sadoulet (1991), 'Peasant Household Behavior with Missing Markets: Some Paradoxes Explained', *Economic Journal*, 101 (409), 1400-17.

Fei, J.C.H. and G. Ranis (1964), *Development of the Labor Surplus Economy*, Homewood, IL: Richard D. Irwin, Inc.

Harris, J. and M. Todaro (1970), 'Migration, Unemployment and Development: A Two-Sector Analysis', *American Economic Review*, 60 (1), 126-42.

Hayami, Y. (1989), 'Community, Market and State', Elmhurst Memorial Lecture in A. Maunder and A. Valdez (eds), *Agriculture and Government in an Interdependent World*, Proceedings of the 20th International Conference of Agricultural Economics, Buenos Aires: Dartmouth Publications Company, UK and Gower Press, USA, 3-14.

Jorgenson, D.W. (1961), 'The Development of a Dual Economy', *Economic Journal*, June, 509-34.

Kuznets, S. (1966), *Modern Economic Growth: Rate, Structure and Spread*, New Haven and London: Yale University Press.

Lewis, W.A. (1954), 'Economic Development with Unlimited Supplies of Labor', *Manchester School*, 22, 155.

Morris, C.T. and I. Adelman (1988), *Comparative Patterns of Economic Development*, Baltimore and London: Johns Hopkins University Press.

Pirenne, H. (1936), *Economic and Social History of Medieval Europe*, New York: Harcourt,

Platteau, J.P. (1991), 'Land Reform and Structural Adjustment in SubSaharan Africa: Controversies and Guidelines', A Report prepared for FAO, Rome.

Rostow, W.W. (1961), *The States of Economic Growth: A Non-Communist Manifesto*, Cambridge: Cambridge University Press.

Sahn, D.E. and A.H. Sarris (1992), 'The Evolution of States, Markets and Civil Institutions in Rural Africa', Working Paper No. 25, Washington, DC and Ithaca, NY: Cornell Food and Nutrition Policy Program.

Thorbecke, E. (1993), 'Impact of State and Civil Institutions on the Operation of Rural Market and Nonmarket Configurations', *World Development*, 21 (4), 591-605.

Thorbecke, E. (1994), *Intersectoral Linkages and Their Impact on Rural Poverty Alleviation: A Social Accounting Matrix Approach*, Austria: United Nations Industrial Development Organization.

Thorbecke, E. and R. Mehra (1994), 'The Evolution of the Pattern of Exchange in Developing Countries', Institute for Policy Reform, Working Paper Series.

World Bank (1990), 'Poverty', *World Development Report 1990*, Oxford: Oxford University Press.

7. Changing Industrial Structure and Economic Development: Prewar Japan Revisited

Tetsushi Sonobe and Keijiro Otsuka*

1 INTRODUCTION

The process of economic development accompanies structural changes from agriculture-based to industrialized economy. Within the industrial sector, the weight shifts from labor-intensive light industries to capital-intensive heavy and then to high-tech industries. The analysis of such changes in industrial structure has been a main subject of development economics, notably in the work of John Fei and Gustav Ranis (1961, p. 533), which focusses on 'the transition process through which an underdeveloped economy hopes to move from a condition of stagnation to one of self-sustaining growth'.

Yet, the recent studies of growth accounting on newly industrialized economies in East Asia deal only with aggregate inputs and outputs without any regard to the structural transformation of the economy (Kim and Lau 1994; Young 1995).[1] They commonly found that these economies achieved high rates of growth for the last few decades due primarily to capital accumulation and, to a much lesser extent, to total factor productivity (TFP) growth. Krugman (1994) took this as evidence for declining returns to capital, which will eventually halt capital accumulation and, hence, the growth of the entire economy.[2] He states explicitly that (p. 67): 'Mere increases in inputs, without an increase in the efficiency with which those inputs are used – investing in more machinery and infrastructure – must run into diminishing returns; input-driven growth is inevitably limited'.

Krugman's hypothesis is correct in the context of the one-sector

* The authors would like to thank Shu-Jen Yeh, Yujiro Hayami, Pan Yotopoulos, and T.N. Srinivasan for their helpful comments, and Tomoya Matsumoto for computational assistance.

growth model, but not necessarily so in the context in which the growth accompanies the transformation of the industrial structure. In the world of the Heckscher-Ohlin model of international trade, for example, Rybczynski (1955) demonstrates that increases in a country's overall capital-labor ratio lead to factor movement away from the relatively labor-intensive to the relatively capital-intensive sectors so as to maintain the factor proportion in each industrial sector, thereby preventing the marginal product of capital from falling. Our own reading of the World Bank's (1993) *East Asian Miracle* strongly indicates that the industrial structure in East Asia economies has changed from labor-intensive to capital-intensive industries with accumulation of capital, which is consistent with the prediction of the Rybczynski theorem.[3]

Furthermore, in his famous argument of the flying-geese pattern of development, Akamatsu (1961) points to the importance of shifting industrial structure from the light to the heavy industries in developing economies in accordance with the ease of technology borrowing from advanced countries.[4] It is obvious that in such a dynamic process of growth, increasing capital accumulation does not necessarily lead to declining returns to capital. In short, the role of changing industrial structure in economic development needs to be reassessed empirically.

The purpose of the present study is twofold. First, we attempt to develop decomposition formulae of capital deepening and labor productivity growth in the economy, which take into account not only capital deepening and TFP growth in each industrial sector but also the shift of resources from labor-intensive to capital-intensive industries and from less productive to more productive sectors. Second, we analyze the Japanese experience by applying these formulae to the disaggregated data from prewar Japan, which covers the 'turning point' (Fei and Ranis 1964) of the Japanese economy at the end of the First World War, as well as the period of rapid heavy industrialization in the 1930s.[5] Since the availability of disaggregated data during the prewar period is limited, our analysis is forced to rely on proxies and rough estimates of key variables for limited time periods. Nonetheless, we believe that our analysis provides strong evidence to indicate the significance of changing industrial structure as a major source of economic growth.

The organization of this chapter is as follows. Section 2 develops the decomposition formulae of capital deepening and labor productivity growth, which will be applied to the empirical data in Section 3. Section 4 discusses the implication of our analysis for the debate on the East Asian Miracle and future studies.

2 DECOMPOSITION FORMULAE

In this section, we first develop a simple formula for decomposing the sources of growth of average capital-labor ratio in the economy into the growth of capital-labor ratios in individual industries and the shift of industrial structure. Second, we construct a decomposition formula of labor productivity growth in the economy, which consists of the effects of capital deepening and TFP growth achieved within individual industries, and the effects of the resource reallocation associated with the structural transformation of industries. Our decomposition formulae are derived simply from the definition of growth rates of capital-labor ratio and labor productivity while applying a series of identities.[6]

Suppose that there are n industries, and industry i uses labor input L_i and capital input K_i to produce output Y_i (i = 1,2, ...,n), which may be measured by value added. Industry i's labor productivity and capital-labor ratio are denoted respectively by y_i and k_i. Average labor productivity in the economy as a whole is given by $y = Y_i/L_i$. It is easy to confirm that the growth rate of the average labor productivity, denoted by $G(y)$, can be expressed as

$$G(y) = \sum_i s_{Y_i} G(Y_i) - \sum_i s_{L_i} G(L_i) \ , \tag{7.1}$$

where s_{Y_i} and s_{L_i} are industry i's shares in output and labor input, respectively. Rearranging (1) and using $G(Y_i) - G(L_i) = G(y_i)$, we have

$$G(y) = \sum_i s_{Y_i} G(y_i) + \sum_i (s_{Y_i} - s_{L_i}) G(L_i) \,. \tag{7.2}$$

The first term on the right-hand side of the above expression shows the weighted average of growth rates of labor productivity in individual industries with the weight being s_{Y_i}. The relation inside the parenthesis in the second term can be rewritten as

$$s_{Y_i} - s_{L_i} = \left[\frac{s_{Y_i}}{s_{L_i}} - 1 \right] s_{L_i} = \frac{y_i - y}{y} s_{L_i} \ . \tag{7.3}$$

Substituting (7.3) back into (7.2), we obtain

$$G(y) = \sum_i s_{Y_i} G(y_i) + \sum_i \frac{y_i - y}{y} s_{L_i} G(L_i) \,. \tag{7.4}$$

The second term indicates that industry i makes a positive contribution to the overall labor productivity growth if it has higher labor productivity than the average ($y_i > y$) and receives additional labor ($G(L_i) > 0$) or if it has lower labor productivity ($y_i < y$) and releases labor to other industries ($G(L_i)<0$). In other words, equation (7.4) demonstrates that the reallocation of labor away from industries with relatively low labor productivity to industries with relatively high labor productivity can be an important source of growth of overall labor productivity.

Similarly, it can be shown that the growth rate of the average capital-labor ratio, $G(k)$, where $k = \Sigma K_i / \Sigma L_i$, consists of the average growth of capital-labor ratios in individual industries, $G(k_i)$, and the reallocation effect of resources from less to more capital-intensive industries:

$$G(k) = \sum_i s_{K_i} G(k_i) + \sum_i \frac{k_i - k}{k} s_{L_i} G(L_i) . \tag{7.5}$$

The above equation shows that even if the capital-labor ratio does not change, that is, $G(k_i) = 0$, in each industry as is assumed in the Rybczynski theorem, the capital-labor ratio of the economy as a whole can increase if resources are reallocated to relatively capital-intensive industries (that is, $k_i > k$ and $G(L_i) > 0$).[7] Thus, the effect of the second term may be termed the Rybczynski effect of capital accumulation.

Now let us assume that the production function of each industry is subject to constant returns to scale and that the equilibrium holds in each industry in which factor shares of inputs are identical to their respective production elasticities. Then, tedious but straightforward manipulation of equation (7.4) leads to

$$\begin{aligned}
G(y) = & \sum_i s_{Y_i} \alpha_i G(k_i) && \text{(i)} \\
& + \sum_i \alpha \frac{k_i - k}{k} s_{L_i} G(L_i) && \text{(ii)} \\
& + \sum_i s_{Y_i} \left[G(y_i) - \alpha_i G(k_i) \right] && \text{(iii)} \\
& + \sum_i \left[\frac{y_i - y}{y} - \alpha \frac{k_i - k}{k} \right] s_{L_i} G(L_i) && \text{(iv)}
\end{aligned} \tag{7.6}$$

where α_i and α stand for factor shares of capital in industry i and the average share in the economy as a whole. The decomposition formula in (7.6) identifies the four sources of overall labor-productivity growth: (i) intra-industry capital deepening; (ii) the Rybczynski effect; (iii) TFP growth within individual industries; and (iv) reallocation of resources from industries with relatively low TFP to industries with relatively high TFP. It can be shown that the sum of the first two terms in (7.6) roughly corresponds to the product of α and the growth rate of the overall capital-labor ratio.[8] Thus, holding the production efficiency constant, or assuming that the third and fourth terms in (7.6) are zero, the average labor productivity increases either through capital deepening in individual industries or through the Rybczynski effect. It must also be pointed out that we duly recognize that structural transformation of industry cannot contribute to industrial growth indefinitely. On the contrary, we argue that the structural change plays an important role in a certain stage of economic development.

Note that the conventional growth-accounting approach measures the TFP growth of the economy by $TFPG = G(y) - \alpha G(k)$. This implies that the measured productivity growth in the conventional approach corresponds to the sum of the last two effects in our decomposition formula. Apparently, the third term is simply a weighted average of TFP growth rates in individual industries, which may be denoted by $TFPG_i$, and the weighted average may conveniently be referred to as the intra-industry TFPG effect.

The effect represented by the fourth term, on the other hand, may be called the TFPG effect of structural transformation, because growth in TFP is achieved by reallocation of resources from less productive to more productive industries. This effect needs further explanation. By using the equality of the value of output and factor payments, the expression in the parenthesis in the fourth term, which represents the structural difference in industry i (or SD_i), can be transformed into

$$SD_i \equiv \frac{y_i - y}{y} - \alpha \frac{k_i - k}{k} = \frac{w_i - w}{w}(1-\alpha) + \frac{r_i - r}{r} \alpha \frac{k_i}{k}, \qquad (7.7)$$

where w_i and r_i are wage rate and rental price of capital, respectively. It is clear that the larger the factor price discrepancies between industries, the larger will be the TFP growth effect of structural transformation, so long as resources move from low-paying to high-paying jobs. Actually, if factor prices are equalized across industries, SD_i becomes zero. Thus, the TFPG effect of structural transformation of industries arises only under disequilibrium situations, which therefore can be interpreted as the dynamic effect of adjustment toward long-run equilibrium. In the absence of such a dynamic effect, $TFPG$ is simply equal to the weighted average of TFP growth rates in individual industries. In the context of economic development, however, the short-term disequilibria can hardly be avoided and, hence, the structural effect of industrial transformation may play a critical role under dynamically changing conditions.

3 STRUCTURAL TRANSFORMATION IN PREWAR JAPAN

In this section, we attempt to apply the decomposition formulae of capital deepening and labor productivity growth to the data from the manufacturing sector classified into nine industrial sectors in prewar Japan. Disaggregated production data including capital stock, value added and factor payments at the two-digit or lower levels of aggregation, however, are not available during the prewar period. Thus, we are forced to rely on proxies and estimates of variables necessary for the decomposition analysis. First of all, we use the amount of horse powers of primary movers to represent capital stock, which is considered to be only a reasonable proxy for capital stock that can be constructed by the industrial sector during the prewar period (Hondai 1992). The Census of Manufactures (Japan Ministry of International Trade and Industry 1961) provides rich information on the horse power from 1909 to 1940, which has been carefully examined and analyzed by Minami (1976). Thus, we use the horse power data classified into nine major industrial categories, supplied by Minami.[9] We must, however, bear in mind the limitation of the Census data that it covers only those factories employing five or more workers. Therefore, the data set used in this study is not representative of the manufacturing sector as a whole in prewar Japan, during which period tiny workshops were quite common. It must be also pointed out that structural change in industries before the 1910s would have been slower than during the 1910s. The number of workers by major industrial sector was well reported by the Census.[10] Since we are interested in the long-term trends of capital accumulation and labor productivity growth, we take five-year moving averages of the variables throughout the analysis. Thus, our sample period for the analysis of capital deepening extends from 1911 to 1938.

The second problem is that value added by industrial sector can be estimated only from 1929 to 1940, by using the value-added ratio in factories covered by the Census, which was estimated by the Economic Planning Agency (1968). The remaining problem is the paucity of data necessary for the estimation of factor shares by industrial sector. Recently, Guan (1995) has estimated capital shares by industrial sector for 1933 based on the production and factor payment data in Tokyo, Nagoya and Kobe. Thus, we perform the decomposition analysis of labor productivity growth only from 1931 to 1938 by using the five-year moving averages of capital-labor (or horse power-labor) ratio and labor productivity (or value added per worker), and the estimates of factor shares of capital by Guan.

We recognize that the data used in this study are admittedly crude and subject to errors. With respect to the characterization of long-term growth patterns, however, we believe that our data provide useful indications, as will become clearer in the analyses conducted below.

3.1 Sources of Capital Deepening

Before estimating the decomposed components of capital deepening shown in equation (7.5), let us examine how the capital-labor ratio in the manufacturing sector as a whole, as well as in industrial sectors, and the industrial structure changed over the period under study.[11] Figure 7.1 compares the trend of the index of the average capital-labor ratio with changes in the index of the wage-rental ratio.[12] The close association between the two indices is striking. This can be explained by the factor substitution along the given isoquant in response to rising wage-rental ratio, the development of capital-using technology,[13] and the structural transformation of industries from labor-using to capital-using industrial sectors. How important is the last effect (called the Rybczynski effect) is a major question to be addressed in this subsection.

Another impressive observation is the rise of the wage-rental ratio from about 1917. This was primarily a result of the increasing real wage rate rather than the declining real rental price or return to capital. The wage-rental ratio began to increase because the Japanese economy had reached a turning point around the end of the First World War in terms of the dual-economy model of Fei and Ranis (1964). Prices of tradable manufactured products soared during the war, which stimulated the expansion of those manufacturing sectors. The demand for labor increased, which pulled up urban wages and attracted labor from rural areas. While prices of tradable products returned to their prewar levels after the war, the real wage did not. This was undoubtedly because the economy had already passed the point where the labor supply facing urban sectors became much less elastic.

A closer examination of Figure 7.1 reveals that the entire period can be demarcated into the three distinct phases: Phase I (1911-18) during which the capital-labor ratio grew despite the relatively stagnant trend of wage-rental ratio; Phase II (1918-31) during which both capital-labor and wage-rental ratios increased concurrently; and Phase III (1931-38) during which both capital-labor and wage-rental ratios changed only sluggishly. In order to explore the extent to which changes in the average capital-

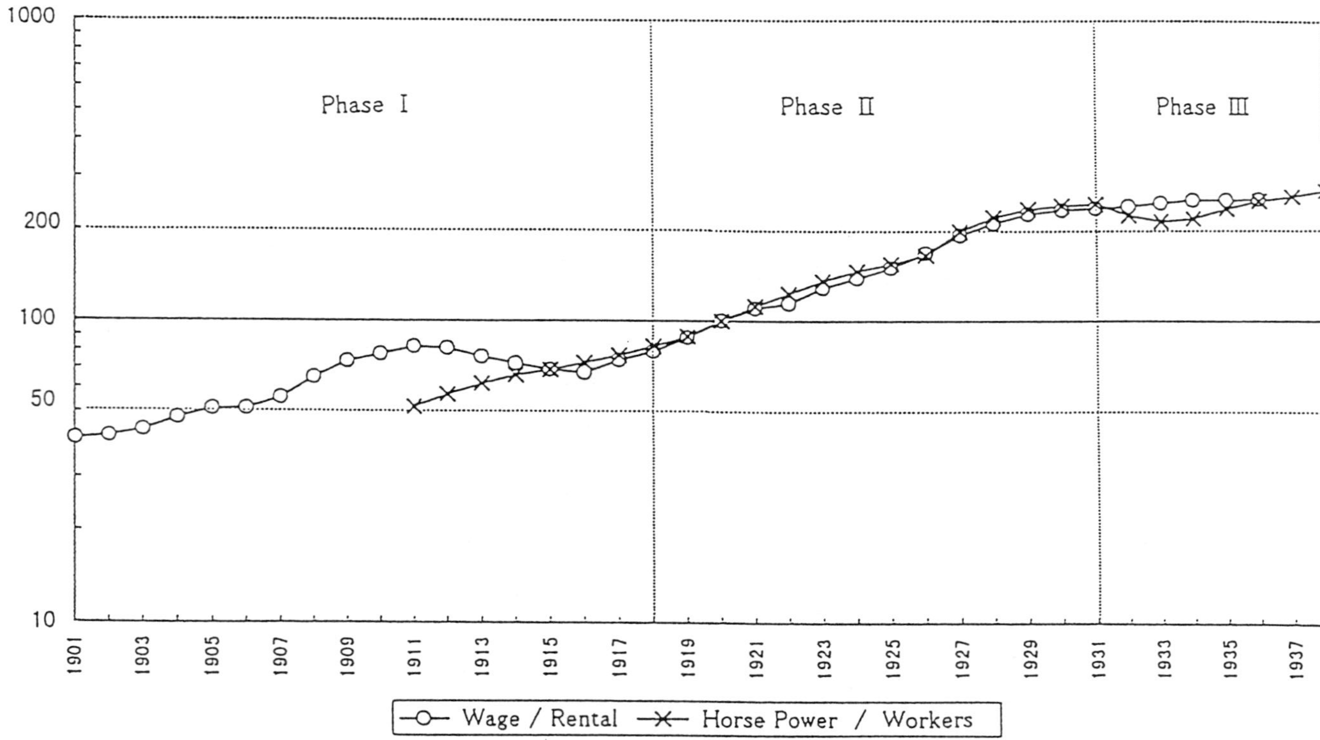

Figure 7.1 Trends in wage-rental ratio and capital-labor ratio, semi-log scale

labor ratio was brought about by changes in industrial structure, Figure 7.2 shows changes in the employment shares of the heavy industries and the machinery industry. An assumption here is that heavy industries are generally more capital intensive than light industries (see Table 7.2 for industrial classification and capital-labor ratios). More disaggregated data by industrial sector are shown in Table 7.1. A glance at Figure 7.2 establishes that heavy industrialization took place during Phase I and Phase III, whereas the industrial structure in terms of the employment share remained largely the same during Phase II. Data in Table 7.1 are consistent with this interpretation.

Observations regarding Phase I indicate that the Rybczynski effect worked in this phase, as the overall capital-labor ratio increased with heavy industrialization and without lowering the rental price of capital relative to wage rate. In contrast, observations regarding Phase III are perplexing because the capital-labor ratio of the manufacturing sector as a whole did not increase while employment shares of heavy industries increased. These observations do not appear consistent with the Rybczynski effect. The Rybczynski effect would not have worked during Phase II, either, because the capital-labor ratio increased without a major change in the industrial structure.

In order to examine changes in the capital-labor ratio within individual sectors, Figure 7.3 compares the trends of capital-labor ratios in the machinery industry, the other heavy industries and the light industries. Table 7.2 shows more disaggregated data by industrial sector.[14] It is remarkable that rapid capital shallowing, rather than capital deepening, took place in the machinery industry during Phase III.[15] According to Hondai (1992), this was due to the fact that a subcontracting system was developed between parent enterprises and enterprises supplying parts and intermediate products during this period, which greatly economized the use of capital equipment by facilitating the division of labor between enterprises. Otsuka et al. (1998) found evidence consistent with this finding; in the machine-tool industry in China, the capital-labor ratio was significantly higher for larger state enterprises, which internally produced most parts and intermediate products by installing all kinds of specialized equipment including those only infrequently used for production.

Capital shallowing also took place in the ceramic industry and the light industries other than the textile industry during the same period (Table 7.2). Yet other industrial subsectors as well as the manufacturing sector as a whole experienced capital deepening. Thus, it is difficult to determine whether the increase in the capital-labor ratio in the manufacturing sector as a whole during Phase III can be attributed to the weighted average of intra-industry capital deepening or to the Rybczynski effect.

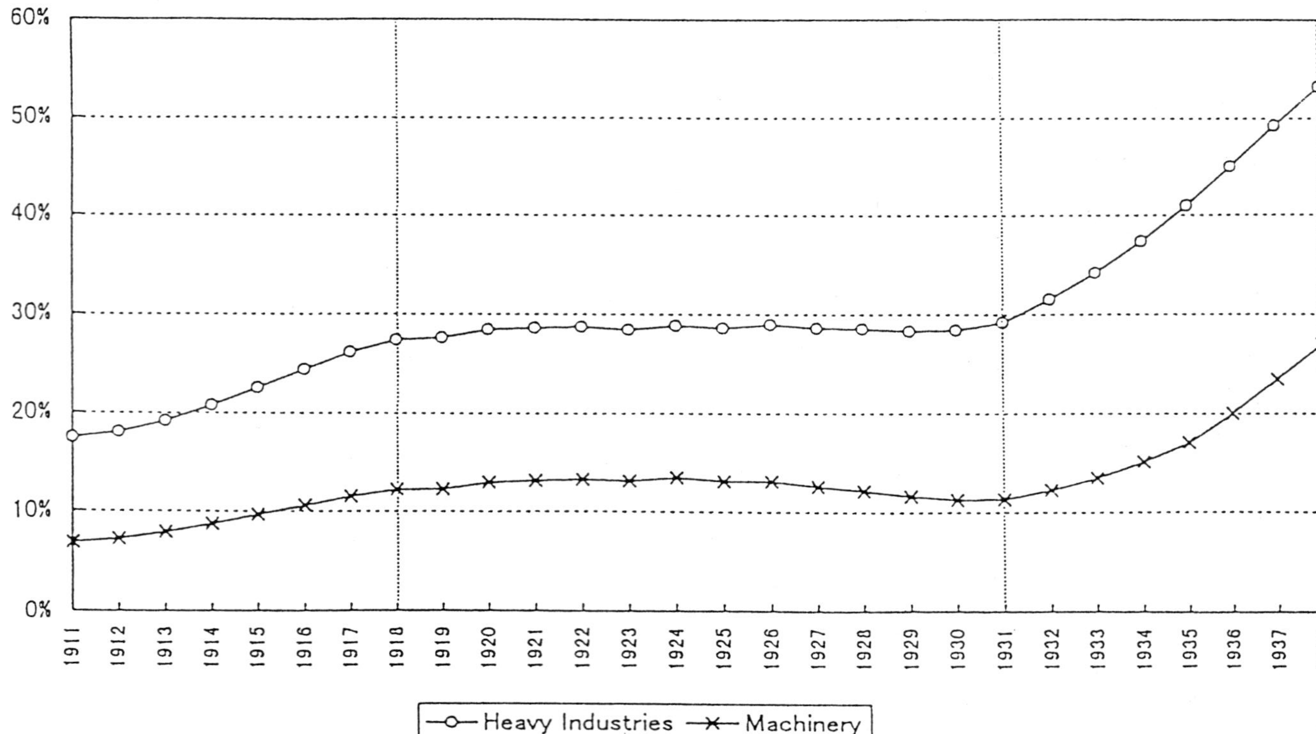

Figure 7.2 Changes in employment shares of heavy and machinery industries

Table 7.1 Changes in employment share by industrial sector (five-year moving averages, %)

Industries \ Years	1911	1918	1931	1938
Heavy industries	17.5	27.4	29.2	53.2
Chemical	3.8	6.1	8.0	10.5
Ceramic, stone and clay products	4.2	4.5	4.0	4.0
Metal industries	2.6	4.7	6.0	11.7
Machinery	6.9	12.2	11.3	27.0
Light industries	82.5	72.6	70.8	46.8
Food and kindred products	8.7	7.1	8.3	6.2
Textile products	63.2	56.4	53.1	31.5
Lumber and wood products	2.9	3.1	3.6	4.0
Printing and book binding	2.8	2.3	3.2	2.1
Miscellaneous manufacturing	4.9	3.7	2.6	2.9

Table 7.2 Changes in horse power per worker by industrial sector (five-year moving averages)

Industries \ Years	1911	1918	1931	1938
All industries	0.4	0.6	1.8	2.0
Heavy industries	1.0	1.2	3.2	2.7
Heavy industries except machinery	1.3	1.7	3.6	4.4
Chemical	2.2	2.3	4.1	5.3
Ceramic, stone and clay products	0.7	0.9	3.0	2.8
Metal industries	0.8	1.5	3.3	4.2
Machinery	0.5	0.7	2.5	1.1
Light industries	0.3	0.4	1.3	1.2
Food and kindred products	0.3	0.5	2.0	1.4
Textile products	0.3	0.4	1.1	1.2
Lumber and wood products	0.7	0.9	2.6	1.7
Printing and book binding	0.1	0.2	0.6	0.6
Miscellaneous manufacturing	0.1	0.3	1.3	0.9

It is also worth noting that capital-labor ratios in all three sectors shown in Figure 7.3 increased during Phase II, whereas they grew only slowly during Phase I. The latter observation supports the hypothesis that the transformation of industrial structure played a major role in raising the overall capital-labor ratio in the manufacturing sector during Phase I.

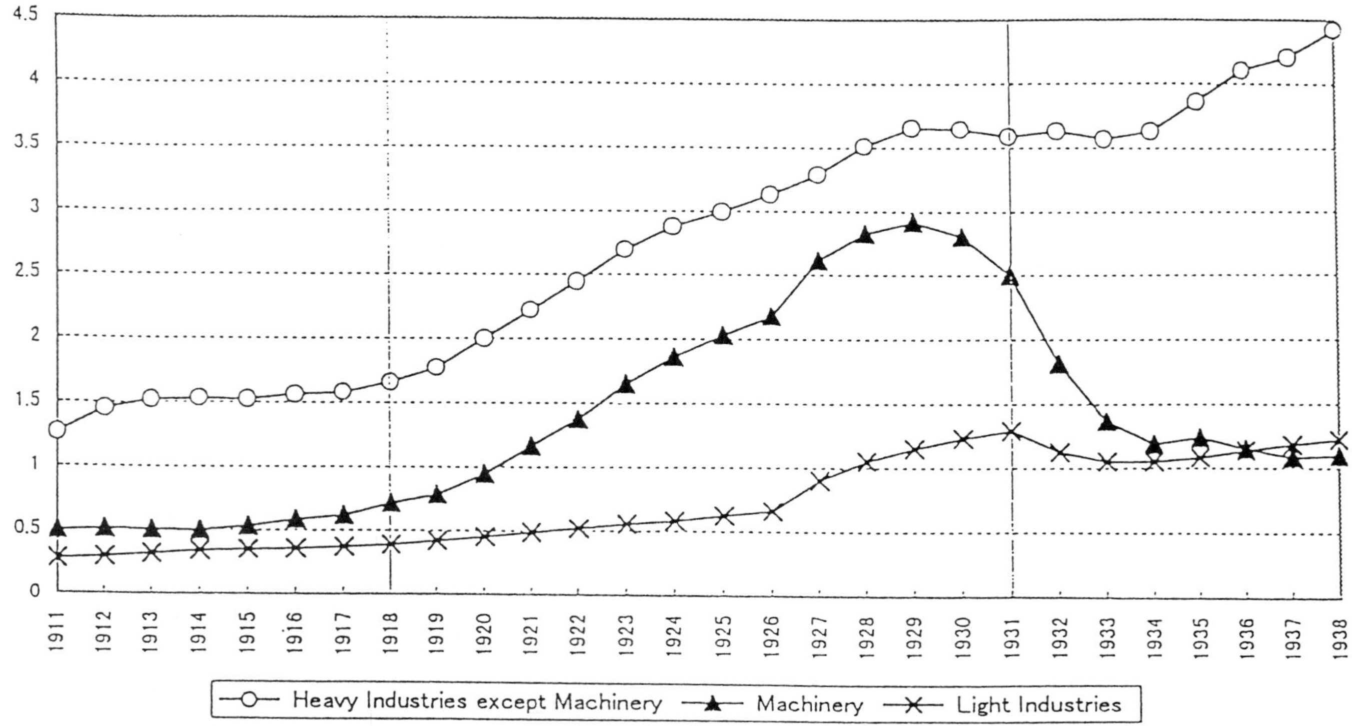

Figure 7.3 Trends in horse power per worker in manufacturing industries (five-year moving averages)

Table 7.3 Decomposition of the growth of the average capital-labor ratio (%)

Periods	Phase I 1911-18	Phase II 1918-31	Phase III 1931-38
Growth of capital-labor ratio $G(k)$	6.6	8.4	1.4
Intra-industry capital deepening	4.4	4.0	−0.8
Rybczynski effect	2.2	0.4	2.2

In order to assess how much of the rise of the capital-labor ratio in the manufacturing sector as a whole was accounted for by the Rybczynski effect, we estimated the decomposition formula shown in equation (7.5) while using data classified into nine industrial sectors. The summary results are shown in Table 7.3. During Phase I, the average capital-labor ratio increased at the annual average rate of 6.6 percent, of which 2.2 per cent or one-third is attributed to the Rybczynski effect.[16] Therefore, it seems reasonable to conclude that the transformation of the industrial structure in the early phase of industrial development in Japan helped mitigate the declining return to capital by means of shifting industrial structure from labor-intensive to capital-intensive industries.

As expected, the Rybczynski effect did not work at all during Phase II. In fact, a negligible portion of the rapidly growing capital-labor ratio was attributed to the shift in the industrial structure during this phase. Somewhat unexpectedly, the Rybczynski effect dominated during Phase III. In this subperiod, the weighted average of growth rates of capital-labor ratio in individual industries was negative, primarily because of the declining capital-labor ratio in the machinery and other industries. On the other hand, the Rybczynski effect was positive and as significant as in Phase I in absolute terms, due to the progress in heavy industrialization. In other words, while the Rybczynski effect was at work during this period, which led to an increase in the capital-labor ratio through the effect of industrial transformation, capital-saving institutional innovation also took place in the machinery industry through the development of the subcontract system.

To conclude, the Rybczynski effect or the effect of structural transformation of industries toward capital-using direction played an important role in the early and last phases of the economic development in prewar Japan. Such a transformation would have helped prevent declining return to capital in the face of capital deepening, even if the rate of technological change was negligible.[17]

3.2 Decomposition of Labor Productivity Growth

Figure 7.4 shows changes in the average labor productivity by industry, that is, y_i's or the real value added per worker, during the third phase. Interestingly enough, the labor productivity in the machinery industry did not decline significantly despite the sharp capital shallowing observed in Figure 7.3. On the contrary, it rose slightly over Phase III. This implies that the development of the subcontracting system led to major efficiency gains in the machinery industry.

Somewhat puzzling is the fact that the heavy industries, excluding the machinery industry, did not achieve a significant rise in their labor productivity levels, even though their capital-labor ratios rose significantly in this phase. It follows that these industries had negative TFP growth. Recall that the wage-rental ratio did not increase appreciably in this phase, so that there would not have been strong incentives to substitute capital for labor. Then, the question arises as to why capital deepening took place in these industries.

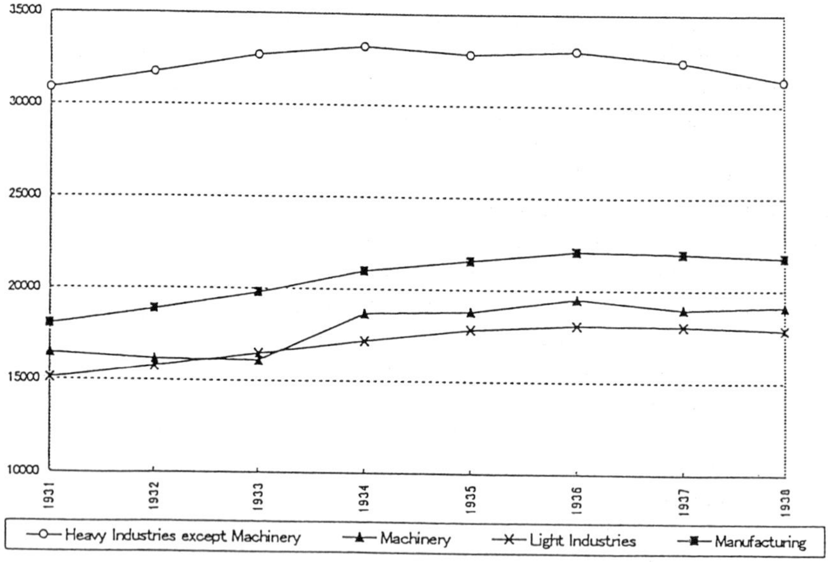

Figure 7.4 Trends in real value added per worker by industry (five-year moving averages)

Table 7.4 shows the result of the decomposition analysis of labor productivity growth during Phase III. The average labor productivity in the manufacturing sector as a whole grew at a modest average rate of 2.7 per cent per year. This growth can be decomposed into the intra-industry effect and the inter-industry resource reallocation effect of capital deepening and productivity growth (see formula (7.6)). In view of the rapid reallocation of resources toward the heavy industries in this phase, it should not be surprising to find that the inter-industry effect accounts for

Table 7.4 Decomposition of labor productivity growth for 1931-38 (%)

Labor productivity growth $G(y)$	2.7
Intra-industry effect	1.4
(i) Intra-industry capital deepening	−0.5
(iii) Inter-industry TFPG	1.9
Inter-industry effect	1.3
(ii) Rybczynski effect	1.1
(iii) TFPG effect of structural transformation	0.2

Table 7.5 Intra-industry growth rates of labor productivity for 1931-38 (%)

Industries	$G(y_i)$	$G(k_i)$	$TFPG_i$
All industries	2.6	1.4	2.0
Heavy industries	0.3	−0.4	0.6
Heavy industries except machinery	−0.1	2.8	−2.1
Chemical	−0.4	3.7	−3.0
Ceramic, stone and clay products	3.1	−1.0	3.7
Metal industries	−1.2	3.3	−2.7
Machinery	2.1	−11.7	6.3
Light industries	2.4	−1.2	2.9
Food and kindred products	0.7	−5.5	5.3
Textile products	3.4	1.0	3.0
Lumber and wood products	−1.9	−6.4	1.3
Printing and book binding	2.1	−0.7	2.2
Miscellaneous manufacturing	0.3	−4.4	2.7

as much as 1.3 percent or nearly a half of the overall growth rate of labor productivity. The further decomposition of this effect shows that the Rybczynski effect, rather than the TFPG effect of structural transformation, accounts for the major portion of the inter-industry effect. The critical role played by the Rybczynski effect conforms to our general hypothesis on the importance of the structural transformation of industries as a source of growth in developing economies.

Despite the capital deepening in the manufacturing sector as a whole, the contribution of the intra-industry capital deepening to the labor productivity growth was negative, that is, −0.5 percent. This is because those industries which had large capital shares, such as the machinery industry, experienced capital shallowing. Thus, the positive intra-industry effect of 1.4 percent is explained by the large contribution of the TFP growth in individual industries or the intra-industry TFP growth, which amounted to 1.9 percent.

The positive average contribution of the intra-industry TFPG effect does not imply, however, that TFP grew in every industrial sector. Table 7.5 demonstrates $TFPG_i$ or the average annual growth rate of TFP by industrial sector. TFP grew in all sectors of the light industries. This observation is consistent with the finding of Otsuka et al. (1988) that new capital-using technologies, such as high-draft ring spinning machines and automatic weaving looms, were rapidly developed and introduced into the cotton textile industries only after the turning point of the economy. As a result, TFP grew rapidly in the 1920s and 1930s.

As may be expected, TFP also grew in the machinery industry, which experienced a declining capital-labor ratio and a slightly increasing labor productivity. In the chemical and metal industries, however, TFP growth rates were clearly negative. As a result, the average annual growth rate of TFP in the heavy industries other than the machinery industry was negative and as large as −2.1 percent. These observations strongly indicate that the heavy industrialization in Japan during the 1930s was achieved at the expense of the production efficiency of the manufacturing sector.

This conclusion is supported by the negligible contribution of the TFPG effect of inter-industry resource reallocation, which was a mere 0.2 percent (see Table 7.4). As was emphasized, this phase of prewar Japanese growth accompanied the significant transformation of industrial structure towards the heavy industries, which is revealed by the significant Rybczynski effect. The resources, however, were not necessarily reallocated to the more productive sectors of the economy during this period.[18] In other words, it may well be that the resource reallocation did not take place in accordance with the changing comparative advantage of industries during this phase of prewar economic growth in Japan.

The facts that the production efficiency generally declined but the capital-labor ratio increased in the heavy industries and that the heavy industrialization failed to achieve significant gains in production efficiency through the inter-industry reallocation effect will not be explained without assuming sizable distortions in the economy. In the 1930s, the government industrial policies were headed toward planned economy in preparation for the war. An early example is the Juyo-sangyo Tosei-ho (Important Industries Control Law) of 1931, which intended to 'build an adequate industrial structure to achieve economies of scale' (Sheridan 1993, p. 106). The government intervention into the economy was further intensified throughout the 1930s, in order to establish a self-sufficient economy with the ability to produce critical commodities for the anticipated warfare. There is therefore no wonder that our decomposition analysis uncovered the perplexing tendencies of capital deepening and productivity decline in the heavy industries.

4 CONCLUSIONS

Recent studies of growth accounting on the long-term growth of advanced countries including Japan and on the cross-section of a large number of countries indicate that the contribution of TFP growth to the growth of overall economy is limited in the early stage of economic development (Hayami and Ogasawara 1997; Collins and Bosworth 1996). In other words, the engine of growth in the early stage of development is capital accumulation based on technology borrowing, which requires massive investments in imported capital equipment. In order to achieve rapid growth through capital accumulation, a sufficient amount of domestic savings must be mobilized. In fact, the savings rate in prewar Japan, the postwar Asian NIEs, and other contemporary East Asian economies increased rapidly to support accumulation-based economic growth.

As Krugman (1994) argues forcefully, such a growth pattern cannot be sustained, if capital accumulation without technological improvement results in a declining return to capital. We hypothesized in this study that the declining return to capital in the face of rapid capital accumulation without substantial technological progress can be avoided by transforming the industrial structure toward capital-intensive industries in line with the conventional theories of international trade. For testing this hypothesis, we first developed the new decomposition formula of economic growth, which is capable of accounting for the contribution of inter-industry resource reallocation effects, in addition to the intra-industry effects of capital deepening and productivity improvement. We then tested the validity of our hypothesis by using the data from prewar Japan.

Our analysis, however, suffers from the serious data limitation. In particular, we failed to apply the decomposition formula of labor productivity growth to the data before the First World War, when capital accumulation was supposed to take place without much technological improvement. Therefore, there is no denying that our empirical analysis is incomplete. Nonetheless, we obtained evidence that capital accumulation took place significantly through the transformation of the economy toward heavy industries in the 1910s. Furthermore, we found that capital accumulation through heavy industrialization played a major role in raising the overall capital-labor ratio and labor productivity in the 1930s. It seems to us that these findings indicate the potential importance of the transformation of industrial structure as a source of economic growth.

Needless to say, the study of economic development is different from that of economic growth with its focus on the role of changing industrial structure in the course of economic growth. Our decomposition analysis incorporates such an element of development economics into the analysis of economic growth. It is fair to say that our analysis provides a new avenue of promising research in economic growth and economic development by broadening the scope of the growth accounting approach. Further application of our decomposition analysis to the growth experience of the East Asian economies will be warranted.

NOTES

1. Similarly, the cross-country studies of economic growth highlight the association between initial conditions and subsequent economic growth at the aggregate level of the economy (see, for example, Barro 1991).
2. Hayami and Ogasawara (1997) base their argument on the historical experience of Japan and the United States and state that the contribution of TFP growth was limited when the economy relied on imported technology but accelerated in later stages of development when human capital is accumulated and organized R&D activities are carried out. Collins and Bosworth (1996) provide new evidence from the recent data in East Asia which is consistent with the Hayami-Ogasawara hypothesis. Also see Odagiri and Goto (1996) for the increasing importance of formal R&D and schooling in industrial innovations after the First World War in prewar Japan.
3. In his earlier work, Young (1992) postulates the hypothesis, based on his theoretical model, that Singapore moved up the ladder of comparative advantage from labor-intensive to capital-intensive industries too fast to benefit from

learning by doing. This hypothesis, however, has never been tested.

4. The essence of Akamatsu's thesis, which looks at the international technology transfer from the viewpoint of developing economies, is the same as the theory of the product cycle advanced by Vernon (1966), which considers the technology transfer from advanced to less-advanced economies.
5. See Ohkawa and Rosovsky (1973) for an overview of economic development in prewar Japan.
6. The idea behind our decomposition formula may not be new, but to our knowledge it has never been incorporated into a formula with clear economic interpretation. Hondai (1992, Appendix I), however, develops a formula for decomposing the capital-labor ratio, which is similar to equation (7.5). Ohkawa and Rosovsky (1973) calculate the productivity effect of labor reallocation between agricultural and non-agricultural sectors, but their formula is quite different from ours. The same remark applies to Denison (1962).
7. While the Rybczynski theorem considers the case in which there are no changes in prices and technologies, the effect captured by the second term in (7.5) includes the effects which arise in the presence of such changes.
8. It can be shown that strict equality holds when the rental price of capital is identical in all industries.
9. More precisely, we use the data of the horse power of primary movers other than motors installed in the case of electric power cuts.
10. The census survey was not conducted in 1910-13 and 1915-18, however. We estimate the number of workers for these years by interpolation.
11. See Fei and Ranis (1965) for capital deepening and factor bias of innovation in the industrial sector during the earlier period from 1891 to 1917.
12. The rental price of capital is estimated by multiplying the price index of machinery by the prevailing discount rate in the Tokyo market for commercial bills. The interest rate data are taken from Okazaki (1997, ch. 2, fig. 22), and the price and wage data are from Ohkawa et al. (1964-88, vol. 8).
13. Hayami and Ogasawara (1997) emphasize the importance of such biassed technological progress in the transformation from the accumulation-based growth to the efficiency-based growth during the prewar period. See also Hayami (1997) for the importance of induced innovation in economic development.
14. In the late 1930s, the horse power-labor ratio in the machinery industry, which may be considered to be a capital-intensive industry, was much lower than the average horse power-labor ratio in the manufacturing sector. The capital-labor ratio in the machinery industry was only about 70 percent of the average capital-labor ratio in the manufacturing sector in the mid-1950s, when income per capita returned to the prewar level. Thus, it is likely that the capital-labor ratio in the machinery sector in the 1930s was as low as the horse power-labor ratio indicates.
15. Ranis (1957) observes capital shallowing in the prewar Japanese economy before the turn of the century.
16. If a finer classification of industrial sectors is possible, a portion of growing capital-labor ratio attributable to the Rybczynski effect is likely to increase.
17. According to the estimate of Hayami and Ogasawara (1997), which covers the

private non-primary sector of the economy, TFPG was very small before the First World War.

18. The average ratio of structural difference (SD_i) was 9.3 percent in the machinery industry, − 11.7 percent in the heavy industries other than the machinery industry, and 1.4 percent in the light industries. Thus, labor was reallocated away from the relatively productive light industries to the much less-productive metal and chemical industries as well as to the highly productive machinery industry.

REFERENCES

Akamatsu, Kaname (1961), 'A Theory of Unbalanced Growth in the World Economy', *Weltwirtschaftliches Archiv*, 86 (2), 196-217.

Barro, Robert J. (1991), 'Economic Growth in a Cross Section of Countries', *Quarterly Journal of Economics*, 106 (2), 407-43.

Collins, Susan M. and Barry P. Bosworth (1996), 'Economic Growth in East Asia: Accumulation versus Assimilation', *Brookings Papers on Economic Activity*, 2, 135-203.

Denison, Edward F. (1962), *The Sources of Economic Growth in the United States and the Alternatives before Us*, New York: Committee for Economic Development.

Fei, John C.H. and Gustav Ranis (1961), 'A Theory of Economic Development', *American Economic Review*, 51 (4), 533-65.

Fei, John C.H. and Gustav Ranis (1964), *Development of the Labor Surplus Economy: Theory and Evidence*, New Haven, CT: Yale University Press.

Fei, John C.H. and Gustav Ranis (1965), 'Innovation Intensity and Factor Bias in the Theory of Growth', *International Economic Review*, 5 (2), 182-98.

Guan, Quan (1995), 'Senzenki no Sangyo Hatten to Gijutsu Kakushin: Tokkyo Data niyoru Bunseki' (Industrial Development and Innovation in Prewar Japan: An Analysis of Patent Data), *Gijutsu to Bunmei,* 9, 49-65.

Hayami, Yujiro (1997), *Development Economics: From the Poverty to the Wealth of the Nations*, Oxford: Oxford University Press.

Hayami, Yujiro and Junichi Ogasawara (1997), 'Changes in the Sources of Modern Economic Growth: Asian NIEs in Japan's Perspective', mimeo, Tokyo: Aoyama Gakuin University.

Hondai, Susumu (1992), *Daikigyo to Chushokigyo no Doji Seicho* (Simultaneous Growth of Large and Small and Medium Enterprises), Tokyo: Dobunkan.

Japan, Economic Planning Agency (1968), *Choki Keizai Tokei no Seibi Kaizen ni kansuru Kenkyu* (Studies on Long-term Economic Statistics), Tokyo.

Japan, Ministry of International Trade and Industry (1961), *Kogyo Tokei 50 Nenshi* (History of the Census of Manufactures (for 1909-58)), Tokyo.

Kim, Jong-Li and Lawrence J. Lau (1994), 'The Sources of Economic Growth of the East Asian Newly Industrialized Countries', *Journal of the Japanese and International Economies*, 8 (3), 235-71.

Krugman, Paul (1994), 'The Myth of Asia's Miracle', *Foreign Affairs*, 73 (6), 62-78.

Minami, Ryoshin (1976), *Doryoku Kakumei to Gijutsu Shinpo* (Power Revolution and Technological Progress), Tokyo: Toyokeizai Shimposha.

Odagiri, Hiroyuki and Akira Goto (1996), *Technology and Industrial Development in Japan: Building Capabilities by Learning, Innovation, and Public Policy*, Oxford: Oxford University Press.

Ohkawa, Kazushi and Henry Rosovsky (1973), *Japanese Economic Growth: Trend Acceleration in the Twentieth Century*, Stanford, CA: Stanford University Press.

Ohkawa, Kazushi, Miyohei Shinohara and Mataji Umemura (eds) (1964-88), *Estimates of Long-term Economic Statistics of Japan since 1968*, 14 volumes, Tokyo: Toyokeizai Shimposha.

Okazaki, Tetsuji (1997), *Kogyoka no Kiseki: Keizai Taikoku Zenshi* (Paths toward Industrialization: A Prelude for the Emergence of Economic Giant), Tokyo: Yomiuri Shinbun.

Otsuka, Keijiro, Gustav Ranis and Gary Saxonhouse (1988), *Comparative Technology Choice in Development: The Indian and Japanese Cotton Textile Industry*, London: Macmillan.

Otsuka, Keijiro, Deqiang Liu and Naoki Murakami (1998), *Industrial Reform in China: Past Performance and Future Prospects*, Oxford: Oxford University Press.

Ranis, Gustav (1957), 'Factor Proportions in Japanese Economic Development', *American Economic Review*, 47 (5), 594-607.

Rybczynski, T.M. (1955), 'Factor Endowments and Relative Commodity Prices', *Economica*, 22, November, 336-41.

Sheridan, Kyoko (1993), *Governing the Japanese Economy*, Cambridge, MA: Polity Press.

Vernon, Raymond (1966), 'International Investment and International Trade in the Product Cycle', *Quarterly Journal of Economics*, 80 (2), 197-207.

World Bank (1993), *The East Asian Miracle. Economic Growth and*

Public Policy, New York: Oxford University Press.

Young, Alwyn (1992), 'A Tale of Two Cities: Factor Accumulation and Technical Change in Hong Kong and Singapore', *NBER Macroeconomics Annual, 1992*, Chicago: NBER, 13-54.

Young, Alwyn (1995), 'The Tyranny of Numbers: Confronting the Statistical Realities of the East Asian Growth Experience', *Quarterly Journal of Economics*, 110 (3), 641-80.

Part III Income Distribution and Development

8. Growth and Changes in Inequality in Labor-absorbing Economies

Chau-Nan Chen and Yun-Peng Chu

1 INTRODUCTION

Between the 1960s and early 1970s, quite contrary to conventional wisdom, Taiwan experienced rapid growth while its income inequality fell. This likely prompted many scholars concerned with the issue to study the topic with zeal. Professor John Fei was one of these scholars. He and his associates Professors Gustav Ranis and Shirley Kuo took the time to investigate what happened and came up with a book, *Growth with Equity: The Taiwan Case*, published by Oxford University Press in 1979. The book has since become one of the most widely read works on Taiwan's economic development and income distribution.

The Fei et al. study covers the period of the 1950s, when Taiwan embarked on import-substituting industrialization, and that of the 1960s and 1970s, when export-led industrialization began and boomed. Data on income distribution were scarce for the former period and the early 1960s. They have become more abundant and reliable since the mid-1960s.

Of the data available for the 1950s and 1960s, those on income inequality among farm households stratified by size of landholdings from the early 1950s to the late 1960s are of reasonably good quality. Fei et al. (1979) report that data and find the following:

1. The Gini coefficient of (nonagricultural) wage income is very small (about 0.06-0.08), and the share of such income in total farm household income increased sharply from less than 6 percent in 1952 to more than a quarter by 1967.
2. The agricultural income Gini is between 0.32 and 0.35 and declining over time. Its share in total farm household inequality fell from 78 to 58 percent between 1952 and 1967.
3. Farm households, income inequality declined sharply in the 1950s and early 1960s. The Gini coefficient dropped from 0.2860 in 1952 to

0.1790 in 1967. This was made possible mainly by the rise in the share of wage income, the distribution of which had been very equal, in total farm households' income.[1]

More data on distribution are available for the late 1960s and afterwards. Inequality of household income is found to have dropped sizably between the late 1960s and early 1970.[2] The phenomenon becomes the center of attention in the Fei et al. (1979) study. Specifically, they apply a method of decomposing the Gini coefficient by different income sources to analyze the fall in inequality between 1964 and 1972.[3] It is found that between 1968 and 1972, the most important factor contributing to the fall was the 'factor Gini effect', or the fall in the Gini of the different types of income by source among households. Within this factor Gini effect, the single largest contributor, accounting for about half of the total fall in income inequality, was the fall in the inequality of wage income among households (ibid., 1979, pp. 102-3).

In the same book, for the period 1964-72, there is another decomposition by two household groups: those headed by farmers and those headed by nonfarmers. Here it was found that 118.5 percent of the fall in the inequality of household income can be explained by the so-called intra-sectoral effect, namely the fall in within-sector inequalities, and −18.5 percent of the fall is attributable to the inter-sectoral effect, namely the between-sector inequality (ibid., p. 246).

These findings have strong implications for theories of income distribution. Most existing theories have been attempts to explain the Kuznets 'inverted-U' hypothesis (see Kuznets 1955), but the Taiwanese case during the period of rapid industrialization does not seem to conform to that pattern.[4] There is need for a different theory. In their book, Fei et al. make several novel attempts at constructing alternative explanations.[5] They argue that the key to the falling income inequality among farm households in the 1950s, and to the falling inequality among all households from the 1960s to the early 1970s, has been the expansion of nonagricultural employment.[6]

In the 1950s, it was the import-substituting, unskilled-labor-intensive industries that provided the employment. In the 1960s, the export-led, unskilled-labor-intensive manufacturing sector provided employment at an even faster speed as exports grew rapidly:

> [E]xports growing at rates of more than 30 percent by the end of the 1961-72 period ... the industries that grew fastest ... were such light consumer goods as textiles and such intermediate goods as electronics. (ibid., 1979, p. 31)

> [R]ates of absorption of non-agricultural labor doubled from 3 percent in the

1950s to more than 6 percent in the 1960s. Despite high ... rates of population growth, the reserve of surplus labor in Taiwan was virtually exhausted by the end of the 1960s. (ibid.)

The distribution of income appears to have improved over the entire 1964-72 period, as it very clearly does after the advent of labor scarcity in about 1968. The pattern after 1968 would be consistent with the views of Lewis ... that equity can be expected to improve along with growth once real wages rise in a sustained fashion after commercialization. (ibid, p. 35)

In the subsequent analysis, various attempts are made by the authors to substantiate the above hypothesis. One attempt is given in their Chapter 4, where the inequalities of wage income among households and among individual workers are analyzed. There it is found that education is the most important factor accounting for the inequality of wages for all three groups of workers-rural, town and city — for 1966. It is also found that the main factor contributing to the disparity of wage income among households in the same year is that some households have more highly educated workers than others.

But that is only a single-year analysis, while the phenomenon in question is the *change* in inequality over time, so the substantiation has not really been completed. Chu's (1996a, 1997) studies are follow-up efforts to bring the substantiation to completion. He uses the Fei et al. 1966 data in grouped form and the 1977 data stored electronically and provided by the Directorate-General of Budget, Accounting and Statistics (DGBAS), Taiwan, to show that the bulk of the fall in the disparity of wage income among individual workers can be attributed to the narrowing disparity of wage income between workers with different years of schooling and different locations of work (urban versus nonurban), age and gender being equal. This result reflects very well the labor-absorption, surplus-labor-exhaustion, employment-expansion stories given in Fei et al. (1979) in explaining the fall in income inequality.

In this chapter, we shall extend the above analysis to cross-country comparisons to see whether the same pattern holds for other countries during their periods of labor-absorbing industrialization. In what follows, Section 2 will revisit the Fei et al. thesis embodied in their decomposition analysis and enlarge it conceptually to allow for possible variations that may be relevant in cross-country comparisons. Section 3 will discuss the cases of Japan and the other three 'tigers' during their periods of labor-absorbing growth by using the concepts developed in Section 2. Section 4 analyzes the situations in Malaysia and the Philippines. Finally, Section 5 will give concluding remarks.

2 THE FRAMEWORK OF ANALYSIS

Dividing the population into groups, some income inequality indices can be decomposed into the sum of within-group and between-group inequalities. The latter is defined as the inequality among group means, that is, the level of inequality that remains when all members in the same group have the same income.

Indices such as the coefficient of variation and the Theil index can be decomposed in this way; they can be called 'groupwise decomposable'. Others such as the Gini ratio cannot be thus decomposed without a residual. Group-wise decomposition of the coefficient of variation is applied in, for example, Chapter 5 of Fei et al. (1979), where households are subject to groupings by (i) farm and nonfarm, (ii) degree of urbanization, (iii) age of household head, (iv) gender of household head, (v) educational attainment of household head, and (iv) number of employed persons in the household. The Theil index (see Theil 1972) is even more widely used in country studies.

Because industrialization is closely related to the growth of the non-agricultural sector relative to that of the agricultural sector, groupwise decomposition is often applied to the grouping of the population by farm and nonfarm sectors. A decomposable inequality index, I, can then be expressed as

$$I = f[I(F), I(N), I_b] \qquad (8.1)$$

where the first two terms are the intra-group inequalities (F for farm households and N for nonfarm households), and the third term is inter-group inequality.

The preferred income variable is the per capita (or per adult-equivalent) household income, in which case I_b is a measure of disparity in per capita household income between the farm and nonfarm households. The more widely used (as in Fei et al., Chapter 5) but less preferred variable is total household income, in which case I_b becomes the inequality in total household income between farm and nonfarm households.

An alternative method of decomposition is to divide income into sources, and then express income inequality as the sum of the contributions of inequalities of sources. This is the primary type of analysis in Fei et al. (1979) presented in Section 1, above. Shorrocks (1982) gives a general account of how inequality indices can be thus decomposed. It is shown there that the 'natural' decomposition by variance is the preferred way, since it meets some intuitive criteria. That is the decomposition used in Chu (1997). Fei et al. use the Gini ratio, the sourcewise decomposition of which is discussed at length there and also appears to be rather intuitive.

Whatever the exact method used, given that wage income from nonagricultural employment is usually an important source of income, it is often instructive to decompose total income into wage and nonwage components:

$$I = g\,[\,I\,(W),\, I\,(NW)\,] \tag{8.2}$$

where W is wage income and NW is nonwage income. The usual income variable used is total household income, divided into wage and nonwage incomes. The preferred income concept is per capita (or per adult-equivalent) household income, divided into per capita wage and nonwage components.

One can apply equation (8.2) to $I(F)$ or $I(N)$ in equation (8.1). In this way (8.2) can be written as

$$I(k) = g[\,I(W_k),\, I(NW_k)\,],\; k = F,\, N \tag{8.3}$$

where W_k and NW_k are the wage and nonwage incomes of the k type of households.

Both equations (8.2) and (8.3) have their strengths and weaknesses. The basic problem with (8.3) is that in most countries, 'farm/nonfarm' households are defined according to the extent of involvement in farming activities, so the 'tags' can change over time. Typically each year more and more farm households no longer fulfill the basic criteria and are reclassified as nonfarm households. This creates problems in the interpretation of results obtained from equations like (8.3).

On the other hand, the distinction of the sector to which a household belongs is often important in the discussion of economic development. Equation (8.2) does not carry such information directly. Fortunately, in many applications it can be rewritten as

$$I = g[\,I(W),\, I\,(NW_f),\, I(NW_n)\,] \tag{8.4}$$

where NW_f *and* NW_n refer to non-wage income from farming and nonfarming activities respectively. Any households with a large (small) NW_f are those closely related with the farming (nonfarm) sector, and the relative share of NW_f in total income, which will be included in the g function in most applications, depends then on the farm/nonfarm income disparity, an important variable in the analysis of income distribution in developing countries.

Since, in the literature, analysis related to both types of concept embodied in equations (8.1)-(8.3) and (8.4) can be seen, we shall review both of them here in terms of how labor-absorbing growth affects changes in income inequality over time.

First, we shall review the groupwise decomposition of equation (8.1) accompanied by sourcewise decomposition of equation (8.3) first. It is obvious that both W_F and W_N in equation (8.3) are affected by the employment and wage rates of the members of households. If for both F and N the poorer households have relatively more members that are un- or underemployed, an expansion in wage-earning employment that is equally accessible to all households will tend to reduce $I(W_k)$, $k = F, N$, other things being equal. Likewise, if the poorer households have relatively more members of lower skill, then a narrowing disparity between wages of skilled and unskilled workers will tend to reduce the magnitude of the same variables, other things being equal. Moreover, given that most wage-earning employment comes from the nonagricultural sectors, and that wages earned in these sectors are usually higher than the income earned from farming activities, an expansion in wage-earning employment among the farm households tends to reduce farm/nonfarm income disparities or I_b, again other things being equal.

Other things are, of course, not always equal. The agriculture/nonagriculture terms of trade will affect the income disparity between farm and nonfarm households. The nature of agricultural development will affect $I(NW_F)$, remembering that farming income is usually the dominant source of income in non-wage income of farm households. Employment opportunities may not be accessible to all. They may be accessible only to the nonfarm households in the nonrural areas. If they are accessible to the rural sector, they may be so only for a selected group of households. In some instances, employment opportunities are shared with migrant workers from other economies. If the expansion of employment is only for skilled workers, the expected result may not be forthcoming either, as better-off households usually have more members of higher skill.

We turn now to equation (8.4). Many of the factors mentioned above are still identifiable. We shall demonstrate how these factors can be incorporated by revisiting the sourcewise decomposition of income of all households in Fei et al. (1979, ch. 3).

Fei et al.'s table 10.2 contains the data needed for a full analysis of decomposition of *changes* in inequality over time. But the analysis actually used in their main body of analysis (their Chapter 3) is only an abbreviation. We shall unfold the full analysis here, as a first step.

Specify equation (8.4) in terms of the Gini ratio and redefine/add some terms as

$$G(y) = (Sw)[sG(W)] + (Sc)[sG(C)] + (Sm)[sG(M)] + (Sa)[sG(pA)] \quad (8.5)$$

where y is total income, and $y = W + C + M + A$, which are wage, capital, transfer and miscellaneous, and agricultural incomes (expressed in nonagricultural goods) respectively; Sj's and $sG(k)$'s are, respectively, the relative shares and pseudo-Gini ratios of the four sources of income, with j and k expressed in lower- and upper-case letters, respectively, and $Sw + Sc + Sm + Sa = 1$. Define N as the sum of non-A income, and equation (8.5) can be rewritten as

$$G(y) = [Sn][sG(N)] + [Sa][sG(A)] \quad (8.6)$$

or

$$G(y) = (1 - Sa)[sG(N)] + [Sa][sG(A)] \quad (8.7)$$

Taking the difference, one obtains

$$\mathrm{D}[G(y)] = \mathrm{D}[sG(N)](1 - Sa) + \mathrm{D}[sG(A)][Sa] + [sG(A) - sG(N)][\mathrm{D}(Sa)] \quad (8.8)$$
$$+ \text{Residual}$$

Applying equation (8.8) to the data in Fei et al.'s table 10.2 generates Table 8.1 and (the 'short version' in) Table 8.2 for the periods of 1964-68

Table 8.1 Decomposition of Gini coefficient in Taiwan: 1964-68

	1964*	1968*	1964-68 decomposed	Percentage contribution
$G(y)$	0.321	0.326		
$sG(N)$	0.308	0.353		
$sG(A)$	0.354	0.178		
Sa	0.275	0.152		
{D[$sG(N)$]}[Avg(1-Sa)]			0.0349	698.49
{D[$sG(A)$]}[Avg(Sa)]			−0.0375	−751.52
[D(Sa)]{Avg[$sG(A)$ $sG(N)$]}			0.0079	158.46
Residual			−0.0003	−5.43
Sum			0.005	100

Note: *Avg*() refers to the average value between the two years.

Source: * Data are from Fei et al. (1979, Table 10.2).

Table 8.2 Decomposition of Gini coefficient in Taiwan: 1968-72

Variables	1968*	1972*	Average
$G(y)$	0.326	0.290	
$sG(A)$	0.178	0.106	
$sG(W)$	0.293	0.260	
$sG(C)$	0.459	0.424	
$sG(M)$	0.363	0.324	
Sa	0.152	0.103	0.1275
Sw	0.507	0.590	0.5485
Sc	0.278	0.258	0.2680
Sm	0.063	0.050	0.0565

	1968-72 decomposed	Percentage contribution
Short version:		
$\{D[sG(N)]\}[Avg(1-Sa)]$	−0.03628	100.81
$\{D[sG(A)]\}[Avg(Sa)]$	−0.00918	25.50
$[D(Sa)]\{Avg[sG(A)-sG(N)]\}$	0.00930	−25.84
Residual	0.00017	−0.47
Sum	−0.036	100
Long version:		
$\{D[sG(A)]\}[Avg(Sa)]$	−0.00918	25.50
$\{D[sG(W)]\}[Avg(Sw)]$	−0.01810	50.28
$\{D[sG(C)]\}[Avg(Sc)]$	−0.00938	26.06
$\{D[sG(M)]\}[Avg(Sm)]$	−0.00220	6.12
$[D(Sw)]\{Avg[sG(W)-sG(A)]\}$	0.01116	−31.01
$[D(Sc)]\{Avg[sG(C)-sG(A)]\}$	−0.00599	16.64
$[D(Sm)]\{Avg[sG(M)-sG(A)]\}$	−0.00261	7.28
Residual	0.00031	−0.86
Sum	−0.036	100

Note: Same as in Table 8.1.

Socure: * Data are from the same source as in Table 8.1.

and 1968-72, respectively. In the former period, Gini of household income rose slightly, from 0.321 to 0.326; in the latter period, it fell sharply to 0.290. It is clear from Tables 8.1 and 8.2 that for 1964-68, the main factor explaining the rise in Gini is the rise in the pseudo-Gini of nonagricultural income or $sG(N)$, as well as the fall in the share of agricultural income or Sa. The main offsetting factor is the fall in the pseudo-Gini ratio of agricultural income.[7] For 1968-72, when the overall Gini registers a sharp fall, the main contributing factor is the fall in the pseudo-Gini ratio of nonagricultural income.

Now let the sectoral terms of trade enter the picture. Let $A=pA'$, where p is the terms of trade and A' is agricultural income in terms of agricultural goods. A rise (fall) in p, other things being equal, would divert labor from nonagricultural to agricultural activities. This would raise (reduce) A'. In the end the share of pA' or A in total income (expressed in nonagricultural goods) has to rise (fall). Within the nonagricultural sector, if the elasticity of substitution is unity, the loss of (gain in) labor would not alter the relative shares of wage and capital income. (Here the transfer and miscellaneous income is assumed to be exogenous and is ignored.) Assume that the distributions of wage and capital incomes (defined in relation to the ranking of total income; so it is the pseudo-Gini concept) do not change; then the nonagricultural pseudo-Gini would remain intact. Assume also that the distribution of agricultural income (in relation to the ranking of total income; again the pseudo-Gini concept) remains the same, then the (marginal) effect of changes in A (as a result of changes in p) in addition to the existing change (when the sectoral terms of trade is constant) on changes in overall inequality is simply the coefficient of $D(Sa)$ in the third term in equation (8.8), or $[sG(A)-sG(N)]$.

Applying this relationship to the period of 1968-72 in Taiwan generates Figure 8.1. The slope of the line is -0.1898. Between 1968 and 1972, Sa fall by -0.049, and the effect on changes in the overall Gini ratio or $G(y)$ is 0.0093, which is small but contrary to the actual sign of changes in $G(y)$. Should Sa fall further due to changes in the sectoral terms of trade, the effect would be for $G(y)$ to fall by a smaller amount. At maximum, when Sa falls to zero, there will be an upward pressure on $G(y)$ of 0.02885, which is large compared to the actual fall of 0.036 during 1968-72. Here numerically one detects the importance of the sectoral terms of trade, which is one of the factors that may not be equal, as indicated above.

If the elasticity of substitution is less than (greater than) unity, the additional labor released to the nonagricultural sector due to a fall in p would raise the capital (labor) share in that sector, and this would raise (reduce) the pseudo-Gini of nonagricultural income, even if the pseudo-

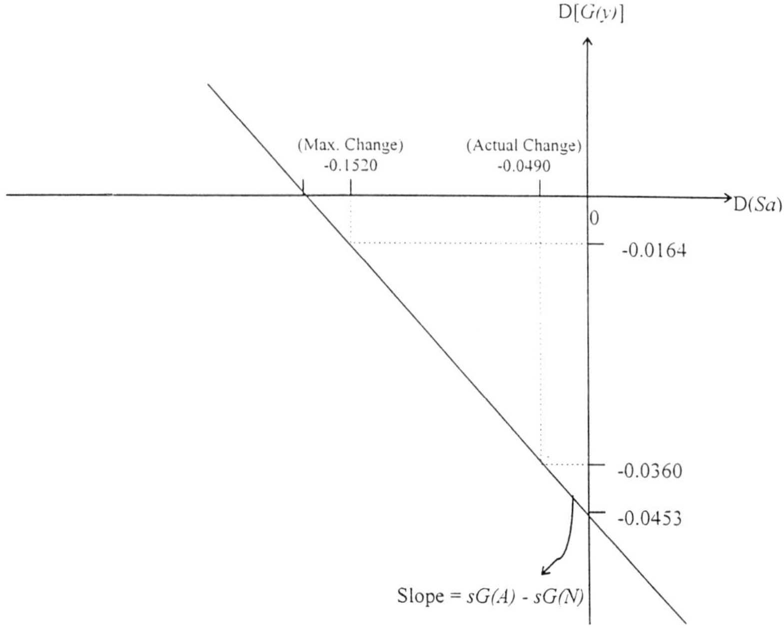

Figure 8.1 Effects of changes in terms of trade on changes in inequality in Taiwan: 1968-72

Gini ratios (defined in relation to the ranking of total income) of wage and capital incomes do not change, provided the former is less than the latter, as is often the case. So the effect of a fall in p on overall inequality would be enhanced (offset). In Taiwan the elasticity of substitution for the nonagricultural sector is likely to be less than unity, noting the gradual rise in the share of wage income over time as capital deepens, the upward pushing effect on overall inequality of changes in the sectoral terms of trade against agriculture would therefore be enhanced.

We shall turn now to the distribution of wage income among households. In Taiwan between 1968 and 1972 when the overall inequality registers a sizable fall, the pseudo-Gini of wage income or $sG(W)$ falls from 0.293 to 0.260, as is clear from Table 8.2. Taking the difference of equation (8.5) and using the relationship that $Sa = 1 - Sw - Sc - Sm$ to re-arrange terms generates the 'long version' in Table 8.2. The coefficient by which changes in $sG(W)$ affects changes in the overall Gini is 0.5485, which is sizable. In fact, changes in $sG(W)$ account for about half of the total change in $G(y)$. If employment opportunities are now less accessible to poorer households, it is likely that $sG(W)$ would not fall by the same amount or even rise. The result would be very different. A stable $sG(W)$, other things being equal, would reduce the fall in overall inequality by half. This shows numerically the importance of the distribution of employment opportunities, a variable that may also not be equal, as indicated above.

Let us summarize the factors that are often at work as an economy embarks on industrialization, in terms of whether they tend to reduce or enhance overall inequality, and according to the interplay of forces described by the variables included in the above equations:

A. Farm/nonfarm or agricultural/nonagricultural income disparity: reduces (raises) overall inequality if it narrows (widens).
B. Terms of trade between agriculture and nonagriculture: reduce (raise) Factor A if they move in favor of agriculture (nonagriculture).
C. Intra-farm and intra-nonfarm inequalities: reduce (raise) overall inequality if they fall (rise).
D. Wage-earning (nonagricultural) employment of unskilled workers in the farm sector: reduces (raises) farm households ('intra-farm') inequality when it expands (falls) if it is accessible to all farm households, provided that poorer farm households have more members of lower skill that are un- or underemployed; also reduces (raises) Factor A above if income from nonagricultural activities is on average higher than that in agriculture.
E. Wage-earning (nonagricultural) employment of unskilled workers in the nonfarm sector: reduces (raises) nonfarm households ('intra-nonfarm') inequality when it expands, if it is accessible to all nonfarm households, provided that poorer nonfarm households have more members of lower skill that are un- or underemployed.
F. Factors D and E combined. Wage-earning (nonagricultural) employment of unskilled workers: reduces (raises) households' overall inequality when it expands, if it is accessible to all households, provided that poorer households have more members of lower skill that are un- or under employed.
G. Wage disparity between skilled and unskilled workers: reduces (raises) overall inequality if it narrows (widens), provided that poorer households have more members of lower skill
H. Agricultural development: raises (holds constant) $I(NW_F)$ if richer farm households benefit more from such development (if benefits are evenly distributed among farm households).
I. Capital income (main source of non-wage, nonagricultural income): tends to raise (reduce) overall household inequality if its share in

total income of all households rises (falls), as its absolute level of inequality is usually higher than wage income, or if its inequality rises (falls).[8]

These factors are different but interdependent. Factors A and C depend mainly on the working of the other factors. The remaining factors either represent independent forces or are directly related to labor-absorbing growth.

The case of Taiwan as presented above has seen the operation of Factors D, F and G moving in the direction of reducing overall inequality. We now turn to the investigation of other economies, based on the same conceptual framework.[9]

3 CROSS-COUNTRY COMPARISONS: JAPAN AND THE OTHER THREE TIGERS

3.1 Japan

From Table 8.3, Japan's inequality fell in the 1960s for either total household income or per capita household income. Mizoguchi and Terasaki (1992) attribute the fall to four factors: (i) a rise in the relative number of employee households; (ii) a decline of inequality among employee households (Table 8.3); (iii) narrowing income disparity between farm and non-farm households (Table 8.3); and (iv) falling

Table 8.3 Income inequality in Japan, 1960-89

	All Households (1)	All households (per capita income) (1)	All Households (2)	Employee Households (2)	Per capita Income: farm households Over nonfarm households (3)
Unit	Gini	Gini	Gini	Gini	Ratio
1960					0.59
1962	0.3726	0.3864	0.373	0.3227	
1965			0.338	0.2942	0.57
1967	0.3517	0.3474	0.352	0.3092	
1970			0.407	0.3310	0.67
1972	0.3487	0.3783	0.349	0.2991	
1975			0.353	0.3059	0.71
1977	0.3581	0.3430	0.342	0.3050	
1980			0.337	0.2641	0.76
1985			0.359		
1989			0.372	0.2950	

Source: Mizoguchi and Terasaki (1992), (1)table 13; (2)table 8; (3)table 3.

inequality among farm households (Table 8.4). Of these, the first one is suspected not to be of major importance. The dominant factor is (ii). Such a finding is very much consistent with the decomposition results in Fei et al. (1979), where it is found that the dominant factor in explaining falling inequalities in Taiwan between the late 1960s and early 1970s was the fall in the inequality of wage income among households.

Mizoguchi and Terasaki (1992) further explore the reasons why inequality among employee households became smaller. They find that in the 1960s, Japan's income disparity among groups of employee households measured either by the total disparity measure (TDM) or by log-variance fell, whether the grouping is based on region (ten regions nationwide), urbanization (five different population densities), or occupation of household head (four types: day laborers, regular workers, non-government staff, government staff).

Such results echo the regression analysis reported in Chu (1997) and Factor G presented in the last section. Region and urbanization are related. From Chu (1997) income disparity between city and noncity workers in the Taiwan case. Occupation is usually highly correlated with education (for both Taiwan and Japan). Again from Chu (1997), income disparity between high-educated and low-educated workers also became smaller in the Taiwan case.

As for factors (iii) and (iv), Mizoguchi and Terasaki (1992) attribute both to the increasing importance of off-farm activities of farm households, made possible by the expansion of non-agricultural employment in less urban areas:

Table 8.4 Relative income of agricultural households in Japan by scale of farm, 1957-81 (average=100)

<table>
<tr><th>Size of farm (hectare)</th><th>1957</th><th>1961</th><th>1971</th><th>1981</th></tr>
<tr><td>0.3<</td><td>85.5</td><td>88.5</td><td>102.6</td><td rowspan="2">101.6</td></tr>
<tr><td>0.3-0.5</td><td>89.4</td><td>92.7</td><td>100.3</td></tr>
<tr><td>0.5-1.0</td><td>91.7</td><td>92.1</td><td>97.8</td><td>99.5</td></tr>
<tr><td>1.0-1.5</td><td>110.5</td><td>97.7</td><td>97.4</td><td>97.8</td></tr>
<tr><td>1.5-2.0</td><td>135.7</td><td>119.1</td><td>98.6</td><td>97.3</td></tr>
<tr><td>>2.0</td><td>172.1</td><td>157.1</td><td>109.9</td><td>101.2</td></tr>
</table>

Note: Japan except Hokkaido.
Source: Mizoguchi and Terasaki (1992, table 12).

> The scarcity of young workers became severe since the late 1950s and the shortage of general workers in the 1960s. Large-scale firms built their factories in local cities in order to employ family members of farm households as regular employees ... [S]hare of farm income in total farm household income sharply declined. In this way the reduction of the income differentials between farm households and non-agricultural households was realized. (p. 26)

This point echoes Factor D (and therefore A) presented in the last section.

Mizoguchi and Terasaki (1992) go on to argue:

> The off-farm employment had also contributed to the improvement of income distribution among farm households ... [O]ff farm employment started from the households on smaller scale of farming ... [There was] a remarkable reduction brought about by off farm incomes in the average income differentials by size of farms. (pp. 26-7)[10]

This is again Factor D, referred to above.

Mizoguchi and Terasaki also note that the beginning of Japan's period of declining inequality coincided with the passing of the turning point from labor surplus to labor scarcity in the late 1950s and early 1960s. They argue:

> [I]t was the scarcity of labor that improved income inequality ... [W]ith labor shortage in the cities, large firms had to move their factories to local areas in order to find workers. Since wages were determined in the same way within the large firm irrespective of location, they were higher than those of local firms [which] were forced to adopt the wage level of the large firms ... In this way the regional differentials of income were reduced. (pp. 30-31)

Another way of saying this is simply that the surplus labor left in the rural areas was also being exhausted.[11]

The paper referred to above is by no means the first one to highlight this aspect of the Japanese experience in the 1960s. Harry Oshima, for example, indicates in 1971 the implication of the growth of labor-intensive industries for income distribution in Japan (Oshima 1971, pp. 172-3; see also Oshima 1970). Mizoguchi in his 1975 study notes:

> [T]he trend toward equalization can be found in the regular employment income of household head[s] after the early sixties ... [A] more fundamental factor is the scarcity of labor. Since the late fifties, the scarcity of young labor became pronounced ... [That] has served to decrease the wage differentials ... [T]he small firms have been forced to revise their pay scheme in order to employ their workers.

He goes on to display a diagram which shows the ratio of job offers to job seekers from 1955 to 1971: it rose from a mere approximate 17 percent in 1955 to a peak of almost 140 percent in 1970 (Mizoguchi 1975, pp. 481-3). Wada (1975) also mentions: 'Our preliminary findings have shown ... the major factor accounting for the downturn in the [previously] widening trend of inequality was the shift in the labor market from surplus to shortage' (p. 557).

Ono and Watanabe's (1976) study reveals that as a result of participation of farm households in nonagricultural activities, the ratio of per capita nominal income of nonfarm households to that of farm households shrank from about 1.6 to 1.3 between 1960 and 1970. The real differential, which allows for differential consumer prices, was slightly smaller but followed the same trend (Ono and Watanabe, 1976, p. 365). Of even more importance, though, in explaining the fall in inequality during the period, they argue, was the fall in inequality within both the nonfarm and farm sectors. The index of income inequality measured by the coefficient of variation among urban-employee households fell from about 115 (1965=100) in 1960 to 90 in 1970. They argue that this was made possible by narrowing wage differentials in the nonagricultural sector. For the agricultural sector, the coefficient of variation also fell: from 46.8 percent for 1959-62 to 44.7 percent for 1968-70, due mainly to the fact that farm households of smaller holdings participated more in nonagricultural employment.

Mizoguchi (1978) also shows a declining (per capita) income differential between agricultural and nonagricultural employee households (classified by the occupation of heads, see ibid., p. 89) after 1960. Agricultural income in total income of agricultural households fell from more than 72 percent in 1953 to 30 percent after 1970, while those with smaller lands derived more household income from non-agricultural income (ibid., p. 93). Both phenomena reflect the influence of the movement of industries from urban to rural areas in response to labor shortages. Among the employee households, when subject to a Rao decomposition by four sources, namely (i) regular employee income of the household head, (ii) bonus or temporary income, (iii) the employment income of other household members and (iv) other kinds of income, Mizoguchi finds regular employee income of the household head to be the dominant factor in explaining the fall in the inequality of total income of such households. It is clear from his table 4 that the Gini coefficient defined on decile of households dropped from 0.2237 in 1963 to 0.1859 in 1970. He notes that one of the dominant factors in bringing down the within-group income inequality of these employee households is the narrowing income disparity among residents of cities of different sizes, again made possible by the same labor-market condition.

The argument is reiterated in Mizoguchi et al. (1980) and in various other works completed in the mid-1970s on the subject, supported by the 'Income and Assets Distribution Research Project, Institute of Economic Research, Hitotsubashi University', from which Mizoguchi et al.'s research originated. It was also put forward in Mizoguchi and Takayama (1984).

Oshima notes in his 1993 book: 'Full employment contributed to income equalization by reducing wage differentials, since small firms had to raise wages to retain their workers. Labor shortages in urban areas forced firms to move to rural areas ... The mechanization of farming accelerated, freeing male workers to take off-farm jobs' (Oshima 1993, p. 212; see also, Oshima 1978, pp. 361-75; and 1987, ch. 10)

So the Japanese experience is most consistent with the story depicted in Fei et al. (1979) and in Chu (1996a, 1997). The turning point arrived about ten years earlier than in Taiwan; and unlike Taiwan, Japan might have experienced an initial (but short) period of rising inequality when the heavy industries were being rebuilt right after the war. But once unskilled-labor manufacturing boomed, the process of equality-enhancing labor absorption began in both economies.[12]

3.2 Hong Kong

As a city-state, Hong Kong does not really have a significant rural sector. So the rural-urban part of the labor-absorbing story does not apply. But the other parts, namely Factors E (or F), G and I still apply. Chau and Hsia (1975) use Census (and By-Census) data to compare the inequality of household income in Hong Kong between 1966 and 1971, during which period Hong Kong's exports of labor-intensive manufactured products soared. They find a significant drop in inequality and they believe that the phenomenon is closely related to the changing structure (sectoral weights) of the working population as well as the between-inequality among and within-inequality of the different sectors to which the working population belongs. In particular, they point to the following factors:

1. The sector to which the household head belongs with the lowest inequality in household income has been manufacturing. and the share of the working population in this sector has been increasing, due to expansion of labor-intensive manufactured exports.
2. Evidence suggests that intrasector distribution narrowed during the period. 'In examining the wage growth of unskilled workers in a

number of industries, we have found that their wage rates grew ... considerably faster than the general rates for the manufacturing sector as a whole'. In addition, during the period there was a decrease in the proportion of employers and self-employed in both the industry and services sectors, with a corresponding increase in the shares of regular employees. Since inequality among the latter has been smaller, such a shift would reduce overall within sector inequality. The shift reflects, they note, 'a tightening of the labour market for which there is ample evidence'(pp. 627-8). Such a fall in intra-sectoral inequality is believed by them to be one of the dominant factors.

3. Inter-sectoral differences of per capita income may also have declined during the period.
4. A related and interesting phenomenon is that there has been a drop in the share of households with five or more persons from 51.4 percent to 47.1 percent. Since inequality among households of smaller size is observed to be higher than that among larger households in 1971, such a change would have caused overall inequality to rise during the period, had the relative inequalities remained constant. But Chau and Hsia suggest that inequality among larger households has fallen during the period, thereby more than offsetting the inequality-raising effects of changing shares. They attribute the suspected decline to the increase in participation rates of 'marginal workers, such as female workers (particularly those over 55 and under 20) and workers who have passed the retirement age of 65'. 'In addition', they note, 'the wage rates of manual, unskilled and female workers have increased more than [the average]. These developments have obviously benefitted the low-income large households and contributed to greater income equality among households of larger size' (p. 627).

Chau (1978) explores the issue further by investigating wage inequality among individual workers using data from manpower surveys. Of the eleven major industries in manufacturing for which there are data, as shown in Table 8.5 below, seven report declining inequality as measured by Gini, between the late 1960s (March 1970 in the case of electronics) and early 1970s, the period when Hong Kong experienced an unprecedented export boom. Inequality was stable for machine shop and metal working, and rose somewhat for 'electrical apparatus and appliances and for building and civil engineering'. For 'textiles', there is no data until during or after the first oil crisis. Chau notes that if the building and civil engineering industry which experienced an unusual construction boom at the time is disregarded, then it is likely that the overall inequality (incorporating both intra-industry and inter-industry inequalities) fell from around 1968 to around 1973.

Table 8.5 Monthly wage income in Hong Kong

Industry	Time of Survey	Employment (person)	Average Income (HK$)	Income Ratio*	Gini ratio
Clothing	March 1969	114,189	411	2.4	0.183
	Nov. 1972	151,550	567	2.3	0.167
	Nov. 1975**	184,128	736	–	0.122
Electrical apparatus	Dec. 1968	13,697	357	3.7	0.176
and appliances	July 1972	16,116	578	3.0	0.207
Electronics	March 1970	32,597	315	–	0.188
	August 1974**	48,203	573	–	0.163
Machine shop and	April 1968	38,835	349	2.3	0.214
metal working	Nov-Dec 1971	45,182	613	2.3	0.228
	Nov-Dec 1974	61,371	740	–	0.213
Plastics	August 1967	60,079	336	1.7	0.227
	June 1972	63,825	546	1.6	0.182
	July 1975**	58,509	631	–	0.215
Printing	August 1969	12,345	439	2.6	0.180
	Aug-Sep 1973	14,242	700	2.1	0.151
Ship building	July 1968	11,198	585	3.0	0.215
and repairs	July-Aug 1974	14,553	1255	2.7	0.209
Textiles	May-June 1973	62,550	701	–	0.150
	August 1975	68,040	779	–	0.170
Building and	August 1968	27,871	517	2.0	0.169
civil engineering	April 1973	55,545	1194	1.6	0.201
	April 1975	45,236	1376	2.0	0.212
Automobile repairs	Dec. 1967	4,996	411	1.9	0.216
and servicing	May 1974	6,745	857	1.3	0.142
Electrical and	Dec. 1968	5,393	429	3.2	0.169
wiring contractors	July 1972	11,805	893	2.1	0.131

Notes:
*The ratio of mean income of technicians to that of unskilled workers.
** With wide income class intervals and concentration of receivers in one or two cells.
Source: Chau (1978, tables 4 and 10).

What caused the inequality of wage income to fall during the period? Chau points to the narrowing disparity among wages of workers at different skill levels and of different sexes. As Table 8.5 shows, for almost all industries, the income ratio of technicians to unskilled workers fell during the period. For all industries as a whole, as Table 8.5 indicates, the wage income of less-skilled workers rose much faster than that of more-skilled. The same general picture holds when gender is introduced in addition to skills, that is, the wage rates of female, low-skilled workers rose faster than those of male, high-skilled workers. – and this occurred amid a sharp rise in female labor force participation (Chau, 1978, p. 36).

The phenomenon was largely the result of an 'upward migration of the general level of skills', as well as a sharp rise in the demand for labor, particularly unskilled labor, from export-led, labor-intensive industries. That was the period when 'Hong Kong evolved from full employment to labour shortage' (ibid. 1978, p. 62).

It seems that the basic picture of declining inequality is evident in Hong Kong as it is in Taiwan, during almost exactly the same period in the same international environment of rising demand for labor-intensive exports. In Taiwan the process works through both the farm and nonfarm sector, whereas in Hong Kong there is only the latter sector. Factors E (or F) and G have been important in bringing down overall inequality.[13]

3.3 Singapore

Rao and Ramakrishnan (1978, 1980) find that the Gini of earnings among workers (including both employees and proprietors) fell from 0.498 to 0.448 between 1966 and 1975, when Singapore was experiencing rapid export-led growth. During the period, real GDP grew at more than 10 percent in most years, and the unemployment rate fell from 8.9 percent to 4.5 percent, in spite of the sharply increasing labor force as a result of the postwar baby boom.

Decomposing inequality by sectors, they find that although there had been significant changes in their structure, the main factors causing inequality to fall were the shrinking disparities within the various sectors. They attribute this to 'the expansion of employment opportunities' (Rao and Ramakrishnan, 1980, p. 175), particularly for young and female workers. It is clear from their table 6 that the percentage of workers aged 10-29 in total employment increased from 40.9 to 52.5 percent between 1966 and 1975, while that of females rose from 20.5 to 28.8 percent. The picture is consistent with the working of Factors E (or F) and G identified above toward income equality.

Decomposing inequality by occupations, they find that both intra- and inter-occupation factors were at work. Of the main intra-occupation factors, the fall in inequality for the lower-income groups (particularly the category of 'production workers, transport equipment operators, labourers, etc.') was dominant. Of the main inter-occupation factors, the narrowing disparity between earnings of the professional, technical and related workers (the top group) and that of the administrative and managerial workers (the second from the top) was significant.[14]

According to them, the latter phenomenon might have something to do with government policies, whereas the former phenomenon was largely the result of an expansion of employment for the young and females in the lower-income occupation groups, which was also largely the result of government policies which were aimed at suppressing wage increases while creating job opportunities for unskilled workers.

Rao (1988) adds that from 1975 to 1979 inequality fell further to 0.424 as measured by the Gini coefficient (his table 2). He attributes this to 'wage increases [catching] up with productivity growth'. So it was very likely the delayed display of the consequence of unskilled labor shortage. Note also that the heavy investment in education helped make possible the eventual exhaustion of surplus labor: in 1966, half of all employees had no formal education while in 1975 the percentage dropped to 30 percent; the percentage of employment with secondary education meanwhile rose from 15.6 to 34.7 percent (ibid., p. 31).

After 1981, however, it seems that inequality was going back up, to 0.443, 0.465 and 0.474 in 1981, 1982 and 1984, respectively. Rao attributes this phenomenon to 'the government signalling a policy of relatively high wages ... for the skilled and professional groups and pursuing a selective immigration policy' (ibid., p. 31). By the latter he means the enhanced immigrant flows of low-skill labor from Malaysia, the Philippines, Sri Lanka and Indonesia, which suppressed the low-skill wage, as well as immigrant flows of top-skilled professionals from the USA, UK and Australia, who demanded high salaries. 'Together, the trends raised the Gini ratio', notes Rao (ibid., p. 31).

Meanwhile, the industrial structure changed, as in Hong Kong, with the rise of the commercial and other service sectors. Since in Singapore as well as in Hong Kong the distribution of earnings within the commerce and finance sector has been higher than manufacturing (Chau 1980, p. 195, and Rao and Ramakrishnan, 1980, p. 176), the fall of manufacturing in GDP *vis-à-vis* the rise of commerce and finance will raise the level of inequality of earnings, other things being equal. However, this is the sequel to rather than the heart of the (unskilled) labor-absorbing story told here.

3.4 Republic of Korea

The situation in the Republic of Korea (hereafter referred to as Korea) is less conclusive than the cases of Japan and Taiwan, but many findings are still consistent with the pattern identified above.

Some of the inconclusiveness is caused by data problems. As noted in Choo (1978), two major sources of data for Korea are the City and Farm Household Income and Expenditure Surveys (CHIES and FHIES).

Between them, however, a number of households are not represented, and researchers have to impute incomes for some groups and ignore those for which imputation is difficult (see ibid., p. 111 for details).

Based on careful imputation, Choo comes up with a result that is reproduced here in Table 8.6. It indicates that between 1964 and 1970, measured by the Gini coefficient or by the Decile Distribution Ratio (the poorest 40 percent over the richest 20 percent), inequality of income among all households fell, that among nonagricultural households fell by a larger degree, and that among agricultural households remained stable.

The finding that inequality among nonagricultural households fell is consistent with that for Taiwan during roughly the same period as analyzed above (Factor C above). In Taiwan, inequality also fell for agricultural households, although it was not the dominant factor in driving down overall inequality; in Korea it did not. There are two possible reasons. One is the problem of data. As Choo (ibid., p. 111) notes, the group of farm households cultivating very small pieces of land and landless agricultural workers are not included in the survey and no imputation is made due to lack of data. However, from the Japanese and Taiwanese experiences, it was precisely the farmers with smaller pieces of land to cultivate who benefitted the most from the expansion of nonagricultural employment opportunities in the rural areas. Therefore, if they have been included in the sample or their incomes could have been imputed, the result would likely be different.

Table 8.6 Choo's estimate of inequality of household income in Korea

	All households	Agricultural households	Nonagricultural households
1964			
Gini	0.36691	0.2386	0.4450
Decile Ratio	18.30/44.06	25.43/35.80	14.39/50.62
1970			
Gini	0.34845	0.2385	0.3565
Decile Ratio	18.76/43.06	23.54/32.97	18.39/44.25
1975			
Gini	0.41475	0.3888	0.4049
Decile Ratio	14.51/47.19	14.67/43.44	15.28/47.33

Source: Choo (1978).

The other possibility is that the development of small-scale, labor-intensive rural industries is less extensive in Korea than it is in Japan or Taiwan. As indicated in Table 8.7, which reproduces Oshima's (1993) Table 7.1, the ratio of nonagricultural to agricultural income for farm households was 105.9 percent in 1970 and 302.7 percent by 1984 in Taiwan; in Japan the ratio rose from 28.3 percent in 1950 to 166.7 percent in 1970 and to 403.4 percent by 1984. In contrast, in Korea it was merely 16.9 percent in 1970, rising to 32.4 percent in 1980 and to 55.1 percent in 1985.

Table 8.7 Ratio of nonagricultural to agricultural income in annual farm household income (%)

China		**Philippines**	
1978	2.6	1965	11.7
1979	3.8	1971	20.5
1980	5.0	1975*	19.3
1981	8.0		
1985	32.7		
Korea (Republic of)		**Thailand**	
1970	16.9	1971	60.0
1975	13.9	1978-79	61.2
1980	32.4		
1985	55.1		
Taiwan		**Indonesia**	
1970	105.9	1985	33.0
1975	120.0		
1980	305.6		
1984	302.7		
1988	312.4		
Japan		**Malaysia**	
1950	28.3	1973	15.5
1960	73.3	1979	39.2
1970	166.7		
1981	393.0		
1984	403.4		

Note: * Sampling and estimation procedure was revised.

Source: Oshima (1993, p. 154).

However, in terms of the disparity between agricultural and non-agricultural incomes, a roughly similar pattern was observed in Korea. Choo's (1978) appendix table 3 reports the per capita farm income and the per capita income of wage and salary earners. It is clear there that while disparity between the two income levels widened in the early 1960s, it narrowed substantially afterwards: from the per capita wage and salary income being almost twice as large in 1967 to no more than 5 percent larger by 1974. Similar results are found in Chung's (1978) table 5.[15]

At any rate, it was the substantial fall in nonagricultural inequality that dominates the scene. What caused this inequality fall? Once again, it was employment expansion (Factor E in Section 2). Choo (1978) notes: 'The improvement in distributive equity ... is primarily attributable to the fruits of rapid economic growth, especially the widened employment opportunities' (p. 116). In observing a trend of declining per capita income differentials between regions and between rural/urban areas in the late 1960s to the early 1970s, Chung (1978) also notes: 'In relation to this phenomenon, we have to point out first of all that new job opportunities in the urban-industrial areas created by the rapid economic growth began to pull out the latent abundant labor force in the rural areas' (p. 142).[16] This is the working of Factor D defined in Section 2.

Table 8.8 reports the long-term time series of the Gini coefficient from a variety of sources, including Choo (1978). It can be seen there that for almost all of the series, it is hard not to see a declining inequality from the mid- or late 1960s to the early 1970s. As for the other three 'tigers', that was the period when the demand from the US market for labor-intensive products was very strong, and exports boomed.[17]

It can be said that Korea's experience, at least, in part, is consistent with the pattern of equality-enhancing labor-absorbing growth mainly through the operation of Factor E, presented in Section 2.

4 THE RECENTLY NEWLY INDUSTRIALIZED ECONOMIES: MALAYSIA AND THE PHILIPPINES

Can the pattern of equality-enhancing labor-absorbing growth described above be applied to the ASEAN countries that are becoming newly industralized economies (NIEs)?

For these countries, export-led growth generally began in the mid- or late 1970s and continued into the 1980s and 1990s (see, for example, World Bank 1993). The general environment was different from that faced by Japan and the four tigers in the 1960s, when the international economy experienced a noninflationary expansion in output. In the 1970s and the early 1980s, there was the oil crisis followed by macroeconomic adjustments. And, finally, there was a significant migration of labor across countries of a scale not seen in the 1960s. In what follows, two ASEAN economies, Malaysia and the Philippines will be discussed to see how the pattern fares.

Table 8.8 Gini of household income in Korea

Source	Choo (1978)	Mizoguchi (1985)	Rao (1988)	Ikemoto (1991)	Oshima (1993)	Medhi (1994)
1964	0.36691					
1965		0.344	0.344	0.343		0.344
1966					0.34	
1967				0.396		
1968				0.425		
1969				0.425		
1970	0.34845	0.332	0.332	0.355		0.332
1971				0.365	0.36	
1972						
1973						
1974						
1975	0.41475					
1976		0.381	0.391		0.37	0.391
1977						
1978						
1979						
1980			0.389		0.39	0.389
1981		0.389				
1982			0.357		0.36	0.357
1983						
1984						
1985					0.41	
1986						
1987					0.46	
1988						0.400

4.1 Malaysia

In Malaysia, from the 1970s to the present, when export-led industrialization took place, inequality on the whole fell. As Shari (1996) notes, the Gini coefficient of household earned income fell from 0.529 in 1976 to 0.446 in 1990 (see Table 8.9). There was a small increase between 1970 and 1976, during which period Malaysia experienced severe inflation, and there was a small increase from 1990 to 1995, when a large amount of migrating labor flocked to the country.

What caused the inequality to fall from 1976 to 1990? Shari notes:

> [N]ot only did more people become employed, but significantly more people were employed full-time. The increase in the labour force participation include a substantial number of Malay women who were employed in the free trade zones and various industrial estates set up around the country ... This gain in real wages is found to be fastest in the lower income brackets, which explain the improvement in urban income distributions of all ethnic groups and hence declining urban inequality as well as the overall inequality. (1996, p. 12)

Indeed, from the 1970s to the 1990s, except for the recession years of 1984 and 1987, there was a general trend of falling unemployment (see Table 8.9). It is also clear from the table that both rural and urban inequalities fell from 1976 to the 1980s, while the disparity between urban and rural incomes narrowed from 1976 to 1990. All these phenomena are consistent with the predictions of Factors D (and therefore A) and E, or F which combines D and E, identified above in Section 2.

As in the case of Japan and the NIEs, in Malaysia the expansion of employment was not simply a gift from heaven. Following the serious ethnic riot in May 1969, the government launched the 'New Economic Policy' or NEP, which attempted to maintain high growth through the expansion of manufactured exports, to increase employment opportunities among the populace, particularly for the residents (predominantly Malay) in the rural areas, and to increase Malay representation in capital ownership. Since in Malaysia the mean income of Malay households has been much lower than that of Chinese (top) and Indians (middle), a policy toward the increase of income among the Malay population naturally tends to reduce inequality. Given that most Malays lived in the rural areas in the 1970s, the policy of enlarged access to nonagricultural jobs in manufacturing for the Malays is consistent with Factor D (and therefore A), depicted in Section 2.

Similar observations can be found in Shari and Mat Zin (1990). They attribute the improvement in the relative position of the Malays to three

Table 8.9 *Household income inequality and employment in Malaysia*

	Overall inequality	Overall inequality	Overall inequality	Rural inequality	Urban inequality	Urban mean houdehold income over rural	Rate of labor force expansion (from prev. yr)	Rate of employment expansion (from prev. yr)	Rate of unemploy -ment
Source	Ikemoto (1991)	Oshima (1993)	Mat Zin and Shari(1990) Shari (1996)	"	"	"	"	"	"
	Gini	Gini	Gini[#]	Gini	Gini		%	%	%
1957*	0.449	0.45	0.414	0.378	0.421	1.79	–	–	–
1970*	0.505	0.51	0.513	0.469	0.513	2.04	–	–	7.5
1976*	0.509		0.529	0.500	0.529	2.12	3.7**	3.9**	6.9(1975)
1979*	0.493	0.49	0.508	0.482	0.501	1.77	3.6 (1980)	3.4 (1980)	5.7(1980)
1984*	–	0.48	0.480	–	–	1.87	3	2.3	6.3
1987*	–	0.44 (1988)	0.456	–	–	1.72	3.8	3.9	7.3
1990	–	–	0.446	0.409	0.445	1.70	2.8	4.6	6
1995	–	–	0.464	–	–	2.00	2.7	2.8	2.8

Notes:
* Peninsular Malaysia only.
** Average annual rate from 1971-75.

Source: # Shari and Mat Zin (1990) for 1957 and Shari (1996) for the rest.

factors: (i) success of several rural development programs for the poorer Malays, (ii) faster increase in educational attainment among the Malays relative to the other ethnic groups, and (iii) 'shift to the labour-intensive, export-oriented industrialization as well as the rapid expansion of the public sector ... [which] led to the expansion of employment opportunities in the second and tertiary sectors' (116). (See also Ikemoto 1985; Rao 1988; and Medhi 1994.)

If other things were held equal, the continued expansion of manufactured exports into the 1990s would have led to still lower inequality according to the theory given above. But other things have not been equal. Shari (1996) notes at least three factors:

1. The large influx of legal and illegal foreign unskilled workers, mainly from Indonesia and Bangladesh. He notes: 'a sizable proportion of new employment opportunities in the 1991-1995 period may go to these migrant workers and thus impede the trends towards [reduced] income inequalities' (ibid., p. 13).
2. '[E]xternal competition has pressured higher skills requirements ... [which] pushed up wages of skilled manpower substantially', notes Shari (ibid., p. 13). The strong demand for skills as well as the increase in supply of migrant unskilled labor together made the disparity between the wages of unskilled and skilled labor wider, contributing to higher inequality (Factor G in Section 2 above, operating towards greater inequality).
3. Shari also points to the possible working of what he calls the 'Williamson phenomenon', where market forces dictate the expansion of modern, higher-productivity industries at the expense of traditional, lower-productivity sectors; since the latter uses unskilled labor in large doses, the demand for unskilled labor softens as do their wages, leading to higher inequality.

While the story of increased supply of migrant unskilled labor is believable and understandable, that of the increased demand for skilled labor needs deeper exploration. The theory behind the stylized pattern predicts the expansion of *unskilled-labor-intensive* industries when unskilled labor is still abundant and cheap. As explained above, productivity of the unskilled-labor-intensive manufacturing sector is higher than that in agriculture, so a movement of labor from agriculture to that sector is consistent with market forces, but it will not result in the softening of the wages of unskilled labor as predicted by Williamson. Quite the contrary, it expedites the movement toward full employment and sharp rises in wages of these workers.

So whether the depression of wages of unskilled Malaysian workers was the sole result of incoming migrant workers or the joint product of supply and demand factors remains to be studied. This said, one may not want to rule out altogether the possibility that the demand factor does play a role, for an important reason: Just as firms might have planned the expansion of their unskilled-labor-intensive production lines while they were cheap, only to find later that their costs rose after these production lines were put into operation, the firms might have planned the expansion of capital- and skill-intensive production lines assuming that the then existing rate of increases in unskilled-labor wages would continue, while in reality that rate softened once the expansion in production was completed. Such an 'over-shooting' would, other things being equal, widen the disparity between wages of unskilled and skilled labor.

How important this force has been remains to be seen. The mechanism, if it exists, would predict a rise in disparity between wages of skilled and unskilled labor as the planned factor intensity overshoots; but it will do so only after the turning point has been reached. Thus it is basically a post-labor-absorbing growth story.

4.2 The Philippines

Growth of per capita GNP had been 1.7, 2.2, 1.9, 3.6, 3.4 and −3.5 percent, respectively, for the periods of 1955-60, 1960-65, 1965-70, 1970-75, 1975-80 and 1980-85. In spite of the positive and sometimes impressive growth rates prior to the 1980s, the percentage of manufacturing in GDP is still low: it rose from 17.5 percent in 1961 to 25.2 percent in 1979. During 1980-92, when the country experienced economic stagnation amid political instability, the percentage gradually declined to about 23 percent in 1994. The country regained higher growth rates only after that year, so it has been a fairly recent phenomenon. The employment in manufacturing as a percentage of the total has been very low, at 10 percent until the late 1970s, while employment in agriculture has been about 50-55 percent until 1994 (Terasaki 1985; Islam and Chowdhury 1997, ch. 15).

As can be seen from Table 8.7, the percentage of non-agricultural income in total farm household income has not been high. Moreover, inside the rural sector, large plantations coexisted with farmers of smallholdings, and neither the commercialization of agriculture, which resulted from the devaluation of the peso in 1960, nor the introduction of new agricultural technology (high-yield varieties, irrigation, fertilizers and so on) was spread evenly among the different regions of the country or among the different households in the same region.[18]

Oshima and Barros (1976) note:

> In the Ilocos Region the expansion of diversified commercial crops ... enabled the better farmers to increase their incomes ... The new rice technology reached only 14 percent of the rice farmers ... by 1971. Similarly in Mindanao, the income disparity increased ... with the migration of farmers from other parts ... to take up commercial farming. In contrast, the position of most of the Muslim peasants probably did not improve ... [I]n the case of Eastern Visayas, the Gini had risen sharply ... due to the increase in the concentration of farm holdings ... also, the spread of the new rice technology had been limited to 16 percent of rice farmers. (pp. 498-99)

These conditions make the Philippine agricultural sector very different from Taiwan's in the 1950s and 1960s. As described earlier, in Taiwan the wage Gini among the farm households is lower than that of agricultural income. In the Philippines, Terasaki (1985, p. 381), found not only that the latter higher than its counterpart in Taiwan, but the former was even higher.[19] This means that not only is nonagricultural employment much less important, as indicated above, but it is also unevenly distributed among farm households, being more abundant in the richer ones

In Taiwan, the increase in agricultural productivity was enjoyed rather evenly by farm households, so the Gini of agricultural income remained low. Consequently, the strong demand for labor in agriculture, which expedites the process of labor absorption, was felt by all farmers. In the Philippines, a large sector of farm households in some regions did not benefit from agricultural technological progress, so there would have been more under-employed labor there (Section 2's Factor H, operating toward greater inequality).

So the benign force of nonagricultural employment for poorer farm households was weak at best, just when these households suffered the most from idle manpower (Section 2's Factor D, operating toward greater inequality).[20] No wonder rural inequality in the Philippines throughout the 1960s rose as reported in Table 8.10. And sourcewise decomposition by Terasaki (1985, p. 381) reveals that in both 1965 and 1971, the factor that contributed most to both overall and rural household income inequalities has been the inequality of wage income. Comparing these sourcewise decomposition results with Table 8.2 and Fei et al. (1979, Table 10.2), we see startling differences. Taiwan's pseudo-Gini ratio of wage income among farm households was 0.187 and 0.238 in 1968 and 1972, respectively, and that among all households was 0.293 and 0.260 in the same two years, respectively; in the Philippines it was 0.52 and 0.56 among rural households, and 0.59 and 0.56 among all households in 1965 and 1971, respectively.

Within the urban sector the situation was better. While rural industries did not really develop, industrialization did take place in the urban areas, and absorbed an increasing amount of labor, particularly unskilled labor. Terasaki (1985) shows that the urban Gini dropped in the 1960s, and a decomposition shows that the dominant factor had been the fall in the wage Gini among urban households. He attributes this to industrialization benefitting unskilled workers more than skilled, as it provided more employment opportunities for the former (Section 2's Factor E operating toward greater equality).

How did overall inequality change? It was stable at a high level as shown in Table 8.10. Groupwise decomposition by Mangahas as cited in Rao (1988, p. 36) shows that within-area rather than between-area (Metro Manila, other urban, and rural) inequality was the dominant factor in explaining overall inequalities in 1961, 1965 and 1971. Given this, and the fact that rural inequality increased while urban inequality fell, it is not surprising that overall inequality followed a flat trend during the period.

Industrialization proceeded more guickly in the 1970s. If it could have spread to the rural areas and remained unskilled-labor-intensive, it might have been able to bring about lower inequality. But unfortunately this was also the period when the government changed its survey methods and gave confusing and sometimes conflicting reports of the inequality situation. Rao (1988) cites attempts of estimation which indicate that inequality remained high. He attributes this to sharply deteriorating agricultural terms of trade during the 1970s due to deliberate government policies (Section 2's Factor B, operating toward greater inequality).

There have been better data since 1985, and they show lower overall inequalities than before (Balisacan 1992). Although it is still questionable that these data can be directly compared to the figures in the 1960s, Rao (1988) thinks that inequality probably was lower in the mid- to late 1980s, in the depth of a recession. Rao describes the situation as 'shared poverty', because more than half of the surveyed households indicated that they survived on gifts, assistance from domestic sources and from abroad. The unemployment rate was high: 7.1 percent and 11.8 percent, respectively, for rural and urban areas in 1985. So the lower inequality, even if it were true, was not really the making of the labor-absorbing story told earlier.

To see if the equity-promoting labor-absorbing mechanism works, one probably has to wait for the results of the recent catching-up in export-led industrialization. GDP grew by 4.5 percent in 1994 and by more than 5 percent in 1995 and 1996. The unemployment rate was still high: 9.7 percent and 9.3 percent in 1994 and 1994, respectively. Islam and Chowdhury (1997) estimate underemployment as being more than 20

Table 8.10 Income distribution in the Philippines

Source	Balisacan (1992) FIES All households	Terasaki (1982) FIES All households #	Terasaki (1985) urban/rural households income Ratio	Rao (1988) FIES and ISH all households	Rao (1988) FIES and ISH rural households	Rao (1988) FIES and ISH urban households
1956				0.48*	0.38	0.49
1957		0.48	2.45			
1961	0.486	0.49	2.47	0.50*	0.40	0.52
1965	0.491	0.49	2.50	0.51*	0.42	0.53
1971	0.478	0.48	2.08	0.49*	0.46	0.45
1975			1.75			
1980				0.56**	0.44	0.51
1983				0.56**	0.48	0.53
1985	0.446			0.46	0.38	0.46
1988	0.445					

Notes:
FIES: Family Income and Expenditure Survey
ISH: Integrated Survey of Households
Calculated from deciles of distribution.
* From International Labor Organization.
** From ISH data.

percent. If the current recovery continues along the line of unskilled-labor-intensive manufacturing, and if industrialization spreads to the countryside, so that both unemployment and underemployment fall, maybe the equalizing force will come. These are, of course, big 'if's, especially on top of the recent currency crisis which may slow down the recovery. More time is needed for a fair assessment.

5 CONCLUSIONS

The experience of Japan and the Asian NIEs indicate that in the process of economic development, the possibility exists that when employment of unskilled labor expands rapidly due to industrialization, income inequality can go down.

When industrialization occurs amid the existence of a large amount of surplus unskilled labor, the rate of increase in their wages may be small, but the expansion of employment opportunities can reduce inequality because (i) the poorer farm and nonfarm households suffer more from the under- or unemployment of their low-skilled members, and (ii) the greater involvement of farm households in nonagricultural activities reduces between-sector income disparities; provided that these opportunities are accessible to all households in both the farm and nonfarm sectors.

In later stages of industrialization, it is possible that wage disparities between skilled and unskilled workers begin to narrow. This can bring down inequality if the poorer households have on average more members of lower skill.

Due to data problems, it is not always possible to directly link existing statistics with the various elements identified in the above statements. But it seems that equality-enhancing effects of employment expansion have been evident in Japan, Hong Kong and Singapore.

In addition, Korea's data for the mid- to late 1960s, which likewise saw the expansion of its labor-intensive exports, support the theses of falling inequality among nonfarm households and the narrowing of between-sector disparities. Malaysia's data from the late 1970s to the 1980s, when that country embarked on export-led industrialization, support the theses of falling inequalities for both farm and nonfarm sectors, and of the narrowing of between-sector disparities.

As for the effects of shrinking wage disparities between skilled and unskilled workers, it seems that these effects are fairly evident in Japan in the 1960s, and in Taiwan from the mid-1960s to the early 1970s. Hong Kong's data from the late 1960s to the early 1970s, when export-led manufacturing boomed, also render support to the thesis that such narrowing of wage disparities has caused household income inequality to fall. Singapore's experience during the 1975-79 period seems to point in the same direction.

Such findings pose a serious challenge to economic theory. Many of the reasons given for the inevitable rise in inequality in the initial stage of industrialization do not hold. New theories paying attention to employment expansion should be forthcoming.[21]

While the above-described process is important, it should not be taken without qualifications. One variable that can operate in an opposite direction is the pattern of rural development. The lack of rural infrastructure would prevent the emergence or growth of rural industries, which have been the most efficient labor-absorption machines in economies that have a sizable rural sector overflowing with surplus labor. The uneven distribution of the adoption of new agricultural technology could raise the inequality of agricultural income among farm households, and the possible increasing concentration of land ownership could make things worse. The Philippine rural sector appears to have been going in such a direction in the 1960s.

Another additional factor is the terms of trade between agricultural and non-agricultural products. When this changes against agriculture, often due to deliberate government policies, as in the case of the Philippines in the 1970s, and when the change is sizable enough, the between-sector disparity can rise to a degree where overall equality is adversely affected.

A third factor, the direct evidence of which is scarce but is nevertheless suspected by many scholars to have been important, is the existence of geological, regional or institutional barriers to the mobility of labor. Lack of labor mobility will prevent rural surplus labor from being absorbed by industries, and will prolong or intensify between-sector income disparities. Mizoguchi (1985), for one, suspects this to be an important reason for the rise in Japan's inequality in the 19th century.[22] A related possibility is the choice of technology, especially the adoption of capital-intensive methods of production when labor is still abundant. Mizoguchi and Terasaki (1992) cite that as one of the reasons for the earlier-mentioned rise in Japan's inequality in the 1950s, when the capital-intensive, heavy industries were being revitalized.[23] The development of Korea since the 1970s seems also to involve this phenomenon, although it was perhaps more a premature response to the potential shortage of labor.

Also, in many economies there have been various *post*-labor-intensive-industrialization stories: when the wages of unskilled labor rise sufficiently, the industry adjusts by resorting to capital- or skill-intensive technologies, and a new situation is created. Or, the relative importance of the manufacturing sector declines when the real exchange rate (between tradables and nontradables) adjusts, thus creating another new situation. Or, there is a large-scale inward or outward migration of labor, thereby creating a third new situation. With the advent of the current currency crisis, there could be still newer situations. Consequently more analysis is needed to tackle these new possibilities.

EPILOGUE

John C.H. Fei was a great teacher and scholar. From very early on, he guided the direction of research of the Institute for Social Sciences and Philosophy, Academia Sinica, beginning in the preparatory stage of its inauguration. The research projects that led to the two papers cited in this chapter (Pyatt et al. 1980, and Chen et al. 1982) could not have been completed without his involvement and encouragement. Over the years, in his capacity as a Member of the Advisory Committee of the Institute, he continued to give valuable advice on academic development. His passing away is a great loss to the Institute. In the more personal realm, both authors had the privilege of having been his friend and co-author. About two months before he passed away, John Fei had lengthy discussions with the second author on a paper on Taiwan's political and economic development, which was presented at the 'Conference on Government and Markets' hosted by Cornell University. That paper once again highlighted Fei's broad range of academic interests and knowledge, by which he will be remembered.

NOTES

1. See also Thorbecke (1979).
2. According to the Directorate-General of Budget, Accounting and Statistics (DGBAS), Taiwan, Gini of (total) household income rose mildly from 0.321 to 0.326 in 1964-68, subsequently fell to 0.291 in 1972, 0.280 in 1976 and then to 0.277 in 1980 when the bottom was reached. After that there has been a rising trend, but Lin (1995), Chu (1997), Fields and Leary (forthcoming) and Schultz (forthcoming) show that the apparent rise has a lot more to do with changes in household composition than with anything else. Kuznets (1980) and Schultz (forthcoming) make the additional point that inequality might not have fallen even in the earlier periods once the size of households is controlled. However, it has been shown in Chu (1996a and 1997) that the direction of the trend in 1966-72 as identified in Fei et al. (1979) is not reversed after changes in the distribution of household size are accounted for.
3. The method is thereafter refined in Pyatt et al. (1980) and in Chen et al. (1982).

4. For recent cross-country studies, see, for example, Anand and Kanbur (1993a and 1993b). See also Saith (1983).
5. See also Liang (1978), Little (1979), Kuo et al. (1981) and Kuo (1983).
6. Chu (1997) stresses an additional point. The gap of per capita income between farm and non-farm households is found to have narrowed in 1952-62, as indicated above. The phenomenon is suspected to be caused also by the process of greater involvement in nonagricultural activities among the farm households.
7. The percentage contributions saw some odd numbers mainly because the denominator, the change in overall Gini, is very small. Therefore it should not cause concern.
8. See Chu (1986) for a model of changes in income distribution when both labor and capital incomes, the latter being derived from the accumulation of savings, are considered.
9. When these 'factors' are identified in the later text, we are referring to their inequality-reducing effects unless otherwise noted.
10. See Ranis and Stewart (1993) for an interesting theoretical discussion of the rural nonagricultural activities.
11. A similar remark can be found in Mizoguchi et al. (1980): 'The shift from a labor-surplus to a labor-scarce economy significantly altered the income inequality trend ... Decreased regional inequalities can be related to the movement of factories to local cities, which was also effective in equalizing income distribution within agricultural households by providing non-agricultural job opportunities' (p. 265).
12. Both economies do have similar initial conditions: a land reform which occurred shortly after the war and a well-developed rural infrastructure after the postwar reconstruction.
13. See also Lin (1985). According to Lin, the unemployment rate fell from 15-17 percent in the mid-1950s to less than 2 percent by the late 1950s. This should have reduced inequality, he notes, but inequality (of household income) remained high in the 1950s presumably because wage disparity between unskilled and skilled labor widened. Inequality really began to fall in the 1960s and 1970s, when employment continued to expand and the wage disparity between skills narrowed as Hong Kong entered the stage of (unskilled) labor shortage. From the late 1970s to the early 1980s, inequality is suspected to have increased. According to Lin, the possible contributing factors are (i) an influx of 350,000 refugees in 1979-80, (ii) the decline in the share of manufacturing and the rise in that of the tertiary sector which traditionally has higher intra-sectoral inequality, and (iii) such demographic factors as shrinking household size.
14. According to the same paper, during the period the mean income of middle-status workers (sales and service) experienced the fastest increase, followed by that of low-status workers, which were in turn followed by top-status workers.
15. These results are important because they give the per capita figure, which is the preferred concept, as noted earlier.
16. In the same article, however, Chung notices a continuously widening wage rate differential between regions and between urban/rural areas. Because the quality of labor is not controlled for in the analysis, it is difficult to assess the findings. Chung nevertheless makes a remark: '[T]here are as yet considerable

productivity gaps between firms located in the industrial centers and those located in the rural areas. Since the late 1960s, many heavy industries such as iron and steel, petro-chemical, electronics, etc. have been established around the metropolitan and large urban areas. [They] can be characterized by their large-scale, capital intensive production methods. It is natural, therefore, that one can expect wide productivity gaps between these new industries and the old ones' (pp. 134-7). This may explain in part why the story in Korea is less obvious than that in Japan and Taiwan, and echoes the point just made about the degree of laborabsorption in the rural areas.

17. Although it appears from Table 8.7 that inequality measured by the Gini coefficient rose from the late 1970s to the 1980s, Medhi (1994) cites a study by Won-Duck Lee to confirm that the inequality of labor income among workers has shown an unambiguous falling trend from 1972 to 1988, as the Gini ratio fell from 0.4022 to 0.3138. Three reasons are given for the phenomenon: (i) the labor market became tighter, as non-farm unemployment declined from 16.4 percent in 1963 to 3.0 percent in 1988; (ii) wage dispersion was reduced by the increase in educational attainment; and (iii) minimum wage legislation and active trade union movements. These comments of Medhi's are consistent with Korea's quintile ratios which he shows in his Table 2.
18. See the interesting and important comparison between Taiwan and the Philippines given in Ranis and Stewart (1993).
19. In terms of pseudo-Gini coefficients.
20. Table 5 in Ranis and Stewart (1993) shows that while in 1956-66 and 1966-80, average annual growth of employment in manufacturing in the rural areas was 4.99 and 10.28 percent, respectively, for Taiwan, it was only 0.57 and 2.03 percent, respectively, in 1967-75 and 1975-88 in the Philippines.
21. See, for example, Chu (1996b).
22. He notes: 'Standard economic analysis assumes a smooth movement of labor. But, in the real world that assumption is rendered invalid and the lack of smooth labor mobility is a factor in income inequality ... This was true of nineteenth century Japan and is true of some contemporary Asian countries ... [I]f a government wants to reduce inequality in a short time, local development policy is required. The Japanese government spent a large amount of money in this way. Its expenditures included not only supports to increase agricultural production but also to shift manufacturing to outlying cities and increase opportunities for nonagricultural employment' (Mizoguchi 1985, p. 320).
23. Since they find inequality to be rising in the 1950s and falling in the 1960s, they mark the trend as an 'inverted-U'. But while Kuznets (1955) uses such a pattern to describe the very long-term trend (hundreds of years) of changes in inequality in the currently advanced countries, Mizoguchi and Terasaki use the term to describe the change between only two decades. So the use of the term is probably more suggestive than pointing out a serious confirmation.

REFERENCES

Anand, Sudhir and S.M.R. Kanbur (1993a), 'The Kuznets Process and the Inequality-Development Relationship', *Journal of Development Economics*, 40, 25-52.

Anand, Sudhir and S.M.R. Kanbur, 1993b, 'Inequality and Development', *Journal of Development Economics*, 41, 19-43.

Balisacan, Arsenio M. (1992), 'Rural Poverty in the Philippines: Incidence, Determinants and Policies', *Asian Development Review*, 10, 125-63.

Chau, Lawrence C. (1978), 'Distribution of Wage Income in Hong Kong', in Oshima and Mizoguchi (1978), 28-66.

Chau, Lawrence C. (1980), 'Economic Growth and Income Inequality in Hong Kong', in Ohkawa and Key (1980), 101-214.

Chau, Lawrence C. and Ronald Hsia (1975), 'An Anatomy of Income Distribution in Hong Kong, 1971', in JERC-CAMS (1975), 600-641.

Chen, Chau-Nan, Tien-Wang Tsaur and Tong-Shieng Rhai (1982), 'The Gini Coefficient and Negative Income', *Oxford Economic Papers*, 34, 473-8.

Choo, Hakchung (1978), 'Probable Size Distribution of Income in Korea: Over Time and by Sectors', in Oshima and Mizoguchi (1978), 109-30.

Chu, Yun-Peng (1986), 'Changes in Income Distribution Over Time in a One-sector Neoclassical Setting', *Journal of Development Economics*, 24, 359-70.

Chu, Yun-Peng (1996a), 'Employment Expansion and Income Inequality', paper presented at the Fifth Convention of the East Asian Economic Association, Bangkok.

Chu, Yun-Peng (1996b), 'The Effects of Off-farm Employment on Inequality: Theories and an Empirical Application to the Taiwan Case', *Journal of Economic Development*, 21, 221-56.

Chu, Yun-Peng (1997), 'Employment Expansion and Equitable Growth: Taiwan's Postwar Experience', mimeograph.

Chung, Young-il (1978), 'Over Time Changes in the Regional and Urban-Rural Income Differences in Korea', in Oshima and Mizoguchi (1978), 131-44.

Fei, John C.H., Gustav Ranis and Shirley W.Y. Kuo (1979), *Growth with Equity: The Taiwan Case*, London: Oxford University Press.

Fields, Gary S. and Jesse Leary (forthcoming), 'Economic and Demographic Aspects of Taiwan's Rising Family Income Inequality', in Ranis et al. (forthcoming).

Galenson, Walter (ed.) (1979), *Economic Growth and Structural Change in Taiwan*, Ithaca, NY: Cornell University Press.

Ikemoto, Yukio (1985), 'Income Distribution in Malaysia: 1957-80', *The Developing Economies*, XXIII, 347-67.

Islam, Iyanatul and Anis Chowdhury (1997), *Asia-Pacific Economies: A Survey*, London: Routledge.

Japan Economic Research Center (JERC) and Council for Asian Manpower Studies (CAMS) (eds) (1975), *Income Distribution, Employment and Economic Development in Southeast and East Asia*, Tokyo: Japan Economic Research Center, and Manila: Council for Asian Manpower Studies.

Kuo, Shirley W.Y. (1983), *The Taiwan Economy in Transition*, Boulder, CO: Westview Press.

Kuo, Shirley W.Y., Gustav Ranis and John C.H. Fei (1981), *The Taiwan Success Story: Rapid Growth with Improved Distribution in the R.O.C., 1952-1979*, Boulder, CO: Westview Press.

Kuznets, Simon (1955), 'Economic Growth and Income Inequality', *American Economic Review*, 45 (1), 1-28.

Kuznets, Simon (1980), 'Notes on Income Distribution in Taiwan', in L.R. Klein, M. Nerlove and T.-S. Tsiang (eds), *Quantitative Economics and Development: Essays in Memory of T.-C. Liu*, New York: Academic Press.

Liang, Kuo-Shu (1978) (in Chinese), 'The Employment and Distribution Effects of Taiwan's Export Expansion', read at the Conference on Income Distribution in Taiwan, Institute of Economics, Academia Sinica.

Little, Ian M.D. (1979), 'An Economic Reconnaissance', in Galenson (1979), 448-508.

Lin, Ching-Yuan (1995) (in Chinese), 'Effects of Changes in Household Composition on Taiwan's Income Distribution', in *Proceedings of Annual Conference of Taiwan Economic Association*, Taipei, 161-78.

Lin, T.-B. (1985), 'Growth, Equity, and Income Distribution Policies in Hong Kong', *The Developing Economies*, XXXIII, 391-413.

Medhi, Krongkaew (1994), 'Income Distribution in East Asian Developing Countries: An Update', *Asian-Pacific Economic Literature*, 8, 58-73.

Mizoguchi, Toshiyuki (1975), 'The Distribution of Household Income in Postwar Japan', in JERC-CAMS (1975), 473-515.

Mizoguchi, Toshiyuki (1978), 'A Note on Sectoral Income Distribution in Japan', in Oshima and Mizoguchi (1978), 84-108.

Mizoguchi, Toshiyuki (1985), 'Economic Development Policy and Income Distribution: The Experience in East and Southeast Asia, *Developing Economies*, XXIII, 307-24.

Mizoguchi, Toshiyuki and N. Takayama (1984), *Equity and Poverty under*

Rapid Economic Growth: The Japanese Experience, Tokyo: Kinokuniya.

Mizoguchi, Toshiyuki and Yasuhiro Terasaki (1992), 'The Impact of Economic, Sociological and Industrial Factors on Changes of Size Distribution of Household Income: A Century of Japanese Experience', mimeograph.

Mizoguchi, Toshiyuki N. Takayama, and Y. Terasaki (1980), 'Over-time Changes in the Size Distribution of Household Income during Rapid Economic Growth: The Japanese Experience', in Ohkawa and Key (1980), 233-66.

Ohkawa, Kazushi and Bernard Key (eds) (1980), *Asian Socioeconomic Development*, Honolulu: University of Hawaii Press.

Ono, Akira and T. Watanabe (1976), 'Changes in Income Inequality in the Japanese Economy', in Hugh Patrick (ed.), *Japanese Industrialization and Its Social Consequences*, Berkeley: University of California Press, 363-90.

Oshima, Harry T. (1970), 'Income Inequality and Economic Growth: The Postwar Experience of Asian Countries', *Malayan Economic Review*, 15, 7-41.

Oshima, Harry T. (1971), 'Labor-Force "Explosion" and the Labor-intensive Sector in Asian Growth', *Economic Development and Cultural Change*, 19, 161-83.

Oshima, Harry T. (1978), 'Comments on the CAMS-Hitotsubashi Income Distribution Seminar', in Oshima and Mizoguchi (1978), 361-75.

Oshima, Harry T. (1987), *Economic Growth in Monsoon Asia: A Comparative Study*, Tokyo: University of Tokyo Press.

Oshima, Harry T. (1993), *Strategic Processes in Monsoon Asia's Economic Development*, Baltimore: The Johns Hopkins University Press.

Oshima, Harry T. and B. Barros (1976), 'Trends in Growth and Distribution of Income in Selected Asian Countries', *Philippine Economic Journal*, 15, 480-521.

Oshima, Harry T. and T. Mizoguchi (eds) (1978), *Income Distribution by Sectors and Overtime in East and Southeast Asian Countries*, Quezon City: Council for Asian Manpower Studies and Tokyo: Institute of Economic Research, Hitotsubashi University.

Pyatt, Grahm, Chau-Nan Chen and John Fei (1980), 'The Distribution of Income by Factor Components', *Quarterly Journal of Economics*, 95, 451-73.

Ranis, Gustav and Frances Stewart (1993), 'Rural Nonagricultural Activities in Development Theory and Application', *Journal of Development Economics*, 40, 75-101.

Ranis, Gustav, Sheng-Cheng Hu and Yun-Peng Chu (eds) (forthcoming), *The Economics and Political Economy of Development in Taiwan into the 21st Century*, Cheltenham: Edward Elgar.

Rao, V.V. Bhanoji (1988), 'Income Distribution in East Asian Developing Countries', *Asia-Pacific Economic Literature*, 2, 26-45.

Rao, V.V. Bhanoji and M.K. Ramakrishnan (1978), 'Structural Changes and Change in Income Distribution: Singapore, 1966-1975', in Oshima and Mizoguchi (1978), 67-83.

Rao, V.V. Bhanoji and M.K. Ramakrishnan (1980), 'Economic Growth, Employment Expansion, and Reduction in Income Inequality: The Singapore Experience, 1966-1975', in Ohkawa and Key (1980), 167-90.

Saith, Ashwani (1983), 'Development and Distribution: A Critique of the Cross-Country U-hypothesis', *Journal of Development Economics*, 13, 367-82.

Schultz, T. Paul (forthcoming), 'Income Inequality in Taiwan, 1976-1993: Aging, Fertility and Family Composition', in Ranis et al. (forthcoming).

Shari, Ishak (1996), 'Globalization and Liberalization: Implications for Growth and Income Inequalities in Malaysia', Fifth Convention of the East Asian Economic Association, Bangkok.

Shari, Ishak and Ragayah Haji Mat Zin (1990), 'The Patterns and Trends of Income Distribution in Malaysia, 1970-1987', *Singapore Economic Review*, 35, 102-23.

Shorrocks, A.F. (1982), 'Inequality Decomposition by Factor Components', *Econometrica*, 50, 193-221.

Terasaki, Yasuhiro (1985), 'Income Distribution and Development Policies in the Philippines', *The Developing Economies*, XXIII, 368-90.

Theil, Henri (1972), *Statistical Decomposition Analysis*, Amsterdam: North-Holland.

Thorbecke, Erik (1979), 'Agricultural Development', in Galenson (1979), 132-205.

Wada, Richard (1975), 'Impact of Economic Growth on the Size Distribution of Income: The Postwar Experience of Japan', in JERC-CAMS (1975), 516-65.

World Bank (1993), *The East Asian Miracle*, New York: Oxford University Press.

9. Income Distribution and Development in Newly Industrialized Countries

Irma Adelman*

1 INTRODUCTION

John Fei was one of the most profound thinkers in economic development. He combined sophisticated theory and mathematics with a concern about the human condition and a broadly based, historical, Kuznetsian view of the development process. His vision of economic development included in the term 'development' not only increases in per capita GNP but also sustained economic growth accompanied by structural change in the economy and in its economic, sociocultural and political institutions and by a wider diffusion of the economic and social benefits of growth.

This chapter reflects John Fei's broad view of the development process. It relates two research themes close to his heart: income inequality and the institutional aspects of development. The chapter examines empirically how economic and institutional change have impacted on income distribution and poverty in a sample of newly industrialized countries (NICs) as of about 1990. Specifically, the study applies the methodology used by Cynthia Taft Morris and myself in our 1967 book *Society Politics and Economic Development* to the analysis of interactions among variables describing: economic, social and political institutions; aggregate economic performance; and income distribution during the late 1980s and early 1990s.

There has been a revival of interest in issues relating to income distribution and poverty. Much of the recent discussion centers around whether the Kuznets curve does or does not exist and whether income distribution and growth go hand in hand or whether there is a tradeoff

* I am indebted to Nobuhiko Fuwa for providing me with the Deiniger-Squire income distribution data set and to Cynthia Taft Morris for her valuable comments. I naturally retain responsibility for any remaining errors.

between growth and equity. We demonstrate in this chapter that this framing of issues is simplistic. Development interacts with distribution in a complex manner. Even in the NICs, not just per capita GNP but structural, institutional, political and socio-cultural change are associated with the distribution of benefits from growth. And growth *per se* is not reliably associated with distributional change; it is only the right kinds of growth, as pointed out long ago by Streeten (1982).

2 THE DATA

The sample of countries included in the present analysis started from the list of 27 institutionally most-developed non-communist developing countries included in our 1967 analysis. From this sample, countries were dropped for three reasons: (i) no reliable income distribution data for about 1990 was given in the 1996 World Bank data compiled by Deininger and Squire (Argentina, Cyprus, Surinam and Uruguay were excluded for this reason); (ii) they had become fully developed by any standard by 1980, the beginning of the time period covered by the present study (Israel and Japan); and (iii) they had retrogressed since the 1960s to a lower level of economic and institutional development (El Salvador, Lebanon, Nicaragua, Paraguay, Peru and Egypt). The final sample therefore consists of: Brazil, Chile, Colombia, Costa Rica, the Dominican Republic, Ecuador, Greece, Jamaica, Korea, Mexico, Panama, Taiwan, Trinidad and Tobago, Turkey and Venezuela.

The list of variables consists of a subset of those used in the 1967 study. It is presented in Appendix 9A, together with short definitions. The static variables reflect an average for the period 1987-92, and the dynamic variables were defined with respect to rates of change between 1980 and 1990. The direction of scoring of the various aspects of development summarized by our variables generally associates higher variable scores with characteristics typical of higher levels of economic development. Thus, higher values for the dualism variable indicate less socioeconomic dualism. There are only four exceptions to this statement: the size of the traditional agricultural sector, the political power of the traditional agricultural elite, and the political power of the military, where it would have been confusing to do otherwise; and the degree of centralization of political power, where a priori theorizing did not suggest a clear direction of association.

Three departures from the 1967 definitions had to be adopted. First, the category limits for most social and economic variables were redefined to better span the entire range of variation reflected in the 1990 data.

Second, the operationalization of the variable describing the extent of leadership commitment to economic development had to be modified since the distinctions used for the 1960s no longer applied to 1990. During the 1960s, the two observable characteristics used to indicate the degrees of seriousness of governments about economic development were: (i) the existence and effectiveness of their central plans and planning agencies, and (ii) the extent and effectiveness of family-planning institutions, an unpopular, but generally acknowledged to be necessary, action to promote development. These characteristics could no longer distinguish among developing-country governments in 1990, since all developing countries now had a family-planning apparatus and central planning has fallen into general disfavor. Instead, in the present analysis, the distinctions among country governments with respect to the seriousness of their commitment to development were based on: (i) the extent of policy reform they had undertaken in liberalizing trade and markets, and (ii) on quality of their macroeconomic stabilization and adjustment policies. These policies reflect the extent of government success in implementing a different set of equally unpopular, but generally considered to be necessary, Washington-consensus-type measures. There is also ample quantitative information (inflation rates, government budget deficits, and current-account imbalances) for assessing differential degrees of success in achieving and maintaining internal and external stability and World Bank country reports provide information on the extent to which trade-liberalization measures have been undertaken and their consistency over time. To highlight this change in definition, the new variable is called 'leadership commitment to stabilization and markets' in the tables summarizing the statistical results of the study presented in this chapter.

Third, a new variable, deemed on a priori grounds to be especially relevant to income distribution, the rate of change of technological dualism, was added. It is defined as the difference between the change in productivity in industry and agriculture over the period 1980-90. Higher scores indicate greater commitment to industrial than to agricultural development.

Fourth, income distribution and poverty indicators were added, based on World Bank data. These included: the shares of income accruing to the poorest 20 and 30[1] percent of the population, the share of income accruing to the richest 20 and 10 percent; the income share of the middle income group; the Gini coefficient; and the share of population living in absolute poverty.[2]

3 THE STATISTICAL TECHNIQUE

As in our earlier study, the statistical technique used in the present chapter is factor analysis.[3] This technique of multivariate analysis is no more familiar to economists now than it was in the 1960s. However, a closely related technique, principal components analysis, has become more familiar due to its use in latent and instrumental variable regressions.

Both techniques start with the correlation matrix among the variables included in the statistical analysis. Both techniques seek to represent the correlation matrix in a lower dimensional space by translating the axes in which the correlation matrix is represented to a set of different axes. The new axes consist of linear combinations of the original dimensions of the correlation matrix. Thus, while the original dimensions of an $(m*m)$ correlation matrix are represented in an m-dimensional space consisting of the m individual variables composing the correlation matrix, the axes along which the correlation matrix is represented in both principal components and factor analyses are orthogonal linear combinations of the original variables. They are extracted from the original correlation matrix by imposing the requirements that (i) the original correlation matrix be represented as closely as possible in the new axes; and (ii) the axes used to represent the correlation matrix are orthogonal to one another. Deriving the new axes involves solving an eigenvector-eigenvalue problem in which: (i) the eigenvectors (factors) represent the new dimensions of the space in which the correlation matrix is portrayed; (ii) the squares of eigenvalues indicate the percentage of variance of the original correlation matrix 'explained' by the associated eigenvector (factor); and (iii) each succeeding eigenvector (factor) captures a smaller percentage of the overall variance.

In principal components analysis, all eigenvectors are calculated, but only the first few, those associated with a statistically significant proportion of the variance, are considered in the interpretation (or subsequent use) of the eigenvectors. In factor analysis, the number of eigenvectors extracted is specified a priori. Thus, factor analysis is identical to principal components analysis except that:

1. only a subset of eigenvectors, that with the largest eigenvalues (which account for the largest proportion of the total variance among all variables), is included;
2. instead of extracting the eigenvectors of the original correlation matrix, in factor analysis the successive eigenvectors are extracted from a modified correlation matrix in which the ones along the diagonal are replaced by the multiple regression R-squares of each variable on all

the eigenvectors included in the analysis; this feature of factor analysis is a direct consequence of the first;
3. the eigenvectors are normalized in length; the normalization used here is the same as that used in our 1967 study in which the length of each eigenvector was normalized to equal its eigenvalue; the successive factors are thus analogous to the dimensions of an ellipsoid; and
4. for ease of interpretation of the results, the eigenvectors are subjected to a rigid rotation.[4] The rotation principle applied in this paper was the same as that used in the 1967 study.[5]

The eigenvectors thus extracted are referred to as factors.

In the tables presented in this chapter, the variables are listed along the rows of the tables; the factors appear in the successive columns, and are labeled F1, F2 and so on. The numbers appearing in the body of the tables are the correlation coefficients of the variable in that row with the factor in that column.[6] Thus, variables with large coefficients in a given factor are closely associated with that factor and those with small coefficients are not. The factors constitute latent variables that are composed of the variables most closely correlated with them. More specifically, if a variable has an entry of, say, −0.50 in the column of the first factor, the first factor 'explains' 25 percent of the overall variance of this variable in the sample. And, if, say, the share of income of the poorest 20 percent has a (statistically significant) positive correlation with the first factor, increased values of the variable in question are systematically associated with lower shares of national income accruing to the poorest 20 percent, on the average.

The order of the rows (variables) in the tables is arbitrary, but the order of the columns (factors) is not. The columns are listed according to the percentage of overall variance in all variables that each factor 'explains',[7] with the factor explaining the largest percentage appearing first. For ease of interpretation, the variables in each table are listed in the order of the factor with which they are most closely associated. Thus, the variables most closely associated with the first factor are listed first; those most closely associated with the second factor next, and so on. The number of factors extracted is limited by both the percentage of overall variance accounted by the included factors and by the share of variance the last factor explains. As in the 1967 analysis, the criterion used to decide on the number of factors extracted is that, provided all factors included account for at least 65 percent of the overall variance among all variables, the last factor extracted should account for at least 108 percent[8] of the overall variance.

In interpreting the results, five different pieces of information will be used: (i) the magnitudes and signs of correlations of each variable with each factor; (ii) the relationship among the signs of the variables with significant correlations within each factor; (iii) the square of the correlation coefficient of the particular distributional indicator with each factor; this indicates the percentage of overall variance of this distributional feature explained by a given factor; (iv) the ratio of the square of the eigenvalues associated with a particular factor to the sum of squared eigenvalues for all factors; this indicates what percentage of the overall variance in all indicators is associated with a given factor; and (v) the factor scores of individual countries on each factor; this indicates how well a particular factor captures the experience of each country. The analysis of results will therefore be based on a rich information base.

4 THE SETTING OF THE STATISTICAL ANALYSES

4.1 Characteristics of the Period

The period covered by the present analysis represents the nadir of economic development for most but not all of our countries. During the late 1960s/early 1970s, the Bretton Woods international monetary system became increasingly inadequate for the liquidity needs of the world economy. When it broke down, the stable, fixed exchange rate system was replaced with a fluctuating exchange rate regime. The resulting sharp effective devaluation of currencies against the dollar contributed to inflationary pressures in Europe and Japan. Productivity growth in developed countries slowed down and wage settlements started outrunning increases in productivity. These fundamental long-run trends were exacerbated by a series of bunched short-term price shocks: a doubling in the price of cereals in 1973; a tripling in oil prices in 1974 and another doubling in 1980. Strong upward pressures on commodity prices and strong inflationary expectations were the result. Inflation rates tripled. Balance-of-payments constraints became binding. As a result, the governments of OECD countries replaced the goal of full-employment growth with the twin objectives of containing inflation and restoring balance-of-payments equilibrium. They moderated their countercyclical budgetary policies; adopted cautious macroeconomic policies; espoused a stance of fiscal restraint; and engaged in protectionist policies. The result was a drastic slowdown in OECD growth. Between 1973 and 1981, the annual real rate of growth of GNP per capita declined to about one quarter of its previous rate and the growth in real world trade fell to less than one half.[9]

In developing countries, a short period of debt-led growth during the 1970s, during which most developing countries borrowed heavily to maintain their growth momentum, came to an abrupt end in 1981. This was followed by a decade of debt crisis, structural adjustment and policy reform. The debt crisis was brought to a head by the inability of Mexico, Brazil and Turkey to meet their debt-service obligations. As a result, banks in developed countries became unwilling to extend further loans to all developing countries. Out of necessity, priorities in developing countries shifted from economic development to achieving external balance.

Adjustment patterns varied. Some developing countries adopted restrictive import regimes, deflationary government expenditure and macroeconomic policies and restrictive wage policies. Others attempted to export their way out of the crisis. They shifted from import substitution to export promotion, devalued to promote expenditure switching among imports and domestic goods, and curtailed their growth rates temporarily. The latter adjustment pattern was considerably more successful. Most developing countries, however, adopted combinations of these policies and shifted among policy regimes in a stop-go fashion.

Rampant inflation, capital flight, low investment rates, drastic declines in living standards, and substantial increases in urban and rural poverty have marked the 1980s in most of our group of countries. Overall, debt-service requirements have led to a net export of capital to the developed world. The debt of developing countries has continued to increase, as most (but not all) of our countries did not achieve a current-balance surplus sufficient to service their debts.

While the average growth performance in our countries during the 1980s was poor, the two East Asian countries in our sample have not only continued but even improved their previous developmental achievements. Perhaps most importantly, the 1980s have also been an era of significant institutional adjustment and policy reform in most countries in this group. Most of our Latin American countries have adopted at least some features of open-trade regimes. Market institutions have been strengthened in all our countries. There have been favorable political developments as well. Military or civilian dictatorships have declined and democracies have increased, although democracy in most of our countries is fragile. In addition, all developing country governments have become convinced of the priority of good economic policy over ideology and politics, though they may or may not adopt it.

Thus, the setting of the 1990s analysis has not been particularly propitious for development. Institutional development, social development (education, literacy, middle class, mass communication), democracy and policy reform have increased, but in terms of growth rates and poverty reduction the 1980s have been a lost decade.

4.2 Characteristics of the Sample

The countries included in the present analysis are heterogeneous: there are two East Asian countries – Korea and Taiwan; two Mediterranean countries – Greece and Turkey; and eleven of the most developed Latin American countries – Brazil, Chile, Colombia, Costa Rica, the Dominican Republic, Ecuador, Jamaica, Mexico, Panama, Trinidad and Tobago, and Venezuela. They differ not only geographically and culturally, but also in their initial conditions and in the development and adjustment strategies they have followed.

The countries in this group are all semi-industrial. On average, their industrial sectors generate about 40 percent of value added; 65 percent of their exports are manufactures; and their rates of increase in industrial output have averaged about 2 percent per year in constant prices. Traditional subsistence agriculture provides for the livelihood of no more than 15 percent of the economically active population; in most of the Latin American countries in our sample, large commercial absentee farms and plantations predominate, but they coexist with a significant share of small commercial owner-operated farming enterprises, while in East Asia farming systems consist of commercially viable owner-operated small farms. Internal transport and power networks are generally adequate for more rapid economic development, though specific bottlenecks still exist in most countries in this sample. Economic institutions are moderately well developed: tax systems are reasonably effective, with a ratio of government domestic revenues to GNP of between 15 and 20 percent and a ratio of direct tax revenues to total government/domestic revenue of at least 30 percent. Their financial institutions are at least moderately effective in attracting private savings and providing long- and medium-term credit to industry and agriculture but their ability to operate has been significantly curbed by hyperinflation or capital flight during a significant portion of the period. The sharp socioeconomic dualism characteristic of lower levels of development has diminished, though, except for East Asia, there are still definite contrasts between an important modern industrial sector and a commercial-agricultural sector using intermediate or traditional technology. Often, however, the traditional subsistence sectors are confined to specific regions and limited to ethnic minorities.

Along social lines, there has been a considerable degree of social development. Sixty percent of the populations of this group of countries reside in cities; literacy rates average 85 percent and secondary school enrollment ratios 65 percent; indigenous middle classes comprise about 20 percent of the population; despite marked social stratification, social mobility is considerable by developing country standards; and crude fertility rates have dropped to around 2 percent.

Politically, during the 1980-90 period there has been a general shift toward greater democracy and away from military regimes, although the military continue to wield considerable political influence. Nationwide democratic parliamentary institutions have operated fairly well during this period, but their effectiveness has been restricted by low voter participation, constraints upon opposition parties, instability of the party system, and/or inexperience with democratic forms. The political influence of tradition-orientated national elites has been moderate but the political influence of commercial and industrial groups, and/or modernizing bureaucrats has been growing. In our countries, the 1980-90 period has been characterized by reasonable political stability without much domestic violence. However, in the later part of the period, the political economy of adjustment has led to increased social tensions with the potential for greater political instability in the near future.

5 RESULTS OF THE STATISTICAL ANALYSIS

The analysis of relations between inequality and development is subdivided into thee sections: influences affecting the economic status of the poor; those affecting the middle income group; and those affecting the relative position of the rich and income concentration.

5.1 The Poor

The results of the statistical analyses portraying the economic status of the very poor are summarized in Tables 9.1-9.2. The explanation of intercountry differences in shares of income accruing to the poorest 20 and 30 percent of the population is presented in Table 9.1; that relating to the percentage of population living in absolute poverty is given in Table 9.2.

The share of income of the poorest 20 percent and poorest 30 percent of the population.

The 20 and 30 percent population shares were chosen so as to cover the entire population in absolute poverty without covering a large percentage of the nonindigent. The average percentage of the population living in absolute poverty in our sample was 23.1; it ranged from 4.5 percent

Table 9.1 Rotated factor matrix for share of income accruing to the poor in 1990 (NICs)

Variable name	F1	F2	F3	F4	R2
Income share of poorest 20%	0.21	0.17	0.73	−0.06	0.62
Income share of poorest 30%	0.28	0.22	0.73	−0.11	0.67
Per capita GNP	0.64	0.57	*	*	0.81
Size of traditional agricultural sector	−0.84	*	*	*	0.76
Extent of use of modern technology in agriculture	0.71	0.57	*	*	0.67
Degree of urbanization	0.67	*	*	*	0.67
Extent of literacy	0.67	*	*	*	0.55
Adequacy of infrastructure	0 .71	*	*	*	0.53
Degree of national integration	0.76	*	*	*	0.74
Degree of centralization	−0.62	*	*	*	0.62
Degree of administrative efficiency	0.76	*	*	*	0.67
Degree of socio-economic dualism	*	0.62	*	*	0.61
Predominant farming system	*	0.82	*	*	0.86
Rate of improvement in human resources	*	0.65	*	*	0.51
Size of the middle class	*	0.57	*	*	0.43
Degree of development of tax institutions	*	0.56	*	*	0.69
Political power of military	*	0.63	*	*	0.67
Gross investment rate	*	*	0.67	*	0.62
Rate of industrialization	*	*	0.63	*	0.86
Extent of modern technology in industry	0.52	*	0.60	*	0.77
Structure of foreign trade	*	*	0.85	*	0.80
Change in technological dualism 1980-90	−0.55	*	0.64	*	0.73
Abundance of natural resources	*	*	−0.67	*	0.49
Political power of traditional landed elite	*	*	−0.76	*	0.68
Degree of democracy	*	*	*	−0.80	0.79
Freedom of opposition and press	*	*	*	−0.78	0.67
Competitveness of party system	*	*	*	−0.74	0.79
Political influence of labor	*	−0.58	*	−0.66	0.78
Commitment to stabilization and markets	*	*	*	−0.54	0.39
Rate of growth of per capita GNP 1980-90	*	*	*	0.60	0.72
Development of financial system	0.54	*	*	0.57	0.67
Degree of social tension	−0.47	*	*	−0.58	0.71

Notes

Bold figures indicate the factor with which each variable is most closely associated. Variables with insignificant correlations with factors are starred. Variables omitted because of insignificant high correlations: extent of social mobility, rate of improvement of financial institutions.

Percentage of overall variance explained by all factors: 68.1 percent; percentage of variance explained by the last factor: 8.1 percent.

Table 9.2 Rotated factor matrix for share of population in absolute poverty in 1990 (NICs)

Variable name	F1	F2	F3	F4	R2
Share of population in absolute poverty	−0.58	0.001	0.33	−0.69	0.92
Degree of socioeconomic dualism	0.60	*	*	*	0.61
Rate of improvement in human resources	0.69	*	*	*	0.52
Predominant farming system	0.84	*	*	*	0.88
Size of middle class	0.55	*	*	*	0.42
Rate of industrialization	0.60	*	−0.48	*	0.84
Degree of development of tax system	0.60	*	*	*	0.69
Political power of military	0.57	*	*	*	0.69
Degree of democracy	*	0.86	*	*	0.77
Freedom of opposition and press	*	0.80	*	*	0.80
Degree of competitiveness of party system	*	0.77	*	*	0.80
Political power of labor	−0.53	0.70	*	*	0.77
Leadership commitment to stabilization and markets	*	0.57	*	*	0.41
Rate of growth per capita GNP 1980-90	*	−0.57	*	*	0.76
Gross investment rate	*	*	−0.64	*	0.59
Structure of foreign trade	*	*	−0.92	*	0.90
Change in technological dualism 1980-90	*	*	−0.69	*	0.71
Abundance of natural resources	*	*	0.60	*	0.41
Political power of traditional landed elite	*	*	0.71	*	
Level of per capita GNP	0.61	*	*	0.66	0.85
Size of traditional agricultural sector	*	*	*	−0.78	0.75
Extent of modern technology in agriculture	0.59	*	*	0.71	0.87
Extent of modern technology in industry	*	*	−0.55	0.59	0.86
Degree of urbanization	*	*	*	0.64	0.66
Extent of literacy	*	*	*	0.59	0.58
Degree of development of financial system	*	−0.52	*	0.61	0.68
Adequacy of infrastructure	*	*	*	0.74	0.56
Degree of national integration	*	*	*	0.80	0.56
Degree of centralization	*	*	−0.47	−0.54	0.62
Degree of administrative efficiency	*	*	*	0.80	0.56
Degree of social tension	*	0.48	*	−0.57	0.68

Notes

Bold figures indicate the factor with which each variable is most closely associated. Variables with insignificant correlations with factors are starred. Variables omitted because of insignificant high correlations: degree of development of financial system, rate of improvement of financial institutions.

Percentage of overall variance explained by all factors: 69.6 percent; percentage of variance explained by the last factor: 7.3 percent.

(Taiwan) to 38 percent (Dominican Republic). In only four countries did the extent of absolute poverty fall outside the 20 to 30 percent range.

The analysis summarized in Table 9.1 explains 62 percent of intercountry variations in the share of income accruing to the poorest 20 percent and 67 percent of the share of income accruing to the poorest 30 percent. An examination of this table indicates that only a single factor, F3, is significantly associated with the share of income accruing to the poorest 20 and 30 percent. Intercountry variations in this factor account for 53 percent (or 0.73 squared) of the variance in these income shares in our sample of NICs. This factor associates higher investment rates in more modern industrial technology, more rapid industrialization, a larger proportion of manufactured exports (structure of foreign trade), and productivity change biased toward manufacturing (change in technological dualism) with higher shares of income accruing to the poor. This big-push, export-oriented, industrial strategy is fostered by a relatively poor resource base and facilitated by reductions in the political power of the traditional agricultural elites, both of which are associated with this factor. This factor summarizes the East Asian development strategy. The high scoring countries in this factor are Korea, Taiwan, Turkey and the Dominican Republic and the lowest scoring country is Venezuela. This factor seems to suggest that, even without the initial land reforms in Taiwan and Korea, the adoption of the export-orientated industrialization strategy would have benefitted the poorest, if it could have been adopted without first weakening the political sway of the landed elites that occurred as a result of their land reforms.[10]

The effects of the other three factors on the share of income accruing to the poorest are negligible. But the negligibility of their effects is interesting in itself. Factor F1 summarizes the country's level of socio-economic development. It combines higher levels of per capita GNP with decreases in the size of the traditional agricultural sector achieved, in part, through improvements in agricultural technology, and, in part, through rural-urban migration that leads to higher urbanization. These processes are enabled by increases in literacy and denser transportation networks linking the countryside to urban centers. They lead to greater national integration. Greater political participation in decision-making (lower centralization) and more effective, less corrupt bureaucracies (greater administrative efficiency) are both causes and effects of the socio-economic development processes summarized in F1. Factor F1 is thus a very Kuznetsian factor. Its negligible impact on the share of population living in indigence suggests that development does not automatically increase the percentage of income accruing to the very poor; rather, it is the nature of development strategies summarized in F3 that matters for extreme relative poverty reduction. This is consistent with the results obtained by Adelman and Morris (1973) and the writings of Anand and Kanbur (1993).

The second factor with a negligible effect on the share of income accruing to the population in extreme poverty is F2. This factor includes most policies generally advocated for poverty reduction: higher levels of per capita GNP (significant secondary correlation with this factor); lower levels of socioeconomic dualism and reductions in rates of increase in technological dualism (change in technological dualism, significant negative secondary correlation); land tenure changes designed to increase the relative importance of commercially-orientated owner-cultivators (improvements in the predominant farming system); the dissemination of more productive techniques in agriculture (significant positive secondary correlation with this factor); improvements in secondary and tertiary school enrollments (higher rates of improvement in human resources); larger middle class; greater reliance on income rather than indirect taxes (more-developed tax institutions); increases in rural credit availability (more-developed financial systems, significant positive secondary correlation); and reductions in social tensions (significant negative secondary correlation with this factor). All of these policies appear to be relatively powerless to better the relative lot of the very poor systematically, essentially because they benefit the non-poor relatively more than they benefit the poor. The poor are generally unskilled landless agricultural workers, or either urban unemployed or employed in the informal urban sector. They own little or no land, so that improvements in land tenure or in agricultural productivity under conditions of excess supply of labor benefit middle- and upper-income groups at least as much as they benefit the poor; their children do not generally go to high school, so that they do not benefit from widening access to secondary or higher education as much as do higher-income groups; their chances of becoming middle class are negligible; their labor is in excess supply under the high unemployment and underemployment conditions generally characteristic of the period in the majority of countries in this group, and they therefore do not benefit as much from reductions in socioeconomic dualism levels as do higher-income groups; and they are virtually unaffected by taxation and do not qualify for credit even when access is widened.

The final factor with a negligible effect on the share of income accruing to the population in extreme poverty is F4. It includes many political influences designed to widen popular participation: increases in democracy; more freedom of oppposition and press; greater competitiveness of party systems; more political influence of labor (who are generally members of the middle class in our group of countries); greater commitment to neoliberal micro- and macroeconomic policies (commitment to stabilization and growth) which have been responsible for lowering the rates of economic growth over the period under consideration and increased social tensions. As we shall see below,[11] greater political participation tends to benefit the middle class rather than the poor.

The overall conclusion from this analysis is that the share of income of the very poor can be increased systematically only through development strategies designed to absorb them in the modern industrial sector. Kuznets effects do not automatically impinge on the relative lot of the very poor. The share of income distributed to the poverty group also appears to be very resistant to policy interventions. It does not respond to general development (F1); nor does it respond to generalized policies (F2); nor does it respond to increases in political participation (F4); or to economic growth *per se* (F4). Appropriate development strategies or targetted anti-poverty programs are necessary to increase the share of benefits flowing to the poorest members of society even in our group of most developed developing countries.

The share of population living in absolute poverty

The results for absolute poverty reduction are considerably more optimistic. This is heartening, but not surprising since the share of the population living in absolute poverty is high either when average per capita income is low, as in Ecuador, or when average per capita income is high but the share accruing to the poor is low, as in Brazil. The proportion of the population living in absolute poverty is, of course, lowest when, as in Taiwan and Korea, both per capita income and the share of income accruing to the poor are high.

Table 9.2 summarizes the results of our analysis of the prevalence of absolute poverty. The analysis explains 92 percent of intercountry variance in absolute poverty incidence. We discuss the factors contributing to absolute poverty reduction in the order of their contribution to variance reduction.

Factor F4, which accounts for 48 percent in intercountry variance in the extent of absolute poverty, represents the country's level of socio-economic development. The composition of this factor is similar to that of F1 in Table 9.1 – a factor that accounted for a negligible proportion of intercountry variance in the *share* of income of the poor. In F4 of Table 9.2, reductions in the prevalence of absolute poverty are associated with higher levels of per capita GNP, a smaller traditional agricultural sector, modern technology in agriculture and industry, higher urbanization and literacy rates, more-developed financial institutions, better transport networks, greater national integration, less political centralization, greater administrative efficiency and lower social tension. Thus the analysis indicates that the Kuznets effect,[12] which was essentially irrelevant for reducing relative poverty, does have a significant systematic impact on absolute poverty reduction.

The next most important cluster of policies for absolute poverty reduction is F1 in Table 9.2, which accounts for about 34 percent of intercountry variance in the prevalence of absolute poverty. This factor is like F2 of Table 9.1, which played an insignificant role in accounting for relative poverty reduction. F1 of Table 9.2 combines reductions in the proportion of the population that lives in absolute poverty with: less socioeconomic dualism, greater improvement in the quality of human resources, more commercially-orientated owner-operated farms (better farming systems), a larger middle class, higher rates of industrialization, more-developed tax systems and greater political power of the military. This factor reflects the contrast between Taiwan and Korea, the countries with the highest positive scores on this factor, on the one hand, and the Dominican Republic and Ecuador, the countries with the most negative scores on this factor, on the other.

The last factor to contribute systematically to absolute poverty reductions is F3 in Table 9.2. It accounts for 11 percent of intercountry variance in absolute poverty and is essentially identical to the sole important factor, F3, which contributed to relative poverty reduction. The factor associates less absolute poverty with more vigorous reliance on an industry- and -export-orientated development strategy encouraged by its attendant political and natural resource initial conditions.

Factor F2 in Table 9.2, which is like factor F4 in Table 9.1, summarizes the political complexion of the government and its consequences for the adoption of neo-liberal policies and economic growth. It combines variables reflecting the extent of political democracy and degree of leadership commitment to stabilization and adjustment policies with their negative consequences for economic growth over the 1980-90 period. It reflects the contrast between Chile, Mexico and Panama, on the one hand, and Trinidad and Jamaica, on the other. As before, this factor has a negligible impact on poverty, whether relative or absolute.

5.2 The Middle Class

The results of the statistical analysis summarizing the economic, social and political influences on the relative economic status of the middle class are given in Table 9.3. The explanation of intercountry differences in shares of income accruing to the middle class is multifaceted, with

Table 9.3 Rotated factor matrix for share of income accruing to the middle-income group in 1990 (NICs)

Variable name	F1	F2	F3	F4	R2
Income share of middle 20%	0.43	0.30	0.48	0.35	0.63
Level of per capita GNP	0.64	*	*	0.63	0.82
Size of traditional agricultural sector	−0.74	*	*	*	0.74
Extent of modernization of technology in agriculture	0.66	*	*	0.65	0.86
Extent of modernization of technology in industry	0.56	*	*	0.51	0.80
Degree of urbanization	0.66	0.57	*	*	0.70
Degree of social mobility	0.61	*	*	*	0.39
Extent of literacy	0.55	*	*	*	0.50
Degree of development of financial system	0.64	0.49	*	*	0.68
Adequacy of infrastructure	0.70	*	*	*	0.53
Degree of national integration	0.79	*	*	*	0.65
Degree of administrative efficiency	0.81	*	*	*	0.70
Extent of social tension	−0.64	0.57	*	*	0.70
Degree of democracy	*	0.87	*	*	0.78
Freedom of opposition and press	*	0.79	*	*	0.68
Degree of competitiveness of party system	*	0.83	*	*	0.79
Political power of labor	*	0.75	*	*	0.79
Political power of military	*	0.53	*	0.47	0.63
Leadership commitment to stabilization and markets	*	0.60	*	*	0.40
Rate of growth of per capita GNP 1980-90	0.45	−0.53	*	*	0.71
Gross investment rate	*	*	0.61	*	0.60
Abundance of natural resources	0.52	*	−0.68	*	0.58
Structure of foreign trade	*	*	0.86	*	0.80
Rate of improvement of financial system	−0.54	*	0.76	*	0.66
Change in technological dualism 1980-90	−0.54	*	0.76	*	0.73
Political power of traditional landed elite	−0.54	*	−0.64	*	0.63
Degree of centralization	−0.51	*	0.56	*	0.68
Degree of socio-economic dualism	*	*	*	0.59	0.63
Predominant farming system	*	*	*	0.87	0.89
Rate of industrialization	*	−0.46	0.52	0.57	0.84
Rate of improvement of human resources	*	−0.58	*	0.66	0.50
Size of middle class	*	*	*	0.52	0.41
Degree of development of tax system	*	*	*	0.68	0.68

Notes

Bold figures indicate the factor with which each variable is most closely associated. Variables with insignificant correlations with factors are starred.

Percentage of overall variance explained by all factors: 69.6 percent; percentage of variance explained by the last factor: 7.3 percent.

most aspects of socioeconomic and political development systematically benefitting the middle class. The overall degree of explanation achieved is 63 percent. Again, we discuss the factors in order of their importance for accounting for intercountry differences in share of benefits captured by the middle class.

The factor explaining the largest share of variance in the income share of the middle class, 23 percent, is F3, the factor depicting the nature of the development-strategy orientation, the vigor with which it is pursued, and some of the economic and political initial conditions making it possible. The analysis suggests that the export-orientated industrialization strategy, vigorously pursued, reliably benefits the middle class, as well as the poor.

The next most significant factor accounting for intercountry variance in income shares of the poor is F1 (18 percent), the Kuznetsian socioeconomic development-level factor. Like F1 in Table 9.1 and F4 in Table 9.2, this factor combines higher levels of per capita GNP, smaller agricultural sector, the use of more modern agricultural and industrial technology, higher degrees of urbanization, social mobility and literacy, more-developed financial institutions, better transport networks linking the countryside with cities, leading to greater national integration, and lower social tensions. The table indicates that socioeconomic development reliably benefits the middle class.

The third most important force accounting for intercountry variance in the relative share of benefits accruing to the middle class is summarized by F4 (12 percent). This is a Lewis-Ranis-Fei factor that associates larger shares of income of the middle class with decreases in socioeconomic dualism, more commercialization of agriculture in viable-sized owner-operated farms, higher rates of industrialization, higher rates of accumulation of human capital, increases in the size of the middle class and more-developed tax systems. One can just see the celebrated Lewis, Fei and Ranis graph at work shifting the distribution of income around the commercialization point toward the (middle-class) workers employed in the modern sector in this factor!

The final factor explaining 9 percent of intercountry differences in middle-class income shares is F2, the political democracy factor analogous to F2 in Table 9.2 and F4 in Table 9.1. The analysis indicates that democracy reliably benefits the middle class, even though it tends to increase commitment to neoliberal stabilization policies which lower growth rates and increase social tensions (significant secondary positive correlation with this factor). As we shall see in the next section, more participatory political institutions systematically benefit the middle class at the expense of the rich. (We saw in the previous section that democracy does not systematically affect either the relative or the absolute lot of the poor.)

The analysis of factors affecting the share of income of the middle class is consistent with that in earlier studies. It confirms the centrality of the Lewis-Ranis-Fei theoretical model of 'Development with Surplus Labor' for development that benefits the middle class. It also confirms two earlier empirical findings of Adelman and Morris (1973): the tendency of socioeconomic development to reliably benefit the middle class; and the tendency of political participation to shift the distribution of income in its favor.

5.3 The Rich and the Degree of Concentration of the Distribution of Income

Table 9.4 combines the results of our analysis of the concomitants of intercountry differences in the share of income captured by the richest 10 and 20 percent with those relating to the Gini coefficient because they are virtually identical. This is not very surprising since the Gini is known to be most sensitive to concentration at the upper end of the income scale. The analysis in Table 9.4 explains between 70 and 74 percent of the variance of each of these variables.

There are two factors in Table 9.4, of almost equal importance, which depict the economic, social and political institutions associated with development that are responsible for systematically decreasing the shares of income and its concentration – F3 and F4. F3 is our old friend, the vigor of pursuit of an export-orientated development strategy and the conditions that make it possible. However, here this factor also includes two other variables, democracy and the degree of centralization of decision-making, that have substantial secondary positive correlations with this factor. They, too, tend to lower the share of income of the rich and decrease the extent of income concentration. F3 accounts for between 35 percent (Gini) and 26 percent (richest 20 percent) of intercountry variances.

F4 includes a subset of the variables depicting the level of socio-economic development included in a single Kuznetsian factor in our previous tables: per capita GNP, the size of the traditional agricultural sector (significant negative secondary correlation), land tenure institutions, and the extent of modernization of technology in agriculture; literacy and rate of improvement of human resources; technological modernization in industry (positive secondary correlation); and degree of development of tax systems. Higher levels of the variables associated with F4 lead to systematic reductions in the share of income of the rich

Table 9.4 Rotated factor matrix for concentration and the share of income accruing to the rich in 1990 (NICs)

Variable name	F1	F2	F3	F4	R2
Gini coefficient	0.25	0.12	−0.59	−0.53	0.71
Income share of the richest 20%	0.32	0.21	−0.51	−0.50	0.74
Income share of the richest 10%	0.31	0.17	−0.56	−0.50	0.70
Size of traditional agricultural sector	0.67	*	*	−0.48	0.74
Adequacy of infrastructure	−0.65	*	*	*	0.54
Development of financial system	−0.67	0.49	*	*	0.69
Degree of urbanization	−0.64	*	*	*	0.70
Extent of social mobility	−0.61	*	*	*	0.40
Degree of national integration	−0.79	*	*	*	0.64
Degree of centralization	0.52	*	0.46	*	0.64
Degree of administrative efficiency	−0.77	*	*	*	0.66
Degree of social tension	0.70	*	*	*	0.63
Size of the middle class	*	0.58	*	*	0.40
Degree of democracy	*	−0.82	0.51	*	0.79
Freedom of opposition and press	*	−0.58	*	*	0.62
Degree of competitiveness of party system	*	−0.73	*	*	0.74
Political influence of labor	*	−0.85	*	*	0.76
Political power of military	*	0.65	*	*	0.69
Leadership commitment to stabilization and markets	*	−0.50	*	*	0.36
Rate of growth of per capita GNP 1980-90	0.47	0.66	*	*	0.74
Degree of socio-economic dualism	*	0.56	*	*	0.61
Rate of industrialization	*	0.74	0.48	*	0.85
Gross investment rate	*	*	0.65	*	0.52
Extent of modern technology in industry	0.52	*	0.53	0.46	0.72
Structure of foreign trade	*	*	0.86	*	0.84
Change in technological dualism 1980-90	−0.54	*	0.74	*	0.71
Abundance of natural resorces	*	*	−0.70	*	0.52
Political power of traditional landed elite	*	*	−0.68	*	0.62
Extent of literacy	−0.45	*	*	0.55	0.59
Rate of improvement in human	*	*	*	0.61	0.55
Level of per capita GNP	−0.54	*	*	0.65	0.83
Predominant farming system	*	*	*	0.74	0.90
Extent of modern technology in agriculture	−0.57	*	*	0.62	0.82
Degree of development of tax institutions	*	*	*	0.84	0.72

Notes

Bold figures indicate the factor with which each variable is most closely associated. Variables with insignificant correlations with factors are starred. Variables omitted because of insignificant high correlations: rate of improvement in financial institutions.

Percentage of overall variance explained by all factors: 68.1 percent; percentage of variance explained by the last factor: 8.1 percent.

and very rich and to decreases in income concentration. The degree of explanatory power of this factor is about 25 percent of variances of all three variables.

The bulk of the rest of the explanatory power of the present analysis is provided by factor F1, which accounts for between 6 and 10 percent of variances of the variables pertaining to the situation of the rich and income concentration. This factor includes the other aspects of socio-economic development left out of F4 that were contained in the single Kuznetsian factor in our prior analyses. It associates higher-income shares for the rich and greater income concentration with greater levels of socio-economic underdevelopment: larger traditional agricultural sectors, less-developed transport networks, financial institutions that do not provide agricultural credit or finance to medium and smaller industries; less urbanization; significant ethnic or social barriers to social mobility; less national integration; greater centralization; more corrupt and less professional bureaucracies; and higher levels of social tension.

The final factor, with insignificant explanatory power for our 'dependent' variables, is F2. It describes a politicoeconomic profile that associates more-developed social and economic institutions and higher growth rates with less-democratic, more-centralized, and more-military political regimes. Specifically, this factor combines: higher rates of growth of per capita GNP; lower degrees of socioeconomic dualism; faster industrialization; a larger middle class; more-developed financial systems (significant positive secondary correlation with this factor); with less-democratic systems; less freedom of opposition and press; less-competitive political party systems; less political influence of labor unions; and greater political power of the military; and less leadership commitment to stabilization and market systems.

6 CONCLUSIONS

The results of this empirical study of the connections between income distribution and various facets of economic, social and political development indicate that they are multifaceted and complex. Simple regression studies relating levels and/or rates of economic growth of per capita GNP to Gini coefficients or income shares cannot hope to capture the full complexity of the relations involved.

Development strategies play a critical role in distribution. Specifically, energetic pursuit of an export-orientated industrialization strategy, *à la* Taiwan and Korea, is a critical influence increasing equity. By expanding modern-sector employment, export-led growth shifts the distribution of income in favor of the very poor, benefits the middle class and reduces concentration and the share of income captured by the rich. It reduces income concentration and augments the absolute income of the poor. Modern-sector employment played a central role in the development theory of Lewis (1954), Fei and Ranis (1964), and Ranis (1978).

Socioeconomic development, of which reductions in dualism are a critical component, increases the absolute incomes of the poor, raises the relative incomes of the middle class and decreases the relative incomes of the rich. Higher per capita GNP levels are only part of the story, and a not very important one at that.[13] Reductions in socioeconomic dualism; modernization of technology in agriculture undertaken while the subsistence sector shrinks, as more formerly agricultural labor is absorbed in the modern industrial sector and surplus labor disappears; land tenure changes which enable commercially-orientated owner-operators of small farms to derive incomes comparable to those of urban workers; and increases in the quality of human resources (literacy for the poor and secondary and higher education for the middle class) all contribute to this process. These are all elements of a development process stressed by John Fei and coauthors (Fei and Ranis 1964 and Kuo et al. 1981) and applied in the East Asia development model.

Most generalized economic policy interventions leave the poor in the same relative position as they were without them. They benefit income groups proportionately to their initial endowments of physical and human assets and, therefore, while they benefit the poor in absolute terms, they are powerless to shift the distribution of income in their favor.

This finding is consistent with that emerging from policy and program simulations with a CGE model of Korea by Adelman and Robinson (1978). A major conclusion from that work was that single policies or programs were dissipated by leakages to upper-income groups soon after they were made and that only large coordinated anti-poverty programs or development strategies could increase the share of income accruing to the poor.

The rate of economic growth *per se* does not affect equity systematically in our sample. The important thing for distribution is how growth is achieved. The centrality of the content of growth was stressed by Streeten (1982) and in the most recent UNDP *Human Development Report* (1996). The desirable content of growth and how growth is achieved are reflected in our results in the choice of development strategy and in the changes in the components of the socioeconomic development level.

Among political forces, increases in democracy benefit only the middle class but not the poor. Democracy tends to empower the middle class, whose political participation is increased. Special measures to empower the poor or to forge an alliance of interest between the poor and the middle class would be required for democracy to better the lot of the poor (Streeten 1982). The critical political factor for distributional equity is how powerful the landed, agrarian, traditional elite is, because its power must be weakened sufficiently to permit adoption of an industrial strategy.

NOTES

1. This share was derived by interpolation from the published data set.
2. With incomes below $600 per capita per year. Calculated by interpolation from the average per capita annual incomes of each quintile.
3. For a rigorous mathematical description of the technique, see Adelman and Morris (1967, ch 3).
4. The rotation represents an angle-preserving rotation of the axes in which the eigenvectors are measured.
5. Specifically, the varimax rotation principle was used. The varimax rotation, which is applied simultaneously to all eigenvectors, makes the coefficient of the variables in each eigenvector as close to either zero (if the original coefficients are small) or unity (if the coefficients are large). The rotation does not affect the results, merely the ease of interpretation.
6. In factor analysis, these correlation coefficients are called 'loadings'.
7. That is, the factors are listed in order of the size of their eigenvalues. As indicated in the text above, the square of the eigenvalue indicates the percentage of the overall variance among all variables accounted for by its associated eigenvector.
8. This is the value of *R*-square which is statistically significant at the 5 percent level.
9. Nevertheless, non-oil imports of developed countries from developing ones grew by 12 percent.
10. This thought is suggested not only by the composition of F3 but also by the statistically insignificant correlation of the variable indicating land tenure condition (predominant farming system) with F3. It runs counter to the writings of John Fei and Gus Ranis with respect to Taiwan and my own writings about Korea.
11. We also found this to be the case in the Adelman and Morris 1973 study.
12. Empirical tests of the Kuznets U-hypothesis relate levels of per capita GNP to shares of income accruing to the poor. Kuznets's own statement of the hypothesis is broader and relates development levels, defined to include not only higher per capita income levels but also changes in technology and structure of production, to income shares. F4 in this table is a closer representation of Kuznets's notion of development than per capita GNP alone.
13. The exclusion of per capita GNP from the factor in which it appears does not perceptibly affect the percentage variance explained by that factor. The

exclusion of GNP per capita from its factor does not change the explanatory power with respect to the share of the poor at all; raises the explanatory power of its factor by 1 percentage point for the middle income group; and reduces the explanatory power of its factor by 1 percentage point for the rich, and the percentage of population in absolute poverty.

REFERENCES

Adelman, Irma and Cynthia Taft Morris (1967), *Society, Politics and Economic Development—A Quantitative Approach*, Baltimore, MD: Johns Hopkins University Press.

Adelman, Irma and Cynthia Taft Morris (1973), *Economic Growth and Social Equity in Developing Countries*, Stanford, CA: Stanford University Press.

Adelman, Irma and Sherman Robinson (1978), *Income Distribution Policy in Developing Countries: A Case Study of Korea*, Stanford, CA: Stanford University Press.

Anand, Sudhir and S.M.R. Kanbur (1993), 'Inequality and Development: A Critique', *Journal of Development Economics*, 40, 42-50.

Deininger, Klaus and L. Squire (1996), 'Measuring Income Inequality: A New Data Base', *World Bank Research Observer*, 10, 565-91.

Fei, John C. and Gustav Ranis (1964), *Development of the Labor Surplus Economy*, Homewood, IL: Richard D. Irwin.

Kuo, Shirley W.Y., Gustav Ranis and John C.H. Fei (1981), *The Taiwan Success Story,* Boulder, CO: Westview Press.

Kuznets, Simon (1955), 'Economic Growth and Income Inequality', *American Economic Review*, 45, 1-28.

Kuznets, Simon (1966), *Modern Economic Growth: Rate, Structure, and Spread*, New Haven, CT: Yale University Press.

Lewis, W. Arthur (1954), 'Economic Development with Unlimited Supplies of Labor', *Manchester School of Economic and Social Studies*, 22, 139-91.

Ranis, Gustav (1978), 'Equity and Growth in Taiwan: How "Special" is the "Special Case"?', *World Development*, 6, 397-409.

Ravaillon, Martin (1997), 'Good and Bad Growth', *World Development*, 25, 631-38.

Streeten, Paul (1982), *First Things First*, Oxford: Oxford University Press.

United Nations Development Program (UNDP) (1996), *Human Development Report,* New York: Oxford University Press.

APPENDIX 9A THE LIST OF VARIABLES

An abbreviated set of definitions of variables is given below. All rate-of-change variables refer to the period 1979/80-1989/90 and all 'level' variables refer to 1987-92. Variables for which the category-limits were changed from the 1960 limits are starred. Full descriptions are given in Adelman and Morris (1967).

Economic Indicators

- Annual Rate of Growth of Real Per capita GNP: between1979/1980 and 1989/90.
- Gross Investment Rate: share to GNP.
- Abundance of Natural Resources: arable land per capita and abundance of fuel and non-fuel. natural resources.
- Extent of Modernization of Technology in Industry: use of power-driven technology and relative importance of modern, large-scale industry.
- Rate of Industrialization: average real annual rate of change of industrial production.
- Predominant Farming System (formerly called Character of Agricultural Organization): this variable ranges from communal ownership of land to viable commercial farming. Intermediate categories are: owner-operated subsistence farming and large scale absentee or owner-operated farms or plantations combined with either subsistence farming or small scale commercial farming.
- Extent of Modernization of Technology in Agriculture: use of mechanical power and fertilizer; and share of non-monetized subsistence farming.
- Adequacy of Infrastructure: transport and power networks.
- Level of Development of Tax Institutions: share of domestic tax revenue to GNP and share of direct to indirect taxes.
- Level of Development of Financial System: effectiveness in attracting private savings and channeling them to investment; and provision of credit to the rural sector.
- Rate of Improvement of Financial Systems: rate of increase of share of demand plus time deposits to GNP.
- Rate of Improvement of Human Resources: weighted average of secondary plus tertiary enrollment rates.
- Structure of Foreign Trade: share of manufactured commodities in total exports plus diversification of exports by commodity and country.

Socioeconomic Indicators:

- Size of Traditional Agricultural Sector: proportion of population engaged in traditional subsistence agriculture. Nets out proportion in commercial agriculture from the total.
- Extent of Socioeconomic Dualism: extent of modernization of methods of production throughout sectors, regions, and scale. Lowest category has very limited development of the exchange sector and preponderance of subsistence production; highest has significant modernization of production in all sectors, regions and scales of production.
- Rate of Change in Technological Dualism: difference between the rate of improvement of industrial and agricultural productivity.
- Degree of Urbanization: percentage of population in cities over 20,000.
- Size of Indigenous Middle Class: percentage of indigenous male population in professional, managerial administrative or technical occupations.
- Degree of Social Mobility: breadth of opportunities for entry into the middle class. Judged by school enrollment ratios; share of middle-class occupations; and extent of ethnic, religious or cultural barriers to entry into middle class occupations.
- Literacy Rate: of adult population.
- Degree of Social Tension: qualitative indicator ranging from countries with no overt signs of social tension or violence to countries with marked social tensions accompanied by substantial violence and social instability.

Political Indicators:

- Degree of National Integration: ranges from countries in which there is a marked absence of national integration as indicated by the absence of a common language and culture, ineffective integration of local and central political systems, and little sense of national unity to countries in which the same criteria indicate that there is a marked degree of national integration.
- Degree of Centralization of Political Power: ranges from countries in which central governments did not maintain effective control throughout important parts of the country to countries with centralized authoritarian governments.
- Degree of Democracy: ranges from countries in which there was little or no practice of nationwide institutional democracy to ones with well-established nationwide democracy, with a least two effective political

parties, freedom of opposition and at least 30 percent of eligible voters participating in national elections.

– Freedom of Opposition and Press: ranges from countries in which political parties were limited to non-political activities and political opposition was banned to countries in which parties were free to organize, operate and oppose the government throughout the period and in which the freedom of the press was restricted at most intermittently.

– Degree of Competitiveness of Political Party Systems: ranges from countries in which there were no political parties effective at the national level to ones in which there were two or more reasonably effective political parties operating at the national level between at least two of which rotation or sharing of government control could be expected.

– Political Strength of the Labor Movement: ranges from countries with negligible or proscribed labor movements to ones in which labor movements were reasonably well established, active and had substantial popular support.

– Political Strength of the Traditional Landed Elite: ranges from countries in which tradition-oriented agrarian elites had little or no political power during most of the period to ones in which landed or other tradition-oriented elites were politically dominant during the greatest part of the period.

– Political Strength of the Military: ranged from countries in which the military had little or no political influence to countries in which the military were in direct political control during an important part of the period.

– Degree of Administrative Efficiency: ranges from countries with extreme bureaucratic inefficiency, with highly corrupt civil service and suffering from serious instability of policy at high levels to countries with a relatively well-trained civil service that did not suffer from instability of policy at high level and that did not have high levels of corruption.

– Extent of Leadership Commitment to Stabilization and Markets: based on extent of shift towards an open trade regime, market-oriented reforms, and internal and external stabilization efforts.

10. Changes in Inequality and Welfare in a Developing Country Experiencing Hyperinflation

John P. Formby and Jacob Kaliyati*

1 INTRODUCTION

The work of Kuznets (1955, 1963), Fei et al. Ranis (1978) and Fields (1980) has firmly established the importance of income distributions in the study of development economics. It is now widely agreed that the welfare effects of growth and development policies require an evaluation of entire distributions of income or consumption. While of interest, measures of macro performance such as real per capita GDP or summary indicators of inequality like the Gini coefficient fail to provide the detailed information needed to rank economic welfare and well-being across time. Evaluating entire distributions requires high quality micro data that are often unavailable for poor countries, particularly those undergoing dramatic changes in economic policy. Peru is an exception. Excellent microdata are available for the mid-1980s and early 1990s, a period characterized by radical policy changes and hyperinflation. The nature of the data makes it possible to analyze changes in income distributions and welfare in urban and rural areas, within major regions of Peru as well as across time. In addition, a subset of the data for Lima residents can be used to measure income mobility during the period of hyperinflation.

The World Bank collected the data using Living Standards Measurement Program (LSMP) survey procedures. Glewwe (1988) and Glewwe and Hall (1994) have used the Peruvian Living Standard Survey (PLSS) micro data to evaluate poverty, inequality and welfare using traditional (descriptive) methods. We bring a fresh approach to the PLSS

*The authors thank Daniel G. Arce John Bishop, Buhong Zheng and Percy Vaughn for helpful discussion. Any errors or omissions, of course, are entirely our responsibility. We also thank the World Bank for making the micro data available.

data by applying powerful dominance techniques that rank entire distributions and provide very general measures of welfare, inequality, poverty and mobility in Peru in the mid-1980s and early 1990s. Compared to the previous work that uses PLSS data, the research reported in this chapter has five distinguishing features. First, as noted above, we use dominance methods, which have proven useful in income distribution studies in developed countries and are increasingly being applied in poor and newly industrialized countries.[1] Second, we apply statistical inference procedures that complement the dominance analysis. This allows us to test explicit hypotheses concerning differences in entire income distributions and welfare. Third, we make adjustments for variations in household size by using several equivalence scales rather than one. This procedure allows us to take economies of scale within households into account and to check the sensitivity of our findings to variations in household size across regions and in rural and urban areas. Fourth, to assess welfare we analyze entire food-share distribution functions. This approach avoids the pitfalls encountered in measuring hyperinflation and using aggregate price indices to deflate incomes and consumption across time. Finally, in addition to inequality, poverty and welfare, we also analyze economic mobility during hyperinflation.

The remainder of the chapter is organized as follows. Section 2 briefly reviews the policy changes in Peru in the mid-1980s and discusses the findings of previous studies that make use of the LSMP data. Section 3 discusses the dominance method and summarizes the inference methods used to evaluate distributions of sample data. Section 3 also discusses extensions of dominance procedures to food-share distribution functions in poor countries. Section 4 discusses the PLSS data. Section 5 summarizes the empirical results. The final section discusses the implications of the findings and provides concluding remarks.

2 ECONOMIC CONDITIONS AND POLICIES IN PERU IN THE 1980s AND EARLY 1990s

We first summarize the changes in economic policies in Peru and the general economic conditions that prevailed in the 1980s and early 1990s. This is followed by brief discussions of previous work relying upon PLSS data and the difficulties encountered with using price deflators to adjust consumption data during hyperinflation.

2.1 Economic Policies and General Conditions in Peru

In the 1980s and early 1990s, Peru went through three radical policy reversals and experienced a dramatic acceleration in prices that reached hyperinflation levels in the late 1980s. A guerrilla movement and civil unrest that waxed and waned during the decade compounded the economic problems. In the early 1980s, Peru followed what has been described as standard IMF/World Bank structural adjustments policies. The thrusts of such policies are well known and consist of two basic types. First, government spending and the size of the public sector are reduced and a general policy of austerity is pursued. Second, exchange rates are allowed to float freely. In combination with international developments including the US recession and a Latin America debt crisis, the effects of these policies were disastrous for Peru. Exchange rates depreciated rapidly, real output fell, net capital inflow decreased, and export revenues declined.

In early 1985, Peru's economy was stagnant, the rate of inflation was 50 percent, and economic conditions were widely perceived as 'alarming' (Paus 1991). This set the stage for a shift in political power to Alan Garcia Perez and the APRA Party in July 1985. On assuming power, APRA immediately abandoned the orthodox economic policy strategies and introduced what came to be called a heterodox program. In particular, APRA rejected the idea that inflation resulted from money creation and excess demand and attributed it to increasing costs caused by devaluations, rising interest rates, and the peculiarities of modern sector price formation in response to declining demand (ibid., p. 415). According to the APRA program, economic revitalization was to be achieved by increasing wages, boosting investment in the education, health, agriculture and transport sectors and stimulating demand. A price freeze (including exchange rates) was an integral part of the heterodox program, which also included arbitrary limits on interest payments on foreign debt, granting of interest-free loans to public sector employees, preferential interest rates for Highland farmers, and general reductions in interest rates and income taxes.

Compared to the early 1980s, the initial effects of the heterodox policies seemed beneficial, but the optimism proved short-lived. By 1988 GDP was again declining and inflation had reached an annual rate of over 1,700 percent and continued to escalate monthly. As a consequence, the APRA government reversed the basic thrust of economic policy; the currency was devalued, interest rates were increased and a policy that forced nominal wage changes to lag behind inflation was imposed. In 1989 and early 1990, APRA introduced additional *ad hoc* policy adjustments, but production continued to fall and inflation soared, going from 1,720 percent in 1988 to 3,400 percent in 1989 and to 7,400 percent in 1990.

A third major policy reversal occurred following Alberto Fujimori's election to the office of President in July 1990. Contrary to his campaign rhetoric, which had promised a moderate program of gradual economic stabilization, Fujimori adopted an orthodox stabilization program that went far beyond the minimum requirements of the standard structural adjustment programs. In brief, the program (now referred to as 'Fujishock') involved privatization, trade liberalization, deregulation, a return to floating exchange rates and tight controls on money creation. The policies of Fujishock are credited with inducing a sharp recession, drastically disinflating the Peruvian economy and eventually halting the deterioration in real wages. By the end of 1992, the rate of inflation was down to 3-5 percent per month and the slide in real wages had ceased.

2.2 Previous Work Using PLSS Data

The World Bank conducted LSMP surveys for Peru in 1985-86, 1990 and 1991. The 1985-86 PLSS data reflect the economic conditions that prevailed at the start and immediately following the adoption of the heterodox policies by the APRA government. The 1990 data reflect the effects of the heterodox policies, hyperinflation and the initial impacts of Fujishock. Glewwe and Hall (1994) analyze primary PLSS data from the 1985-86 and 1990 as well as secondary data to assess poverty, inequality and living standards in Lima. Glewwe and Hall's work is wide ranging and we note only three general findings and a conjecture concerning overall inequality. First, they use conditional mean per capita consumption expenditures at deciles adjusted for inflation as an indicator of welfare across time. Without apparent recognition of the theoretical literature, their procedure is equivalent to simple numeric (zero variance) first-order dominance comparisons of real consumption expenditures. The results indicate that all decile groups experienced declines in the value of both real food and total consumption expenditures. The decreases were quite large; 1990 conditional means were about half the 1985-86 level. Glewwe and Hall interpret this result as suggesting that the poorest deciles suffered the most. Based on this, they conclude that inequality seemed to have deepened in Lima between 1985-86 and 1990.

Second, Glewwe and Hall investigate headcount poverty in Lima across time. Like most countries, Peru does not have an official poverty line. Using quite reasonable procedures, different poverty lines are constructed and PLSS data are used to estimate headcount poverty in

Lima in 1985-86 and 1990.[2] Irrespective of the poverty line used, the results indicate that headcount poverty increased dramatically across time. Third, Glewwe and Hall review secondary data on health and education in Lima and find little evidence of deterioration; in some instances the evidence suggests improvement. Finally, Glewwe and Hall (1994) use Glewwe's (1988) evidence for the entire 1985-86 PLSS and argue that for Peru (as distinct from Lima) consumption may have been more equally distributed in 1990 than 1985-86. The logic underpinning this conjecture is that almost half of the poorest 10 percent of Peru's population are engaged in rural agriculture. These households are more or less self-sufficient, particularly in food consumption. Therefore, it may be the case that for Peru as a whole, welfare was more equally distributed in 1990 compared to 1985-86.

2.3 Difficulties with Price Deflators in Hyperinflation

There is an important question relating to the reliability of price deflators in hyperinflation. This is apparent from the brief review of Glewwe and Hall's (1994) analysis of Peru summarized above. Their table 1 reports a consumer price index (CPI) (1980 = 100) of 3,474 for 1985 and 40,216,592 for 1990, which suggests that the average price level rose by more than 11,500 percent over the period studied. Here is the difficulty: Peru was a very poor country in 1985-86 and applying the price deflator suggests that conditional mean consumption fell by more than half in every decile of the distribution. Thus, the people of Lima were more than twice as poor in 1990 as five years earlier. If this were true we should expect mass social disruptions, interruptions of education, higher infant mortality, declining health and even starvation. None of these things happened! Real consumption apparently did not decline by anything resembling the magnitude suggested by applying price deflators to the hyperinflated consumption expenditures reported in PLSS data for Lima.

Glewwe and Hall are clearly aware of the potential difficulties associated with using the Peruvian price deflators to adjust hyperinflated consumption expenditures and report on procedures followed to try to verify their finding that welfare declined between 1985-86 and 1990. In fact, they examined food shares which they interpret (ibid., p. 696) as providing supporting evidence for dramatic declines in welfare. However, our inference-based analysis of food shares reported below indicates Peru's CPI is so unreliable that results based upon deflated expenditure data are seriously suspect. We follow Bishop et al. (1996) and use food-share distribution functions as the basic welfare indicator and apply inference procedures to test explicit dominance hypotheses concerning welfare. To show the magnitude of the differences in the results of the two approaches, we present some of our dominance results for both food shares and deflated consumption expenditures. The differences in the implications are startling.

3 INFERENCE-BASED DOMINANCE METHODS FOR EVALUATING ENTIRE DISTRIBUTIONS

Lorenz dominance is acknowledged to be the most general method available for evaluating relative inequality, while rank or first-order dominance provides an equally compelling technique for assessing distributions of absolute income or consumption expenditures. Both procedures are based upon ordinal rankings of entire distributions and provide partial orders of relative inequality and absolute distributions of income or consumption. The appeal of the dominance approach is traceable to three features of the methodology. First, it rests upon very general and nonrestrictive assumptions that often yield unambiguous conclusions. Second, the dominance method is easily implemented and has proven to be quite powerful in empirical studies of a number of distributions. Third, beginning with the work of Beach and Davidson (1983) a series of statistical inference procedures that complement and refine the dominance method have been developed. A possible drawback to empirical use of dominance techniques is that they may provide only a partial order of the distributions of interest, which means that it may not be possible to rank some distributions due to crossing Lorenz curves or distribution functions. But there is growing awareness that a crossing provides the researcher with valuable information about the distributions of interest.

3.1 Lorenz Dominance

The Pigou-Dalton principle of transfers holds that the redistribution of a small amount of income from a person ranked in higher positions in the ordered distribution to a person ranked in a lower position *always* decreases inequality. Atkinson (1970) used this assumption to demonstrate that if two Lorenz curves cross it is always possible to find competing summary inequality indices that have contradictory implications concerning relative income inequality in the two distributions. It is well known that such conflicts are avoided if, and only if, one Lorenz curve dominates the other. Thus, Lorenz dominance avoids the multiplicity of index numbers problem and it is this attribute that

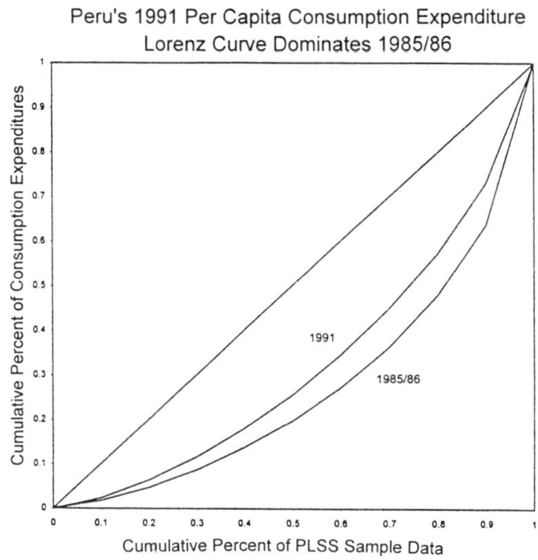

Figure 10.1 Lorenz dominance and inequality

ensures that it is the most general of all inequality measures satisfying the Pigou-Dalton transfer principle.

Figure 10.1 illustrates the Lorenz dominance ranking criterion by comparing per capita consumption showing the Lorenz curves, which are derived from PLSS data for 1985-86 and 1991. Initially we ignore the problem of statistical inference and conclude by inspection of Figure 10.1 that Lorenz dominance holds; inequality is uniformly more equal at every decile in 1991 than in 1985-86. Thus, all inequality indices will yield the same qualitative conclusions concerning inequality in Peru over this time period.

Kolm (1969) and Atkinson (1970) show that Lorenz dominance implies greater welfare when the income distributions being compared have the same mean and a symmetric welfare function is assumed. However, as stressed by Sen (1973), if the means of the distributions being compared are different, as they almost always are in empirical studies, Lorenz dominance is devoid of welfare content. It continues, of course, to be the most general of all inequality measures.

3.2 First-order (Rank) Dominance

Saposnik (1981, 1983) addresses the welfare question associated with income distributions in the most direct and straightforward manner possible by applying first-order dominance techniques. This intuitively appealing criterion is implemented by comparing absolute incomes or

Consumption expenditures in ranked (ordered) positions of the inverse distribution function. First-order dominance is underpinned by the strong Pareto principle and anonymity, two assumptions that command wide acceptance. Therefore, first-order dominance is also referred to as the anonymous Pareto principle. To facilitate comparisons of populations of different sizes, first-order dominance also makes use of the population principle (compare Dasgupta et al. 1973). In an important contribution, Saposnik uses these two assumptions to prove that the statistical cumulative distribution functions (cdf) and its inverse, referred to as the quantile function, contain sufficient information to unanimously rank welfare.

First-order dominance of consumption expenditures are illustrated in Figure 10.2 with plots of the per capita food expenditure quantile functions for the 1985-86 and 1991 PLSS data. Consumption expenditures are adjusted for hyperinflation using consumer price indices of the sort routinely employed to adjust for inflation in time-series data. If the inflationary adjustments are believed, then per capita consumption declined in every decile with reductions ranging between 84 and 92 percent. Figure 10.2 suggests that the bottom eight deciles in 1991 were worse-off on average than the lowest decile in 1985-86. For the

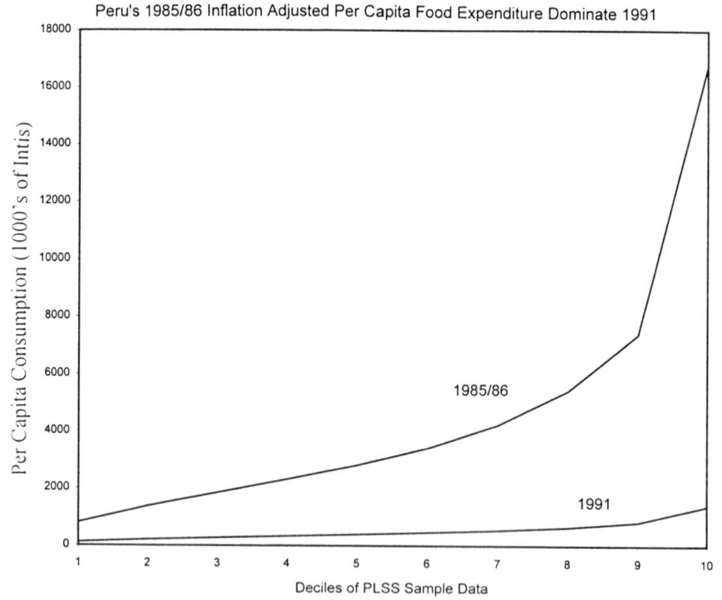

Note: * Expenditures are in thousands of Intis at June 1, 1990 prices.

*Figure 10.2 First order dominance – per capita food expenditures**

reasons explained in Sections 2.3 above, and 5.2 below, it is difficult to believe that price indices used to deflate consumption in Peru's hyperinflation are reliable in welfare and poverty analysis.

3.3 Food Expenditure Shares, Well-being and Food-Share Distribution Dominance

This section summarizes and illustrates how food-share distribution functions can be used to avoid the problem created by the lack of reliable price deflators in hyperinflation. Bishop et al. point out that there is a long tradition of using food expenditure shares to gauge the economic well-being of individual families, which is traceable back to Engel (1883). Further, budget studies that focussed upon food expenditures provided pivotal evidence that led to Friedman's (1957) permanent income hypothesis and to the now widely accepted view that consumption provides a better indicator of welfare than income, particularly in poor counties. To make welfare comparisons in Peru, we follow in the Engel tradition and use food shares to compare well-being across time.[3] Specifically, we assume that the share of a household's budget that is devoted to food can be used to infer living standards. Thus, households spending the same proportion of their income on food are assumed to have equivalent standards of living. As household food expenditures decline, economic well-being improves because more nonfood discretionary spending is made possible. More generally, unambiguously smaller food expenditure shares are associated with higher standards of living and improved economic well-being.

To implement the Engel approach we follow Bishop et al. (1996) and estimate food-share quantile functions using conditional means at deciles of the distribution. For poor countries the crucial assumption we make is not at all stringent. Poor households have little choice but to use available resources to meet the basic requirement of food subsistence before spending on other goods and services. If there is agreement that Peru was in fact poor in 1985-86, 1990 and 1991, then there should be wide agreement with ordinal rankings of welfare based upon statistical comparisons of entire food distribution functions. The chief advantage of this approach is that, under the assumption of utility maximization, the prices of food and all other goods are fully taken into account when the optimal allocation of real income and expenditure is made. Hence, the well-being of families across time can be compared using food shares without adjusting for the price variations. A second advantage is that under the assumption that within families each member is equally well-off in terms of food distribution, one can compare the well-being of groups across time and among regions. As a consequence, not only does the food-share approach avoid the distortions caused by hyperinflation, it also evades the necessity of adopting a specific and inevitably arbitrary equivalence scale. Further, the food-share distribution approach is operational in the sense that it can be applied using expenditure data that is common to virtually all modern income distribution surveys in poor countries such as the World Bank's PLSS data. Finally, as shown by Bishop et al. (1996) inference tests for first-order dominance can easily be adapted to test for differences in food-share quantile functions.

In contrast to income and consumption quantile distributions, which are ordered from the smallest to the largest, food-share distributions are ordered from the largest to the smallest. Ordering food-share distributions in this manner reflects the assumption that welfare is a decreasing function of food share. Given the food shares calculated from sample data across time, welfare comparisons can be carried out by making pairwise comparisons of entire food share distributions. Since smaller food shares imply greater welfare, dominance is indicated by one food share distribution lying below another at one or more quantiles and *not* lying above at others. However, if two food-share distribution functions cross, then unambiguous welfare conclusions cannot be drawn. The absence of a crossing is likely to lead to wide acceptance of the welfare implications of food-share dominance.[4]

Figure 10.3 illustrates food-share welfare dominance using 1985-86 and 1991 PLSS data. Note that ordering food shares from largest to smallest necessarily implies that all food-share distribution functions slope negatively. If statistical inference problems are ignored, it is apparent by inspection of Figure 10.3 that the quantile functions do not cross and 1985-86 lies below 1991 over much of the range of the food-share data. Therefore, 1985-86 first-order dominates 1991 in terms of food shares; which implies greater urban welfare.

The differences between Figures 10.2 and Figure 10.3 are quite striking. Figure 10.2 suggests enormous declines in welfare throughout the distribution. In contrast, Figure 10.3 shows either zero or small decreases in the lower deciles and modest declines in the upper deciles. The statistical analysis sheds more light on this issue, particularly as it relates to poverty. But it is apparent from Figures 10.2 and 10.3 that using price indices to adjust for hyperinflated consumption expenditures grossly overstates the decline in welfare. Figure 10.3 suggests that welfare decreased in Peru but the fall was nothing like the mammoth decline suggested by deflated consumption expenditures.

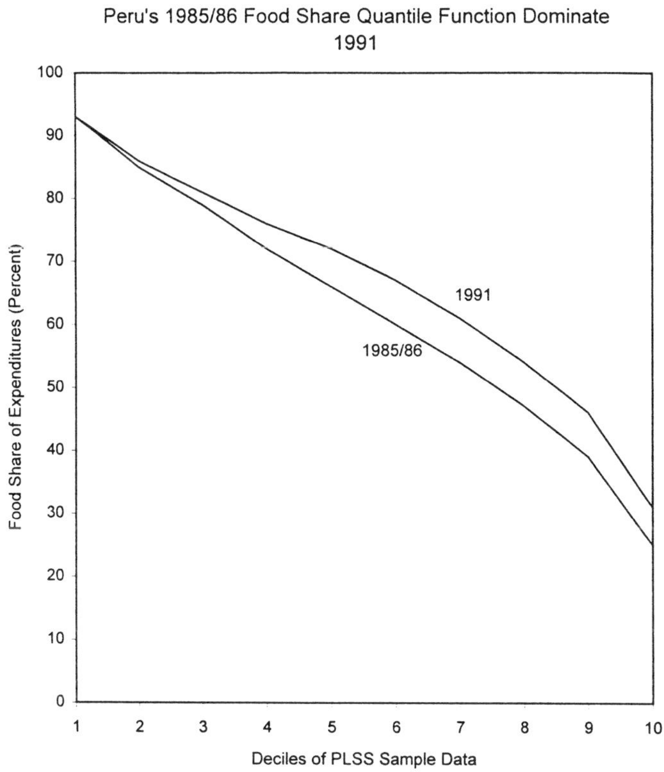

Figure 10.3 First order dominance —food-share expenditures

3.4 Statistical Inference Procedures

We estimate the Lorenz curves and quantile functions at deciles, which means that in comparing Lorenz curves of consumption we test at nine points and for quantiles of consumption and food shares the joint tests are at ten points in the distribution. Considering this limited set of quantiles recognizes the tradeoff between a better approximation of the distributions of interest (more quantiles) and the efficiency of the variance estimates (fewer quantiles).[5]

The essence of the inference procedure can be illustrated with a test for *Lorenz dominance* using the 1985-86 and 1991 PLSS data that are depicted in Figure 10.1. Statistically, three outcomes are discussed in the dominance literature (Bishop et al. 1989, 1992). *Lorenz dominance* is defined as $L^t(p) \geq L^{t+1}(p)$ with at least one strict inequality prevailing; *Lorenz equivalence* requires strict equalities at each ordinate and *Lorenz*

Crossing occurs when $L^t(p) \geq L^{t+1}(p)$ at some p, and $L^t(p) \leq L^{t+1}(p)$ at some other p. Likewise, dominance, crossing or equivalence relationships are possible when we statistically evaluate food-share quantile functions.

Tests at each of the $k = 9$ Lorenz curve ordinates are sub-hypothesis (T_i) of the joint test of the equality of two vectors of cumulative incomes. Similarly, tests at each of the $k = 10$ food-share quantile function ordinates are sub-hypothesis (T_i) of the joint test of the equality of two vectors of conditional food share expenditures. To maintain the size of this joint test, the critical values are determined from the Student Maximum Modules (SMM) distribution. That is, an approximately α level test of the equality of two vectors of conditional means rejects each of the sub-hypotheses if $T_i > m_\alpha(k, \infty)$, where $m_\alpha(k, \infty)$ is the upper α critical value of the SMM distribution with ∞ degrees of freedom.[6] One aspect of the inference procedures that are particularly relevant to our analysis of the PLSS data warrants emphasis. The statistical tests are valid for independent samples and there is a panel feature to the PLSS data that creates the possibility of some dependence in data samples across time. As described in the next section, we adjust for this problem by dropping observations that create statistical dependence.

If dominance is found the statistical analysis allows us to distinguish further between *strong dominance* and *weak dominance*. In Lorenz comparisons *strong dominance* exists if $L^t(p) > L^{t+1}(p)$ for all p. *Weak dominance* prevails if $L^t(p) > L^{t+1}(p)$ for some p and equalities exist at others. Strong and weak dominance can also be distinguished in analyzing quantile functions. We emphasize that only weak dominance is required to achieve a unanimous ranking in terms of the dominance theorems underpinning this approach to the study of inequality and applied welfare economics. Nevertheless, whether an inequality or welfare comparisons involves dominance at all deciles or only some deciles is of empirical interest and in summarizing our results we distinguish between weak and strong dominance.

4 THE PLSS DATA

This section provides a brief discussion of the World Bank's Living Standard Measurement Program (LSMP) and the three PLSS data sets used in the analysis reported below. The problems of data comparability and quality are well known to researchers who study income distributions and inequality. In the late 1970s, the World Bank recognized the limitations imposed on policy analysts by low-quality and noncomparable income distribution statistics. The LSMP was designed to provide reliable and consistent samples of consumption data in both the urban and rural sectors of poor countries. Glewwe (1988) provides an excellent summary of the LSMP and the compelling logic that led to using consumption (including market values of in-kind consumption) as the basic indicator of well-being.

LSMP surveys have now been conducted in a large number of countries and are extensively used by World Bank economists. By special arrangement, the data for some countries is made available to outside researchers. Three Peruvian LSMP surveys covering 1985-86, 1990 and 1991 are used in this study. The data sets do not cover exactly the same populations across time. Differences in sample coverage limits the types of dominance comparisons that can meaningfully be made within the regions of Peru and across time. Table 10.1 summarizes pertinent information concerning the PLSS data sets and shows the constraints on the types of comparisons that are both possible and meaningful given the comparability and statistical independence requirement.

Our objective is to evaluate welfare, inequality and poverty in Peru in the mid-1980s and early 1990s. To accomplish this necessitates extracting comparable subsets of PLSS data that satisfy the statistical requirement of independence,. Extracting and comparing subsamples for the same set of geographical regions ensures comparability. Thus observations in certain

Table 10.1 An overview of the Peruvian living standard surveys

	1985-86	1990	1991
1. Sample size (no. of households)	5,120	1,500	2,304
2. Geographic area	Geographical coverage and percent of sample size		
Coast urban	14.3	–	15.9
Coast rural	6.2	–	–
Highlands urban	10.9	–	22.2
Highlands rural	33.5	–	26.3
Jungle urban	2.9	–	–
Jungle rural	6.8	–	–
Metropolitan Lima	25.4	100	35.6
3. Panel data sets l	1985 86 to 1990 727 households	1990 to 1991 545 households	540 households span All three years

Notes:

*The samples overlap across time which gives rise to the panel aspects of the data. Using the match merge criteria suggested by the World Bank identifies 727 'panel dwellings' for the 1985-86 and 1991 surveys and 540 for the 1990 and 1991 surveys. The 540 households are a subset of the 727 and appear in each PLSS survey.

regions are dropped when these regions were not covered in one of the time periods being compared. There are reasons to believe that incomes of individuals are correlated across time. As a consequence, to satisfy the requirement that the samples being compared across time are independent, we also drop observations of panel households from one of the two time periods being compared. For statistical prudence such households are dropped from the larger of the two data sets being compared. This ensures that the subsamples used in the analysis are the largest possible and yet still satisfy the independence requirement.

5 RESULTS

We first summarize the findings concerning inequality. This is followed by a discussion of first-order dominance and welfare. The implications for poverty and some of the results from our analysis of economic mobility are then reviewed briefly.

To condense numerous statistical tables and a great deal of information we make use of the following notation:

1991 $\underset{\text{SLD}}{>}$ 1985-86	indicates 1991 strongly Lorenz dominates 1985-86
1985/86 $\underset{\text{WLD}}{>}$ 1990	indicates 1985-86 weakly Lorenz dominates 1990
Rural $\underset{\text{LD}}{=}$ Urban	indicates Lorenz equivalence; the null hypothesis of no differences in Lorenz curves cannot be rejected
Rural $\underset{\text{LD}}{\times}$ Urban	indicates a statistically significant Lorenz crossing

Similar notation is used for first-order dominance.

5.1 Lorenz Dominance and Inequality

Table 10.2 provides an example of the many pairwise comparisons of Lorenz curves across time, among regions, and for urban and rural areas of Peru. It corresponds to the Lorenz curves depicted in Figure 10.1. The differences in Lorenz ordinates of per capita consumption are quite large and the SMM statistics are all far larger than the critical values at every decile. Therefore, the inference test reveals strong Lorenz dominance.

Table 10.2 Lorenz dominance comparisons for Peru[1] 1985-86 and 1991[2] per capita total consumption expenditure equivalence

Decile	Lorenz ordinate 1985-86 (%)	Lorenz ordinate 1991 (%)	Difference in lorenz ordinates	SMM statistics[3]
1	0.0174 (0.0002)	0.0234 (0.0003)	−0.60	*****
2	0.0470 (0.0005)	0.0635 (0.0007)	−1.65	*****
3	0.0868 (0.0009)	0.1159 (0.0010)	−2.91	*****
4	0.1367 (0.0013)	0.1794 (0.0014)	−4.27	*****
5	0.1972 (0.0017)	0.2550 (0.0017)	−5.78	*****
6	0.27.08 (0.0023)	0.3441 (0.0021)	−7.33	*****
7	0.3620 (0.0029)	0.4487 (0.0025)	−8.67	*****
8	0.4786 (0.0036)	0.5733 (0.0028)	−9.47	*****
9	0.6378 (0.0043)	0.7323 (0.0031)	−9.45	*****
10	1.000 (0.0000)	1.000 (0.0000)	0.00	—

Notes:
1. Standard errors are shown in parenthesis.
2. Sample sizes are 3,676 and 2,304 respectively.
3. ***** Indicates a large number, far above the critical value, which is 2.63 at the 90 percent confidence level.

Clearly, inequality in Peru was much less in 1991 than in 1985-86.

It is well known that inequality findings can be sensitive to the treatment of household size and composition. Simply looking at households ignores economies of scale while only considering per capita consumption assumes that adults and children are equivalent. Researchers now routinely consider several equivalence scales, with per capita consumption being one extreme. We use household size and composition data within the PLSS and make estimates using the following four equivalence scales:

1. per capita consumption,
2. varying adult weights for children of different ages (weights of 0.2, 0.3

and 0.5 are assigned to children aged 0 to 6, 7 to 12, and 13 to 17, respectively),

3. constant adult weights for all children (each child below the age of 18 is assigned a weight of 0.5), and
4. the square root rule, which assigns weights using the following formula

Table 10.3 Summary of Lorenz dominance comparisons of per capita consumption expenditures in Peru[1] (selected years and various regions using comparable and independent samples[2])

Regions compared	Years Compared	Sample sizes	Results[3]
All but rural coast and jungle regions	1985-86 1991	3,676 2,304	$1991 \underset{SLD}{>} 1985/86$
Lima only[4]	1985-86 1990	1,348 771	$1985/86 \underset{WLD}{>} 1990$
Lima only[4]	1990 1991	954 845	$1991 \underset{SLD}{>} 1990$
Rural v/s urban excluding Lima	1985-86	R – 2,231 U – 1,409	$\text{Rural} \underset{WLD}{>} \text{Urban}$
Rural vs urban highlands region	1991	R – 594 U – 502	$\text{Rural} \underset{LD}{\times} \text{Urban}$
Rural vs urban highlands region	1985-86 1991	1601 594	$1991 \underset{SLD}{>} 1985/86$
Urban vs urban excluding the jungle area	1985-86 1991	4306 1710	$1991 \underset{SLD}{>} 1985/86$

Notes:

1. Joint 10 percent tests are conducted at deciles.
2. The samples are comparable and independent in the sense that the same geographic areas are being compared, panel households are excluded from the largest of the two PLSS subsamples being compared.
3. The notation $\underset{WLD}{>}$ indicates weak Lorenz dominance,
$\underset{SLD}{>}$ denotes strong Lorenz dominance and
$\underset{LD}{\times}$ means that there is a statistically significant crossing in the Lorenz comparison.
4. The difference in the sample sizes for 1990 is explained by the necessity of dropping panel households from the larger of the two data sets being compared to maintain statistical independence. For 1985-86 no households are dropped from 1990 PLSS because the 1985-86 sample is so much larger. However, in the 1990-91 period, the Lima sample for 1990 is larger than 1991, so panel households are dropped from 1990.

Adult Equivalence = $\sqrt{A + 0.4C}$ where A and C are the number of adults and children.

The last three equivalence scales take household size and composition into account and also reflect economies of scale within the household. The scale with variable weights for children is the same as the one employed by Glewwe (1988) in his analysis of PLSS data. The scale with a constant child weight is used widely by researchers to analyze the Luxembourg Income Study (LIS) data (compare Buhmann et al. 1988). The square root rule is extensively used in the United States (compare Cutler and Katz 1992 and Blackburn 1994) because it provides a smooth approximation of results that are obtained by applying the Orshansky scale, which is the official scale used in measuring poverty in the USA.

Tables 10.3 and 10.4 summarize the results of the inequality analysis. Table 10.3 presents seven pairwise comparisons across time and among regions and areas using per capita consumption expenditures as the metric. Row 1 of Table 10.3 refers to the same Lorenz dominance comparison as reported in Table 10.2 and Figure 10.1 The details are suppressed and only the overall statistical ranking is reported. For all seven pairwise comparisons in Table 10.3 the tests reveal strong Lorenz dominance in four, weak Lorenz dominance in two and one significant crossing. Across time, inequality rose between 1985-86 and 1990, but decreased between 1990 and 1991.

Table 10.4 shows the seven Lorenz comparisons for each of the four equivalence scales. Column 2 again shows per capita consumption results and thus repeats the information in Table 10.3. There are two important results in Table 10.4. First, when strong Lorenz dominance exists, it is consistently found for all equivalence scales. Thus, in these comparisons the dominance results are unaffected by the treatment of household size and composition. This suggests that we can have great confidence in these inequality rankings. Second, the urban and rural inequality comparisons as well as the 1985-86 to 1990 comparison of Lima are sensitive to the equivalence scale used in the analysis. For example, in the Lima comparison across time three equivalence scales result in weak Lorenz dominance of 1985-86 over 1990, which means inequality rose. But in applying the square root scale we cannot reject the null hypothesis that there are no differences in the Lorenz curves across time. Statistically, Lorenz equivalence prevails, which suggests that inequality did not change.

Table 10.4 Lorenz dominance and inequality in Peru1[1] using four different equivalence scales[2] selected years and various regions using comparable and independent samples[3]

Pairwise Lorenz comparison (1)	Equivalence Scales: Per capita consumption (2)	Varying weights for children of different ages[4] (3)	Constant weights for children of different ages[5] (4)	The square root scale[6] (5)
1985 vs 1991	1991 $\underset{SLD}{>}$ 1985/86	1991 $\underset{SLD}{>}$ 1985-86	1991 $\underset{SLD}{>}$ 1985-86	1991 $\underset{SLD}{>}$ 1985-86
1985-86 vs 1990	1985-86 $\underset{WLD}{>}$ 1990	1985-86 $\underset{WLD}{>}$ 1990	1985-86 $\underset{WLD}{>}$ 1990	1985-86 $\underset{LD}{=}$ 1990
1990 vs 1991	1991 $\underset{SLD}{>}$ 1990	1991 $\underset{SLD}{>}$ 1990	1991 $\underset{SLD}{>}$ 1990	1991 $\underset{SLD}{>}$ 1990
Rural vs Urban1985\86	Rural $\underset{WLD}{>}$ Urban	Rural $\underset{WLD}{>}$ Urban	Rural $\underset{WLD}{>}$ Urban	Rural $\underset{LD}{=}$ Urban
Rural vs Urban1991	Rural $\underset{LD}{\times}$ Urban	Urban $\underset{WLD}{>}$ Rural	Urban $\underset{WLD}{>}$ Rural	Urban $\underset{WLD}{>}$ Rural
Rural vs Rural	1991 $\underset{SLD}{>}$ 1985-86	1991 $\underset{SLD}{>}$ 1985-86	1991 $\underset{SLD}{>}$ 1985-86	1991 $\underset{SLD}{>}$ 1985-86
Urban vs Urban	1991 $\underset{SLD}{>}$ 1985-86	1991 $\underset{SLD}{>}$ 1985-86	1991 $\underset{SLD}{>}$ 1985-86	1991 $\underset{SLD}{>}$ 1985-86

Notes: 1. Joint 10 percent tests are conducted at deciles.

2. The notation $\underset{WLD}{>}$ indicates weak Lorenz dominance,

$\underset{SLD}{>}$ denotes strong Lorenz dominance, and

$\underset{LD}{\times}$ means that that there is a statistically significant crossing in the Lorenz comparison and

$\underset{LD}{=}$ indicates that we cannot reject the null hypothesis that the two come from the same population.

3. The samples are comparable and independent in the sense that the same geographic areas are being compared panel households are excluded from the largest of the two PLSS subsamples being compared.

4. Adult equivalence weights of 0.2, 0.3, and 0.5 are assigned to children aged 0-6, 7-12, and 13-17, respectively.

5. Adult equivalence weights of 0.5 are assigned to all children under the age of 18.

6. By the square root rule adult equivalence is determined by the formula: Adult Equivalence $\sqrt{A + 0.4C}$

Table 10.5a First-order dominance comparisons of inflation[1]-adjusted household food expenditure in Peru,[2] 1985-86 and 1991[3]

Decile	Quantile ordinates 1985/86	Quantile ordinates 1991	Difference in quantile ordinates	SMM statistic[4]
1	805	122	683	75.06
	(0.8948)	(0.1657)		
2	1374	208	1166	100.02
	(1.1448)	(0.22)		
3	1841	272	1569	112.18
	(1.383)	(0.2089)		
4	2312	330	1982	127.37
	(1.5339)	(0.2618)		
5	2802	393	2409	127.21
	(1.8726)	(0.2824)		
6	3408	463	2945	117.96
	(2.4739)	(0.3367)		
7	4225	543	3682	123.95
	(2.948)	(0.3657)		
8	5400	647	4753	107.21
	(4.4053)	(0.4962)		
9	7373	826	6547	96.23
	(6.7666)	(0.7076)		
10	16777	1390	15387	46.26
	(33.1818)	(2.3173)		

Notes:
1. Mean decile expenditure figures (quantile ordinates) are in thousands of intis, at June 1, 1990, prices.
2. Standard errors are shown in parenthesis.
3. Sample sizes are 3676 and 2304 respectively.
4. The critical value of the SMM statistic is 2.56 at the 90 percent confidence level.

5.2 First-order Dominance and Economic Welfare

Table 10.5 provides detailed results for the first-order dominance comparisons of the quantile functions depicted in Figures 10.2 and 10.3. Table 10.5a corresponds to the deflated food expenditures in Figure 10.2 and Table 10.5b shows the results of the analysis of food-share distribution functions in Figure 10.3. The first thing to note is that the statistical inference results strongly indicate that using price indices to adjust hyperinflated consumption is a seriously misleading gauge of economic welfare in Peru. The SMM statistics for differences in real food expenditures are enormous and strong first-order dominance exists.

Table 10.5b First-order dominance comparisons of household food expenditure shares and welfare in Peru,[1] 1985-86 and 1991[2]

Decile	Quantile ordinate 1985/86	Quantile ordinate 1991	Difference in quantile ordinates	SMM statistic[3]
1	0.93 (0.2125)	0.93 (0.2408)	0.00	0.00
2	0.85 (0.1967)	0.86 (0.2196)	−0.01	−0.34
3	0.79 (0.1848)	0.81 (0.2062)	−0.02	−0.72
4	0.72 (0.1811)	0.76 (0.2046)	−0.04	−1.46
5	0.66 (0.1730)	0.72 (0.2037)	−0.06	−2.25
6	0.60 (0.1711)	0.67 (0.2047)	−0.07	−2.62
7	0.54 (0.1704)	0.61 (0.2103)	−0.07	−2.59
8	0.47 (0.1716)	0.54 (0.2236)	−0.07	−2.48
9	0.39 (0.1724)	0.46 (0.2288)	−0.07	−2.44
10	0.25 (0.1934)	0.31 (0.2692)	−0.06	−1.81

Notes:
1. Standard errors are shown in parenthesis.
2. Sample sizes are 3676 and 2304 respectively.
3. The critical value of the SMM statistic is 2.56 at the 90 percent confidence level.

However, for food shares the SMM statistics are far smaller and eight out of ten are below the critical values for a 10 percent test. In deciles six and seven, the test statistics are larger, which means that weak first-order dominance of 1985-86 over 1991 prevails. Thus, we conclude that welfare declined in Peru but not so severely as the deflated consumption expenditures in Figure 10.2 and Table 10.5a suggest.

Table 10.6 summarizes the food-share and welfare dominance results for the seven pairwise comparisons discussed in the inequality section above. Row 1 of Table 10.6 provides the overall statistical ranking shown in Table 10.5b, but suppresses the details of the statistical inference underpinning the analysis. Three interesting results stand out in Table 10.6. First, urban dwellers outside Lima are better off than rural dwellers. Second, when comparing urban to urban and rural to rural (excluding Lima) the null hypothesis of no change in welfare cannot be rejected.

Table 10.6 Summary of first-order dominance comparisons of food expenditure shares and welfare in Peru[1]-selected years and various regions using comparable and independent samples[2]

Regions\areas compared	Years compared	Sample sizes	Results[3]
All but rural coast and jungle regions	1985-86 1991	3,676 2,304	1985/86 $\underset{WFOD}{>}$ 1991
Lima only[4]	1985-86 1990	1,348 771	1985/86 $\underset{FOD}{=}$ 1990
Lima only[4]	1990 1991	954 845	1991 $\underset{FOD}{=}$ 1990
Rural vs urban excluding Lima	1985-86	R – 2,231 U – 1,409	Urban $\underset{SFOD}{>}$ Rural
Rural vs urban highlands region	1991	R – 594 U – 502	Urban $\underset{WFOD}{>}$ Rural
Rural vs rural highlands region	1985-86 1991	1601 594	1991 $\underset{FOD}{=}$ 1985-86
Urban vs urban jungle area excluded	1985-86 1991	4306 1710	1991 $\underset{FOD}{=}$ 1985-86

Notes:
1. Joint 10 percent tests are conducted at deciles.
2. The samples are comparable and independent in the sense that the same geographic areas are being compared panel households are excluded from the largest of the two PLSS subsamples being compared.
3. The notation $\underset{WFOD}{>}$ indicates weak first-order dominance,
$\underset{SFOD}{>}$ denotes strong first-order dominance and
$\underset{FOD}{=}$ means that that the hypothesis that the two food shares are drawn from the same population cannot be rejected.
4. The difference in the sample sizes for 1990 is explained by the necessity of dropping panel households from the larger of the two data sets being compared to maintain statistical independence. For 1985-86 no households are dropped from the 1990 PLSS because the 1985-86 sample is so much larger. However, in the 1990-91 period, the Lima sample for 1990 is larger than 1991, so panel households are dropped from 1990.

Third, for Lima only there are no statistically discernible differences in food-share quantile functions and welfare between 1985-86 and 1990 or between 1990 and 1991. The first Lima result goes against the findings of Glewwe and Hall who also compared welfare in Lima between 1985-86 and 1990, but used deflated food expenditures as the basic indicator of welfare.[7]

5.3 Poverty

Glewwe and Hall (1994) conclude that welfare declined in Lima between 1985-86 and 1990 and that the poor suffered the brunt of the fall in living standards. Our food-share dominance analysis reveals that in Peru as a whole, welfare decreased from 1985-86 to 1991, but did not change in Lima. We now focus on the question of poverty in Peru during the tumultuous policy changes and hyperinflation of the late 1980s and early 1990s. Usually, poverty is counted by first establishing one or more poverty lines and adjusting them with price indices across time. Since the work of Sen (1976) it has become standard procedure in poverty analysis to also consider poverty gaps and the distribution of income among the poor. But the poverty index approach necessarily begins with a fixed poverty line, which must be adjusted for inflation if the indices are to make sense.

The analysis of poverty in Peru can be misleading due to the shortcoming of price indices as deflators during hyperinflation. The problem is that the poverty lines across time are not comparable time due to distortions created by imprecise measures of inflation on economic well-being. Fortunately, theoretical advances in poverty measurement over the last decade and our inference-based dominance analysis of food shares and welfare make it possible to draw some conclusions concerning headcount poverty using dominance comparisons. The theoretical advances are primarily due to the work of Atkinson (1987) and Foster and Shorrocks (1988) and result in ordinal poverty rankings that are consistent with the Foster et al. (1984) class of distribution sensitive poverty indices. The advantage of the dominance approach is that it generates poverty orderings that are robust with respect to the location of the poverty line and the choice of poverty indices. Foster and Shorrocks (1988) prove a fundamental theorem that says, in essence, that if one distribution, say F, first-order dominates a second, say G, then headcount poverty in F can never exceed that of G, *regardless of the poverty line chosen*. Therefore, truncating the quantile function at some maximum point that can be interpreted as a poverty line and testing for first-order dominance on the truncated distribution provides a general headcount poverty ordering over a wide range of alternative poverty lines.[8]

The dominance approach to poverty measurement has immediate implications for Peru. Consider Figure 10.3 and Table 10.5b, which provide first order dominance analysis of welfare in 1985-86 and 1991. If one inserts a poverty line at *any point in the bottom half of the food share distribution function*, then by the Foster and Shorrocks (1988) first-order dominance theorem we can conclude that the null hypothesis of no change in headcount poverty cannot be rejected. Therefore, we conclude that the poverty did not increase across this time span. Further, the more equal distributions of consumption shown in Figure 10.1 and Table 10.2 strongly reinforce this conclusion.

5.4 Economic Mobility in Hyperinflation

The dominance analysis discussed above rests upon the anonymity assumption and the panel aspects of the PLSS data are ignored. But most researchers and policy analysts (compare Atkinson et al. 1988 and Geweke et al. 1986) agree that when panel data is available, economic and welfare mobility should be explored. It is of interest to know how much movement, particularly among the poor, occurs across time. Further, it is well known that substantial mobility implies that inequality of permanent income is less than observed inequality in any cross-section of survey data. There is an additional reason for investigating mobility in the PLSS data. To our knowledge no researcher has been able to explore economic mobility in hyperinflation. This section reports briefly on the degree to which Peruvian households exchanged welfare positions across time.

Table 10.7 Mobility matrices of per capita household consumption in Lima, 1985-86 to 1990

Percentages of row totals*

1985	1990 decile										
decile	1	2	3	4	5	6	7	8	9	10	Total
1	**33**	24	11	8	10	7	3	3	1	0	100
2	25	**19**	14	12	10	7	6	6	1	1	100
3	16	18	**11**	7	15	10	7	8	6	3	100
4	15	10	15	**11**	17	8	4	8	7	6	100
5	4	6	12	16	**10**	26	11	10	3	3	100
6	3	7	16	14	8	**14**	16	11	4	7	100
7	1	7	6	14	11	8	**19**	8	15	10	100
8	1	7	4	6	10	7	11	**19**	23	12	100
9	0	3	3	3	10	8	11	16	**23**	23	100
10	0	1	8	8	1	6	11	11	18	**36**	100
Total	10	10	10	10	10	10	10	10	10	10	**100**

Note: *The sample size is 727. Rows and columns contain either 72 or 73 households.

Two related approaches to measuring mobility are available; namely, Lorenz-concentration curve analysis and transition or mobility matrix analysis. In this chapter we rely upon the latter and use it to describe changes in welfare rankings that are associated with the dramatic swings in economic policy that occurred in Peru during the hyperinflation. This approach is intuitive and the measures are readily understood. Mobility matrices are constructed using panel data sets and can be used to trace the movement of households within distributions across time.[9] Like Lorenz curves, mobility matrix analysis is invariant to the method of deflating incomes across time. Therefore, Peru's hyperinflation does not distort the mobility measures within a matrix.

Matching and merging the 1985-86 and 1990 PLSS data yielded 727 Lima households. The decile mobility matrix for this panel is shown in Table 10.7. The rows show the 1985-86 deciles, while the columns show the 1990 deciles occupied by the same households. The percentage on the diagonal for decile 1 (33 percent) shows the proportion of the 72 households that did not move or change their relative welfare positions across time. It follows that 67 percent of the poorest households moved out of decile 1. Inspection reveals that 14 percent moved to decile 5 or higher. Note that households in decile 1 in 1985-86 could only remain poor or move up to higher deciles in 1990. On the other hand, households in decile 10 in 1985-86 could remain at the top or move down to lower deciles in 1990. Households in deciles 2-9 could move in either direction with those at higher deciles having more room to move down than up and vice versa.

We point out that in this mobility analysis we do not consider growth or decline in total consumption, so the mobility is relative or what sociologists call pure mobility. As a consequence, if one person moves up another must move down. Thus, income mobility is like a 'zero-sum game', absolute incomes and consumption are ignored and only the churning and changes in relative positions are considered. Nevertheless, it is still possible to make inter-matrix mobility comparisons. We apply a simple procedure for doing this by summing the diagonal elements and expressing the sum as a percentage of all households in the sample. The result is a normalized measure of the households that do not change positions. It follows that the sum of the off-diagonal elements expressed as a percentage of the sample size is an index of mobility for the entire matrix. In this way it is possible to carry out simple inter-matrix mobility comparisons.

Table 10.8 provides a second mobility matrix derived from the PLSS data for 1990 and 1991. Recall that this period involves the Fujishock policies and the beginning of Peruvian disinflation. The sample size is

Table 10.8 Mobility matrices of per capita household consumption in Lima, 1990-1991

Percentages of row totals*

1990	1991 decile										
decile	1	2	3	4	5	6	7	8	9	10	Total
1	**29.6**	22.2	14.8	7.4	13.0	7.4	3.7	1.9	0.0	0.0	100
2	20.0	**29.6**	10.9	14.5	3.6	10.9	10.9	5.5	0.0	3.6	100
3	13.0	16.7	**14.8**	9.3	14.8	11.1	5.6	5.6	1.9	7.4	100
4	9.1	9.1	12.7	**20.0**	10.9	10.9	9.1	3.6	7.3	7.3	100
5	7.4	9.3	9.3	13.0	**13.0**	13.0	13.0	13.0	5.6	3.7	100
6	1.8	9.1	10.9	12.7	12.7	**18.2**	10.9	7.3	10.9	5.5	100
7	9.3	7.4	7.4	3.7	9.3	3.7	**14.8**	18.5	14.8	11.1	100
8	7.3	0.0	9.1	10.9	5.5	14.5	9.1	**18.2**	18.2	7.3	100
9	1.9	5.6	7.4	3.7	11.1	3.7	13.0	14.8	**14.8**	24.1	100
10	0.0	1.8	1.8	5.5	5.5	7.3	9.1	12.7	25.5	**30.9**	100
Total	9.9	10.1	9.9	10.1	9.9	10.1	9.9	10.1	9.9	10.1	**100**

Note: *The sample size is 545. Rows and columns contain either 54 or 55 households.

545 in contrast to 727 in the 1985-86 to 1990 panel. The mobility in the year-to-year change seems remarkably high. Seventy percent of those in the bottom decile in 1990 moved to a higher decile in 1991 and, of those that moved, almost 70 percent jumped by two deciles or more. The movement out of the top decile was equally dramatic. For Table 10.8 the sum of the households in the off-diagonal elements as a percent of the sample size is $M_{90\text{ to }91} = 439/545 = 0.81$. Thus, more than 80 percent of the Lima panel moved by at least one decile. In contrast, in Table 10.7 for the much longer period 1985-86 to 1990, the households in the off diagonal elements as a percent of the sample size yields $M_{85\text{-}86\text{ to }90} = 565/727 = 0.78$. The results indicate that mobility in the one-year period following Fujishock was as great and possibly greater than the comparable mobility in the four-year period of heterodox policies and hyperinflation.

In concluding the discussion of mobility we point out that as with inequality analysis, the equivalence scale used may affect the results. The per capita consumption mobility reported in Tables 10.7 and 10.8 involves only one of many possible equivalence scales that could be used. We also constructed mobility matrices for the other three equivalence scales used in the inequality analysis discussed above, but we do not report these results in this chapter. We note, however, that the use of different equivalence scales to adjust for household size and composition seems to have negligible effects on the findings concerning economic mobility.

6 CONCLUSIONS

This study applies inference-based dominance methods to study welfare, inequality, and poverty in Peru during the latter half of the 1980s and early 1990s. In addition, we present mobility matrices and make comparisons of changes in economic positions of the same households during hyperinflation and the disinflation accompanying the Fujishock policies that ended Peru's period of international isolation and heterodox policy. Peruvian Living Standards Survey (PLSS) micro data for 1985-86, 1990 and 1991 are used to evaluate changes in welfare, inequality, poverty and mobility across time.

A number of conclusions emerge from the study. First and perhaps foremost, inference-based dominance comparisons of food expenditure shares across time strongly suggest that deflated consumption expenditures provide misleading indicators of economic welfare in Peru. During periods of hyperinflation using consumer price indices to deflate consumption expenditures introduces distortions into the dominance comparisons of consumption and welfare. Therefore, in this study we rely upon comparisons of values that are invariant to the scale of prices. These include food expenditure shares to measure welfare, Lorenz curves to gauge inequality, truncated food-share quantile functions to provide ordinal poverty orderings and mobility matrices to measure movements up and down the income distribution.

Additional conclusions that warrant emphasis follow.

- Application of dominance tests to the largest and most representative PLSS samples for Peru as a whole reveals that welfare declined between 1985-86 and 1991, but by nothing like the magnitude suggested by deflated consumption expenditures. At the same time, inequality substantially decreased. Further, headcount poverty did not change for any poverty line drawn within the five bottom deciles of the PLSS samples. Urban welfare is greater than rural welfare in both years. Finally, urban versus rural inequality comparisons in both 1985-86 and 1991 are sensitive to the equivalence scale used, but major changes in the degree of relative inequality in rural and urban areas seem to have occurred.
- The first-order dominance tests for 1985-86 versus 1990 are for Lima only and reveal no change in welfare or poverty. The food

shares were uniformly higher in 1990 but none of the test statistics reached the critical value. The Lorenz curve tests suggest that inequality probably increased during the period. Three of the four equivalence scales suggest weak Lorenz dominance while the fourth yields test statistics that fail to reject the null hypothesis of no difference in Lorenz curves.

- Between 1990 and 1991, inequality decreased substantially in Lima. However, the test statistics for first-order dominance are small and the null hypothesis of no change in welfare and headcount poverty cannot be rejected.

Mobility comparisons of samples of Lima households between 1985-86 and 1990 and 1990 and 1991 indicate that in the one-year period following Fujishock, mobility was as great or greater than the comparable mobility in the four years of heterodox policies and hyperinflation.

NOTES

1. See, for example, Chiou's (1996) dominance analysis of Taiwan's income distribution across time and Bishop et al.'s (1996) evaluation of regional differences in income distributions and welfare in China.
2. The first and highest poverty line is based on the cost of a minimum consumption basket of food for a family of six. The family is assumed to comprise two adults and four children, and the basket should provide 2168.8 kilocalories and 62.3 grams of protein per day. After making the necessary adjustments, this translates into a poverty line of 1,477,650 intis per adult equivalent per month. Two additional poverty lines based upon the 1985 minimum wage evaluated at June 1, 1990 prices, and the actual minimum wage on June 1, 1990 yielded poverty lines of 695,000 and 1,391,000 intis respectively.
3. A substantial literature in the 1950s and 1960s made use of food expenditure data. For example, in addition to relying upon Brady's (1952) food expenditure saving budget studies in developing the permanent income hypothesis, Friedman (1957) used food shares to compare the well-being of families of different size compositions (see Friedman 1952). Prais and Houthakker (1955) also used food shares as a welfare indicator and referred to this method as the 'standard commodity approach'. The US Bureau of Labor Statistics (1960) used food shares to devise scales of equivalent income and referred to the proportion of expenditures devoted to food as 'one of the most generally acceptable measures of level of living' (1960). Orshansky (1965, 1969) used food expenditures as a key ingredient in developing the poverty line that later was adopted to implement official US government measures of poverty.
4. Note that in making food-share dominance comparisons, we also make several assumptions that are standard in the dominance literature (for example

anonymity and the population principle), which are discussed above.

5. Beach and Davidson (1983) provide the formulae used to calculate the asymptotically distribution-free covariance matrices for the conditional means and Lorenz ordinates. Bishop et al. (1989, 1992) extend the test procedures to first-order dominance. Bishop and Formby (1994) summarize the test procedures and survey numerous applications. See Bishop and Formby (1997) for a discussion of simulation studies that provide information on the power of the test.
6. The SMM critical values are obtained from Stoline and Ury (1979). The 10 percent critical values for $k = 9$ is 2.51 and for $k = 10$ (the food-share tests) is 2.56.
7. It should be noted that our sample for Lima is not exactly the same as Glewwe and Hall's (1994). To maintain statistical independence we drop the 540 households that overlap in the two surveys from the 1990 Lima data set, which is the larger of the two PLSSs.
8. For a more complete discussion of the dominance approach to poverty measurement, see Ravallion (1993). Zheng (1997) provides a general survey of poverty measurement that includes the dominance approach. For a recent application of statistical inference procedures to poverty dominance see Bishop et al. (1995).
9. For a detailed discussion of mobility matrices, see Atkinson (1983).

REFERENCES

Atkinson, A.B. (1970), 'On the Measurement of Inequality', *Journal of Economic Theory,* 2, 244-63.

Atkinson, A.B. (1983), 'The Measurement of Economic Mobility', in *Social Justice and Public Policy*, Cambridge, MA: MIT Press, 61-73.

Atkinson, A.B. (1987), 'On the Measurement of Poverty', *Econometrica*, 55, 749-764.

Atkinson, A.B., F. Bourguignon and C. Morrison (1988), 'Income Distribution and Wealth Inequalities: Earnings Mobility', *European Economic Review*, 32, 619-32.

Beach, C.M. and R. Davidson (1983), 'Distribution-free Statistical Inference with Lorenz Curves and Income Shares, *Review of Economic Studies*, 50, 723-35.

Bishop, J.A. and J.P. Formby (1994), 'A Dominance Evaluation of the Distribution of Income and the Benefits of Economic Growth in the United States', in J. Bergstrand, T. Cosimano, J.W. Houck, and R.G. Sheehan (eds), *The Changing Distribution of Income in an Open U.S. Economy,* Amsterdam: North Holland, 66-103.

Bishop, J.A. and J.P. Formby (1998), 'Tests of Significance for Lorenz Partial Orders', in Jacques Silber (ed.), *Income Inequality: From*

Theory to Measurement, Amsterdam, Kluwer Academic Press: forthcoming.

Bishop, John A., John P. Formby and Paul D. Thistle (1989), 'Statistical Inference, Income Distribution and Social Welfare', in Daniel J. Slottje (ed.), *Research on Economic Inequality*, Vol. 1, Greenwich CN: JAI Press, 49-82.

Bishop, J.A., J.P Formby and P.D. Thistle (1992), 'The Convergence of South and Non-south Income Distributions, 1969-1979', *American Economic Review,* 82, 262-72.

Bishop, J.A., J.P. Formby and L.A. Zeager (1995), 'The Impact of Food Stamps on U.S. Poverty in the 1980s: A Marginal Dominance Analysis', *Economica*, 63, 141-62.

Bishop, J.A., J.P. Formby and B. Zheng (1996), 'Regional Income Inequality and Welfare in China: A Dominance Analysis', *Asian Economic Journal*, 10, 139-69.

Blackburn, M.L. (1994), 'International Comparisons of Poverty', *American Economic Review*, 84, 371-4.

Brady, Dorothy (1952), 'Family Savings in Relation to Changes in the Level and Distribution of Income', in *Research in Income and Wealth,* Vol. 15, New York: National Bureau of Economic Research, 103-28.

Buhmann, B., L. Rainwater, G. Schmaus and T. Smeeding (1988), 'Equivalence Scales, Well-being, Inequality, and Poverty: Sensitivity Estimates Across Ten Countries Using the Luxembourg Income Study (LIS) Database', *Review of Income and Wealth*, 30, 115-42.

Chiou, Jong-Rong (1996), 'A Dominance Evaluation of Taiwan's Income Distribution', *China Economic Review*, 7, 57-75.

Cutler, D. and L. Katz (1992), 'Rising Inequality? Changes in the Distribution of Income and Consumption in the 1980s', *American Economic Review*, 82, 546-51.

Dasgupta, P., A.K. Sen and D. Starrett (1973), 'Notes on the Measurement of Inequality' *Journal of Economic Theory*, 6, 180-87.

Engel, Ernst (1883), 'The Cost Value of Man', Economic Issues of the Time, 37/38, Berlin.

Fei, John C.H., Gustav Ranis and Shirley W.Y. Kuo (1978), 'Growth and the Family Distribution of Income By Factor Components', *Quarterly Journal of Economics*, 92, 17-53.

Fields, Gary S. (1980), *Poverty, Inequality, and Development,* Cambridge: Cambridge University Press.

Foster, J., J. Greer and E. Thorbecke (1984), 'A Class of Decomposable Poverty Measures', *Econometrica*, 52, 761-6.

Foster, J.E. and A.F. Shorrocks (1988), 'Poverty Orderings', *Econometrica*, 56, 173-77.

Friedman, Milton (1952), 'A Method for Comparing Incomes of Families Differing in Composition', in *Research in Income and Wealth*, Vol. 15, New York: National Bureau of Economic Research, 1-19.

Friedman, Milton (1957), *A Theory of the Consumption Function,* New York: National Bureau of Economic Research.

Geweke, J., R.C. Marshall and G.A. Zarkin (1986), 'Mobility Indices in Continuous Time Markov Chains', *Econometrica*, 54, 1407-23.

Glewwe, Paul (1988), 'The Distribution of Welfare in Peru in 1985-86', *LSMS Working Paper* No. 42, Washington, D.C., World Bank.

Glewwe, P. and G. Hau (1994), 'Poverty, Inequality, and Living Standards during Unorthodox Hall, Adjustment: The Case of Peru, 1985-1990', *Journal of Economic Development and Cultural Change*, 42, 689-717.

Kolm Serge (1969), 'The Optimal Production of Social Justice', in J. Margolis and H. Guitton (eds), *Public Economics*, London: Macmillan, 115-200.

Kuznets, Simon (1955), 'Economic Growth and Income Inequality', *American Economic Review*, 45, 1-28.

Kuznets, Simon (1963), 'Quantitative Aspects of the Growth of Nations: VIII Distribution of Income by Size', *Economic Development and Cultural Change*, 11, 1-80.

Orshansky, Mollie (1965), 'Counting the Poor: Another Look at the Poverty Profile', *Social Security Bulletin*, 28, 3-29.

Orshansky, Mollie (1969), 'How Poor is Measured', *Monthly Labor Review,* 92, 37-41.

Paus, Eva A. (1991), 'Adjustment and Development in Latin America: The Failure of Peruvian Heterodoxy, 1985-90', *World Development,* 19, 411-34.

Prais, S.J. and H.S. Houthakker (1955), *The Analysis of Family Budgets*, New York: Cambridge University Press.

Ravallion, Martin (1993), *Poverty Comparison,* New York: Harwood Academic Publishers.

Saposnik, R. (1981), 'Rank Dominance in Income Distribution', *Public Choice*, 36, 147-51.

Saposnik, R. (1983), 'On Evaluating Income Distributions: Rank Dominance, the Suppes-Sen Grading Principle of Justice, and Pareto Optimality', *Public Choice*, 40, 329-36.

Sen, A.K. (1973), *On Economic Inequality,* Norton: New York.

Sen, A.K. (1976), 'Poverty: An Ordinal Approach to Measurement', *Econometrica*, 44, 219-31.

Stoline, M.R. and H.K. Ury (1979), 'Tables of the Studentized Maximum Modulus Distribution and an Application to Multiple Comparisons Among Means', *Technometrics*, 21, 87-93.

US Bureau of Labor Statistics (1960), 'Estimating Equivalent Incomes or Budget Costs by Family Type', *Monthly Labor Review*, 83, 1197-200.

Zheng, B. (1997), 'A Survey on Aggregate Poverty Measurement', *Journal of Economic Surveys*, 11, 123-67.

Part IV Institution and Development

11. Growth, Poverty and Inequality in the Philippines

Arsenio M. Balisacan

1 INTRODUCTION

The Philippine economy's current episode of growth, starting in 1993, appears to have a fundamentally different character from previous ones. During most of the last three decades, each episode of boom, fueled largely by massive foreign borrowing and capital-intensive import-substituting industrialization, was soon followed by bust and stagnation. The period also saw heavy government regulation of the market economy, as well as political instability, natural disasters and major shocks in global trade and finance. For these reasons, the country acquired the unenviable image as Asia's 'sick man'. In contrast, the current growth is taking place in an environment of political stability, economic deregulation and institutional reforms. While policy coordination problems (for example, in public investments) still persist, it cannot be denied that the country is now closer to a market economy than it ever was in the past.

Doubts linger, however, as to whether the present growth has the desired quality consistent with poverty alleviation and equity objectives. Indeed the common themes in policy discussions of the growth-poverty-inequity nexus are that (i) economic growth has not been broadly based and that (ii) the growth has not been benefitting the poor. Unfortunately, official data on poverty have not helped much in informing the discussion. As elaborated elsewhere (Balisacan 1997), the official approach to assessing poverty appears to be yielding not only relatively high poverty lines but also inconsistent ranking of spatial and intertemporal poverty profiles – 'inconsistent' in the sense that two persons with the same command over basic consumption goods are not treated the same way. The official estimates show, for example, that poverty incidence is about three times higher in the Philippines than in Indonesia, even though the former is either ahead of (or on a par with) the latter in terms of almost all other aspects of human development.[1]

Critics of development policy in the Philippines often point to the relatively large mean income differences between Metro Manila (the country's capital) and neighboring Southern and Central Luzon regions, on the one hand, and the other regions of the country, on the other, as a prime cause of the high income inequality and poverty in the Philippines (ILO 1974; Lamberte et al. 1993). The widely held view is that development policy has favored Luzon and discriminated against Visayas and (especially) Mindanao. Moreover, the poor performance of the Philippine economy over the last three decades has been attributed partly to the relatively large variation in access to infrastructure and social services between the major urban centers and rural areas (for example, Ranis and Stewart 1993; Balisacan 1993; Bautista and Lamberte 1996). Spatial variation in certain summary measures of human development—particularly those incorporating literacy rate, mortality rate and poverty incidence—is also evident (UNDP 1996).

If indeed spatial income disparities are at the core of the poverty problem in the Philippines, then policy reforms aimed at reducing these disparities have to be central elements of the country's poverty reduction program. This may also promote efficiency goals: important dynamic externalities can arise from targetting by area or sector-specific characteristics (Bardhan 1996; Ravallion and Jalan 1996). Investment in physical infrastructure (such as roads, communications and irrigation) in backward areas, or in the rural sector in general, may improve the productivity of private investment, influence fertility through its effect on labor allocation and educational investment decisions, promote the development of intangible 'social capital' (in the form of social networks, peer group effects, role models, and so on), and mitigate erosion in the quality of life in urban areas through its effect on rural-urban migration decisions. In Taiwan, public investment in rural areas appears to have induced such externalities, thereby contributing to the country's broadly based pattern of economic growth during the last three decades (Park and Johnston, 1995).

However, if disparity in incomes and human achievements *within* each of the regions or areas of the country is itself the major problem, a different approach to poverty reduction would have to be found. It is possible, for example, that systematic differences in levels of human capital between low- and high-income groups within a geographic area translate into considerable differences in earning opportunities between these groups. Indeed, as shown in Balisacan and Bacawag (1994), differences in living standards within regions dominate differences between regions. In this case, the policy prescription to reduce overall income inequality and poverty would have to involve expanding the access of the low-income groups to basic social services, technology and infrastructure.

This chapter reexamines the nature of the growth-poverty-inequality nexus in the Philippines during the second half of the 1980s and first half of the 1990s, a period of economic liberalization and institutional reforms. The next two sections give new estimates of national and spatial poverty during the period, assess the relative contributions of growth and redistribution to the observed changes in poverty measures across space and over time, and examine the link between growth and poverty, as well as between growth and income inequality. The chapter then examines the determinants of regional poverty, using a consistently assembled regional data set for the period. The final section provides concluding remarks.

2 POVERTY ESTIMATES: LEVELS, CHANGES AND PROXIMATE CAUSES

Identification of the poor requires the use of a broad indicator of a person's standard of living. The Philippine government uses current household income in its poverty assessment. However, as is well known, income may overestimate or underestimate living standards. If a person can borrow or use his or her savings, his or her standard of living is not constrained by current income. Even in underdeveloped regions, households typically have some capability to buffer their welfare from temporary variations in income, such as by saving money or goods. Moreover, a household that can share in the income of others may have a higher welfare level than its current income would permit.[2] Current consumption would thus be a better indicator of welfare level than current income. Indeed, using standard arguments in microeconomic theory, it can be claimed that since welfare level is determined by 'life-cycle' or 'permanent' income, and since current consumption is a good approximation of this income, current consumption can be justified as a better measure of current welfare. This does not, of course, suggest that consumption does not vary over time. It does, and the change over the life cycle is sometimes large. This is especially true among the poor who do not have access to capital markets (or to interhousehold transfers) and whose current consumption is thus constrained by current instead of life-cycle income. But even in this case, current consumption is as good an approximation of life-cycle income as current income. Hence, in this chapter, consumption is preferred to income as a broad indicator of a person's living standard.[3]

In aggregating the information on the poor into a single measure of poverty, a common procedure is to simply count the proportionate number of the population deemed poor. The resulting *headcount index,* conventionally interpreted as a measure of the 'incidence' of poverty, is what appears in official reports on poverty in the Philippines. This measure, however, is silent about the depth and severity of poverty. Two other popular measures are reported below to capture these aspects of poverty. The *poverty-gap index,* defined by the mean distance below the poverty line as a proportion of that line (where the nonpoor are counted as having zero poverty gap) gives a measure of the 'depth' of poverty, while the *distribution-sensitive measure,* defined as the mean of the squared proportionate poverty gaps, reflects the 'severity' of poverty. The latter index pertains to the familiar FGT (Foster-Greer-Thorbecke) measure incorporating a society's 'moderate' aversion to poverty (Foster et al. 1984).

Table 11.1 provides two sets of estimates of poverty for the 1980s and early 1990s. The first set, referred to as official estimates, reflects the government's approach to estimating poverty. In brief, the approach uses current household income as the indicator of living standards, as well as poverty lines constructed from actual consumption patterns in each region or area of the country.

Table 11.1 Poverty estimates based on two approaches (in percent)

Year	Aspect of poverty		
	Incidence	Depth	Severity
FLOL approach*			
1985	32.7	9.4	3.8
1988	26.9	6.9	2.5
1991	26.6	7.1	2.7
1994	23.4	5.9	2.1
Official approach**			
1985	49.2	17.0	7.9
1988	45.3	15.0	6.7
1991	45.2	15.4	7.0
1994	40.2	13.2	6.0

Notes:
*Based on fixed-level-of-living poverty lines and on consumption expenditure as an indicator of living standard.
**Based on official poverty lines and on current income as an indicator of living standard.

As shown in Balisacan (1997), the problem with the approach is that the poverty lines estimated for the various regions and years tend be inconsistent — 'inconsistent' in the sense that two persons with the same command over basic consumption needs are not treated the same way. Put differently, the poverty lines applied for various regions, areas and years imply different levels of living standards, tending to underestimate (overestimate) *systematically* the reduction (increase) in absolute poverty in economically more progressive (backward) regions or sectors, or during periods when the overall economy is expanding (contracting).[4] In contrast, the second set of estimates in Table 11.1, hereafter referred to as fixed-level-of-living (FLOL) estimates, uses the official norm about nutritional calorie requirement (that is, 2,000 kilocalories per person per day) but imposes the desirable consistency feature of a poverty norm by holding the poverty line fixed in real terms over time or across regions/areas of the country.[5]

At least three points are apparent in Table 11.1. First, poverty in the Philippines is much lower than indicated by official figures. The incidence estimates are broadly comparable to those obtained by the World Bank (1996) using an internationally comparable poverty line of one US dollar (at 1985 purchasing power parity) per capita per day. Second, while both estimates show considerable progress in poverty reduction during the period under investigation, the reduction displayed by the FLOL approach is more 'impressive' considering that the initial-year poverty level is relatively much lower in the FLOL than in the official approach. Third, the FLOL approach indicates that a good deal of the poverty reduction took place between 1985 and 1988 (a period of considerably high consumption growth), while the official approach shows that this occurred from 1991 to 1994 (a period of low consumption growth).

Clearly, the construction of a poverty norm greatly affects the profile of aggregate poverty. But how robust are the observed *changes* in poverty over time? To check whether the intertemporal poverty pattern is robust to the choice of poverty lines and of poverty index, a first-order dominance test is applied.[6] Figure 11.1 compares pairs of cumulative distributions of per capita consumption; two nonintersecting cumulative distribution (CD) curves indicate that the change in poverty during the period is unambiguous. This is the case for 1985 and 1988 as well as for 1991 and 1994. In both periods, poverty fell unambiguously, regardless of the assumed (but plausible) poverty norm and the chosen poverty index. Note that the vertical distance between the 1985 CD curve and the 1988 CD curve is wider for almost all levels of per capita expenditure than that between the 1991 CD curve and the 1994 CD curve, suggesting that the

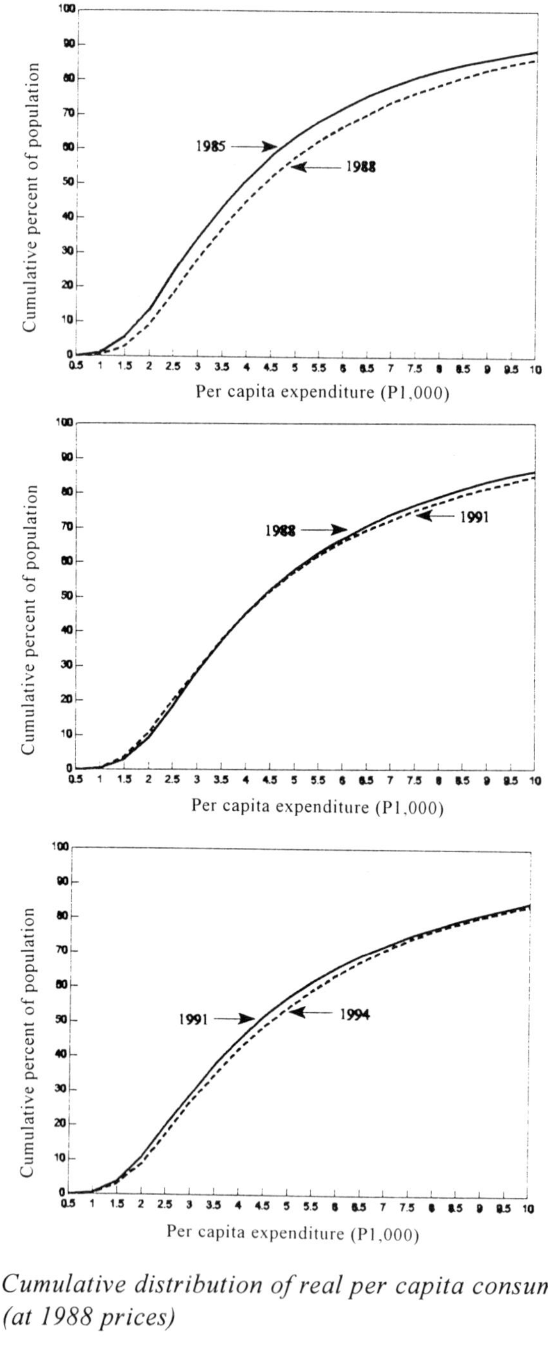

Figure 11.1 Cumulative distribution of real per capita consumption (at 1988 prices)

poverty reduction in 1985-88 is greater than in 1991-94. The possibility of disagreement on the direction of poverty change applies to 1988 and 1991 where the CD curves intersect. Indeed, both the FLOL and the official estimates indicate inconsistent ranking of 1988 and 1991 by the three poverty indices.

Viewed from an international perspective, the rate of poverty reduction during the second half of the 1980s and early 1990s was broadly comparable to those for China and Indonesia, but much slower than the average for developing Asian and Pacific countries (Table 11.2). However, this performance is remarkable considering that economic growth during this period was considerably lower in the Philippines than in virtually all developing East Asian and Pacific countries, especially China and Indonesia. Even more significant is the contrast of this period with the 1960s and 1970s when economic growth in the Philippines was respectable by international standards, but poverty during the period appeared not to have responded well to that growth (Ranis and Stewart 1993; Balisacan 1993; Bautista and Lamberte 1996).

The growth (and stagnation) of real consumption per capita may well have been an important factor in the changes in poverty measures observed in Table 11.1. Indeed real consumption per capita grew fastest during the 'boom' of 1985-88, a period of relatively rapid poverty reduction, and slowest during the deep 'bust' of 1991-94 (Table 11.2). But another 'proximate' cause for the observed poverty reduction during the 1980s and early 1990s may well be the changes in the distribution of living standards. The consumption Gini changed only slightly during this period (Table 11.3), but as shown below, even such changes could have considerable impact on aggregate poverty.

Table 11.2 Poverty reduction, Philippines versus other developing countries

Country	Period	Percentage-point reduction per year	Growth of GNP per capita, 1980-94 (%/year)
Philippines	1985-1994	1.0	1.7
East Asia and the Pacific (excluding China)	1987-1993	1.6	6.9
China	1987-1994	0.7	7.8
Indonesia	1984-1996	0.9	6.0

Sources: For the Philippines, Table 11.1 (about the same figure for both FLOL and official estimates); East Asia, the Pacific, and China, World Bank (1996b); Indonesia, Hill (1996) and BPS (1997).

Table 11.3 Consumption growth and inequality

Period	There-year growth of real consumption per capita (%)	Inequality in living standards*	
		Gini ratio, end year	Ratio of richest 20% to poorest 20%, end-year
1985		0.43	7.9
1985-1988	10.3	0.42	7.1
1988-1991	6.0	0.45	8.9
1991-1994	1.6	0.42	8.2

Note: *Based on distribution of real consumption expenditure per capita.
Sources: National Statistics Office, *Family Income and Expenditures Survey*, various years.

It is possible to determine the relative importance of growth and distributional change to poverty measures through some simple counterfactual experiments. One such experiment would be: what would have been the change in poverty during a given period if all consumption groups had shared equally in the growth that occurred? Another would be: how much further would poverty have increased (decreased) during the period if not for the growth (decline) that did occur? The latter experiment requires simulating the poverty measures that would have been observed at the end-year of the period if mean consumption did not change but inequality did as actually observed.

The two experiments correspond to components of a poverty change, that is, the growth and the redistribution components of observed changes in the poverty measures employed in this chapter.[7] Put differently, the growth component is the change in the poverty measure due to a change in mean consumption per capita while holding the consumption distribution constant at some reference level. The redistribution component, on the other hand, is simply the change in consumption distribution while keeping the mean consumption constant at some reference level.

The end-period poverty levels corresponding to the two experiments—one with no change in inequality and the other with no growth in mean consumption—are summarized in Table 11.4. Clearly, poverty measures would have been lower at the end of each period if the distribution of consumption did not change. A distribution-neutral growth would have, for example, led to a drop of 5.4 percentage points in poverty incidence from 1991 to 1994, instead of 3.2 percentage points. Similarly, during the 'boom' years of 1985-88, the drop in poverty incidence would have been 8.5 percentage points, instead of 5.8 percentage points. The other poverty indices show generally comparable qualitative results.

It is thus the changes in real mean consumption, rather than changes in its distribution, that have mainly contributed to the observed changes in poverty in recent years. This result runs counter to the common claim in policy dialogues that recent episodes of growth have largely not benefitted the poor.

Table 11.4 Simulated poverty measures

	Aspect of poverty		
	Incidence	Depth	Severity
1985-1988			
1985 (actual)	32.7	9.4	3.8
1988 (actual)	26.9	6.9	2.5
1988 (with no change in inequality)	24.2	6.1	2.3
1988 (with no growth in mean consumption)	36.2	10.4	4.2
1988-1991			
1988 (actual)	26.9	6.9	2.5
1991 (actual)	26.6	7.1	2.7
1991 (with no change in inequality)	24.9	6.1	2.2
1991 (with no growth in mean consumption)	28.6	7.9	3.0
1991-1994			
1991 (actual)	26.6	7.1	2.7
1994 (actual)	23.4	5.9	2.1
1994 (with no change in inequality)	21.2	5.2	1.8
1994 (with no growth in mean consumption)	28.4	7.7	3.0

3 HOW MUCH CAN GROWTH PERFORMANCE EXPLAIN REGIONAL POVERTY REDUCTION?

Poverty varies considerably across regions of the country (Table 11.5).[8] Metro Manila, which accounts for about 14 per cent of the population, had the lowest poverty and contributed not even one percent of the national poverty in 1994. This is true for both incidence and severity indicators of poverty. On the other hand, Bicol, the Visayas regions, and Western and Northern Mindanao had much higher poverty levels than the average for all regions of the country; these regions contributed about 60-70 per cent of the national poverty, depending on the year and the poverty measure employed. Poverty was more severe in Bicol and Central Visayas than in any other region of the country, as indicated by the marked increase in the contribution of the two regions to national poverty when the assessment moved beyond headcount to include as well the distribution of poverty among the poor.

Table 11.5 Regional poverty profile, 1985 and 1994 (in percent)

		Population share		Poverty measure				Contribution to national poverty, 1994	
				Incidence		Severity			
		1985	1994	1985	1994	1985	1994	Incidence	Severity
Philippines		100.0	100.0	32.7	23.4	3.8	2.1	100.0	100.0
NCR	Metro Manila	14.0	13.8	3.5	0.4	0.2	*	0.2	0.3
I	Ilocos	7.2	6.8	31.8	18.7	2.4	1.1	5.5	3.5
II	Cagayan Valley	4.6	4.5	34.6	25.0	3.4	2.0	4.9	4.3
III	Central Luzon	9.9	10.5	10.6	8.4	0.6	0.4	3.8	2.0
IV	Southern Tagalog	12.5	13.0	31.4	17.5	3.3	1.3	9.9	8.0
V	Bicol	6.8	7.1	47.7	39.1	5.4	4.5	12.1	15.1
VI	Western Visayas	8.9	9.0	44.7	26.6	4.4	1.6	10.4	6.8
VII	Central Visayas	7.6	7.2	57.3	37.8	9.3	4.6	11.8	15.7
VIII	Eastern Visayas	5.4	5.2	53.0	42.3	8.1	4.8	9.6	11.8
IX	Western Mindanao	5.1	5.1	38.7	33.3	4.4	3.6	7.4	8.7
X	Northern Mindanao	6.1	5.9	48.3	39.2	7.0	4.1	10.0	11.5
XI	Southern Mindanao	7.3	7.2	32.4	22.5	3.3	1.7	7.0	5.8
XII	Central Mindanao	4.5	4.8	35.0	34.8	2.7	2.8	7.3	6.4

Note:
Provinces under the Cordillera autonomous region (created in 1987) and the autonomous region for Muslim Mindanao (created in 1990) were lumped into their regional classification in 1985.
* denotes less than 0.1%.

It might be expected that achieving a given absolute reduction of poverty would be easier (more difficult) for regions with initially high (already low) poverty levels. The correlation, however, is rather weak (Table 11.6). Bicol and Western Mindanao, two of the poorest regions, had lower poverty reduction than the average for all regions. It was not that growth was absent in the two regions. The observed consumption growth during the period would have reduced poverty in both regions by more than the reduction achieved for the entire country if the growth were distributionally neutral, which it was not. In Western Mindanao, the poverty-increasing effect of a rise in consumption inequality almost totally wiped out the poverty-decreasing effect of growth, hence the little reduction in poverty between 1985 and 1994. In Central Mindanao, the effect of growth on poverty was insufficient to offset the poverty-increasing effect of redistribution. Ilocos Region and Southern Tagalog had initially low levels of poverty *vis-à-vis* the average for all regions, but the observed poverty reduction in the two regions was higher than the national average. In both cases, the growth effect was considerably high *vis- à-vis* the redistribution effect. In Western and Central Visayas, two of the poorest regions, the positive effect of improved distribution on poverty complemented that of growth.

To what extent do differences in mean living standards account for the variation in regional poverty estimates? The data set for the four survey years and 13 geographic regions of the country shows a strong negative relationship between the consumption mean and the three poverty indices (Figure 11.2). It is also apparent that the relationship is not linear. Taking logs of the variables deals well with this nonlinearity; the regression coefficient of the logarithm of a poverty measure on the logarithm of real consumption per capita is 2.5 for the head-count regression, 3.0 for the poverty-gap regression, and 3.4 for the distribution-sensitive measure regression. These estimates indicate a highly elastic response of poverty to changes in average living standards. It is well known, however, that such regressions are likely to be biassed since cross-region comparisons of levels are quite prone to problems of measurement and related errors. For example, any omission of region-level fixed effects correlated with the consumption variable will bias the estimate of the impact of consumption growth on poverty. Moreover, since the estimation of poverty uses the information on consumption, any errors in measuring consumption are reflected in the estimates of poverty and, hence, of the regression parameters.

A convenient way to resolve these problems is to focus on *rates* of growth in poverty and consumption, rather than on levels. Differencing eliminates region-level additive fixed effects that may bias conventional

Table 11.6 Decomposition of poverty change between 1985 and 1994, by region (in percentage points)

	Growth component	Redistribution component	Residual	Total change
Incidence				
Philippines	−15.88	6.64	−0.46	−9.70
NCR Metro Manila	−2.11	−2.22	1.19	−3.14
I Ilocos	−21.31	11.78	−3.54	−13.07
II Cagayan Valley	−17.38	12.63	−4.91	−9.66
III Central Luzon	−8.10	9.06	−3.25	−2.29
IV Southern Tagalog	−16.72	1.52	1.30	−13.90
V Bicol	−19.61	9.56	1.45	−8.60
VI Western Visayas	−20.07	−1.91	3.95	−18.03
VII Central Visayas	−16.76	−4.05	1.24	−19.57
VIII Eastern Visayas	−20.13	11.52	−2.15	−10.76
IX Western Mindanao	−18.47	17.11	−4.03	−5.39
X Northern Mindanao	−23.89	13.91	0.88	−9.10
XI Southern Mindanao	−19.87	13.04	−3.06	−9.89
XII Central Mindanao	−22.65	24.32	−1.83	−0.16
Severity				
Philippines	−2.33	1.58	−0.89	−1.64
NCR Metro Manila	−0.13	−0.12	0.09	−0.16
I Ilocos	−2.03	2.13	−1.39	−1.29
II Cagayan Valley	−2.38	2.26	−1.19	−1.31
III Central Luzon	−0.45	2.60	−2.29	−0.14
IV Southern Tagalog	−2.13	0.37	−0.30	−2.06
V Bicol	−3.20	3.54	−1.28	−0.94
VI Western Visayas	−2.57	−0.14	−0.08	−2.79
VII Central Visayas	−4.63	−0.36	0.32	−4.67
VIII Eastern Visayas	−4.32	2.17	−1.19	−3.34
IX Western Mindanao	−2.92	4.00	−1.93	−0.85
X Northern Mindanao	−4.60	4.21	−2.52	−2.91
XI Southern Mindanao	−2.62	2.86	−1.84	−1.60
XII Central Mindanao	−2.10	5.47	−3.27	0.10

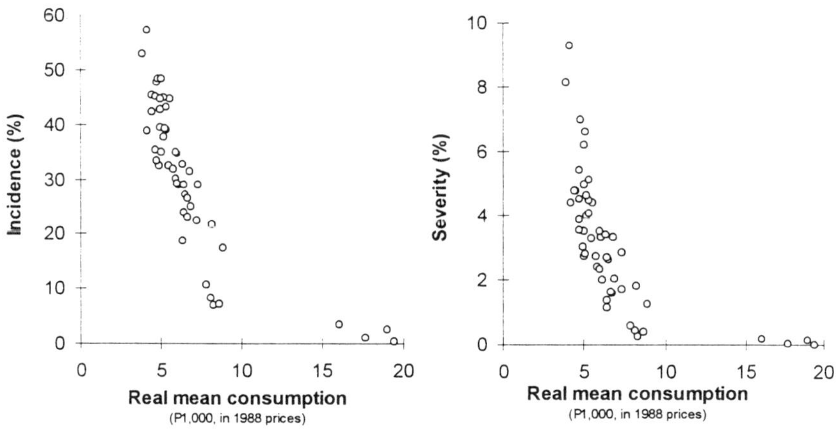

Figure 11.2 Real mean consumption versus poverty

regressions. Instead of using survey consumption means, we employ the (largely independent) estimates of the growth rate in mean consumption per capita reported in the national income accounts. This should take care of the measurement problem noted above. The regression results are[9]

$$H_t/H_{t-1} = 0.923 - 0.935[(C_t/C_{t-1}) - 1], \qquad R^2 = 0.20$$
$$(30.59)\ (-3.09) \qquad \text{Mean of dep. var.} = 0.880$$

$$PG_t/PG_{t-1} = 0.927 - 1.482[(C_t/C_{t-1}) - 1], \qquad R^2 = 0.27$$
$$(23.46)\ (-3.72) \qquad \text{Mean of dep. var.} = 0.858$$

$$DSM_t/DSM_{t-1} = 0.937 - 1.864[(C_t/C_{t-1}) - 1], \ R^2 = 0.29$$
$$(19.71)\ (-3.91)\ \text{Mean of dep. var.} = 0.850$$

Evaluated at mean values, the implied elasticities of the poverty measures with respect to consumption per capita are 2.6 for the incidence (headcount) index, 3.1 for the depth (poverty-gap) index, and 3.2 for the severity (distribution-sensitive) measure. The higher absolute values of the elasticity for poverty measures that are sensitive to the depth and/or severity of poverty indicate that the effects on the poor of growth (and contraction) in average living standards are not confined to those living near the poverty lines. Thus, *contrary to popular perception, the growth process across regions of the Philippines in recent years has not had a strongly adverse impact on the position of the poor.*

However, these elasticities are somewhat low (in absolute values) by 'international' standards. Using comparable data on poverty from a cross-section of 16 developing countries in the 1980s, Ravallion (1995) estimated poverty elasticities of 3.4 for the head-count index and 5.6 for the distribution-sensitive measure. Thus, *while poverty in the Philippines responds elastically to growth, the economy's ability to translate growth to poverty reduction appears weaker than for the 'average' developing country.* Indeed, the (above) regressions of the rate of change in poverty on the rate of growth of real consumption per capita could account for only 20-30 percent of the observed variation in poverty changes across regions during the second half of the 1980s and early 1990s.

4 HOW IMPORTANT ARE INITIAL CONDITIONS ON ECONOMIC INEQUALITY TO RURAL POVERTY ALLEVIATION?

As shown above, poverty alleviation varies substantially across regions. So is the relative importance of growth to poverty changes in recent years. The rural sector accounts for more than three-quarters of poverty in virtually all regions. Within each region (excluding Metro Manila), the agricultural sector is the biggest contributor — more than 80 percent — to poverty (Balisacan 1997). It thus appears that the search for a solution to the country's poverty problem has to involve an understanding of the conditions and processes impinging on the performance of the rural sector, as well as on the responses of rural areas to certain growth stimuli.

The 'initial' conditions of rural areas — distribution of physical and human assets, infrastructure and institutions — are expected to influence significantly the responses of rural welfare to growth stimuli, such as those provided by agricultural growth and/or export (urban) demand growth. Indeed, success in rural poverty alleviation has been associated with the growth not only of agriculture but also of rural nonfarm activities, especially in economies with a fast-growing labor force (Ranis and Stewart 1993; Mellor 1995; Otsuka 1996). High inequality in access to land, poor state of rural infrastructure, low level of human capital, and unfavorable policy environment would not only impede rural industrialization and growth but could also disproportionately harm the economic prospects of the poor, especially those in low-productivity agriculture.

How important are these factors in explaining regional differences in poverty alleviation? In addressing this issue systematically, we have estimated reduced-form functions relating to three aspects of poverty — incidence (given by the headcount index), depth (given by poverty-gap index), and severity (given by the distribution-sensitive FGT measure). The poverty data pertain to FLOL estimates using the 1985, 1988, 1991, and 1994 FIES rounds. These data are supplemented by regional indicators obtained from various sources.

In each function, we have included the following (three-year lagged) explanatory variables: functional literacy, defined as the proportion of adult population that can read and write simple messages and in addition possess numeracy skills such as elementary addition and subtraction; land inequality, given by the landholding Gini ratio which has extreme values of one (perfect inequality) and zero (perfect equality); average farm size; incidence of tenancy, defined as the ratio of area of farms under share tenancy to total area of farms; irrigation, expressed as the ratio of irrigated to total farm area; agricultural terms of trade, defined as the ratio of the price of agriculture to the price of nonagriculture; road wealth, quality-adjusted road length per square kilometer of land; and electricity, defined as the proportion of households with access to electricity. The functional-literacy variable reflects the predetermined quality of human capital endowment in the region. The irrigation variable is a proxy for land quality. The terms-of-trade variable reflects the relative price incentives for agriculture. Road wealth and electricity are proxies for access to markets and off-farm employment.[10] Three-year dummy variables are also included to capture significant differences in political and economic environment during the period of interest: 1985 was a period of severe macroeconomic difficulties (Marcos regime); 1988 was the peak of the short-lived economic recovery in the 1980s (Aquino regime); 1991 was the lowest ebb of the relatively long recession beginning in 1989 (severely weakened Aquino regime); and 1994 was the early period of the economic recovery and of renewed policy and institutional reforms (Ramos regime). All the regression equations take a double-log specification. Hence, the coefficients, except for the dummy variables, can be conveniently interpreted as poverty elasticities. In all regressions Metro Manila is excluded since agricultural production is not an important part of economic activity in the region. The regression results are given in Table 11.7.

Functional literacy is highly significant in all regressions. Its coefficient suggests a very elastic response of poverty to improvement in human capital. Poverty incidence falls by about 15 percent if functional literacy rate improves by 5 percent, all other things remaining the same. For the poverty measure capturing the severity of poverty, the reduction

Table 11.7 Poverty determination functions

Explanatory variable	Incidence	Depth	Severity
Functional literacy	−3.120	−4.070	−4.637
	(−5.07)	(−5.38)	(−5.25)
Land inequality	2.579	3.406	3.946
	(6.92)	(7.42)	(7.36)
Farm size	−0.358	−0.468	−0.499
	(−2.82)	(−2.99)	(−2.73)
Tenancy	0.045	0.057	0.080
	(0.43)	(0.44)	(0.53)
Agricultural terms of trade	−0.255	0.115	0.609
	(−0.50)	(0.18)	(0.82)
Irrigation	−0.175	−0.307	−0.404
	(−3.51)	(−5.00)	(−5.63)
Road wealth	−0.427	−0.613	−0.727
	(−3.17)	(−3.70)	(−3.77)
Electricity	−0.148	−0.317	−0.394
	(−1.64)	(−2.11)	(−2.18)
Year-1988 dummy	−0.066	−0.140	−0.184
	(−0.87)	(−1.48)	(−2.68)
Year-1991 dummy	−0.190	−0.209	−0.203
	(−2.05)	(−1.84)	(−1.53)
Year-1994 dummy	−0.230	−0.328	−0.376
	(−2.70)	(−3.13)	(−3.08)
Constant	−0.076	−1.060	−1.858
	(−0.27)	(−3.01)	(−4.52)
Adjusted R^2	0.867	0.887	0.890
F-value	28.97	34.65	35.63

Note: All variables, except year dummies, are in natural logarithms. Figures in parentheses are t-ratios. Data pertain to regional aggregates for rural areas.

would be 23 percent. These results confirm the popular story emanating from the development experience of the so-called East Asian economic miracles, suggesting that substantial improvements in human capital formed part of the building blocks for sustained economic growth and poverty reduction (World Bank 1993; Ranis 1995).

The land-inequality variable is consistently significant in all regressions, thereby also affirming the common observation in development literature concerning the negative association between landholding inequality and rural poverty. Furthermore, the elasticity of poverty with respect to this variable increases with the degree of importance given to the consumption shortfalls of the poor. Thus, for a 5 percent increase in land Gini index, the poverty incidence rises by about 13 percent, while poverty severity rises by about 20 percent, all other factors remaining the same. Even more interesting is that these elasticities reflect the national picture, that is, the responsiveness of national poverty to the consumption Gini index (Balisacan and Bacawag 1994).

Farm size and irrigation are also important determinants of poverty in regions other than Metro Manila. The consistently negative and significant coefficient of the irrigation variable suggests that improvements in land quality offer an important avenue for reducing poverty, both in agriculture and in rural nonfarm areas.

Road wealth is highly significant in all equations. Electricity is significant for the depth and severity regressions but not for the incidence regression. At the very least, both variables suggest that access to markets and off-farm employment opportunities influence poverty. The importance of road wealth in explaining the variation in regional poverty is particularly interesting because previous attempts to capture the effect of market access and off-farm employment opportunities on poverty in agriculture through the use of conventional measures such as road density and urbanization (usually expressed as the ratio of urban population to total population) proved unsuccessful (see Balisacan 1993).

The terms-of-trade variable is insignificant. It is possible that this variable could not capture adequately the regional biases of commodity pricing policies and hence the relative profitability of agriculture.

Interestingly, tenancy is not significant in any of the regressions. What this observation, as well as many other recent theoretical and empirical studies (for example, Hayami and Otsuka 1993), suggests is that tenancy by itself is not as important and compelling a correlate of poverty as expected: the variation in incomes within tenure classes (reflecting the effect of farm size, yield, cropping intensity, land quality, and so on) has been found to be much greater than the variation between classes.

Finally, note that the year dummy variables are generally significant, indicating that changes in the overall macroeconomic and political regimes influence the incidence, depth and severity of poverty, as expected.

5 CONCLUSIONS

Contrary to popular perceptions, recent episodes of growth in the Philippines have not been anti-poor; the bulk of the poverty reduction since the mid-1980s, a period of wide-ranging economic deregulation and institutional reforms, has come from the beneficial effects of growth on the poor. The importance of growth in poverty alleviation varies greatly, however, across administrative regions and sectors of the economy. For the entire country, the agricultural sector led the way to poverty alleviation during the 1980s and early 1990s despite its sluggish growth (Balisacan 1997). The self-employed workers, the large majority of whom were dependent on agriculture, gained more than proportionately to the overall growth, mainly because their consumption grew more rapidly than those of other groups. For faster poverty alleviation, the development of agriculture and the rural sector, which still accounts for more than three-quarters of the poor, has to be a central element of the country's development strategy. Priority should be given to rural infrastructure development, human capital formation, agricultural research and small- and medium-scale industrial development, and improvement of access to land. As the East Asian experience demonstrates, these investments, together with sound 'fundamentals' (that is, fiscal and monetary restraint), are critical to the building of initial conditions for broad-based growth and development.

The high inequality of landholding weakens, though perhaps not eliminates, the potential of agricultural growth in leading the way to poverty alleviation in rural areas. Several land reform programs have been launched since the 1930s, but their performance has been poor in relation to their objectives, as well as to similar programs undertaken in East Asian countries. In general, their very limited success in promoting either equity or efficiency stems not so much from lack of 'political will' but from faulty designs arising from unrealistic expectations and virtual disregard for financial, economic and political landscapes. It is high time that an alternative paradigm for reforming agrarian relations in the Philippines, as elsewhere in developing Asian countries, be found. The 'new' paradigm needs to exploit the virtues of decentralized decision-making, rely upon market forces for land transactions, and impose compatibility of incentives with program objectives (that is, the intended beneficiaries have the incentive to seek program benefits, while the unintended beneficiaries do not have the incentive to preempt these benefits).

The finding that economic growth in recent years has been beneficial to the poor, even in the short run, is a stark contrast to earlier findings for the 1960s and 1970s when the 'trickle-down' effects of growth on poverty were comparatively small (see, for example, Balisacan 1993; Ranis and Stewart 1993; Bautista and Lamberte 1996). It is possible that the structure of the economy has changed in ways that now allow greater participation of the poor during episodes of growth. But what has changed, and how have specific policy reforms in recent years influenced the observed outcomes on poverty? The analysis undertaken in this chapter provides some answers, but the story on what explains the country's unenviable record in growth and poverty alleviation is far from complete.

NOTES

1. The official estimate of the proportion of the population deemed poor was about 14 percent in 1993 and 11 percent in 1996 for Indonesia, while this was 40 percent in 1994 for the Philippines. Using an internationally comparable poverty line of one US dollar (at 1985 purchasing power parity) per capita per day, the World Bank (1996b) estimated the poverty incidence in the early 1990s to be about 15 percent for Indonesia and 20 percent for the Philippines.
2. Cox and Jimenez (1995) found evidence of substantial interhousehold income transfers in the Philippines typically from the relatively rich households to poor households.
3. For an extensive discussion on conceptual and empirical issues in poverty assessment, see Ravallion (1996).
4. It is well known that as household incomes rise, consumption of cheap sources of calories tends to decline as consumers shift to higher quality and more varied, but not necessarily more nutritious, food sources. Put differently, the income elasticity of demand for calories is typically much lower than that for food as a group (Bouis 1996; Subramanian and Deaton 1996). The shift is invariably associated with improvement in living standards. On the implication of this issue on poverty assessment, see Ravallion (1994).
5. Poverty lines in the official approach are sensitive to overall mean expenditure (income), suggesting that what is partly captured by the poverty assessment is *relative* poverty. Put differently, poverty is intimately identified with the distribution of living standards. In developed countries, poverty assessment is commonly anchored on such a notion of poverty. However, for developing countries such as the Philippines, where the immediate policy concern is the reduction of *absolute* poverty, this concept is of limited value. As is well known, a relative measure of poverty may underestimate the progress being made in the reduction of absolute poverty. From a policy viewpoint, the two concepts have different implications for the choice of poverty-reduction strategies. Redistributive programs (for example, social welfare payments) characterize a development policy focussed on reducing relative poverty. Economic growth alone may not help much in reducing this type of poverty. On the other hand, the reduction of absolute poverty may require no less than overall expansion of employment opportunities sustained over a long period of time. In this case, development policy anchored on poverty reduction may have to focus on creating a favorable environment for sustained employment growth (for example, investment in infrastructure and human capital).
6. On the application of stochastic dominance theory to poverty assessment, see

Foster and Shorrocks (1988).

7. The methodology follows that suggested by Datt and Ravallion (1992) for decomposing poverty change into growth and redistribution components.
8. For reasons indicated in the preceding section, this section uses spatial poverty estimates based on the fixed-level-of-living (FLOL) approach.
9. Ramset reset test for functional form (using powers of fitted values) gave 1.41 (distributed as F) for the headcount, 0.99 for the poverty gap, and 0.62 for the distribution-sensitive measure. The tests are satisfactory, suggesting the appropriateness of the functional form. The White-Weisberg test for heteroskedasticity gave 0.03 (distributed as chi-square) for the headcount, 0.81 for the poverty gap, and 0.35 for the distribution-sensitive measure. These tests indicate the absence of the heteroskedasticity in the regressions.
10. Road wealth is preferred to the conventional road-density measure (total road length expressed as a ratio of land area) since the former better reflects regional differences in the quality of road stock.

REFERENCES

Balisacan, Arsenio M. (1993), 'Agricultural Growth, Landlessness, Off-Farm Employment and Rural Poverty in the Philippines', *Economic Development and Cultural Change*, 41, 533-62.

Balisacan, Arsenio M. (1994), 'Targeting Transfers to the Poor: The Case of Food Subsidies', *Journal of Philippine Development*, 21 (First and Second Semesters), 179-220.

Balisacan, Arsenio M. (1995), 'Anatomy of Poverty during Adjustment: The Case of the Philippines', *Economic Development and Cultural Change*, 44, 33-62.

Balisacan, Arsenio M. (1997), 'Poverty during Episodes of Boom and Bust', in E.F. Esguerra and K. Ito (eds), *Employment, Human Capital and Job Security: Recent Perspectives on the Philippine Labor Market*, Tokyo: Institute of Developing Economies, 165-79.

Balisacan, Arsenio M. and Rhoda Theresa Bacawag (1994), 'Inequality, Poverty, and Urban-Rural Growth Linkages', in A.M. Balisacan et al., *Spatial Development, Land Use, and Urban-Rural Growth Linkages in the Philippines*, Pasig: National Economic and Development Authority, 106-48.

Bardhan, Pranab (1996), 'Efficiency, Equity and Poverty Alleviation: Policy Issues in Less Developed Countries', *Economic Journal*, 106, September, 1344-56.

Bautista, Romeo M. and Mario M. Lamberte (1996), 'The Philippines', *Asian-Pacific Economic Literature,* 10, November, 16-32.

Bouis, Howarth E. (1996), 'A Food Demand System Based on Demand for Characteristics: If There is "Curvature" in the Slutsky Matrix, What Do the Curves Look Like and Why?', *Journal of Development Economics*, 51, 239-66.

Cox, Donald and Emmanuel Jimenez (1995), 'Private Transfers and the Effectiveness of Public Income Redistribution in the Philippines', in Dominique van de Walle and Kimberly Nead (eds), *Public Spending and the Poor: Theory and Evidence*, Baltimore, MD: Johns Hopkins University Press for the World Bank, 321-46.

Datt, Gaurav and Martin Ravallion (1992), 'Growth and Redistribution Components of Changes in Poverty Measures: A Decomposition with Applications to Brazil and India in the 1980s', *Journal of Development Economics*, 38, 275-95.

Foster, James E., Joel Greer and Erik Thorbecke (1984), 'A Class of Decomposable Poverty Measures', *Econometrica*, 52, 761-66.

Foster, James E. and A.F. Shorrocks (1988), 'Poverty Orderings', *Econometrica*, 56, 173-7.

Hayami, Yujiro and Keijiro Otsuka (1993), *The Economics of Contract Choice: An Agrarian Perspective*, Oxford: Clarendon Press.

Hill, Hal (1996), *The Indonesian Economy since 1966: Southeast Asia's Emerging Giant*, Cambridge: Cambridge University Press.

International Labour Organization (ILO) (1974), *Sharing in Development: A Programme of Employment, Equity and Growth in the Philippines*, Geneva: ILO.

Lamberte, Mario, et al. (1993), *Decentralization and Prospects for Regional Growth*, Makati: Philippine Institute for Development Studies.

Lipton, Michael and Martin Ravallion (1995), 'Poverty and Policy', in J. Behrman and T.N. Srinivasan (eds), *Handbook of Development Economics*, Vol. III, Amsterdam: North Holland, 2552-657.

Mellor, John W. (ed.) (1995), *Agriculture on the Road to Industrialization,* Baltimore, MD: Johns Hopkins University Press.

Otsuka, Keijiro (1996), 'Rural Industrialization in East Asia', Paper presented at the International Economic Association Round Table Conference on the Institutional Foundation of Economic Development in East Asia, Tokyo, December 16-19.

Park, Albert and Bruce Johnston (1995), 'Rural Development and Dynamic Externalities in Taiwan's Structural Transformation', *Economic Development and Cultural Change*, 44, 181-208.

Ranis, Gustav (1995), 'Another Look at the East Asian Miracle', *World Bank Economic Review*, 9, September, 509-34.

Ranis, Gustav and Frances Stewart (1993), 'Rural Nonagricultural Activities in Development: Theory and Application', *Journal of*

Development Economics, 40, 75-101.

Ravallion, Martin (1993), 'Poverty Alleviation through Regional Targeting: A Case Study for Indonesia', in Karla Hoff, Avishay Braverman, and Joseph E. Stiglitz (eds), *The Economics of Rural Organization: Theory, Practice, and Policy*, Oxford: Oxford University Press for the World Bank, 453-67.

Ravallion, Martin (1994), *Poverty Comparisons*, Chur: Harwood Academic Publishers.

Ravallion, Martin (1995), 'Growth and Poverty: Evidence for Developing Countries in the 1980s', *Economics Letters*, 48, 411-17.

Ravallion, Martin (1996), 'Issues in Measuring and Modeling Poverty', *Economic Journal*, 106, September, 1328-43.

Ravallion, Martin and Jyotsna Jalan (1996), 'Growth Divergence due to Spatial Externalities', *Economics Letters*, 53, 227-32.

Subramanian, Shankar and Angus Deaton (1996), 'The Demand for Food and Calories', *Journal of Political Economy*, 104, 133-62.

United Nations Development Program (UNDP) (1996), *Philippine Human Development Report*, Manila: UNDP.

World Bank (1993), *The East Asian Miracle: Economic Growth and Public Policy,* Washington, DC: World Bank.

World Bank (1996a), *A Strategy to Fight Poverty: Philippines*, Washington, DC: World Bank.

World Bank (1996b), *Poverty Reduction and the World Bank: Progress and Challenges in the 1990s,* Washington, DC: World Bank.

12. The Founding of the Bretton Woods Institutions: A View from the 1990s

Anne O. Krueger*

1 INTRODUCTION

The history of the founding of the Bretton Woods institutions presents something of a puzzle. As early as the lend-lease agreements, and continuing with the Atlantic Charter, Britain and the United States committed themselves to establishing a regime of free and open multilateral trade at the end of the Second World War. As Gardner (1956, p. 13) notes, "the best short description of the Administration's basic objective in international affairs would be the reconstruction of a multilateral system of world trade". Cordell Hull, the Secretary of State, was powerful in the administration and a firm believer in free trade.[1]

Yet, in 1944, delegates met at Bretton Woods and agreed upon the articles for the International Monetary Fund (IMF) and the World Bank. Congress approved the legislation for these organizations in 1945.[2] By contrast, the *first* meeting of delegates to agree upon an international trade organization did not convene until November 1945, a charter was not negotiated until 1948, and, of course, it was never ratified.

The United States was not only first among equals: it was clearly dominant. With the American government committed to a multilateral trade organization, why did this not come about simultaneously with the Bretton Woods agreements? Why did the international financial institutions (IFIs) – the World Bank and the IMF – get established, apparently so readily, while the trade organization never came into being?

This is a political economy puzzle of some interest. Conventional wisdom regarding the founding of the Bretton Woods institutions is approximately the following. Because of wartime pressures, economists (especially Keynes) were free to develop the plan for the three postwar international economic institutions. It was only the curmudgeonly

* I am indebted to Evren Ergin for research assistance in preparation of this chapter.

American Congress that partially thwarted the plan by failing to ratify the proposed articles for the International Trade Organization (ITO). The world was therefore left with the IMF, the World Bank, and a small GATT – which was an 'agreement' which did not require congressional approval – which was all that could be done in support of an open multilateral trading system in light of Congress's refusal. Further, it is widely believed that the proposed ITO would have stood as a strong bulwark for free trade, while the weaker GATT in effect could only gradually assume the functions intended for the ITO.[3]

While this interpretation has substantial validity, the truth is significantly more complicated and somewhat different. There is no question but that the IMF was intended to anchor an international monetary system that would support an open trading system. The political economy puzzle becomes all the more remarkable when it is recognized that the Fund and the World Bank both required far larger initial resources from the United States than would the ITO.

The World Bank[4] was conceived as facilitating international capital flows, since it was believed that the events of the 1930s had effectively precluded any resumption of private long-term capital flows on an adequate scale. But underlying both of these conceptions, as well as that of the ITO, was a perceived tension between the goals just stated and concerns about the future evolution of the world economy in light of Keynesian economics.

A reexamination of what happened, and why, is of interest not only in its own right, but also because of the light it sheds on certain issues in political economy. The founding of the postwar international economic institutions (including the failure to bring the ITO into being) was considerably more complicated than the generally held view, and there are several points that are either erroneously reported or forgotten.

The purpose of this chapter is to attempt to interpret events that were unfolding in the 1940s from the viewpoint of political economy. I shall argue that bureaucratic politics and personalities, the power of ideas, budget constraints and even accidents all mattered. The pressures and confusions of wartime precluded the carefully reasoned discussion and debate over the Bretton Woods institutions that might have taken place in calmer times,[5] but also permitted their inauguration more readily than could have happened in peacetime.

Section 2 provides an outline of events that were significant in the evolution of the postwar international economic system. Sections 3 and 4 then view these events in light of the ideas that underlay them, focussing on the power of ideas in shaping the institutions. Section 5 examines the reasons for the demise of the ITO, contrasted with the relative ease with which the International Bank for Reconstruction and Development (IBRD) (now World Bank) and the IMF were established. It will be argued that political power and personalities, especially in the American administration, made a significant difference to the outcome. Section 6 concludes.

2 WHAT HAPPENED?

In the 1940s, economists and policy-makers were still in shock over the Great Depression. This had several important consequences:

1. it was widely believed that the world would revert to recession or depression at the end of the war[6] unless there was overt governmental action;
2. it was generally thought that 'competitive devaluations' and other 'beggar-thy-neighbor' policies, including the successive rounds of heightened tariffs and retaliation, had greatly intensified the Great Depression;[7]
3. Keynesian thought supported the proposition that government intervention was essential to achieve a 'good' equilibrium of full employment and the corollary that free trade *à la* Ricardo and Smith was desirable only in a context where the good equilibrium had been achieved; and
4. many interpreted the lessons of the Great Depression to include the proposition that countries could not individually (or perhaps even bilaterally) avoid depressions and that international cooperation (and presumably international institutions) would be required.[8]

Proposals for all three international institutions had been developed in 1942-43,[9] primarily between the British and the Americans.[10] John Maynard Keynes and James Meade were members of the British team which negotiated with the Americans and which met several times prior to Bretton Woods.[11] An American proposal for an organization supporting an open multilateral trading system was circulated in 1943, but there were significant differences between the Americans and the British on it (as discussed below).[12]

2.1 Events Leading to the Establishment of the Bank and the Fund

Discussions for international monetary arrangements culminated in the Bretton Woods conference of 1944, with participation by representatives of 45 countries.[13]

Although all accounts indicate that it was agreed that there would be three international institutions – to oversee trade arrangements,[14] to underpin the international monetary system, and to supplement private long-term capital flows – only the IMF and the IBRD articles were drawn up and approved at Bretton Woods.

Proposals for the international monetary facility were considerably more controversial between the Americans and the British than were those for the IBRD.[15] As is well known, Keynes initially proposed an international bank-money, called 'bancor'. The proposal focussed upon increasing world liquidity, and assumed that exchange controls and quantitative restrictions would persist in the international economy. The clearing union would be one in which members had virtually automatic drawing rights (like overdrafts), up to some specified limit. This proposal was firmly grounded in the Keynesian view of a world in which secular stagnation would be the chief problem and the solution would involve measures to stimulate demand. He therefore also initially proposed that a significant part of the adjustment of any payments imbalance be placed on the surplus country.[16]

The initial American proposal, by contrast, focussed on exchange rates as the key issue, and stabilization of rates as the chief purpose of the Fund. It was anticipated by all that the dollar would be a surplus currency.[17] Changes in nominal exchange rates were regarded as inimical to private foreign investment and to trade (see Horsefield 1969, ch. 3. p. 46). Although Harry Dexter White proposed a 'unitas', it was to be a bookkeeping unit of account and would be strictly limited in its issuance.

Underlying this difference in emphasis was the real issue: the extent to which the future IMF would provide resources freely to its members. The British, anticipating deficits, wanted as much access with as few restrictions as possible; the United States, concerned that it would be the source of resources, wanted less access and more restrictions.[18] The US plan placed no part of the burden of adjustment on creditor countries. There was also an issue over the extent of Fund control over changes in exchange rates. On that question, not surprisingly, the British wanted final control over the sterling exchange rate, while the American position would have required Fund consent for an exchange rate change. The final wording was, of course, a compromise, although it was much closer to the American plan than the British. As Skidelsky reports,

> The Bretton Woods Agreement, signed on 22 July 1944, after two difficult negotiating sessions in Washington, reflected American rather than British views. British and American conflicts on such matters as exchange rate management,

> access to reserves, tariff policy, and responsibility for adjustment reflected national interests ... Britain's negotiating achievements were limited to obtaining safeguards, postponements, and derogations within the framework of the American plan. The chief British success was to secure a 'scarce currency' clause which allowed debtor countries to discriminate. (Skidelsky 1966, p. 101)

As will be argued below, it was over this issue that one of the fundamental problems with ideas at the time arose; the notion of a 'fundamental disequilibrium' in the balance of payments has never been satisfactorily defined.

Negotiations over the Fund were carried out until sufficient agreement was reached so that a British-American 'Joint Statement by Experts on the Establishment of an International Monetary Fund' was released to other countries' capitals in the fall of 1943. Although neither the American nor the British government at that time officially endorsed the text, it was in fact the basis for detailed negotiations that led to the IMF articles (see Dan 1982, pp. 84ff, and references therein).

The IBRD articles generated less attention and disagreement than did the Fund's. The only real issue was the magnitude of the IBRD's resources, and the split over that issue was not dissimilar to that over the Fund's resources and scope.

At Bretton Woods, remaining questions were resolved and the negotiators initialed their assents.[19] Thereafter, the articles were rapidly submitted to the US Congress and other national legislatures for their ratification. In the case of the USA, the Roosevelt administration submitted both sets of articles to Congress in January 1945, with an appeal for speedy approval. While by that time the Allied forces were clearly winning the war, it was still wartime.

This fact is critically important in understanding what happened. The Bretton Woods conference was conducted during wartime, and while there was a definite mandate to the policy community concerned to provide for a postwar international economic order, the focus of public attention was clearly on winning the war. Even then, when the IMF and IBRD articles were debated before being ratified by the US Congress, 'the American Treasury set in motion a powerful publicity campaign to win support for the two institutions' (Gardner 1956, p. 129).

There was opposition to the Bank and Fund Articles. Senator Taft was a key opponent, claiming that

> in this case we are giving our money to a board which is controlled by the debtors, the very fellows who are going to borrow .... I do not think anybody has ever proposed to give away American money as this Fund proposes to give it away, to

> people who themselves will control its disposition. (Quoted in Gardner 1956, p. 130)

There were also significant questions about the scarce currency clause, with concerns that American exports might be restricted.

By contrast, the US Treasury over-promised. It stressed the extent to which the Fund's presence would support American exports. One Treasury official even testified that the Fund's establishment would result in a rapid end to all exchange controls. Even so, when Congress approved the Articles of Agreement, it stipulated that there should be another institution to prevent the replacement of controls over payments with controls over trade.

By July 1945, Congress had voted to approve the Bank and Fund articles. It had the support of most groups, and only a minority of Republicans (led by Senator Taft) continued to oppose the Bank and fund.

2.2 Negotiations for a Trade Organization

As already mentioned, the commitment to an open multilateral trading system was already embedded in the lend-lease agreements and the Atlantic Charter. In both cases, the clauses were there at US insistence, despite some resistance from the British who were simultaneously in a very weak bargaining position because of their need for American resources.

Opposition to US views was strong, and surfaced in early meetings between American and British officials over the possible outlines of a postwar institution.[20] While the Americans were advocating open multilateral trade, others (and especially the British) were concerned that their circumstances in the initial postwar period would require exchange controls; in addition, they placed much more emphasis on the necessity for maintaining domestic freedom of action when there was incipient recession or depression than did the Americans.[21]

Consequently, it was not until 1945 that the United States published and circulated Proposals for Expansion of World Trade and Employment. This was put forward as a proposal prepared in consultation with the British, although in fact that 'consultation' was negotiation over the Anglo-American loan of 1946 (in which the British sought $6 billion and finally achieved a loan of $2.75 billion). Thereafter, several draft charters were published after successive conferences in London, New York, Geneva, and finally Havana in 1948.[22]

As these discussions were proceeding, in 1947 there was – at US instigation[28] – a first round of multilateral tariff negotiations in Geneva to reduce tariff levels. The General Agreement was drawn up as a mechanism to permit the agreed-upon tariff reductions to go forward without being in effect nullified by other trade measures.[24]

It was anticipated that there would be future reciprocal tariff negotiations, that they would take place under the auspices of the ITO then being negotiated, and that the General Agreement would be incorporated into the final articles for the organization.

As Dam (1970) points out, the GATT essentially enshrines the US position as earlier articulated by Cordell Hull[25] and other representatives of the US. The State Department was the lead agency in the negotiations. Essentially, all nontariff barriers should be eliminated, while tariffs should be reduced to the lowest possible levels on a multilateral basis. Effectively, after multilateral tariff negotiations, countries would 'bind' their tariffs (until the next round of negotiations, although in practise that never happened and tariff concessions, once made, tended to be permanent, with the next negotiations starting from the lower tariffs negotiated in the previous round). They could not then increase them unless 'injured', and then had to pay 'compensation' to countries whose exports were reduced due to findings of injury in the form of alternative tariff reductions.

There were several bases of foreign opposition to an open multilateral trade organization which incorporated only the GATT principles. First, many policy-makers in other countries were concerned, especially in the immediate postwar period, that they would be confronted with very high demands for imports relative to their export capabilities. This was certainly true of the British. Second, the belief that the world (and especially the United States) might revert to recession/depression led many to believe that free trade was a goal that should be subordinate to concerns with regard to domestic employment and income. Finally, as mentioned earlier, the British were desirous to maintain special relationships with Commonwealth countries, and also the imperial preferences.[26]

The GATT articles were therefore regarded as interim, to be incorporated into the ITO agreement, and it was clearly understood during the Geneva negotiations that the Havana conference would be held and the articles augmented in ways that would address these concerns.

In the negotiations leading up to the Havana Charter, the United States gave ground on all three issues. Countries were to be entitled to use exchange controls and quantitative restrictions on imports for balance-of-payments reasons; countries were to be able to rescind their tariff concessions whenever there were domestic employment objectives with which they were inconsistent; and preferences were to be allowed.

There were entire chapters on exceptions arising from domestic economic concerns. There were chapters on 'Employment and Economic Activity', 'Economic Development and Reconstruction', 'Restrictive Business Practices', and 'Intergovernmental Commodity Agreements'. These additions to the GATT articles in effect permitted countries to impose trade restrictions whenever deemed necessary to achieve domestic economic objectives.

Once delegates had signed the Havana Charter, it had to be ratified. At that time (1948), European reconstruction needs were dominant, and the Truman Administration was proposing, and putting its efforts into achieving support for, the Marshall Plan. The Administration therefore did not even present the Articles to Congress in 1948. As reported by Diebold (1956, p. 6),

> As a result, the Charter was held over until the new Congress met in 1949. In April of that year President Truman sent the Charter to the Hill and asked for a joint resolution authorizing American participation. But by then Congress was busy with the North Atlantic Treaty, the Military Defense Assistance Program, and legislation for the second year of ECA [Economic Cooperation Administration in charge of administering the Marshall Plan]. The Administration apparently agreed with Congressional leaders that it was better not to press for quick action on the ITO since these other foreign affairs measures took precedence. The slight recession of mid-1949 brought on a series of complaints about unemployment allegedly traceable to imports, thus helping to create a sour atmosphere for the ITO. Not until April and May 1950 did the House Committee on Foreign Affairs hold hearings on the joint resolution. The Committee did not report, and the matter never came to the floor of the House.

In the meantime, British opposition to the ITO also arose. Of course, few nations would in any event have ratified the agreement if they knew that the United States would not become a member of the organization. But Gardner (1956, p. 371) concludes that 'It was doubtful that Britain would ratify the ITO, even if the United States should choose to do so'.

In 1950, of course, the Korean War began. Later that year, the Truman Administration announced that it would not again be asking for approval of the ITO, and it was in fact dead. The GATT Secretariat was gradually assuming some of the functions that an ITO would have undertaken, and over the years filled that role amazingly well.[27] And, not germaine to the present analysis, the success of the GATT, and the corresponding liberalization and expansion of world trade, finally led the members to negotiate a World Trade Organization in the early 1990s, which came into being in 1995, incorporating the GATT and considerably more.

3 THE ROLE OF IDEAS

In assessing the role of ideas, I focus primarily on the US position. This is in part because the US was the dominant country, and in part because it was US support of the IFIs and failure to ratify the ITO charter that resulted in the birth of two, and not three, international organizations.

However, for the IMF and the ITO, British views were also important. They were important in part because the British negotiators were widely respected in the United States. and therefore influential disproportionately to the UK's power. They were also important because they gave rise to many of the chapters in the ITO Charter that can be regarded as having been crucial in undermining the support of key constituencies for free trade in the United States.

Underlying the conceptions of the three international institutions were strong legacies from the ideas that came out of the Great Depression. There is little doubt that the United States placed more emphasis on economic origins of the war than did the British, but in both countries the idea that prosperity would be conducive to maintaining the peace was generally accepted. It was widely believed that the beggar-thy-neighbor policies and Hawley-Smooth tariffs had significantly intensified the depression. Cordell Hull's commitment to free trade had been important. Even during the Great Depression, he had been able to secure the passage of the Reciprocal Trade Agreements through Congress. Hull is widely quoted from the 1930s as having insisted on an open multilateral trading system not only as an economic goal, but as an essential element or prerequisite for peace. In his *Memoirs* (1948, Vol. 1, p. 9), he wrote:

> unhampered trade dovetailed with peace; high tariffs, trade barriers, and unfair economic competition, with war. Though realizing that many other factors were involved, I reasoned that if we could get a freer flow of trade ... so that one country could not be deadly jealous of another and the living standards of all countries might rise, thereby eliminating the economic dissatisfaction that breeds war, we might have a reasonable chance of lasting peace.

The American view seems clearly to have had 'an exaggerated emphasis on economic policy' (Gardner 1956, p. 8) as a lynchpin of the postwar system to guard the peace.

Following on the idea that a healthy international economy would be essential to preserve the peace was an insistence that this could best (if not only) be achieved by founding appropriate international organizations. They were clearly thought to be important and underpinned the Keynes Plan and the US proposals and planning for the postwar period.[28] The US administration, however, insisted on international organizations for even deeper reasons. Multilateralism was regarded as an essential element of policy (on this see ibid., p. 16). This, too, implied reliance on international organizations but also a downplaying of any special relationships (such as that with Britain).

Thus, there was complete agreement that there should be international economic institutions, and both sides of the Atlantic agreed early on three institutions. However, agreement stopped shortly after that point.

As already seen, with regard to the IMF (and World Bank), the disagreement focussed over the extent of resources to be available from the Fund and the conditions under which countries could draw upon them.[29] Britain, expecting to be a borrower, clearly wanted large resources and virtually unrestricted access.[30] The fact that the United States effectively held the purse strings necessarily enabled resolution of this particular disagreement largely in accord with American preferences. This implied the imposition of conditions on lending from the IMF, which in turn was used to assure all but the Taft faction of the Republican Party that borrowing would not be 'excessive'.

With the American ideas prevailing, the focus of the IMF was to be on the exchange rate regime. But, from that starting point, Keynes's ideas won the day. On one hand, he believed in fixed exchange rates – as did the United States. On the other hand, he also believed that the British difficulties of the late 1920s had been a result of repegging sterling to gold at the 'wrong' exchange rate in 1925.

A focus on 'fixed but adjustable exchange rates', which was the Bretton Woods world from 1946 to 1973, was not entirely logically consistent. The insistence that exchange rate changes could be made only in cases of 'fundamental disequilibrium',[31] without a definition of that term, left to a considerable degree an unresolved intellectual tension. It was also important that the compromise insisted that the Fund could not insist on any change in domestic policies *instead of* exchange rate changes when it was deemed that there was 'fundamental disequilibrium'.

The difficulties inherent in the notion of fundamental disequilibrium are obvious. Yet it is probably the case that use of the notion was what was able to bring about coherence between the Keynesian ideas, on the one hand, and the principles that the Americans were willing to support, on the other.

With regard to the ITO, the situation differed. First, with the end of the war and the emergence of such nations as India from under colonial rule, the dialogue and discussions took place among a larger number of participants who could be effective in expressing their views. Virtually all, except the United States, were concerned that America might go into recession. The Keynesian theories had seemingly provided a case in which free trade might not be optimal from the viewpoint of an individual country (and perhaps the world): when resources were unemployed and a tariff might result in their utilization, imposition of a tariff would increase domestic output and employment and hence be desirable. Developing countries wanted to be able to protect newly established industries in conformity with the idea that import-substituting industrialization was necessary for development;[32] Europe wanted to be able to use protection during the period of reconstruction and was, in any event, less committed to free trade than was the United States.

Consequently, when conferences were held regarding the ITO, American delegates were more 'surrounded' by opposition than they had been in reaching agreement leading up to and at Bretton Woods. The GATT articles essentially already reflected American concerns; most of the additional chapters were the result of compromises between the American position and that of virtually all other countries.

Despite that, the US delegation proceeded to negotiate an ITO Charter at Havana. It reflected both the American commitment to open multilateral trade (in the GATT articles which were incorporated in it) and the many exceptions insisted upon by the rest of the world. Unlike the IMF and World Bank negotiations, there were no American resources at stake that might have 'persuaded' other countries to accept something closer to the American position.

Hence, whereas the IMF articles reflected a compromise based on a fuzzy idea that papered over differences, the ITO document was really the result of two sets of ideas; and in the ITO Charter, permitted exceptions could in fact be expected to offset most of the GATT principles much of the time.

4 BUREAUCRATIC POLITICS AND PERSONALITIES

There are several important aspects of bureaucratic structure and personalities that were important in determining the outcome.

It was obviously critical that President Roosevelt decided that the American Treasury, rather than the State Department be the lead agency in the monetary negotiations (see Moggridge 1992, p. 722). This was almost certainly the result of Roosevelt's much closer relationship to Henry Morgenthau than to Cordell Hull.[33] Once the Treasury had the lead responsibility, Harry Dexter White could assume a key role in formulating a proposal and in the negotiations.[34]

The fact that the US Treasury was the lead agency for the IMF and

World Bank while the State Department was the lead agency for the ITO was also crucial in another way. That is, the State Department was largely overwhelmed by the pressing matters of dealing with allied countries during the war.[35] Despite Hull's commitment to the principle of free trade, his other commitments were so pressing that he could not provide the active leadership for trade that the Treasury could for the IMF and World Bank. It is significant that, in Hull's almost 900 pages on the wartime years in his *Memoirs,* there is only one paragraph which even mentions the IFIs, and even then there is no formal mention of their name.[36]

Although it is arguable that the clash of ideas over the ITO, along with the absence of desperately-needed resources to enforce American views, was responsible for its demise, it is also clear that the delay in bringing the ITO proposals forward until late 1945, with Havana not until 1948, was critical. During the war, attention was focussed elsewhere, and Congress could ratify the Fund and Bank articles with strong Treasury leadership. There were few other issues on which the Treasury had to spend its 'political capital' during the war, and government borrowing to finance the war was so large that the budgetary consequences were probably not as seriously examined as they might have been at a later date. Once the war had ended, the State Department's leadership was altered, the political agenda for the State Department was crowded, and, in any event, the clash of ideas underlying the ITO charter was considerably more fundamental than that which underlay the IMF and World Bank.

Keynes's personality was also an important determinant of the outcomes. Keynes himself was committed to the IMF and World Bank, even if they did not fully live up to his initial conception. He was much more schizophrenic regarding trade issues, as already seen. Keynes's influence was important in several ways. First, when it became evident that the United States would not accept British proposals, it was usually Keynes who proposed a compromise. Keynes was widely respected in Washington as well as in Britain, and he was probably therefore a more effective negotiator with the Americans than others might have been.[37] In addition, Keynes vigorously supported the proposed Bank and Fund Articles when they were under discussion in the United Kingdom (see Moggridge 1992, pp. 730ff).

It is questionable whether Keynes, had he lived, would have been equally active in the discussions leading up to the ITO, or would have participated in the final negotiations. His role in bringing the Bretton Woods negotiations to closure cannot be disputed. For the IFIs, Keynes was supporting a scaled-down version of what he was committed to, and believed to be strongly in the interests of Britain. Although he initially proposed an organization for international trade, his schizophrenic views on free trade might have diminished his input in discussions, even had he lived. But, had he been as committed to an international trade organization as he was to the Bank and Fund, he could, quite clearly, have made a difference.

5 WHY DID THE BANK AND THE FUND EMERGE AND THE ITO DIE?

We now have the pieces to be put together. To the extent that the British (and others) disagreed with the American conception and formulation of the IMF and World Bank, it was because they wanted more of a good thing. Said another way, they agreed on the idea, but simply got less of it than they wanted. For the Americans, support was forthcoming because of the 'vague feeling of guilt'and commitment to international organizations when the war was still in progress. Indeed, American negotiators had consistently had the necessity for congressional approval in view, and had limited the extent of IMF and World Bank resources to be consistent with what they deemed could meet with congressional approval.

There are two interesting questions. First, if Roosevelt had given the lead to the State Department, would the Bank and Fund articles have emerged in a form similar to that derived at Bretton Woods? The probable answer is 'yes'. There does not appear to have been significant difference with the State Department over the Bank and Fund articles, although the State Department might have tended to be more generous in initial funding for the IFIs. However, overburdened as the State Department was, there are significant questions as to whether it could have organized the Bretton Woods conference in 1944 and whether it could have lobbied effectively for congressional approval.

That, then, raises the second question. If the Bretton Woods conference had taken place a year later, and the results sent to Congress under peacetime conditions, would Congress have ratified the agreement? Here, the answer must be much more in doubt. The fact that it was wartime and that hopes for a future peace were high certainly helped gain congressional approval. Once the Cold War had begun, and disillusionment set in with international organizations (especially the United Nations), it is arguable that passage through Congress would not have happened.

Turning to the ITO, several points are obvious. First, there was no consensus on the principles underlying the proposed organization. For that reason alone, support in both Britain and the United States was diluted. Second, and as emphasized by Diebold (1952) and to a lesser extent by Ikenberry (1993), the document that emerged from Havana was therefore one that pleased no one. Protectionists did not want an international organization for open multilateral trade. Free traders did not want an organization with so many loopholes. While the American negotiators believed that they had beaten back demands for exceptions to the maximum extent possible, those supporting free trade (including the business community) were far more skeptical, although many finally gave lukewarm support. The absence of a strongly supportive pro-free-trade group made opponents far more effective.

Finally, the ITO charter was not available for public discussion until late in 1948. By that time, disillusionment over the United Nations had increased. The Cold War had become official and, with it, the hope that international organizations could keep the peace was substantially lessened.

6 CONCLUSIONS

Several themes in political economy are evident. Clearly, the power of ideas is important. Those ideas – at least in principle if not in well-articulated detail – were present for the IMF and the World Bank. They were not as widely accepted in the case of the ITO.

Then, too, the notion that there are 'windows of opportunity' during which new ideas of technocrats and policy-makers can be implemented without quite the normal degree of political scrutiny certainly holds in the case of the contrasting fates of the three proposed inter-organizations. In 1944, there was such a window of opportunity, as the political focus was largely on the war effort. By 1948, it was much more 'politics as usual' and the scope of reform was more limited.

Finally, bureaucratic politics do matter. That the State Department had the lead for the trade organization almost certainly meant that the window of opportunity was missed; as a corollary, it could not devote its political resources into supporting the ITO (because of commitments to the UN, the Marshall Plan and other important agenda items).

In the end, however, the question must be: who got it right? The architects of the three charters, or the American political process? In light of recent economic history, it must be concluded that the American political process was closer to the truth. The 'Bretton Woods System' served the world well for a quarter of a century despite the vagueness of some of the ideas; even after the move to floating exchange rates, the Bank and the Fund have continued to play important roles in the world economy.

Likewise, the GATT served the world well; and, by the early 1990s, the need for an international organization was evident and acted upon. Although a stronger international trade organization might have achieved more, the ITO Charter might also have been used in ways which thwarted some of the trade liberalization which did in fact take place under the GATT. Had all of the exceptions to the principles of open multilateral trade been enshrined in ratified ITO articles, that could well have retarded the process of trade liberalization in the postwar era, and hence, have dampened the very successful growth of the international economy.

NOTES

1. It is arguable whether he believed in unilateral free trade or only in reciprocal free trade. He certainly viewed the reciprocal trade agreements as a politically viable means of achieving free trade. Whether he would have advocated unilateral free trade in the absence of such agreements is more questionable. Hull was, of course, instrumental in the wording and drafting of the lend-lease agreements (1940) and the Atlantic Charter (1941). See Hull (1948).
2. There had, of course, been preparatory work and exchanges of drafts before that date
3. See, for example, Johnson (1965, pp. 36ff.) for this interpretation.
4. The proposed institutions were the International Monetary Fund (IMF), the International Bank for Reconstruction and Development (IBRD) (now a part of the World Bank group which includes the International Development Association, the International Finance Corporation and several other international economic agencies) and the International Trade Organization (ITO). For simplicity I shall refer to the IBRD as the World Bank unless the distinction between the various components of the World Bank group matters with regard to the point being made.
5. On observing debates of international economic issues such as fast-track legislation in the 1990s, however, one wonders how reasoned any such debate might have been.
6. This was the 'secular stagnation' doctrine, which held that the great investment opportunities of the 19th and early 20th centuries had been exhausted, and that there was a chronic tendency for *ex ante* savings to exceed *ex ante* investment. Perhaps the name most closely associated with this view was that of Alvin Hansen, a professor at Harvard. See Van der Wee (1983, p. 302).
7. Eichengreen and Sachs (1985) have questioned the extent to which this belief was correct.
8. Van der Wee (1986, p. 31) cites 'a vague feeling of guilt'on the part of the American elite for US isolationism in the interwar years. Isolationism (and failure to participate in the international institutions after the First World War) was regarded as a major contributor to the disasters of the 1930s and US support

for postwar plans was based partly, if not largely, on the belief that an international economic system could prevent repetition. It is difficult with hindsight to recall that the predominant view was that the postwar problem would be one of the resumption of recession/depression.

9. The Atlantic Charter, propounded in 1941, termed one objective of the war effort to be 'to bring about the fullest collaboration between all nations in the economic field' (quoted in Diebold 1952, p. 2). The lend-lease agreements between Britain and the United States. also contained provisions stipulating aspects of the postwar international economic organization.
10. Representatives of other governments had been involved in the discussions to some degree. Both the French and the Canadians submitted alternative plans. Nonetheless, the dominance of Britain and the United States meant that the negotiations between representatives of those two governments were determinate of the outcome.
11. Ikenberry (1993, pp. 164ff.) cites the emergence of a consensus in the 'community of policy experts' during these talks, and believes that there was a consensus of views. And it is certainly clear that the British and American representatives had great leeway in devising the postwar architecture. However, a reading of such documents as the Meade-Robbins (Moggridge and Howson 1990) diaries gives the flavor of considerably more disagreement between the British and the American policy-makers, and considerably more decision-making under pressure than the Ikenberry account conveys. Moggridge (1992) reports great haste in drafting, noting that Keynes was unaware of some provisions (which had been opposed by the British and were not within his terms of reference as a British representative) in the IMF Articles until after the British delegation had returned to London.
12. Keynes's initial proposal called for four functional institutions. The fourth, which never came to fruition, was an organization to oversee and stabilize prices of primary commodities through the operation of buffer stocks. The proposal for the fourth was abandoned, although the Havana Charter contained provisions for the World Trade Organization to undertake activities geared to commodity price stabilization. See Moggridge (1992, pp. 676ff).
13. These 'countries' included India as well as representatives of countries then under German rule. See James (1996, p. 48) for details.
14. Agreements with regard to trading arrangements were a part of the lend-lease agreements, providing for recovery plans to include movement toward 'the elimination of all forms of discriminatory treatment in international commerce; to the reduction of tariffs and any other trade barriers' (quoted in Diebold 1952, p. 3).
15. The atmosphere is best captured in the Meade-Robbins diaries. See Moggridge and Howson (1990). Skidelsky (1996, p. 101) describes the two negotiating sessions between the British (led by Keynes, Robbins and Meade) and Americans (led by Harry Dexter White) as being 'mixtures of extraordinary eloquence, verbal as well as intellectual, and extraordinary rudeness to and about the Americans.' After Bretton Woods, Keynes supported the Bretton Woods agreements wholeheartedly.
16. Keynes is quoted in Horsefield (1969 ch. 3, p. 13) as stating: 'It is widely held

that the control of capital movements, both inward and outward, should be a permanent feature of the post-war system — at least as far as we (that is the British) are concerned. If control is to be effective, it probably involves the machinery of control for all transactions, even though an open general license is given to all remittances in respect of current trade. But such control will be more difficult to work ... by unilateral action than if movements of capital can be controlled at both ends. It would therefore be of great advantage if the United States and all other members of the Currency Union would adopt machinery similar to that which we have now gone a long way towards perfecting in this country'. The British dropped these plans in response to American opposition.

17. See Moggridge (1992). However, the British felt that the Americans underestimated the severity of their postwar prospects.
18. Dam provides on quantification of the difference: the White Plan would, at one time along the negotiations, have cost the United States about $5 billion while the Keynes Plan would have cost the United States around $30 billion. See Dam (1982, p. 83).
19. There were many minor disagreements: for example, the United States held out for full-time resident Executive Directors, whereas Keynes strenuously opposed the idea. This, and other disagreements, are detailed in the Meade-Robbins diaries, Gardner (1956), and Moggridge (1992), among other sources.
20. Dam (1970, Ch. 1), believes that American insistence on enshrining principles in legal doctrine was a key flaw in the American proposals. He argues that this confused the role of the rule of law with substantive issues.
21. It should be recalled that Keynes was apparently schizophrenic on the question of the desirability of free trade.
22. Dam (1970, pp. 10-11, footnote 2) provides a detailed account of the published documents and meetings that took place from 1945 to 1948.
23. The United States apparently wanted the 1947 round for two reasons (aside from the belief that trade liberalization was a good thing). First and most pressing, the President's authority to reduce tariffs was to expire in 1948 before the ITO charter could be ratified. Second, the United States was supportive of the formation of closer economic integration within Europe, but wanted to see it achieved in the context of multilateral trade liberalization.
24. Otherwise, nations having cut tariffs could immediately have imposed quantitative restrictions on imports or taken other steps to maintain or even increase protection, and the tariff cuts would have been meaningless.
25. Hull resigned as Secretary of State (because of ill health) in November 1944. He was succeeded by Edward Stettinius and then Dean Acheson. Acheson was Secretary of State at the time of the Havana Conference and seems to have supported the Hull position.
26. Several United States actions led to increased opposition to the United States position abroad. On one hand, the United States negotiated a trade agreement with the Philippines in 1946 which provided for a 20 year phaseout of the Philippines' special position with regard to tariffs; the Philippines were initially to maintain duty-free entry of their exports to the United States This led to charges that the United States was inconsistent in its demands for the end to British preferences.

Second, President Truman enlarged the domain in which the escape clause could be applied. Third, just as the Geneva conference was starting, Congress passed a bill increasing the tariff on wool and setting high domestic price supports.

27. As Dam (1970, p. 16) commented in 1970, 'In one of the happiest examples of ingenuity in the history of international organization, the GATT has risen above the legalistic confines of the text of the General Agreement and has improvised numerous procedures'.
28. See Gardner (1956, pp. 6ff). for an array of quotes from influential people at the time, all of whom insisted that international *economic* organization would be essential for the postwar peace. Many blamed Hitler's rise on the economic difficulties of the earlier era, and they, in turn, were thought to have been caused in significant part by the absence of United States cooperation in the League of Nations.
29. There are two related issues that appear not to have been recognized at the time. On one hand, multiple exchange rates were permissible 'with the approval of the Fund', although a unified floating rate was not. Even as late as 1956, one-fifth of Fund members had *Fund-Approved* multiple exchange rates (see Dam 1982, p. 131). Also, the ability of a country to replicate the effects of a devaluation, at least with respect to transactions in goods and services, by appropriate tariffs and subsidies, was apparently not recognized in the anticipated division of labor between the IMF and the proposed ITO.
30. It is often forgotten how much relative economic power shifted between the late 1930s and the late 1940s. It is estimated that US GNP in 1948 was 65 percent above that of 1938, while British GNP was only 6 percent higher (Van der Wee 1983, p. 30). While part of that shift was anticipated (especially by the British), it seems clear that Americans were less acutely aware of the economic difficulties facing Britain and the rest of Europe (see Skidelsky 1996, pp. 102ff). See also the Meade-Robbins diaries for a series of entries commenting upon the differences in perception (Moggridge and Howson 1990).
31. See Gardner (1956, pp. 114). for a description of Keynes's shift to the notion of fundamental disequilibrium when the proposals for a much larger and more automatic facility were rejected by the Americans.
32. See Krueger (1997) for an analysis of these views in the context of the time.
33. Hull's biography repeatedly refers to Morgenthau's 'meddling' in State Department business (see for example, Hull 1948, pp. 207-8 and 1676).
34. White's biographer strongly suggests that White's ideas regarding the need for multilateral institutions had been formed in the 1930s, and that White's influence with Morgenthau was a key factor in enabling him to shape the American position (see Rees 1973).
35. Hull in fact retired of exhaustion under doctor's orders late in 1944.
36. There is considerable discussion of postwar planning, but almost all of it refers to the United Nations. In the only paragraphs on the new economic organizations, Hull described a bit about them very briefly. Referring in the same description to the Food and Agriculture Conference, the Relief and Rehabilitation Conference, the International Labor Conference, and the Monetary and Financial Conference (at Bretton Woods), he wrote: 'The State Department was not the leading

department in these conferences, but we of necessity had to negotiate with other nations for their organization and operation, and many officials of the Department took part in them. The conducting of these conferences was in the hands of the chiefs of other departments ... These conferences arrived at valuable decisions on food supply, on relief, on the improvement of labor standards, and on the creation of an international monetary fund and an international bank. To us at the State Department they had the additional value of serving as a barometer of the degree of cooperation we could expected from the other United Nations in the establishment of the postwar security organization' (Hull 1948, p. 1654).

37. However, that does not mean all went smoothly. Meade described the sessions in the following terms: 'What absolute Bedlam these discussions are! Keynes and White sit next to each other, each flanked by a long row of his own supporters. Without any agenda or any prepared idea of what is going to be discussed they go for each other in a strident duet of discord which after a crescendo of abuse on either side leads up to a chaotic adjournment of the meeting' (Moggridge and Howson 1990, p. 127).

REFERENCES

Dam, Kenneth W. (1970), *The GATT: Law and the International Economic Organization*, University of Chicago Press, Chicago.

Dam, Kenneth W. (1982), *The Rules of the Game*, Chicago: University of Chicago Press.

Diebold, William, Jr. (1952), 'The End of the I.T.O.', *Essays in International Finance*, No. 16. Princeton.

Eichengreen, Barry and Jeffrey Sachs (1985), 'Exchange Rates and Economic Recovery in the 1930's', *Journal of Economic History*, 65, 925-46.

Gardner, Richard N. (1969), *Sterling-Dallar Diplomacy*, 2nd edition, New York: McGraw Hill Book Company.

Horsefield, J. Keith (1969), *The International Monetary Fund 1945-1965*, Washington, DC: International Monetary Fund.

Hull, Cordell (1948), *The Memoirs of Cordell Hull*, Vols 1 and 2, New York: MacMillan.

Ikenberry, G. John (1993), 'The Political Origins of Bretton Woods', in Michael D. Bordo and Barry Eichengreen (eds), *Retrospective on the Bretton Woods System*, Chicago: University of Chicago Press.

James, Harold (1996), *International Monetary Cooperation since Bretton Woods*, New York and Oxford: International Monetary Fund and Oxford University Press.

Johnson, Harry G. (1965), *The World Economy at the Crossroads*, Oxford:

Clarendon Press.

Krueger, Anne O. (1997), 'Trade Policy and Economic Development: How We Learn', *American Economic Review*, March, 1-22.

Moggridge, D. (1992), *Maynard Keynes. An Economist's Biography*, London and New York: Routledge.

Moggridge, D. and S. Howson (eds) (1990), *The Wartime Diaries of Lionel Robbins and James Meade 1943- 1945*, St. Martin's Press, New York.

Rees, David (1973), *Harry Dexter White,* New York: Coward, McCann & Geohegan.

Skidelsky, Robert (1996), *Keynes,* Oxford and New York: Oxford University Press.

Van der Wee, Herman (1986), *Prosperity and Upheaval: The World Economy l945-80*, Berkeley: University of California Press.

13. Democracy, Conflict and Development – Three Cases

Frances Stewart and Meghan O'Sullivan*

1 INTRODUCTION

What Samuel Huntington has called 'the third wave of democracy' (see Huntington 1991) – the spread of democracy in southern Europe in the late 1970s, to Latin America in the 1980s, and parts of Asia, Africa, Eastern Europe and the former Soviet Union in the late 1980s and early 1990s – carried with it a tide of optimism. The sudden espousal of democracy by so many disparate countries was proclaimed to provide a foundation for the resolution of both domestic and international problems, to mutual advantage. Even when difficulties along the road of democratic transition became apparent (Carothers 1992) the notion of 'democratic deliverance' was not abandoned, as Clinton placed 'democratic enlargement' at the centre of his foreign policy agenda (Brinkley 1977).

The promotion of democracy is seen as desirable by Western governments not only given the widely touted belief that democracies do not go to war with one another, but also due to the perception that democracies make better partners in trade and diplomacy. While there is great debate about whether a proliferation of democratic states would actually usher in a more peaceful international order, is there any basis to assume that democracy will bring *domestic* peace and stability to those countries who embrace it? Are democracies really less likely to suffer internal strife? Given the proliferation of conflicts *within* states today, this is a critical question for those concerned with human suffering and social and economic development.

Civil conflict is not only immediately damaging to the people directly involved, but also involves large development costs, as noted by John Fei: 'We must realize that, under conditions of social unrest, political upheaval

* We are grateful to Richard Sandbrook, participants at the Taipei meeting and an anonymous referee for helpful comments on a previous draft.

and wars, economic modernization is impossible' (Fei 1997, p. 510). Over recent decades, the presence of civil conflict appears to be one of the major causes of underdevelopment: six of the worst ten performers in the world, judged by the Human development index (HDI) or GNP per capita, are countries which currently have, or have recently had, severe civil wars. An investigation into the countries worst affected by conflict in the 1970s and 1980s showed the heavy economic and social costs that typically arise, and therefore the importance, from a development perspective, of controlling conflict (Stewart et al. 1997).

This chapter explores the connections between democracy, conflict and development by examining the experience of three countries: Kenya, Uganda and Sri Lanka. This is a small sample, and not one chosen for its especial representativeness. So the lessons must be suggestive rather than conclusive. But the stories of the three countries do appear to challenge some accepted views. Even a rapid overview of their stories suggests a more complex relationship than the simple equation of democracy with peace and development:

1. Uganda has had episodes of democracy, dictatorship and near anarchy, involving very widespread conflict leading to huge numbers of deaths with greatly damaging effects on development.
2. Kenya has not had sustained democracy in any real shape at the national level, but has had a certain amount of local democracy and has mostly maintained development.
3. Sri Lanka has had democratic institutions, but also longstanding conflict. Nevertheless, economic development has broadly been sustained.

The following matrix shows the combinations of democracy, conflict and development in the three countries.

Country	Democracy	Conflict	Development
Uganda	occasional	+	– (mainly)
Kenya	very limited	–	+ (mainly)
Sri Lanka	+	+	+

A quick look at the matrix (which is a vast oversimplification of complex and changing events) shows that no simple generalizations are possible. By exploring the story of these three countries in more depth we hope to arrive at some conclusions about the nature of the interactions between democracy, conflict and development, which will permit a critique of the simplistic view currently being purveyed by the international community.

While our prime concern is the relationship between democracy and conflict, we shall also consider how these cases illuminate the connection between economic development and conflict, since development, like democracy, has been heralded as a 'cure' for conflict (Nafziger 1996).

The chapter is organized as follows: Section 2 explores the cases of Kenya and Uganda; it shows that democracy does not appear to be effective in avoiding conflict, and indeed may encourage it, but suggests that, perhaps, this is due to the *form* of democracy, rather than democracy as such. This is the view of political scientists such as Lijhart and Horowitz, presented in Section 3. They argue that if democratic structures are designed appropriately, they will encourage ethnic accommodation. Their hypothesis is explored in the case of Sri Lanka in Section 4, where democratic institutions appear to have been structured to encourage such accommodation. Yet, this too, appears to be over-optimistic. Indeed, even apparently well-designed institutional crafting may encourage conflict. The final section comes to some conclusions about appropriate political and economic policies in conflict-prone societies, in the light of the earlier analysis.

2 THE CASES OF KENYA AND UGANDA[1]

Kenya and Uganda both acquired political independence from the British in the 1960s (Uganda in 1962 and Kenya in 1964). At a superficial level, they appeared similar at that time, for example, with respect to the economy, social indicators and multi-ethnic composition. Both started the independence era with democratic structures of government. However, in the years since then, Uganda has had among the worst records of recurrent mass violence on the continent, involving the deaths of more than one million people, while in Kenya, violence has been episodic and relatively minor. The heavy economic and social cost of the violence in Uganda underlines the importance of avoiding civil conflict not only for the immediate human suffering it causes, but also for the achievement of development objectives.

Both countries had been subject to British colonial rule from the late 19th century and together, along with Tanzania, formed the East Africa Protectorate. They had similar-sized populations composed of a number of major ethnic groups around which local administrative boundaries had been drawn. Kenya had 30 recognized ethnic groups, nine of which each constituted more than 1 percent of the population, with the centrally located Kikuyu accounting for about a fifth of the population; Uganda had 15 large ethnic groups, with the Baganda, also centrally located, forming about 30 percent of the population (Table 13.1). While aggregate per capita incomes were higher in Kenya in 1960, African incomes were very similar as were such indicators as life expectancy, adult literacy and access to safe water.[2]

In both countries, the constitutions adopted at independence embodied democratic multiparty institutions. In each, there were many factors making it unlikely that such institutions would be maintained, including the past (non-democratic) colonial experience, economic inequalities, low levels of education, and ethnic divisions. In practice, both countries abandoned elements of their democratic structures soon after independence. In each, aspects of democracy have been restored periodically, typically following international pressure. But the 'democratic' periods have not succeeded in promoting peaceful development, but rather have been accompanied by rising tensions, leading to violence.

The countries present strong contrasts in terms of political stability and conflict over the period since independence. Uganda has been much less stable politically and has experienced conflict on a massively greater

Table 13.1 Size and location of largest ethnic groups in Kenya and Uganda

Kenya			Uganda		
Ethnic group	Share of pop.1989 %	Province-location	Ethnic group	Share of African pop. 1969 %	Regional location
Kikuyu	20.8	Central	Baganda	28.2	Southern
Luyha	14.4	Western	Banyanko	12.2	Western
Luo	12.4	Nyanza	Basogo	10.0	Eastern
Kalenjin	11.5	Rift Valley	Batoro	6.1	Western
Kamba	11.4	Eastern-south	Nubians	6.1	Northern, West Nile
Kisii	6.2	Nyanza	Bakedi	5.6	Eastern
Meru	5.1	Eastern	Langi	5.3	Northern
Masai	1.8	Rift Valley, South	Acholi	4.9	Northern
Embu	1.2	Eastern-central	Bagisu	4.5	Eastern

Sources: Republic of Uganda, MFEP (1966); Republic of Kenya, *Population Census 1989*; Encyclopedia of World Culture, Vol. IX.

scale (Table 13.2). The country is now under its seventh national leader since independence, whereas Kenya has had only two presidents, the second having been deputy of the first. The comparative history of the two countries sheds considerable light on the role democratic structures can play in countries which are potentially divided and subject to conflict, and how this in turn impacts upon development.

2.1 Uganda

Each of the four distinct periods of Ugandan post-independence political history has been marked by political violence, with much the worst episodes during the Amin period and the second Obote regime.

Uganda's post-independence history cannot be understood separately from its Colonial past – in particular the special position given to the Baganda by the British. The 1900 Agreement with Buganda, establishing the British protectorate, gave the Baganda a special role. A colonial law of 1908 awarded land to the Kabaka (King of Buganda), his family and major chiefs. In the system of 'indirect rule', the British appointed Baganda to administer much of the country outside Buganda, and Buganda was allocated land taken from neighboring territory.[3] Cash crops were encouraged in the south generally (including Buganda) and education was promoted. Westerners and northerners, lacking economic opportunities in their own territories, came to Buganda as low-paid labourers.

At the same time, there was a deliberate policy of ethnic imbalance in the army, which was recruited almost entirely from the people from the North and the East. In every other respect Buganda, located in the south of the country, had a privileged role. This, together with the attitudes of the Baganda to the rest of Uganda and of others to them, which had antecedents in the pre-colonial era but was much strengthened by colonial policies, left a deep faultline in the centre of the Ugandan polity, with northern domination of the army accentuating potential dangers to political stability.

The Independence constitution in Uganda was quite peculiar: Buganda alone was given some autonomy in a federal relationship with the centre and the Kabaka was made President of the whole country; other areas had much less autonomy. This was an early example of an institutional innovation intended to solve one political problem, but creating others. The intention was to persuade the Baganda to join independent Uganda. But in practice such a constitution could scarcely be expected to endure as non-Baganda were unlikely to find the solution acceptable, while the illogicality of the constitution appeared to justify an absence of respect for it.

Table 13.2 Violence in Kenya and Uganda, estimated deaths

	Kenya		Homicide and deaths in custody p.a	Uganda		Homicide
1950s	Mau Mau	15,000	n.a	—	—	n.a.
1960s	Shifta	3,000	n.a.	Riots after referendum on lost counties. Narulabye Massacre. Battle of Mengo	2,500	n.a.
1970s	—	—	920[1]	Amin Terror, 1971-79 esp. against Acholi and Langi	300,000	n.a.
1980s	—	—	1,410[2]	1979 attack on West Nile 1984-85: massacre of Buganda in Luwero Triangle	300,000 +	n.a.
1990s	Ethnic Clashes, Rift Valley (94/5) Mob Violence	1,500 192	2,000[3]	1986-96 rebellions in North and West	10,000+	1,720[4]
Total (est)		19,692	1,780		606,500	1,720 (annual)

Notes

1. Based on two years
2. Based on one year.
3. Est includes 819 deaths in custody, 1994-95.
4. 1991-94 average.

Source: Kenya Human Rights Commission (1995); *Africa Watch* (1993); Sivard (1992); Govt of Kenya *Statistical Abstract* (1981, 1985); Uganda Country Paper.

Obote I regime: 1962-1971

The ethnic composition of the country meant that no one tribe could achieve a majority, and some coalition among tribal groups was essential for a party or person to gain power in a democratic system.

Political parties at independence followed a combination of religious and ethnic divisions; for example, the Democratic Party (DP) was formed in 1954 by the Baganda to represent Catholics; the Kabaka Yekka (YK – King Alone) was formed by the elite Protestant Baganda to improve the position of the Kabaka; and the Uganda People's Congress (UPC), led by Milton Obote, had Protestant backing, and was essentially an anti-Baganda party.

Milton Obote, himself an Acholi from the north, came to power following an election, through an unlikely alliance between the UPC and the KY, parties which had previously been strongly opposed to each other. As soon as he could manage without the support of the Baganda, Obote initiated policies which alienated them. In 1966, he suspended the constitution, displacing the Kabaka and assuming the presidency himself, denying Buganda its federal status. Government troops attacked the Kabaka's palace, killing an estimated 2000. Obote became increasingly authoritarian, alienating many groups by abuses of human rights and promotion of his own people, while relying on the military for support. A state of emergency was extended throughout the country. In 1969, Obote proscribed political parties, and proposed that the presidency should be his for life. Political and religious leaders were arrested.

The Amin faction in the army carried out a coup while Obote was abroad in January 1971.

The Amin regime: 1971-1979

Initially the Amin coup gained wide support from the many groups who had been alienated by Obote.[4] But slaughter of civilians and members of the armed forces soon began. Idi. Amin used the occasion of abortive coups to attempt to eliminate Acholis and Langis from the army, with massive killings. Expulsion of groups of foreign nationals followed, first, Israelis, then the 50,000 Asians, who together owned and controlled perhaps half of the country's wealth. Their assets were given to Amin followers, chiefly from his own tribe.

A 1973 decree empowered the Military Police to arrest people without a court order or an arrest warrant (Bwengye 1985). The army was brought directly under Amin's control and a Defence Council was created, encroaching on the duties of the Cabinet. Violence and murders became institutionalized. Disappearances of people and summary executions were common. Many prominent people were killed, including the Chief Justice.

The independence of the judiciary and the rule of law had been destroyed. Many Ugandans fled to other countries, particularly the well-educated middle class.

The regime was brought to an end in 1978, when Amin invaded north-western Tanzania, and the Tanzanian People's Defence Forces together with Ugandan opposition groups attacked central and western Uganda, defeating Amin's army.

The Era of the Uganda National Liberation Front (UNLF): 1979-1980

From 1979-80, three administrations held office as rival groups jockeyed for power. During the confusion, Acholi and Langi soldiers in the Uganda National Liberation Army proceeded to revenge the massacres of Amin, with indiscriminate killings in West Nile, Amin's home area. According to the United National High Commissioner for Refugees (UNHCR), over a quarter of a million refugees from West Nile fled to neighbouring countries (Karugire 1980).

In 1980 a general election, supervised by a group of Commonwealth observers, was contested by the traditional political parties, as well as a new party, the Uganda Patriotic Movement (UPM), led by Yoweri Museveni. Although Obote was declared the winner by the Military Commission, a result endorsed by Commonwealth observers, the results of the election had clearly been rigged (Mudoola, 1988).[5] In the face of election fraud, the National Resistance Army (NRA), led by Museveni, along with some other opposition groups, launched an armed struggle against the new government

Obote II Regime: 1980-1985

Obote's second period of leadership was marked by continual, mounting and at times horrific violence by the regime in its attempt to suppress the Museveni uprising. The Baganda were especially victimized. Conservative estimates are that about 300,000 people may have been killed during these years and another 500,000 displaced in Buganda alone (Mutibwa 1992). Many commentators suggest that the extent of human rights abuse under Obote II exceeded that in the Amin years.

In January 1986, the NRA captured Kampala and Museveni became President by decree.

Museveni regime: 1986 onwards

The government appointed by Museveni was broad based politically and ethnically, although it has been accused of giving Ankole disproportionate jobs and influence. Prominent members of the various political parties and the different regions and religions in the country gained positions in the administration, the balance favoring the western and central regions. Despite declared democratic intentions, elections were delayed, and the role of traditional political parties was severely circumscribed. A presidential election – *without political parties* – was finally held in March 1996, resulting in an easy victory for Museveni.

The regime aimed to incorporate all the various military forces into a single national army, with a balanced ethnic composition (Mudoola 1988), including not only the various forces that had fought against Obote, but also soldiers from Obote's army and later Amin supporters from West Nile.[6]

The Museveni regime has faced chronic violent opposition, especially in the north and west. In both these areas, the persistent violence is intertwined with the situation in neighboring countries; in the north, the Sudanese helped the rebels, while the Uganda government supported the opposition forces in Sudan. In the west, Ugandan government forces assisted the Zairean rebels and the Mobutu government supported the anti-Museveni forces. But violence has persisted after the defeat of Mobutu.

2.2 Kenya

The Kikuyu in Kenya parallel the Baganda in Uganda, in being the largest tribe, located centrally and privileged economically. But during the colonial era, far from being favored by the British, they were the group that lost their land to the settlers. This eventually led to the Mau Mau rebellion. This rebellion gave Jomo Kenyatta, a Kikuyu leader detained by the British, the status of national leader with support throughout the colony. This coming together against the British reduced the force of divisions within Kenya initially, in contrast to the situation in Uganda.

Kenya's post-independence history is not stained by the mass violence that has marked Uganda. Yet there have been episodes of conflict in Kenya since the 1950s, as indicated in Table 13.2. The major violent movements include the Shifta Wars and ethnic clashes in the Rift Valley and Western Province and more recently around Mombasa, as well as growing criminality.

There was a steady centralization of power in the Office of the President during the Kenyatta era. The Preservation of Public Security Act permitted detention without trial. A one party system became the rule *de facto* as the Kenya People's Union was banned and its leader, Oginga Odinga, detained. The regime was also allegedly involved in political assassinations of potential rivals to Kenyatta. A diverse array of patronage rewards especially favored the Kikuyu. The Kenyatta period saw the growth of Kikuyu dominance over economic as well as political realms, and Central Province prospered. Contemporary reports in the media refer to a belief among 'peripheral' groups that the process of Kenyanization was really one of 'Kikuyuization'.

Nonetheless, taken as a whole the system of state patronage incorporated the leaders of virtually all ethnic groups apart from the Luo (Throup 1996). Moreover, electoral competition at the local level appeared vibrant with regular elections to the National Assembly. Critics of the Kenyatta regime (such as the Law Society and the churches) were allowed to express their opinions, and parliamentary critics were often elected. 'Political life remained remarkably open and its press comparatively free by African standards' (ibid., ch. 2). Provided that they remained within the party (which did not entail any strict ideological constraints) and did not criticize the President, there was considerable freedom for individual politicians. The regime managed to be responsive to popular demands despite the restrictions on democracy, while the regular (semi-competitive) elections helped diffuse potential conflict.

During the Kenyatta regime, the only systematic organized violence was the 'Shifta' War, when the people of the north, who had voted in a referendum in the early 1960s to secede and join Somalia, took up arms against the state. The government relied on punitive and repressive measures which provided extraordinary powers to the authorities to enter homes, search them, seize property and detain, and, in certain proscribed areas, shoot people on sight, destroy any building and seize or destroy livestock. The original unity among the secessionists, however, gradually broke down (Sora 1995, p. 6). A peace agreement was reached in 1968.

On the death of the first President, his deputy, Daniel arap Moi, took control. Coming from the 'periphery' (Tugen/Kalenjin), he faced fierce resistance from most of the Kikuyu establishment who perceived their privileged position to be under threat. The early Moi years were characterized by populist measures that sought to appeal to the poorer elements in Kenyan society, bypassing established patrons and undermining the potential bases for political competitors. Moi sought to broaden the base of development in Kenya and benefit his allies in the Rift Valley, Western and Coast Provinces.

The prominence of Kikuyu in government and the civil service was gradually reduced. Most of the Kikuyu elite, nonetheless, managed to adapt to the new order with a continued presence in both business and parliamentary arenas. However, after an unsuccessful coup attempt in 1982 by the (Kikuyu-dominated) air force, supported by university students, the Kikuyu were systematically excluded from positions of influence within the government (Nelson 1986) and the regime became increasingly repressive. A constitutional amendment made the state formally a one-party regime. Kalenjin and Luyha interests were promoted within the ruling party (KANU), and party membership became a virtual pre-requisite for civil service advancement, access to loans and so on (Throup 1996, ch. 3). Resort to detentions without trial and repression of union and other potential opposition continued (see Holmquist et al. 1994). The press began to exercise greater self-censorship in response. Electoral rigging escalated and a system of queue voting (replacing secret ballot), introduced in 1986, facilitated voter intimidation.

In the early 1990s, international pressures for political liberalization grew, culminating in the suspension of aid in 1991. In response, President Moi acceded to multi-party elections and controls over the media were relaxed. Three main parties and five much smaller ones emerged to oppose KANU, but were unable to unite effectively. During the presidential campaign, Moi relied on the security forces for surveillance and disruption of the opposition. Most notoriously, his political tactics extended to direct sponsorship of ethnic clashes in the Rift Valley (*Africa Watch*, 'State Sponsored Ethnic Conflict in Kenya', 1993). Fifteen hundred deaths occurred, and at least 300,000 were displaced. Homes and granaries were burnt, crops destroyed just prior to harvest, property was looted and livestock stolen. The primary aggressors were male youth, known as 'Kalenjin warriors'. The government portrayed the clashes as a fulfillment of the forecast repercussions of a multiparty system. Several detailed studies,[7] however, concluded that the regime was closely implicated in the clashes. Senior government figures were alleged to have promoted violence through sponsorship of private armies and inflammatory public statements. The domestic security apparatus failed to control the violence, or arrest the perpetrators. Although the clashes had a clear anti-Kikuyu dimension, it should be noted that the violence was focussed against the smallholder Kikuyu, while large farmers were left relatively unscathed. Violent incidents on a small scale continued. Insecurity prevails among the displaced, many of whom did not return to their former homes.

The clashes served the regime both in creating a sense of insecurity so that voters would prefer the certainty associated with the status quo and in changing the ethnic balance in the Rift Valley – a crucial area in electoral terms accounting for 44 of the 183 seats.

Although the outcome of the election did not provide a majority endorsement of the President, with 36.5 percent of the vote, Moi obtained the largest share in the face of the divided opposition.

Unrest occurred again in 1997, this time centered around Mombasa, as new elections (due in early 1998) were anticipated; there have also been violent clashes between the government and opposition in Nairobi; again it is believed that these were been provoked by the regime.

There have been other violent occurrences during the Moi period. Reports of the Kenya Human Rights Commission and Africa Watch suggest that significant episodes of violence in the larger urban areas are not uncommon. Attacks on government agents are frequent in the northeast. Unsupervised private armies have emerged in Northeastern Province with an effective abdication of power by the government (Umar 1995, p. 68). But the scale of violence over the Moi period has been small compared with that found in Uganda.

2.3 Democracy, Violence and Development in Uganda and Kenya

Neither country has sustained democratic institutions. Uganda has had episodes of 'democracy', followed by violence and sharply reduced democratic and human rights. Kenya has been a one-party regime for most of the time, with human rights also curtailed, but not so severely as Uganda, and with violent episodes preceding national elections. The history of the two countries suggests that, if anything, democratic institutions have led to violence rather than preventing it.

The Obote I period started democratically; however, once in power, Obote progressively suspended democratic institutions, using the army to sustain power. Amin completed and extended the process of eliminating democratic processes and human rights, undermining the legal system. Obote II might appear to constitute a 'democratic' era. It was ushered in by a multiparty election approved by international observers, while the regime soon received the support of Western countries and the International Financial Institutions (IFIs). Yet the 1980 election was clearly fraudulent, and human rights abuse was enormous. It was the misuse of democratic institutions which led to the NRA revolt, the horrific violence that ensued in Obote's attempts to suppress it, and eventually the fall of the regime.

The Museveni regime was not democratic at all for a decade. Presidential elections, without political parties, followed after ten years. The government, however, appears broadly to have been an inclusive one, incorporating people from all over the country and all political parties in political positions and economic benefits, and not seeking revenge. There has been a gradual restoration of the institutions of civil society including the legal and educational systems.

Kenya rarely fulfilled international demands for multiparty democracy, effectively having a one-party system for most of the period. When multiparty democracy occurred it was the occasion of rising violence, with the clashes in the Rift valley in the early 1990s and around Mombasa in 1997. Yet the one-party system in Kenya incorporated a number of ethnic groups: under Kenyatta most were involved in government other than the Luo; under Moi, the powerful Kikuyu have been largely disenfranchised. But because most other groups were included, it was difficult for the excluded to mount a serious challenge to the government. Moreover, successful economic and social performance diminished popular support for opposition, particularly violent opposition. The existence of some limited political freedom may also have helped diffuse opposition.

The economic and social record of the two countries suggests that economic stagnation is the outcome rather than the cause of conflict. There was fairly widespread improvement in economic and social indicators during the first Obote regime, with progress in per capita income, infant mortality rates, school enrollment, adult literacy and access to health services (Tables 13.3 and 13.4) and a rapid rate of growth

Table 13.3 Economic performance in Kenya and Uganda

		GDP, growth, (% p.a.)	GDP, per capital growth (% p.a.)	private consumption growth, (%p.a.)	Inflation, (% p.a.)	Invest-ment GDP (%)
1960s	Uganda	6.0[1]	2.3[1]	5.6	2.4[1]	1965
						11
	Kenya	6.2[2]	2.8[2]	2.9	2.7[2]	14
1970s	Uganda	−1.2	−4.1	−4.0	47.4[4]	1980
						6
	Kenya	4.4[3]	5.9[4]	5.9	10.1[4]	25
1980s	Uganda	3.1	0.2	3.2[5]	92.7	1987
						12
	Kenya	4.2	0.5	4.7[5]	11.8	25
1990-94	Uganda	5.6	2.7		22.7	1994
						14
	Kenya	0.9	−2.5		30.8	21

Notes:
1. 1962-71.
2. 1964-72.
3. 1972-81.
4. 1970-82.
5. 1980-93.

Sources: World Bank, *World Development Reports* (various).

Table 13.4 Social developments in Kenya and Uganda, 1962-97

	Calories per person		Calories (% required)		Prmary school enrollment (%)		Seconday school enrollment (%)		Population per doctor		Population with access to safe water		Adult literacy (%)		Infant mortality rate (per 1,000 live birth)	
	Ug.	Ken.	Ug.	Ken.	Ug.	Ken.	Ug.	Ken.	Ug.	Ken.	Ug.	Ken.	Ug.	Ken.	Ug.	Ken.
1960	2383[5]	2289[5]	na	na	49	47	3	2	15050	10690	na	na	25	20	133	112
1970	2096[6]	2117[6]	90	91	54[6]	58	4	9	9210	8000	35[10]	17[10]	44	32	117	102
1980	1778[7]	2056	80	88	50	110	5	19	26810	7890	161	28	43[11]	47	113	83
1990 or near	2180[1]	2075[8]	93[1]	89[4]	67[2]	95[8]	11[2]	29[8]	21681[3]	10130	34[9]	53[9]	54[2]	69	114[4]	61[4]

Notes:

1. 1988-90.
2. 1991.
3. 1989-90
4. 1993.
5. 1965.
6. 1974.
7. 1981.
8. 1992.
9. 1990-95.
10. 1975.
11. 1985.
12. 1983.

Sources: UNDP (1996); World Bank (1996a;1989); *World Development Reports* (various); UNDP, *Human Development Reports* (various).

of GDP (of 6.0 percent per annum). In contrast, the Amin terrorism saw regress in economic and social indicators; GDP fell by 1.2 percent per annum, tax revenue and government expenditure collapsed, while military expenditure rose sharply. Social expenditure fell from 4.5 percent of GDP in 1972 to 0.5 percent 1981. Social indicators worsened. In the early years of Obote II there was some economic and social recovery, as resources flowed in from the international community and the tax base expanded. However, the severe war from 1984 disrupted this recovery.

The Museveni years have been ones of considerable and sustained economic recovery in both economic and social terms. IFI support was soon forthcoming, and the government adopted orthodox programmes, quite generously financed, without demur. Uganda indeed is seen as a model performer by the IFIs. Economic growth from 1990-94 was 5.6 percent per annum. This improvement occurred during a nondemocratic era, despite continuation of localized episodes of violence.

Kenya succeeded in maintaining economic growth and expanding social services for most of the post-independence era (Tables 13.3 and 13.4). In the 1960s the experience was similar to Uganda, with growth of over 6.0 percent per annum. Growth was maintained at 4 percent per annum in the subsequent two decades, far better than Uganda in the Amin era, and also during Obote II. However, Uganda has outperformed Kenya during the Museveni period, especially in the 1990s when Kenya's economic performance deteriorated markedly. Kenya's investment rate has been persistently and substantially higher than in Uganda, reaching 25 percent in the 1970s and 1980s.

In comparison with Uganda, Kenya continued to sustain a much higher share of revenue in GDP and social expenditure as a proportion of total government expenditure. Consequently, even in the 1990s, social expenditure as a proportion of GDP was more than three times as great in Kenya as Uganda (Table 13.5). As a consequence, Kenya has outpaced Uganda on all indicators of social performance. By 1990, Kenya's primary school enrollment rate was 95 percent while Uganda's was 67 percent; infant mortality in Kenya was 61 per 1000 compared with 114 in Uganda. It is clear from a comparison decade by decade (Table 13.4) that again it was during the worst periods of political instability in Uganda that the two countries diverged sharply.

Both countries have shown marked divergencies in access to services, employment and incomes across regions. The northern region of Uganda has been historically deprived and the central region privileged. Like Uganda, Kenya shows quite sharp regional differences in economic and social performance. In fact the coefficient of variation of various dimensions of performance – a summary measure of regional disparities –

Table 13.5 Government expenditure and revenue, Uganda and Kenya

	Govt. revenue (% GDP)		Govt. exp. (% GDP)		Defence (% govt. exp.)		Social exp. (% govt. exp.)		Social exp. (% GDP)	
	Ug	Ken	Ug	Ken	Ug	Ken	Ug	Ken	Ug	Ken
1972	13.7	18.0	21.8	21.0	23.1	6.0	20.6	29.8	4.5	6.3
1981	0.7	23.5	3.2	28.4	34.5	10.7	14.9	28.4	0.5	8.1
1990	7.4	22.4	14.6	28.1	26.9	10.0	16.7	25.3	2.2	7.1
1994	8.2	23.5	18.4	29.9	(87-92)	6.2	(87-92)	24.2	(87-92)	7.2

Source: World Bank, World Development Reports (various); World Bank, World Development Indicators Data Set.

is typically as great, and sometimes greater, in Kenya than in Uganda. One might have expected, therefore, that such economic differences would have given rise to similar ethnic and political tensions. But there are some economic reasons why they did not. The most important one is that the general advance in social and economic indicators was widely shared (including by the most deprived regions). In contrast, with economic regress in Uganda, differentials became even more resented. Moreover, the pattern of development in Kenya created sharper *vertical* inequalities (that is, between economic classes within ethnic groups) which tended to offset the political effect of *horizontal* (that is, regional or ethnic) inequalities. The vertical inequalities created divisions within regional and ethnic groups, since the richer elements were gaining from the system and had much to lose from violence of any significant magnitude. In addition, over time the horizontal inequalities showed some diminution.

Economic factors help explain why the Kikuyu have tolerated their loss of political power under Moi. The Kikuyu have continued to maintain economic advantages, with many large Kikuyu businessmen and farmers prospering. Potentially such people have a great deal to lose from serious political conflict. Central Province, where the Kikuyu are concentrated, has by far the largest share of formal employment opportunities. Although their previous advantage in terms of per capita income has been eroded, the province has the lowest rate of infant mortality and the highest adult literacy. Relatively high economic integration in Kenya compared with Uganda, and a much larger private sector, mean, first, that more people have more to lose from violence; and second, that economic opportunities are not completely dominated by the state so that political control is of less overwhelming importance for generating economic opportunities.

2.4 Conclusions from the Kenya/Uganda comparison

The history of these years illustrates the complexity of the relationships between democracy, freedom from conflict and development. It is apparent, in the context of countries with many deep divisions, low incomes and low levels of education, that the introduction of democratic institutions does not guarantee their continued existence, or avoid conflict. Indeed, the reverse may be the case. Political parties tend to accentuate ethnic divisions to gain support, while government forces may incite violence in order to strengthen their position and avoid democratic challenges.

The violence does not obviously appear to have been the result of failed development, as such, since the worst episodes in Uganda followed economic progress (from 1962-70, and 1980-83) not regress. Relative, rather than absolute, deprivation appears to predispose to violence, especially in the context of economic stagnation. Most of the localized violence in both countries does seem to be associated with relative deprivation.

Where there are strong economic differences which are combined with ethnic ones, political parties may represent and use these differences in a way that can provoke violence, and if this spreads it can destroy development. In such societies widely shared economic and social development may be a necessary *precondition* for a democratic and peaceful society rather than the other way round. Inclusive government is what is needed in order to create 'cultural nationalism', as emphasized by John Fei, an essential initial stage in development which he recognized (see Fei 1997). This is very difficult to attain. The examples of Kenya and Uganda over these years suggest that imposing democracy from outside is not an effective mechanism. Outsiders may play a more effective role in monitoring gross abuses of power, and promoting shared development through aid and policy conditionality.

3 DOES THE STRUCTURE OF DEMOCRATIC INSTITUTIONS INFLUENCE DEMOCRACY'S ABILITY TO CONTAIN CONFLICT?

The experiences of Uganda and Kenya seem to indicate that democracy has little conflict-solving potential. But before discarding democracy unceremoniously as a method of solving conflicts, it is necessary to undertake a more sophisticated evaluation of democracy's impact on conflict, differentiating between forms of democracy. Such an appraisal must recognise that certain democratic systems can actually cultivate conflict. For example, an ethnocracy – where one ethnic group dominates the institutions of government and the resources distributed by the state – can fuel ethnic tensions by promoting one group at the expense of the other or persecuting smaller groups having no access to power. Where one ethnic group comprises a majority of the population, an ethnocracy can be the result of democratic elections, as has been the case in Sri Lanka in the past. Clearly, to be democratic – in the conventional sense of competitive elections, limited government power, and public expressions of preference – is not enough to mitigate conflict. For that, what is required is not simply a democratic system in the strict sense of the word, but a system that incorporates all groups or individuals in such a way that they benefit from it and therefore have a stake in its perpetuation and respect the institutions of mediation offered by it.

This realization has underpinned a substantial body of conflict management literature which is devoted to 'political engineering' or, in other words, to exploring how institutional structures can reduce conflict. For example, Lijhart, one of the best-known scholars in this field, advocates a political structure based on elite cooperation. His prescriptions for group accommodation dictate a 'grand coalition of elites' from all groups, a mutual veto in decision-making for the representative of each group, group proportionality in the allocation of certain offices and opportunities, and some sort of federal structure allowing for a measure of group autonomy (Lijhart 1977, 1968). Calling such an institutional arrangement 'consociationalism', he promotes it as holding the best prospects for peaceful governance in all divided societies (Lijhart 1969, 1977, 1983), despite the fact that his formulations arose out of an examination of Western states, the Netherlands in particular.

Other scholars advocate a variety of innovative institutional forms as being those most likely to guarantee that each group, and each individual as part of a group, feels incorporated into the system (see Lapidoth 1992; Esman 1973; Coakley 1994). One of the approaches felt to hold the most promise for controlling conflict is the sophisticated institutional engineering best exemplified by the work of Donald Horowitz.[8] His work has focused on conflict-ridden countries and the effects that their various institutional arrangements have had on ethnic accommodation. Conscious of how different economic situations, distributions of ethnic groups, geographies, and social histories shape the ability of institutions to promote ethnic accommodation, Horowitz has provided examples of situations where institutions did contribute to ethnic accommodation and where they encouraged polarization and conflict. (Horowitz 1971, 1985, 1991). While his desire to include all the relevant variables in his analysis necessarily precludes any simple 'across-the-board' policy recommendations, he argues that it is possible to prescribe institutions that stand the greatest chance of promoting accommodation by taking into account the environment in which they operate.

For Horowitz, the purpose of institutional engineering is to structure the institutions of a divided society in a way which provides incentives for cooperation across the relevant cleavages, whether they be racial, ethnic, or linguistic; the ideal institutions in a given society are those which make it the self-interest of political actors to pursue policies of accommodation. While he does not advocate the same set of institutions for all countries in conflict, the ultimate *goal* of his institutional engineering in ethnically divided societies is the same: to induce the formation of *multi-ethnic coalitions of commitment*. A coalition of 'commitment' differs from one of 'convenience' as it requires an electoral pact between parties representing different ethnic groups before elections.[9] Such an agreement precludes either party from campaigning on a platform of ethnic chauvinism and requires at least a modicum of consensus on what measures to be adopted. In contrast, multi-ethnic coalitions of convenience are formed *after* elections, often between parties with conflicting platforms, out of desperation to achieve parliamentary majorities. Often these coalitions, having no common vision, result in competition, conspiracy and chaos, leading to further conflict in themselves. A classic example of this is the coalition of convenience formed by Obote after the 1962 election in Uganda, between an anti-Baganda party (UPC) and the royalist Baganda party (KY).

According to Horowitz, the manipulation of institutions – particularly the electoral system and devolution – can create the conditions most conducive to the formation of these multi-ethnic coalitions of commitment. He argues that once group fragmentation, party proliferation, intra-group conflict, regional competition, and incentives for inter-ethnic bargaining characterize the political landscape – all encouraged through the carefully prescribed use of institutions – the ground is fertile for the formation of multi-ethnic coalitions of commitment. While Horowitz is well aware of the potential for disappointment, the failures he considers, such as that of Northern Ireland in the 1970s,[10] do not lead him to question the ability of multi-ethnic coalitions of commitment to foster ethnic accommodation, but rather allow him to focus on the difficulties in evoking them.

4 THE CASE OF SRI LANKA

Sri Lanka, in the decades following independence, often captured the praise of the development community as a society meeting the basic needs of its population despite its low income per capita. More recently, international attention on Sri Lanka has focussed not on its achievements, but on its intractable and brutal civil war between the majority Sinhalese and the minority Tamils. Post-independence shifts in the political leadership of the Sinhalese elite from a secular, liberal attitude toward a more chauvinistic, nationalistic one led to changes favoring the Sinhalese in linguistic, economic and political spheres. The consequent alienation of the Tamils grew, until in 1976, the main political representative of the Tamil population began advocating a separate state in the Northern and Eastern Provinces. Rising militancy of the Tamil movement, Sinhalese insecurities and unsatisfactory progress in devolution discussions have contributed to the more or less sustained violence between the two communities during the past 14 years.

Examining Sri Lanka's experience contradicts the usual hypotheses concerning democracy, conflict and development. First, it is important to note that hostilities between communities developed during the decades after independence in the context of a vibrant parliamentary democracy. Moreover, these burgeoned into violence within a democratic context and, although at times the conflict has jeopardized Sri Lanka's institutions of liberal democracy, democratic structures have never been suspended nationwide. Therefore, even the bare outline of Sri Lanka's history discredits the notion that democracy necessarily abates conflict. Second, in the 1970s and 1980s constitutional changes were introduced along the lines which Horowitz prescribes. An examination of this experience thus provides some test of the question of how far democratic forms can be designed to reduce conflict. Third, unlike most conflict-ridden countries, Sri Lanka has enjoyed sustained economic growth and continued overall improvement in human indicators even while suffering violent conflict on a large scale.[11] This experience, therefore shows that economic development in itself does not guarantee reduced conflict, nor does conflict invariably prevent economic growth.[12]

Sri Lanka underwent a period of Horowitz-style institutional changes during the late 1970s and 1980s, the very time during which some of the most intense conflict occurred. The 1978 Constitution, ushered in by the new United National Party government of the time, transformed the political structure from a Westminster-like parliamentary system to a system much like the current French one, with a strong president as well as a parliament and prime minister. Moreover, the new constitution replaced the first-past-the-post (FFP) electoral system based primarily on small single member constituencies with a list proportional representation system[13] operating along much larger district lines. Although these changes were not specifically enacted in response to the ethnic discord between the majority Sinhalese and the minority Tamils, the motives behind the institutional structuring are irrelevant in evaluating its impact on ethnic accommodation.[14] In contrast, the 1987 Indo-Lanka Accord between the governments of Sri Lanka and India, and the territorial system of provincial councils which it established, was a specific attempt to quell the violence in the island by providing the Tamil population with a significant measure of autonomy in the northeastern areas.

Of course, the consequences of these institutional changes for ethnic accommodation were multiple and varied, and it would require an extensive study to evaluate all of the relevant repercussions. As such a comprehensive assessment is beyond the scope of this chapter,[15] it will concentrate on one dimension of how institutional change altered the scope of the conflict. In examining how institutional structuring affected the Muslim community and their politics, it is possible to assess the ability of institutions to bring about that ultimate objective of institutional engineering, a multi-ethnic coalition of commitment. Constituting almost 8 percent of the island's population, the Muslims of Sri Lanka are the second-largest minority in the country. Geographically dispersed, two-thirds of the community live among the Sinhalese in the provinces in the southwest, outside the main region of violent conflict in the northeast. While maintaining a distinct identity, the Muslims in these areas have been integrated into Sinhalese society. This intermingling is manifested by the Muslims' recent willingness to learn Sinhala, the language of the majority community among whom they live, although historically the Muslims of Sri Lanka were a Tamil-speaking people. In contrast, the remaining third of the Muslims lives among the Tamils-in the northeast area which has been immersed in war for much of the last 14 years. There, the Muslims constitute one-third of the population of the Eastern Province. Remaining distinct from their Tamil neighbours in religion, these Muslims maintain linguistic as well as cultural traditions in common with the Tamils. Today, the southern and eastern Muslims differ not just in their language, but also in their economic profiles. Southern Muslims have, for the most part, been involved in trade and business, while their eastern counterparts are primarily engaged in agriculture.

Despite the significant differences between the two segments of the Muslim population, the entire community has historically been politically represented by Muslims operating within the Sinhalese national parties. While distinct from their Sinhalese and Tamil neighbors in cultural and religious terms, the Muslims did not extend this separateness to embrace a distinct political agenda as other communities on the island had.[16] However, the institutional changes implemented over the conflict period were critical in transforming this Muslim sense of separateness into a viable, significant, Muslim political formation represented by a Muslim political party, the Sri Lankan Muslim Congress (SLMC). First, as anticipated, the election of the president by a single transferable vote proportional representation (PR) system – where the second and third preferences of voters could decide the outcome of an election – did encourage presidential candidates to seek out alliances with minority leaders. While this did promote moderation in the platform of the presidential candidates, it also gave leaders, local Muslim leaders in the east in particular, leverage to extract concessions and support for the building of their own political entities. Second, the PR system provided incentives for a Muslim regional party in the east where the Muslim population was geographically concentrated by allowing Muslim votes, formerly spread across smaller constituencies, to count toward the election of a candidate running on an exclusively Muslim platform. Lastly, although the provincial council system instituted under the Indo-Lanka Accord was ultimately a failure, the desire of the Sri Lankan and Indian governments to give the first elections in the northeast a sense of legitimacy motivated them to lend significant support to political parties, such as the SLMC, who were willing to contest the elections in 1988.

Given these institutional arrangements and the incentives they furnished, it is not surprising that local Muslim leaders formed the first political party, the Sri Lankan Muslim Congress, campaigning on an exclusively Muslim platform. Emphasizing the need to link Muslim political and religious leadership and utilizing mosques as well as religious groups, leaders, and symbols heavily in their campaign, the SLMC gathered a substantial following in the east and a fair-sized one in other parts of the country.[17] Naturally, the rise of this new Muslim political formation had repercussions elsewhere. As garnering the vote of one community is most easily done by creating an enemy out of another, in encouraging an exclusively Muslim party platform, the institutions also promoted anti-Tamil rhetoric. This fed local Muslim-Tamil tensions in the northeast and undoubtedly contributed to the rise in Muslim-Tamil violence there in the late 1980s and early 1990s. Moreover, as the Muslims of the southwest and those of the northeast espoused varying interests and conceptions of how best to promote them, the rise of a Muslim political party based in the east, yet speaking for the community as a whole, encouraged intra-group rivalry within the Muslim community. Lastly, the success of the SLMC at the polls siphoned away support traditionally thrown behind the national Sinhalese parties. Anticipating this shift of preferences of Muslim voters, the major Sinhalese parties made pre-election agreements with the SLMC. While in the 1989 election, the connection between the United National Party (UNP) and the SLMC was not formalized, in the 1994 parliamentary election, the People's Alliance (PA) and the SLMC struck an explicit electoral pact involving vote pooling. When the PA found themselves several seats short of a parliamentary majority, as expected, it turned to the SLMC[18] to form a multi-ethnic coalition of commitment.

In evaluating the capacity of Sri Lanka's institutions to facilitate conflict management, it is evident that institution crafting – by promoting a new ethnic actor, the SLMC – did contribute to a restructuring of the political system along the lines that Horowitz cites as being conducive to ethnic accommodation and conflict management. There was a fragmentation of ethnic groups, a rise in intra-ethnic rivalry, a proliferation of political parties, and an increase in competition at the regional level. Most importantly, as hoped for, these conditions led the way to a formation of a multi-ethnic coalition of commitment, the supreme objective of institutional engineering.

While it may be tempting to conclude there, claiming a victory for institutional engineering, a responsible analysis goes one step further. Has this restructuring of the political system truly created the new incentives for ethnic accommodation as Horowitz promises and as common sense would have us believe? In Sri Lanka's case, the answer is an unequivocal no. In fact, it could even be argued that the current institutional system creates incentives which encourage continued marginalization of the Tamils. First, the prominence of the Muslims in recent politics has at times enabled Sinhalese governments to relinquish responsibility for resolving the conflict by pitting the Muslims and Tamils against one another, as was the case in the 1989 All Party Conference. Second, by providing the Sinhalese parties with an alternative partner when faced with the need to form coalitions and cater to minority interests, the Muslim political formation, which the institutional changes encouraged allowed the Sinhalese majority to continue to evade compromise with the Tamils. Moreover, although exclusion of Tamils from government does not necessarily imply the oppression of them, the incentive structure created by current institutions permits and may encourage government policies which neglect or even persecute Tamil citizens. As seen earlier, institutions have invited the Muslim party to take an anti-Tamil position in the east in order to win votes. Not only has this fomented conflict at the regional level, but it provides no reassurances, rather the opposite, that a Sinhalese-Muslim coalition of commitment would not also be an anti-

Tamil coalition. Additionally, a permanent political split between the Muslims and the Tamils, with the former in government and the latter outside it, may contribute to an uneven balance of resources in the east where both communities live, thereby further exacerbating the conflict at the regional level.[19] Lastly, if we are to be truly cynical, the Muslim leadership, which has gained access to power and patronage by leveraging the weight of its community against the Tamils, could conclude that perpetuation of the conflict is in its own interests.[20]

The experience of Sri Lanka does not tell us what the usual cases do about institutional engineering. It does not suggest simply that institutional change may be unsuccessful in bringing about the desired conditions, as was the case in British Guyana, or that the desired conditions, such as intra-group rivalry and incentives for inter-ethnic cooperation, do not always lead to multi-ethnic coalitions of commitment, as in Northern Ireland. Rather, more disturbingly for the Horowitz case, the Sri Lankan experience indicates that even when institutional structuring does in fact produce the intended outcomes supposedly conducive to ethnic accommodation, these multi-ethnic coalitions of commitment – the supposed guarantors of ethnic accommodation – may not only be insufficient to promote peace, but can even be recipes for further conflict.[21]

Institutional engineering failed, even after it successfully created a multi-ethnic coalition of commitment, because it ignored certain factors which are critical in understanding the relations between ethnic groups. Perhaps the most important issue which must be considered in the search for ethnic accommodation is the role that differential rates of economic advancement play in shaping ethnic hostilities. In Sri Lanka, the Muslim community gained political salience not only due to encouraging institutional mechanisms, but also because a history of social and economic tension between the Muslims and the Tamils, and, to a lesser extent, the Sinhalese, formed the foundation for an exclusive, and sometimes chauvinistic, Muslim political agenda.

In the southwest, a rising Muslim middle class became frustrated with a government it felt was preoccupied with Sinhalese economic interests and uninterested in aiding Muslim socioeconomic advancement. As a result, Muslim leaders increasingly turned to Arab nations to finance community development projects. Although such endeavors did not promote Muslim development on a wide scale, they did have the effect of increasing Sri Lankan Muslim identification with the Muslim world. Already wary of the Tamil minority and its links to India, the majority Sinhalese frowned on another minority with significant international connections. In the east, certain patterns of socioeconomic development stoked tension between the Muslim and Tamil communities living side by side. Policies geared toward promoting Sinhalese – such as land colonization – created scarcity which intensified competition between Muslims and Tamils. Similarly, as both Muslims and Tamils in the east were educated in the Tamil language, policies to promote Muslim education siphoned resources and jobs away from the Tamil community, adding to a legacy of resentment. Institutional engineering is in no way responsible for these difficult socioeconomic relations between the Muslims and other groups; it only allowed these sentiments to find expression in a Muslim political party.

4.1 Conclusions from Sri Lanka's Experience

The experience of Sri Lanka, like the cases of Uganda and Kenya, cautions us against being overconfident in the conflict-reducing potential of democracy. While the experience of Sri Lanka shows that we should not ignore the form of democratic institutions, as they are critical in influencing the actors that promote or destroy prospects for ethnic reconciliation, the course of events in Sri Lanka further suggests that even the most successfully engineered democratic structures are not capable, in themselves, of eliminating conflict and may even encourage it. Moreover, the case of Sri Lanka has demonstrated that legacies of uneven development can be more potent in fueling conflict than current growth is in abating it. This finding leads us to dismiss general reassurances that economic growth by itself will reduce conflict.

5 CONCLUSIONS

The three case studies have demonstrated that the interaction between democracy, development and conflict is much more complex than is commonly supposed. Clearly, the belief that democracy or development in themselves can guarantee peace and stability is erroneous.

In Uganda, democratic institutions were manipulated in a way that fomented conflict, both in the 1960s and in 1980. The experience shows that imposing democratic structures can result in leaders manipulating identities and worsening ethnic tensions, especially where sharp economic differences broadly coincide with ethnic ones. In contrast, the experience of Kenya is of a country which was able to achieve relatively inclusive development with comparatively low levels of violence, despite limited manifestations of democracy. Indeed, the adoption of democratic structures at the behest of the international community in the early 1990s directly heightened levels of violence as the president orchestrated ethnic violence in order to maintain political power.

A possible conclusion from the cases of Uganda and Kenya is that while the *form* democracy took in these countries may have fueled conflict, alternative democratic institutions might have avoided doing so by encouraging ethnic coalitions. The analysis of Sri Lanka, however, tends to refute this hypothesis. It shows how democracy, even when well established, may not only be incapable of managing or preventing conflict, but can actually encourage it. Moreover, Sri Lanka's case challenges the claim that it is the form of democracy, not democracy *per se,* which fuels conflict. By exemplifying how even the most carefully 'engineered' democratic system may still contribute to conflict rather than mitigate it, Sri Lanka's situation calls on us to evaluate the merits of democracy as a whole from the perspective of conflict management. Furthermore, Sri Lanka's unusual experience of continued conflict within the context of economic growth indicates that a positive rate of economic growth may be less important in abating conflict than a pattern of economic and social development which is perceived to be shared fairly among potentially conflicting groups.

The differing experiences of the three countries suggest that two factors are of the utmost importance in mitigating conflict. The first crucial component is a politically *inclusive* government which incorporates people from most or all major groups at a political level, and consequently gives these groups a stake in the system, an interest in its perpetuation and the maintenance of avenues of mediation. The second critical element is the realization of an economic and social system which *spreads the fruits of progress widely,* extending the benefits to all significant regions/ethnicities/religious groups, and thus avoids the destabilizing consequences of uneven development, that is what is required is *economically* inclusive government.

This model of inclusive development, politically and economically, was very approximately achieved for much of the last 40 years in Kenya and since 1986 under Museveni in Uganda — in neither case with full — multiparty democracy.

Our findings suggest that, while not impossible, the type of inclusive system described is very difficult to achieve through the democratic process in conflict-prone societies, for a number of reasons. First, as Sri Lankan experience shows, the mere existence of democracy does not preclude the existence of ethnic nationalisms, and can actually encourage them. Clearly, a system — democratic or not — based on exclusive ethnic identification is unlikely to adopt an inclusive development program or to incorporate other groups into government decision-making. Second, the nature of democracy encourages each elected representative to cultivate a support base, something achieved most easily through the extension of political patronage. In societies where ethnic-based parties are likely to dominate, the distribution of political patronage by the parties in government is likely to exacerbate economic inequalities among ethnic or regional groups rather than to decrease them. Lastly, as the experience of Uganda and Sri Lanka shows, whether inside or outside democratic institutions, conflict can undermine civil society and other institutions. Without a strong civil society, a framework establishing the rule of law, a reasonably free press – all institutions which are eroded during conflict – a 'democratic' process is even more likely to result in a system dominated by one or two groups committed to selective developmental aims.

It follows that in highly divided societies, especially immediately after conflict, some sort of government of unity which incorporates members of all major groups[22] may be more developmentally orientated and inclusive than a multiparty democracy. But such a regime is difficult to secure or sustain. Problems with nondemocratic regimes can be anticipated. They often exacerbate economic divisions among ethnic groups by selective patronage, and undermine civil society through repression. In some cases, such as that of Kenya, a nonelected regime may promote inclusive development but simultaneously undermine important institutions. An additional obstacle is that rulers are typically reluctant to give way to democratic pressures when the path for democratic transition has been laid. Yet in these cases, as economic development proceeds, it is likely that internal pressures for democracy will mount, making it increasingly difficult for nonelected regimes to maintain power.

While perhaps sounding much like the consociational system we rejected earlier, the key difference is that our inclusive, developmentally orientated regime would be intended to be temporary in nature. The objectives of such a system would be explicitly to promote even development and decrease economic inequities between groups, to establish a working legal framework, and to encourage the growth of civil society. Once these aims were achieved (granted, a difficult judgment to make), the transitional government would be expected to be prepared to relinquish power through elections. But even after such a 'democratic transition' the need to maintain inclusivity remains essential if democratic institutions and the absence of violent conflict is to be sustained. Such considerations should inform both constitutional arrangements and external influences concerning political and economic choices.

Undoubtedly, the decision about the most appropriate regime in conflict-prone societies is not an easy one. The potential damage from a 'bad' nondemocratic regime may be worse than that liable to arise from a democratic one. All we can conclude is that where external actors intervene they do so in ways that are liable to promote peace rather than exacerbate conflict. They should be sensitive to the actual context. When peace is fragile, external actors should be wary of demanding democracy as a condition for their support, and should focus on securing inclusive government and balanced development combined with respect for some fundamental human rights. Not only can democratic structures fuel conflict, but domestic 'ownership' of such structures is even more important than ownership of economic conditionality, because without it democracy certainly will not work.

NOTES

1. This section draws heavily on some work on Kenya by Jeni Klugman (see Klugman and Stewart 1997). We are grateful for her agreement to use some of the material here.
2. The difference in per capita incomes between the two countries was due to non-African incomes being significantly greater in Kenya.
3. Bunyoro: this land came to be known as the 'lost counties'.
4. These included religious and ethnic groups (see Mudoola 1992).
5. It appears clear that the DP won the majority of votes – the early results strongly favoured the DP, whereupon the head of the Military Commission announced that all further results would be declared by the Military Commission. From that point, the UPC and Obote were declared the winners. A decree announced that anyone who talked about the results would be subject to imprisonment (Mudoola 1988).
6. Soldiers who had served in the Obote army were sent to camps for screening and 'political education'.
7. Including that of a parliamentary committee of the (then) KANU – only National Assembly, the National Council of Churches of Kenya (NCCK) and Africa Watch.
8. For his most comprehensive work, see Horowitz (1985).
9. Horowitz refers to this phenomenon as 'vote pooling' (see Horowitz 1991).
10. Horowitz (1991), delineates how the single transferable vote system did create incentives for intergroup compromise in the 1973 election in Northern Ireland, but still did not lead to the formation of a coalition advocating accommodation.
11. This derives from indicators available for Sri Lanka during the conflict period, most of which, however, exclude data from the northeast, the area of conflict.
12. For an account of how Sri Lanka managed to sustain economic growth during conflict (see O'Sullivan 1996).
13. Under the list proportional representation system, the percentage of popular vote won by a party (in a district in Sri Lanka's case) secures the proportional number of parliamentary seats in the district for that party.

14. As Horowitz has noted, much institutional engineering is 'inadvertent' (see Horowitz 1991, p. 155).
15. For the impact of these institutional changes on minority voters in the southwest as well as the impact of the preference voting system on intra-party conflict, see de Silva (1989).
16. Of course, this is a bit of an oversimplification. The simple existence of a 'Muslim' community was a political construct, created over time in contestation to other identities such as a 'Moor community' or a 'Tamil-speaking' one.
17. The support for the SLMC in areas outside the northeast declined in the 1990s, for a range of reasons.
18. The PA also needed to incorporate into the government the one MP from the Upcountry Tamil People's Front to reach a one-seat majority of 113 seats.
19. This has already happened to some extent with the opening of the South Eastern University in the east, an institution which unofficially caters to the educational needs of the Muslims.
20. Muslim leaders would not be unlimited in their ability to promote conflict as they were elected by their constituents not only to gain access to patronage, but also to secure peace and stability.
21. Some might respond to this analysis of Sri Lanka by proposing more institutional structuring which would promote moderation between Tamil and Muslim parties at a regional level. It might work, but it is likely that such a change would alter the balance elsewhere in the political structure. For example, an alternative voting proportional representation system for parliament might engender the formation of a moderate Muslim-Tamil party in the east. Yet the existence of such a party might encourage national Sinhalese parties to adopt anti-Tamil rhetoric in order to win the support of more strident Muslim voters. This turn of events could result in fewer seats for a moderate Muslim party and more for the Sinhalese national party, dispensing with the need for a coalition at the center.
22. These group representatives may themselves be elected.

REFERENCES

Brinkley, D. (1997), 'Democratic Enlargement: The Clinton Doctrine', *Foreign Policy*, No. 106, Spring, 111-27.

Bwengye, F.L. (1985), *The Agony of Uganda: from Idi Amin to Obote: Repressive Rule and Bloodshed*, London: Regency Press.

Carothers, T. (1992), 'Democracy Without Illusions', *Foreign Affairs*, 76 (1), 88-99.

Coakley, J. (1994), 'Approaches to the Resolution of Ethnic Conflict: The Strategy of Non-territorial Autonomy', *International Political Science Review*, 15 (3), 297-314.

de Silva, C.R. (1989), 'Preference Voting: Some Remarks on the Sri Lankan Experience, 1987-1989', Paper presented at the 18th Annual

Conference on South Asia, Madison, Wisconsin, November 3-5.

Esman, M. (1973), 'The Management of Communal Conflict', *Public Policy*, 21, Winter, 49-78;

Fei, J.C.H. (1997), *Lectures on China's Economy.*

Holmquist, F., F. Weaver and M. Ford (1994), 'The structural development of Kenya's political economy', *African Studies Review*, 37 (1), 69-105.

Horowitz, D. (1971), 'Three Dimensions of Ethnic Politics', *World Politics*, 23 (2), January , 232-44.

Horowitz, D. (1985), *Ethnic Groups in Conflict*, Berkeley: University of California Press.

Horowitz, D. (1991), 'Ethnic Conflict Management for Policymakers' in J. Montville (ed.), *Conflict and Peacemaking in Multiethnic Societies,* New York: Lexington Books.

Huntington, S. (1991), *The Third Wave: Democratization in the Late Twentieth Century*, Norman: University of Oklahoma Press.

Karugire, S. (1980), *A Political History of Uganda*, Nairobi: Heinemann Educational Books.

Kenya Human Rights Commission (1995), *Quarterly Repression Report,* Nairobi.

Klugman, J. and F. Stewart (1997), 'Socio-economic Causes of Conflict: A Comparative Study of Kenya and Uganda', Paper prepared for the OECD Development Centre, Paris: OECD.

Lapidoth, R. (1992), *Autonomy: Flexible Solutions to Ethnic Conflict*, Washington, DC: United States Institute of Peace Press.

Lijhart, A. (1968), *The Politics of Accommodation: Pluralism and Democracy in the Netherlands*, Berkeley: University of California, Press.

Lijhart, A. (1969), 'Consociational Politics', *World Politics*, 21, January, 207-25.

Lijhart, A. (1977), *Democracy in Plural Societies*, New Haven: Yale University Press.

Lijhart, A. (1985), *Power-sharing in South Africa*, Berkeley: University of California Press.

Mudoola, D. (1988), 'Political Transitions Since Amin: A Study in Political Pathology', in H.B. Hansen and M. Twaddle (eds), *Uganda Now: Between Decay and Development*, London: James Currey.

Mutibwa, P. (1992), *Uganda Since Independence; A Story of Unfulfilled Hopes,* Kampala: Fountain.

Nafziger, W. (1996), 'The Economics of Complex Humanitarian Emergencies', *WIDER Working Paper*, No. 119, Helsinki: WIDER.

Nelson, H. (ed.) (1986), *Kenya: A Country Study*, Washington, DC: The

American University.
O'Sullivan, M. (1996), Paper prepared for Queen Elizabeth House project on Economic and Social Consequences of Conflict, Oxford: Queen Elizabeth House.
Republic of Kenya (1981), *Statistical Abstract 1981*, Nairobi: Republic of Kenya.
Republic of Kenya (1985), *Statistical Abstract 1985*, Nairobi: Republic of Kenya.
Republic of Kenya (1996), *WMS II*, Nairobi: Republic of Kenya.
Republic of Uganda (1971a), *Statistical Abstract 1971*, Department of Statistics, Ministry of Finance and Economic Planning.
Republic of Uganda (1971b), *The Birth of the Second Republic*, Entebbe: Government Printer.
Republic of Uganda (1972), *Uganda's Third Five Year Development Plan 1971/2-1975/6*, Entebbe: Government Printer.
Republic of Uganda (1973), *Report on the 1969 Population Census*, Vol. III, Entebbe: Government Printer.
Republic of Uganda (1996), *Statistical Abstract 1996*, Entebbe: Government Printer.
Republic of Uganda, Ministry of Finance and Economic Planning (MFEP) (1996), *Report on the Uganda National Integrated Household Survey, 1992-3*, Vol. III, Kampala: MFEP.
Sen, A. (1994), 'Freedoms and Needs: An Argument for the Primacy of Political Rights', *The New Republic,* January 10, 34-5.
Sivard, R. (1993), *World Military and Social Expenditures 1993,* Washington, DC: World Priorities Inc.
Stewart, F., F. Humphrey and N. Lee (1997), *Oxford Development Studies*, February.
Talbott, Strobe (1996), 'Democracy and the National Interest', *Foreign Affairs*, 75 (6), 47-63.
Throup, D. (1996), *The Triumph of the System: The Kenyan Struggle for Multiparty Democracy*, London: James Currey.
Umar, A. (ed.) (1995), *Sustainable Development for North East Kenya,* Nairobi: Crescent of Hope.
UNDP (1996), *Uganda's Human Development Report*, Kampala: UNDP.
Wilson A.J. *The Gaullist States of South Asia.*
World Bank (1989), *African Economic and Financial Data*, Washington DC: World Bank.
World Bank (1993), *Uganda: Social Sectors*, Washington, DC: World Bank.
World Bank (1996a), *African Development Indicators 1996*, Washington, DC: World Bank.

World Bank (1996b), *Uganda: The Challenge of Growth and Poverty Reduction*, Washington, DC: World Bank.

Index

A

adverse selection 19, 119
aggregation 132, 194
Ak model 80, 82, 83
authoritarianism 35

B

balanced growth 7, 81, 84
Bretton Woods 258, 335, 336, 337, 338, 339, 344, 345, 347, 349, 351, 353, 354

C

capital deepening 125, 191, 193, 194, 195, 198, 202, 203, 204, 205, 206, 207, 208
capital fundamentalism 77, 78, 79, 80, 83, 92, 93, 101, 103, 104
capital shallowing 198, 203, 205, 209
capital-using technology 195
competitive-devaluation trade 111
currency substitution 108, 109, 110, 118, 119, 120, 139

D

democracy 6, 20, 21, 30, 31, 32, 33, 34, 35, 38, 138, 260, 261, 263, 266, 268, 270, 271, 274, 278, 355, 356, 357, 358, 365, 367, 372, 375, 380, 381, 382, 383
development phases 158
distribution-sensitive measure 316, 323, 327, 333
dollarization 119
domestic-demand driven 127, 132
dominance 157, 297, 298, 299, 300, 301, 304, 305, 306, 318, 332, 350, 365

Dual-dual framework 160

E

East Asian Miracle 39, 43, 78, 155, 190, 191, 211, 253, 334, 335
economic fundamentals 33
endogenous growth 11, 31, 33, 79, 80, 82, 83, 85, 89, 91, 92, 97, 98, 100, 101, 104, 108, 113, 114, 115, 117, 137, 144, 149
engine of growth 25, 27, 80, 84, 164, 165, 206
exchange configurations 169, 170, 177, 178, 181, 184, 185

F

Fel'dman Mahalanobis model 13
foreign exchange 23, 107, 108, 109, 111, 113, 115, 117, 119, 120, 121, 122, 125, 126, 127, 128, 138, 139
free riding 19
free-currency markets 108, 109, 110, 118, 119, 122, 137

G

GATT 336, 341, 342, 343, 345, 349, 352, 353
Gini coefficient 214, 220, 228, 232, 233, 235, 237, 249, 256, 270, 271, 273
good governance 108, 121, 122, 126, 138
government failures 18
growth accounting 49, 50, 53, 77, 78, 100, 101, 104, 190, 206, 207

H

handmaiden of growth 25
hard and soft currencies 108
Harrod-Domar model 11
head-count index 327
human capital 9, 15, 24, 25, 31, 35, 49, 51, 54, 56, 63, 64, 66, 67, 69, 70, 72, 73, 78, 79, 82, 83, 84, 103, 104, 165, 207, 269, 314, 327, 328, 329, 331, 332
hyperinflation 123, 261, 300, 301, 302, 304, 305

I

IMF 37, 188, 335, 336, 337, 338, 339, 340, 343, 344, 345, 346, 347, 348,

349, 350, 352
incomplete markets 107, 109, 138, 139
inequality 4, 5, 33, 145, 213, 214, 215, 216, 217, 218, 219, 222, 223, 224, 225, 226, 227, 228, 229, 230, 231, 232, 233, 234, 235, 237, 238, 239, 240, 242, 243, 245, 246, 247, 248, 249, 254, 262, 298, 301, 304, 305, 314, 315, 320, 321, 322, 323, 327, 328, 329, 331
initial conditions 8, 9, 15, 137, 144, 145, 170, 208, 248, 260, 268, 269, 331
institutional economics 4
intangible capital 49, 51, 53, 54, 56, 57, 59, 64, 68, 69, 70, 71, 72, 73, 75
intermediate-goods-based growth model 85, 90
intersectoral linkages, 160
ITO 336, 337, 341, 342, 343, 345, 346, 347, 348, 349, 351, 352

J

Japan 4, 17, 45, 46, 52, 53, 54, 59, 62, 64, 65, 67, 68, 69, 70, 71, 75, 76, 80, 92, 93, 96, 97, 98, 101, 102, 103, 104, 107, 108, 112, 118, 122, 126, 127, 128, 129, 130, 131, 133, 134, 135, 136, 137, 138, 139, 140, 141, 143, 146, 155, 165, 168, 189, 191, 194, 202, 206, 207, 208, 210, 211, 216, 224, 225, 226, 227, 228, 233, 234, 235, 236, 238, 245, 246, 249, 251, 253, 254, 259

K

Kuznets contour 151, 152
Kuznets hypothesis 5

L

labor productivity 191, 192, 193, 194, 195, 203, 204, 205, 207
labor-using industrial sector 195

M

'market failure' view 6
'market enhancing' view 6
'market-friendly' view 6
macroeconomic crises 27
mobility 8, 75, 246, 249, 261, 263, 268, 269, 271, 272, 301, 302, 303, 304, 305, 307

moral hazard 19, 172, 175

N

natural growth rate 7
neoclassical growth model 7, 11, 77, 78, 79, 81, 82, 83, 85, 87, 90, 91, 92, 96, 99, 100, 101, 102, 104
nonconvexities 8, 10

O

openness 6, 25, 26, 27, 28, 34, 37, 114
opportunistic behavior 18, 19, 20
outward orientation 24, 26

P

Peru 254, 297, 298, 300, 301, 302, 304, 305, 308
pluralistic economic development 108, 126, 128, 132, 134
poverty 160, 161, 162, 163, 164, 165, 168, 243, 254, 256, 259, 260, 262, 263, 264, 265, 266, 267, 268, 274, 275, 300, 301, 304, 305, 306, 307, 313, 314, 315, 316, 317, 318, 319, 320, 321, 322, 323, 324, 325, 326, 327, 328, 329, 330, 331, 332, 333
poverty indices 292
purchasing power parity 4, 111, 317, 332

R

R&D 10, 28, 39, 40, 49, 51, 52, 54, 55, 56, 58, 60, 62, 64, 66, 67, 68, 69, 70, 72, 74, 75, 76, 84, 85, 97, 208
revisionist, 107, 136
Rostow contour 150, 152, 154
Rybczynski effect 192, 193, 195, 198, 199, 202, 204, 205, 206, 209

S

social capital 22, 314
stages of growth 145, 148, 153
subcontracting system 198, 203

T

tangible capital 51, 52, 53, 56, 57, 59, 61, 64, 65, 68, 71, 72, 73, 75

technical progress 6, 8, 10, 14, 45, 46, 47, 48, 49, 50, 51, 52, 53, 54, 56, 59, 60, 61, 62, 63, 64, 68, 69, 71, 73, 74, 75, 79, 81, 83, 91, 92, 93, 99, 102, 103, 104, 151, 153
total factor productivity 24, 28, 45, 56, 64, 74, 75, 114, 190
transactions cost 5
turning point 134, 191, 196, 205, 226, 228, 241

W

warranted rate of growth 7
welfare 6, 8, 12, 13, 14, 16, 18, 36, 71, 79, 127, 133, 135, 298, 299, 300, 301, 302, 304, 305, 306, 315, 327, 332
World Bank 5, 17, 22, 23, 42, 43, 63, 78, 114, 119, 130, 140, 143, 155, 164, 189, 190, 211, 236, 253, 254, 255, 256, 276, 308, 317, 320, 329, 332, 334, 335, 336, 337, 344, 345, 346, 347, 348, 349, 368, 369, 371, 386, 387